An Introduction to Religious and Theological Studies

Second Edition

An Introduction to Religious and Theological Studies

Second Edition

CYRIL ORJI

 CASCADE *Books* · Eugene, Oregon

AN INTRODUCTION TO RELIGIOUS AND THEOLOGICAL STUDIES
Second Edition

Cascade Books
An Imprint of Wipf and Stock Publishers
199 W. 8th Ave., Suite 3
Eugene, OR 97401

www.wipfandstock.com

PAPERBACK ISBN: 978-1-5326-8591-0
HARDCOVER ISBN: 978-1-5326-8592-7
EBOOK ISBN: 978-1-5326-8593-4

Cataloguing-in-Publication data:

Names: Orji, Cyril, author.

Title: An introduction to religious and theological studies, second edition / Cyril Orji.

Description: Eugene, OR : Cascade Books, 2021 | Includes bibliographical references and index.

Identifiers: ISBN 978-1-5326-8591-0 (paperback) | ISBN 978-1-5326-8592-7 (hardcover) | ISBN 978-1-5326-8593-4 (ebook)

Subjects: LCSH: Christianity and other religions. | Religions.

Classification: BL80.3 .O75 2021 (print) | BL80.3 .O75 (ebook)

JANUARY 5, 2021

Affectionately dedicated to my students.
Without you I would not be the teacher that I am today.
You are the best. You'll Never Walk Alone (YNWA).

Contents

Preface

THE FIRST EDITION OF *An Introduction to Religious and Theological Studies* was undertaken to meet a need. At the time, it was hard to come by any book for undergraduate study of Christian theology that addressed topical issues in all the four traditional areas of Christian theology: systematic, historical, biblical, and theological ethics. While there are plethora of good books for study of Christian theology, they usually treat only one or two of the aforementioned areas. College professors have had to rely on multiple texts, which can be both cumbersome and expensive. It was as part of the effort to ameliorate this problem that the first edition was written. The goal was to bring together in a single text some key topical issues in all the four traditional areas of Christian theology and examine them within the broader context of Christianity's shared values with the two other Abrahamic religions— Judaism and Islam. The chapter on Tribal Religions vis-à-vis African Tradition Religions (ATRs) was added to give the hint that Christian religion must move beyond its Abrahamic roots and dialogue with native or indigenous religions whenever and wherever it encounters indigenous cultures. The reception of the first edition has been overwhelmingly positive, thereby necessitating a second and expanded edition.

This second and expanded edition makes the hint that Christianity must dialogue with other religions more explicit. In the light of the new global consciousness, particularly in the push to put to rest the ghost of Christendom and make students of Christian theology understand Christianity's relationship with other religions, the goal of this expanded edition remains the same—to help students grasp how and why Christianity must understand other religions, if it is to engage them in dialogue. As a world religion, Christianity has to understand the worldviews, cultures, practices, and ethos of peoples of other religions in the Christian encounter with the other. It is precisely for this reason that the second edition has added three new chapters—Asian religions (Daoism and Confucianism), Hinduism, and Buddhism.

This expanded edition has a total of fourteen chapters. It is divided into two sections. The division into two sections means that the chapters have to be slightly rearranged. Section I with its ten chapters retains its focus on Abrahamic religions. Section II with its four chapters focuses on non-Abrahamic religions. The chapter on Islam, which has been conveniently located in Section I, has been expanded and infused with some new informative material. At the end of each chapter are some good discussion questions that the teacher can use to stimulate class discussion (see Appendix). For exam purposes, these questions can be adapted for use as essay or multiple-choice questions.

Acknowledgments

MY THANKS TO ALL the good people, too numerous to mention here, who made this book possible. However, I will be remiss if I do not mention the noble students I had during my graduate student years at Marquette University, Milwaukee, Wisconsin, and the good students of the University of Dayton, Ohio. The students of these two institutions made me develop love for teaching survey course in Christian theology/religion. In their various ways they helped shape my identity as a teacher, particularly through their persistent questioning, unrelenting desire for meaning-making, and heartwarming embrace. Special thanks also to Profs. Bradford and Christine Firer Hinze (now of Fordham University, New York) who believed in me as a teacher during my graduate student years at Marquette. They encouraged me to be a teacher-scholar and created the environment that gave me my first teaching opportunity. To you all I will forever be indebted.

PART I

Christian Theology
and the Three Abrahamic Religions

1

The Complex Matter of Religion

THE PHENOMENON THAT GOES under the umbrella term "religion" is one of the many ways individuals and communities engage in human search for meaning. From the beginning of humanity, religion has served as a unique response to the fundamental human question, "Who am I?" At a recent conference on the environment and economic sustainability in Copenhagen, Denmark, a young man from Brazil gave a fascinating account of their primary school curriculum. According to this young man, at a very early age Brazilian children are exposed to three different cultures: the cultures of the indigenous peoples of Brazil, African cultures, and Portuguese culture. The first African slaves arrived in Brazil in the sixteenth century to replace the indigenous labor. At the time Brazil was occupied by the Portuguese crown. Modern Brazilians trace their ancestry to at least one or two of these cultures that have mixed over time. What they are trying to find out in essence is their roots—who they are as Brazilians. We all confront the same dilemma as humans: Who are we? Where do we come from? And why are we here? For some, this is a question about the mystery of life.

Questions about the mysteries of life are much more common during times of distress, war, famine, earthquake, or other disasters. On January 12, 2010, a 7.0 earthquake left about 230,000 Haitians dead and about 1.3 million others homeless. A 9.0 earthquake hit Japan the following year in March, triggering a tsunami that left hundreds of people dead. The tsunami also hit parts of Japan where their radiation plants were located, setting off a radiation crisis in the region. The impact of this calamitous event was felt beyond Japan. For example, the tsunami brought about 1.5 million tons of debris from Japan to the west coast of the United States, fueling further fears of radiation crisis and irregular climate patterns. Natural disasters and wars in general produce calamities and destruction. The instability they produce can and does raise serious questions about the human person, the world, and our place in it.

The question "Who am I?" is ultimately related to the matter of our place in the world—the question of human agency. The question of human agency is a fundamental "religious" question: How are we related to the earth or planet? In 1991 what used to be Yugoslavia collapsed. The breakdown led to a series of armed conflicts from 1991 to 2001 (the Balkan War) between then Yugoslavia's multiethnic groups—Serbs, Bosnians, Croats, etc. As the country disintegrated the world saw grotesque pictures of massacred innocent people, particularly women and children. The International Court of Justice called the massacre of Bosnian Muslims at Srebrenica in 1995 an act of genocide. By the time the war was over more than 200,000 people had lost their lives and a thousand others had been displaced from their homeland. The end result was a divided Yugoslavia federation that split along ethnic lines: Serbia, Slovenia, Bosnia, Croatia, Kosovo, and Macedonia. In situations such as these, when people are faced with questions that touch the core of their existence, they turn to religion for answers. We return to our question of human agency that religion addresses: How are we related to one another? How are we related to the planet? What does our relationship to the planet and to others say about who we are—question of personal identity?

The way Western cultures conceive personal identity is somewhat different from the way non-Western cultures conceive it. Although those of us in the West acknowledge that there are many factors (family, school, environment, etc.) that shape who we are, we still think of personal identity as a rather personal thing to be resolved by the individual. The individual self is often conceived as an independent and autonomous entity. But that is not so in non-Western cultures where the emphasis is on community—personal identity is a rather communal thing. We should keep in mind that the difference between the Western conception of personal identity and the non-Western conception of personal identity invariably affects their respective definitions or conceptions of the activity we call "religion."

WHAT IS RELIGION?

The activity we call religion is an ancient human phenomenon that predates Western culture itself. Before Christianity and Islam, indigenous peoples all over the world were always religious, although they may not have had a word to capture that religious activity. Indigenous peoples lived their lives in the particularities of their culture, community, and language, and expressed their belief in divine realities in the context of these. Religion, for them (if we may use the term), was not limited to worship of deity, but was rather for them a way of responding to the challenges posed by the harshness of their environment and the world at large. Religion and culture were, for them, one and the same reality, and participation in religious practices was considered part of what it means to be a member of the community. What we call "religion," in a nutshell, was for them a way of being human and a way of answering questions concerning the mystery of human life. In other words, they confronted questions posed by the mysteries of life in the larger context of what it means to be human: Why are we here? Who made us? Who or what is God? Do angels or spiritual beings exist? Why do we suffer? What is the meaning of suffering? Why is evil in the world? Do our actions here on earth have eternal consequences? Is there a life after death? They transmitted their answers to these questions orally from generation to generation, often embedding them in folklores, rituals, songs, dances, proverbs, customs, and ethical codes.

In its technical sense, the term "religion" is a Western concept. The term has a history—it was used at a particular time in human history to capture practices and ideas that are considered religious. What is technically called "religion" is an attempt to answer the same questions indigenous peoples have grappled with: What is humanity? What is the meaning of human life? Why are we here? Why suffering? Does suffering have a purpose? Why death? "What, finally, is that ultimate inexpressible mystery which encompasses our existence: whence do we come, and where are we going?"[1] All peoples, in some sense, answer these questions, but they do so somewhat differently. Some answer them categorically, while others answer them unconsciously.

1. See Paul VI, *Nostra Aetate*.

Important Terms for Understanding the Meaning of Religion		
Term	**Meaning**	**Examples of Persons/ Cultures**
Syncretism	Religions, like cultures, sometimes come in contact with each other. When this happens, blending takes place. The blending that takes place when two cultures come in contact is known as acculturation. The blending that takes place when two religions come in contact is known as syncretism. Syncretism seems unavoidable in religion, the same way acculturation is unavoidable in culture.	Hinduism began as an intermingling of Aryan and Harappan cultural and religious traditions. The Harappan people lived in the Indus Valley region (modern-day India) around 200,000 BCE, before they were invaded by the Aryans. The intermingling of their religions resulted in Hinduism. Judaism borrowed aspects of Canaanite religion. The Canaanites called their gods or shrine *El*, and Jews would call God *El-ohim*. Christianity borrowed aspects of Judaism, e.g., Jewish scripture.
Theism	Belief in a personal deity or god.	Judaism, Christianity, Islam, Zoroastrianism, Hinduism, African Traditional Religions (ATRs), and Native American religions.
Atheism	The idea that there is no deity or god.	Contemporary atheists like Richard Dawkins and Christopher Hitchens. Some self-proclaimed atheists in the United States protest against Christian or religious holidays. They also want the words "in God we trust" removed from US currency.
Agnosticism	The idea that, since we do not know for sure whether God exists, we should doubt it.	Some Hollywood celebrities and TV stars claim to be agnostics.

Deism	Throughout history there have been different expressions of deist ideas. But in its simple term, deism is the idea that God created the world and absconded; that God does not actively engage in the world.	Some of the US founding fathers, like Thomas Jefferson and Benjamin Franklin, espoused deist views. This led to the idea of separation of church and state.
Monotheism	Belief in one God.	The three Abrahamic monotheistic religions: Judaism, Christianity, and Islam. Two non-Abrahamic monotheistic religions: Zoroastrianism and Egyptian civilization (during the reign of Akhenaton).
Polytheism	Belief in the existence of multiple deities or gods.	Hinduism, which has about 333 million gods; Greek and Roman religions.
Pantheon	Belief in the existence of multiple gods, hierarchically structured	In the Greek Pantheon the gods live on Mount Olympus, and Zeus is the leader.
Scientism	The idea that only what can be proven by science is correct and that disbelief in God is a scientific hypothesis that can be rationally demonstrated.	The New Atheists, such as English evolutionary biologist Richard Dawkins, Anglo-American literary critic Christopher Hitchens, and American philosopher and neuroscientist Sam Harris.
Rationalism	The idea that only what can be proven by reason is valid and that faith is not a form of knowledge.	Philosophers, like David Hume and Bertrand Russell, and the New Atheists.

Unconscious Religiousness

Whenever human existence is threatened, as in war, famine, or violence, religious and non-religious people alike look for answers. Religious people look up to the heavens for answers because they believe God is the origin and end of human life and therefore God must have an answer. Non-religious people, for their part, may look to the heavens but in a slightly different way, perhaps somewhat "unconsciously," if we may borrow the use of that term from the Auschwitz survivor and psychologist Viktor Frankl (1905–97). Whenever I teach a class on religion I get two or three students who tell me off the bat that they are not "religious" or that they don't believe in any deity. But when I ask how many people in the class have done volunteer work to help the needy some of these same people who are not "religious" tend to be in the forefront. When I ask them why they volunteer or give their time to help others they often tell me they do it because it is the right thing to do. Frankl says this kind of activity is motivated by one's "spiritual unconscious" or "unconscious religiousness." According to him, life does not mean something vague, but something real and concrete, and so questions about the meaning of life cannot be answered by sweeping statements.[2]

In Frankl's analysis of the human condition, everyone (religious and non-religious alike) has an "unconscious religiousness." It is this unconscious religiousness that makes us go beyond ourselves (transcendence) and reach out to others (actualize ourselves in freedom). Human existence, according to Frankl, insofar as it has not been neurotically distorted, is always directed at something or someone other than oneself. This reaching to something other than oneself he calls "self-actualization" or "self-transcendence." According to Frankl, self-actualization is not easy to attain. Like success, self-actualization can be elusive; the more one strives for it the more one misses it. "Don't aim at success," writes Frankl, "the more you aim at it and make it a target, the more you are going to miss it. For success, like happiness, cannot be pursued; it must ensue, and it only does so as the unintended side-effect of one's personal dedication to a cause greater than oneself or as the by-product of one's surrender to a person other than oneself."[3]

Viktor E. Frankl (1905–97)

Viktor Frankl was an Austrian psychiatrist and holocaust survivor. He was born into a Jewish family in Vienna, Austria, in 1905. As a student Frankl was fascinated by the works of the Austrian neurologist who later became known as the father of modern psychoanalysis, Sigmund Freud (1856–1939), and his student Alfred Adler (1870–1937). Frankl built on their works and went beyond them. He studied medicine at the University of Vienna and later concentrated in neurology. He was particularly interested

---

2. Frankl, *Man's Search for Meaning*, 98.
3. Frankl, *Man's Search for Meaning*, 17.

in matters pertaining to depression and suicide. While studying neurology in Vienna, Frankl was part of a team that worked in a "suicide pavilion" that treated over 30,000 women who suffered from depression and were near suicide. Frankl always put to his patients who suffered torment the question, "Why do you not commit suicide?" From their answers he discovered that there is always a deep or fundamental reason why suicide was not an option—that "hunger, humiliation, fear and deep anger at injustice are rendered tolerable by closely guarded images of beloved person, by religion, by a grim sense of humor, and even by glimpses of the healing beauties of nature." From this Frankl derived what he called "logotherapy," an existential analysis whose central theme is "to live is to suffer, to survive is to find meaning in the suffering. If there is purpose in life at all, there must be a purpose in suffering and dying. But no man can tell another what this purpose is. Each must find out for himself, and must accept the responsibility that his answer prescribes."

When the Nazis took over Austria in 1938 Frankl was prevented from treating any Aryan patients because he was a Jew. In September 1942 Frankl and his wife, Tilly, together with his parents and his brother and sister, were deported to the Theresienstadt Ghetto by the Nazis. In October 1944 he and his wife were sent to the concentration camp in Auschwitz, where he spent five months working as both a slave laborer and physician. In Auschwitz he was separated from his wife, who was sent to a nearby concentration camp, Bergen-Belsen, where she died. His mother, Elsa, died in the gas chambers of Auschwitz. His father and brother also died in a concentration camp. In total, Frankl spent about three years in different concentration camps. During that time Frankl discovered the importance of finding meaning in life. He returned to Vienna in 1945 after the American troops liberated Auschwitz, and then continued his work as a psychiatrist. In 1959 he wrote his famous book *Man's Search for Meaning*, in which he described his experiences in the concentration camps. The book was his way "to convey to the reader by way of a concrete example that life holds a potential meaning under any conditions, even the most miserable ones."

Self-actualization is implicit in the notion of religion. Many people who consider themselves "religious" can relate to Frankl's idea that the more one forgets oneself by giving oneself to a cause greater than oneself the more one fully actualizes oneself. Religious people think that self-actualization is fully realized only when one has found or discovered God—that this is what makes a person fully human. This is not to say that people who do not believe in God or who do not consider themselves "religious" are not fully human, but rather that to be religious is to be human in a unique way. One theologian who described this very well was twentieth-century German Jesuit theologian Karl Rahner (1904–84). Rahner raised the question regarding whether a human person can know God, and answered in the affirmative. According to Rahner, we know God in our reflections on the meaning of life and existence. As human beings we experience our limitations when we face difficult situations such as natural disasters or human tragedy. It is when we experience our limitations that we begin to experience that which is beyond us. In such experience we begin to grasp the mystery of human existence and life in general. As we go through this experience we not only begin to go beyond (transcend) ourselves, we also begin to know ourselves as "mystery." Rahner calls this process of self-discovery "transcendental experience." It is in transcendental experience that we also experience God. When we start to speak of our experience of God, it is then that we begin to come to knowledge of who we really are in the true sense of the word. The God that we experience is mediated to us through religion.[4] The prison experience of Viktor Frankl may be a good example of a transcendental experience. Frankl suffered a great deal in Auschwitz. There he saw the highest level of human degradation and brutality. But rather than despair, he turned his experience into something positive. His prison experiences made him come to terms with himself as an authentic human person who is capable of enduring suffering. More than enduring suffering, an authentic human person is one who has learned to surrender self through a "religious" experience.[5] This then leads us to the question: What is religion?

---

4. Rahner, *Foundations of Christian Faith*, 44–71.

5. Lonergan, *Method in Theology*, 104.

Other Important Terms for Understanding the Meaning of Religion		
Term	**Meaning**	**Examples of Persons/Cultures**
Animism	The idea that spirits inhabit everything.	Shinto is an ancient religion of Japan that was founded around 1000 BCE. Shintoists believe that spirits, which they call *kami*, live everywhere.
Pantheism	The belief that God is in everything.	In the Hindu philosophical text the Upanishads, there is the idea that although Brahman is the foundation of all reality, God is everything and everything is God.
Henotheism	The belief that there are several gods but some are more important than others.	This idea is found in religions like Hinduism and Greek and Hellenistic religions.
Monolatry	The idea that one may acknowledge and choose to worship one deity while not denying the existence of other deities.	Egypt during the time of Akhenaton (1360–1344 BCE) advocated worship of Aton, one of the several deities in Egypt.
Morphology	The study of the changing forms or structure of religion.	Hinduism is a good example of a religion that has gone through several changes. It has assumed new forms in different phases.
Anthropomorphism	The idea of depicting God in human form and assigning human characteristics to God.	Christianity, Judaism, and Islam often speak of God as if God were human. In both the Bible and the Quran God is described as "walking in the garden," "speaking to Abraham," and being disappointed with Adam and Eve. These are human characteristics ascribed to God.
Theriomorphism	The depiction of gods in animal forms.	Polytheistic religions, like Hinduism and ancient Egyptian religions, have animal gods.

THE MATTER OF RELIGION RECONSIDERED

Raimon Panikkar (1918–2010), the Spanish-born Roman Catholic priest who had a Spanish Catholic mother and an Indian Hindu father, argued long ago against the idea of a universal theory of religion. His reason was that any universal theory of religion will be "loaded with political overtones"[6] and will inevitably be derived from the particular culture of those providing the theory.[7] The merits of Panikkar's objection notwithstanding, we still need a working theory of religion. We need to define the ideas and practices we consider religious. The field of religion is very broad. Religion is as ancient as humanity itself. From the very beginning of human existence, human beings have been religious. Ancient civilizations, like Egypt (ca. 3100 BCE), Mesopotamia (ca. 3000 BCE), and Babylon (ca. 1792 BCE), were great not just because they had strong systems of government or because they engaged in commerce and trade with their neighbors, but also because they built their dynasties on strong religious (and ethical) systems. The legacy of their civilizations includes not only economics, but profound religious systems as well. They articulated in a unique way their "perception of that hidden power which hovers over the course of things and over the events of human history."[8] The Code of Hammurabi, named after King Hammurabi, who ruled from ca. 1792 to 1750 BCE, is a well-ordered religious and political text comprised of law codes put together for the good functioning of society. It stands in comparison to earlier law codes of ancient civilizations, like the Code of Ur-Nammu (ca. 2050 BCE) of King Ur, the Laws of Eshnunna (ca. 1930 BCE), and later Hittite laws, Assyrian laws, and even the laws of Moses in the Hebrew Scriptures.

The word "religion" derives from the Latin *religio*, which was used to denote the act of performing a ritual with reverence or care. *Religio* itself may also have been derived either from the Latin *relegere*, which denotes people who were careful in their ritual actions, or *religare*, meaning "to bind." Early Latin Christian writers may have used the word *religio* to distinguish what they thought was true religion from false religion. For them *religio* would not extend to what we now know as "world religions" (like Hinduism, Buddhism, Islam, etc.). They applied the word only to what they thought was genuine and true worship, which for them was the Christian religion.[9] But a modern understanding of religion goes beyond the narrow definition of

---

6. Panikkar, "Invisible Harmony," 136.

7. See Schweitzer, *Contemporary Christologies*, 102.

8. See Paul VI, *Nostra Aetate*, §2.

9. Kessler, *Eastern Ways of Being Religious*, 19.

the ancient Christian writers and incorporates different historical traditions and practices—Islam, Hinduism, Buddhism, African Traditional Religions (ATRs), etc. Broadly defined, then, religion is "a system of symbols, myths, doctrines, ethics, and rituals for the expression of ultimate relevance."[10] The subject matter of religion is the human person, while God or deity may be considered the object or goal of religion. Viktor Frankl observed how those who died the quickest in the concentration camps were those who had lost self-determination and did not have anything to live for. He also observed that most of those who survived the horrors of the camps were those who had something to live for, such as their children or other loved ones, and who had attained self-actualization or self-transcendence—God. To better understand the meaning of religion we need to understand each of the five component parts of our broad definition.

A. **Symbol**: Why do Christians wear the cross around their necks? Why do Muslims who make the pilgrimage to Mecca wear white robes? Why do traditional Jewish men come to prayer with their *tallit* (prayer shawl)? A symbol is like a sign in the sense that it is used to represent something. A symbol is also like an icon because it presents something to the senses that ultimately needs to be interpreted. But more than a sign or icon, a symbol embodies that which it represents. A sign, for example, represents the object or idea to which it refers only in an arbitrary way. The relationship between the sign and the representation is determined merely by social convention. For example, we know by social convention that a red light means traffic must stop, but the red color of the light and the traffic's ability to stop are not inherently related in any way. It is just an arbitrary connection that can be changed whenever it is decided that there is a better way of signaling traffic to stop. But a symbol points to something beyond itself in a more evocative way. A symbol also has different levels of meaning. A symbol is better appreciated when it can be interpreted.

Christians wear a cross around their necks to "symbolize" who they are—followers of the man Jesus, who died on a cross, and rose on the third day. Muslims on pilgrimage to Mecca wear simple white robes to symbolize the equality of all human beings and the purity that God expects of everyone. Jews come to prayer wearing the *tallit* to show that they remember the commandments given to them by Yahweh. Somebody on the outside may not be able to interpret or even appreciate a symbol the way a person on the inside does. This is because

10. Carmody and Brink, *Ways to the Center*, 1.

there is a difference between an insider's view and an outsider's view of religion.

Symbols are foundational to religion. Symbols, when used in religion, are meant to transport us out of our ordinary or mundane existence to the realm of the ultimate.[11] Religious symbols also inspire commitment on the part of those who belong to that religion. A cross is a Christian symbol that inspires commitment on the part of Christians. The crescent is a Muslim symbol that inspires a commitment on the part of Muslims. Symbols are not meant to be "believed," but revered.[12] Because they evoke reverence, symbols arouse passion. Religious people defend their religious symbols dutifully. What religious people do when they use a symbol is communicate something of deep significance that means the world to them.

B. **Myth**: Myth is usually confined to the realm of legends. We usually think of a myth as a story about a hero or an event that cannot be factually proven, or something that defies explanation. This common-sense definition assumes that a myth is not verifiable and not factual. But when used in religion, myth does not necessarily imply that we are dealing with an unverifiable fact. Rather than make factual claims, myths are to be understood as stories told and retold to express certain values. The question to be asked is not whether the truth claim of a myth can be verified, but whether the values it purports to convey can be vindicated.[13]

There is an episode in the life of Prophet Muhammad known as the *Miraj* (Ascension), which is referenced in Quran 17:1; 53:1–18. According to the way the story is told, the prophet was miraculously transported on a winged beast from Mecca to Jerusalem, where he ascended through the seven levels of heaven to the throne of God, and along the way met Moses, Jesus, and Abraham. The issue here is not whether we can factually determine that there are seven levels of heaven or whether a winged beast can transport a human person to heaven. Muslims who pray and venerate at the Dome of the Rock in Jerusalem (the site where Muhammad's heavenly journey began) are not concerned with such trivial matters. They are rather more concerned about preserving the sacred places of worship in Mecca and Jerusalem

11. Carmody and Brink, *Ways to the Center*, 6.
12. Carmody and Brink, *Ways to the Center*, 6.
13. Carmody and Brink, *Ways to the Center*, 6.

that the Quran prescribes.[14] The same thing can be said about the creation account in Genesis 1. The manner in which the story is told can be said to be a myth; it cannot be verified by the science of archeology. But the truth it expresses about the relationship between God and human beings and its basic assertion that God made man and woman in God's own image and likeness can be vindicated.

C. **Ritual**: "Rituals are prescribed, formalized actions that dramatize religious symbols."[15] Like myth and symbol, the primary purpose of ritual is "to connote some profound understanding or evoke some commitment within the person who hears the myth or participates in the ritual."[16] Because of the profound significance of the Quran in the daily life of Muslim believers, they engage the text of the Quran, both in their public and private recitation of it, in a variety of ways that might be considered ritualistic.[17] They engage in ritual behaviors like kissing the Quran, requesting a blessing from the Quran, weeping as the Quran is read, and placing the Quran in the home or somewhere outside the mosque as a sign of personal and communal devotion. These are prescribed obligatory rituals Muslims must perform.[18] In addition, Muslims also have a powerful ritual that is prescribed before prayer called *wudu* (ablution). Before prayer a person must clean with water his or her mouth, face, nostrils, forearms, elbows, feet, ears, and head. The only time one is exempted from this obligatory ritual is for women during menstruation. Christians likewise have prescribed obligatory rituals (like kneeling and standing at prescribed times during worship) they perform. In many cases, particular times for rituals are prescribed. For example, Catholic Christians are required to go to church on Ash Wednesday to receive ash on their forehead to mark the beginning of the Lenten season of fasting and abstinence, which lasts for forty days. The Jews eat the Sabbath meal at sundown on Friday, and what they eat and drink at this important meal are prescribed. Thus, often times "rituals are repeated in order to attain or sustain,

14. See Kaltner, *Introducing the Qur'an*, 52.

15. Carmody and Brink, *Ways to the Center*, 7.

16. Carmody and Brink, *Ways to the Center*, 8.

17. Kaltner, *Introducing the Qur'an*, 32.

18. Kaltner, *Introducing the Qur'an*, 32–33.

the individual's contact with ultimate relevance and to consolidate the cohesion of the community."[19]

D. **Ethics**: People expect certain modes of behavior from religious persons. When a person who professes belief in deity acts in a way that is untoward or unbecoming, we usually express disappointment. This is because religions express values and have ethical prescriptions that hold their adherents to a very high standard. For example, the Ten Commandments forbid lying, stealing, killing, bearing false witness, etc. These are ethical prescriptions for Jews and Christians, who accept these as divinely decreed by God. Buddhism prescribes the Middle Way (that one should avoid the extremes of sensual pleasure and the extremes of abstinence) and Eightfold Path: right speech, right understanding, right livelihood, right action, right effort, right mindfulness, right concentration, and right thought.

E. **Doctrine**: Religions have their own categorical statements about God, the origins of human life, sin, salvation, afterlife, etc. These are collectively called doctrine. In the Jewish prayer book (Siddur), the first two words, Shema Yisrael ("Hear O Israel"), are a fundamental statement about God that takes center stage at Jewish morning and evening prayer services. It is a statement about the unity of God taken from Deuteronomy 6:4–9. A Jewish child learns the Shema and commits it to memory. An adult Jew is required to recite the Shema at least twice a day, once in the morning and once in the evening. Orthodox Jews cover their eyes with their right hand as a sign of reverence when it is recited in the synagogue. Buddhist doctrine is encapsulated in the Four Noble Truths: all life is suffering; the cause of suffering is desire; stopping desire will stop suffering; and the Eightfold Path is the best way to stop desire.

To be religious is therefore to be fully human. When we say this, however, as we pointed out earlier, we are by no means implying that people who do not consider themselves religious are less human. What we are saying unequivocally is that to be religious is to be human in a unique way. For religious people the knowledge of God, the supreme truth, brings radical change to a person's life in such a way that he or she lives no longer for self, but for others and God. "The human person cannot find fulfillment in himself that is apart from the fact that he exists 'with' others and 'for' others. This truth does not simply

19. Carmody and Brink, *Ways to the Center*, 7–8.

require that he live with others at various levels of social life, but that he seek unceasingly—in actual practice and not merely at the level of ideas—the good, that is the meaning of truth."[20]

IS RELIGION DIFFERENT FROM THEOLOGY?

Earlier we pointed out how Raimon Panikkar objected to the idea of having a universal theory of religion because of its implicit political overtones. He suggested that what is needed instead is a "theology for a post-colonial era."[21] Hints from Panikkar's suggestion already indicate that theology differs from religion. Religion seeks ultimate relevance. Theology attempts a reflection on religion and brings to light the significance and value of religion in a given culture.[22] The subject matter of theology (God) is also different from that of religion. Religion seeks to understand the human person as he or she expresses ultimate relevance. Theology attempts to understand God and God's response to human invocations. In the latter understanding, we can speak of a plurality of theologies—Christian theology, Islamic theology, Jewish theology, etc. Theology, like religion, has a history which has been understood differently, even by people of the same era. In Christian theology, for example, the early Christians had different understandings of Jesus. These different understandings led to divergent theologies of the person of Jesus Christ (Christology). Those who sought a political messiah who would deliver them from Roman oppression thought Jesus was a leader like Moses—a political liberator. Others who saw salvific value in their human suffering saw Jesus as one who would liberate them from sin and eternal punishment—a savior and religious leader.

The word "theology" is derived from the two Greek words, *theo* (God) and *logos* (discourse or study). From this etymological derivation theology can be conceived as the study of or reflection about God. Within a Christian context it denotes a person's reflections on the revelation given in and by Christ Jesus.[23] Christians, from the very beginning, have reflected on their understanding of God, i.e., how God has been revealed throughout human history, particularly in the Jewish and Christian scriptures. These reflections, as already indicated, have often led to different theologies. The reflections of the author of the Fourth Gospel (sometimes referred to as the

---

20. Pontifical Council for Justice and Peace, *Compendium of the Social Doctrine*, 73.

21. Schweitzer, *Contemporary Christologies*, 102.

22. See Lonergan, *Philosophy of God and Theology*, 22.

23. Lonergan, *Method in Theology*, 296.

Johannine community), for instance, have some marked differences with the reflections of the writer of Mark's Gospel (the Marcan community). The reflections of the writer of the Gospel of Luke (the Lukan community) are also different from the reflections or theology of the writer of the Gospel of Matthew (the Matthean community). Even between Peter and Paul, the two great leaders of the early Christian community, we see some differences in their theologies and understandings of Jesus. These marked differences may account for why Paul saw his own mission as that of an apostle to the Gentiles (Rom 11:13) and Peter as an apostle to the Jews (Gal 2:8). From these examples we see that even though theology attempts a reflection on God, "when we talk about God, we are also talking about ourselves in our contexts in nature, history, and culture."[24] We cannot talk about God without talking about ourselves, the human condition, and our search for meaning and ultimate relevance.

In the Catholic tradition the idea of theology has a complicated history. As reflection about God, theology was first carried out wherever there was a believing community. For some early Christians, like Clement of Alexandria (ca. 150–220), theology was understood as "knowledge of divine things." The term "theology" could be used to describe the writings of ancient Greek writers like Homer, since the writings of these authors reflect their knowledge of divine realities, even if those divine realities are not Christian.[25] But more specifically, Christians of the third century used the word "theology" to mean only "talking about God in a Christian way," which means that they saw the study of theology as systematic thinking and articulation of the fundamental ideas of Christianity, i.e., the "intellectual reflection on the act, content, and implications of the Christian faith."[26] At this time theology was something that only monks and pastors engaged in. Theology did not develop into an academic discipline until the Middle Ages, the time of the scholastics, or "Schoolmen" as they were known (ca. 800–1500). With these Schoolmen came the growth of universities and centers of learning, like those in Paris, Bologna, Oxford, Rome, and Naples. Theology then ceased to be the prerogative of bishops and pastors and developed into an academic discipline or science that was vigorously pursued by anyone interested in learning about divine realities, like the Schoolmen, monks, and abbots did. The Schoolmen were the first to reflect on the nature of theology as a science and address the question of its definition. They made the science of theology rigorous and methodical, researching, classifying, and interpreting

24. Portier, *Tradition and Incarnation*, 148.

25. Cunningham, *Catholic Heritage*, 107.

26. McGrath, *Theology*, vii.

commentaries on the books of the Old and New Testaments, as well as the works of eminent writers before them. One such example is the systematic compilation of Christian theology in the *Book of Sentences* (1150 CE) by Peter Lombard (1100–1160). For Schoolmen like Lombard, "theology became a way of knowing God's revelation more deeply, protecting it from erroneous understanding, and the advancement of some newer understanding of that revelation by the application of human intelligence."[27] An examination of a few definitions of theology from the time of the Schoolmen to contemporary times will show us how the understanding of theology has evolved over time.

Anselm of Canterbury (1033–1109)

A famous scholastic, monk, archbishop, and doctor of the church, St. Anselm of Canterbury, was one of the first to offer a systematic definition of theology. He is regarded as one of the fathers of scholastic theology. He became famous for introducing Aristotelian logic into medieval thought. Before he became the archbishop of Canterbury, Anselm served as the prior (religious superior) of the Abbey of Bec. He spent his time teaching and providing counsel to the monks under his care. The two major works for which he is known are the *Monologion*, which literally means "an address to God," and the *Proslogion*, another work in which he gave a systematic presentation of the existence of God known as the "ontological argument."

Anselm did not see much need for a rational proof of God's existence. In the medieval era in which he lived faith was taken for granted and philosophy was assumed to be a "handmaid" of theology. As a leader of a large community, Anselm wanted to reach out to those monks who were vigorously involved in pastoral and intellectual activities. Wanting to encourage them and give them reasons why they should not despair in the face of difficulties, he gave a detailed account in the *Proslogion* of how God exists both as a concept and in reality. Starting with the notion that God is "that than which nothing greater can be conceived," Anselm argued that what exists in reality must be greater than that which exists only in the mind, and since God is that than which nothing greater can be thought, God must exist in reality. Anselm understood his project to be *fides quaerens intellectum* ("faith seeking understanding"). In other words, rather than seeking rational proof for God's existence, he derived his understanding from a simple act of faith. Addressing God in the *Proslogion*, he exclaimed,

27. Cunningham, *Catholic Heritage*, 108.

> Permit me, at least from afar or from the deep, to look upwards toward your light. Teach me to seek You, and reveal Yourself to me as I seek; for unless you instruct me I cannot seek You, and unless You reveal Yourself I cannot find You . . . For I do not seek to understand in order to believe but I believe in order to understand. For I believe this: that I shall not understand unless I believe.[28]

Fides quarens intellectum, which speaks to Anselm's search for ultimate meaning, has been taken by many Catholic theologians to be a classical definition of theology. Anselm's definition was influenced by the theological debate of the time concerning essence and existence. The debate, dating back to the time of Aristotle, suggested that everything comes into being by virtue of two principles: essence and existence. The essence of a thing (what makes a thing what it is) is different from its existence. There was also the debate as to whether or not existence precedes essence. In his *fides quarens intellectum*, Anselm accepted the notion that in God essence and existence are one and the same. For some of Anselm's peers who were trained in Aristotelian philosophy, the notion that God is that than which nothing greater can be conceived was easily understandable, for such a notion squares well with the Christian adaptation of the Aristotelian theory of essence and existence. Regardless, some of Anselm's contemporaries still questioned Anselm's definition on philosophical grounds.

Thomas Aquinas (1224/5–74)

At the time of Aquinas what we call "theology" was known as "natural theology." In book 6 of *Metaphysics* Aristotle, whom Thomas admired as an intellectual giant, treated natural theology as part of philosophy. Not satisfied with this Aristotelian treatment, Thomas needed another term for natural theology. He chose the term *sacra doctrina* ("sacred doctrine"), since it deals with the wisdom of God that comes to us from revelation. In book 1, chapter 4 of *Contra Gentiles*, Aquinas gives three reasons why it is difficult for some people to engage in diligent inquiry for truth: some are prevented because their physical disinclination makes them not disposed to learning, others are prevented because of the pressures of family life, and still others are prevented because of laziness. Aquinas suggests that the reason why a person learns metaphysics (the study of divine realities) is because the pursuit of truth requires such a considerable effort, which unfortunately many are not willing to give. He argues that there are two ways of knowing the

---

28. Anselm of Canterbury, *Proslogion*, ch. 1.

truths about God. The first is through natural reason, as in the case of those truths that have been conclusively proved by philosophers. The other is through revelation, by which we know those things that exceed the capacity of human reason, like the mystery of the Trinity (the fact that God is three persons in one being).

Aquinas defined theology as the "science of faith," and went to great lengths to discuss the nature of this science, contending that it is necessary for the salvation of the human person that there be a knowledge revealed by God that goes beyond philosophical science. Those truths that exceed human reason, according to Aquinas, are known by revelation, for without revelation "truth about God such as reason could discover would only be known by a few, and that after a long time, and with the admixture of many errors."[29]

In the *Summa Theologiae* Aquinas devotes ten articles to investigating the nature and extent of *sacra doctrina*: (1) Whether it is necessary?; (2) Whether it is a science?; (3) Whether it is one or many?; (4) Whether it is speculative or practical?; (5) How it is compared with other sciences?; (6) Whether it is the same as wisdom?; (7) Whether God is its subject matter?; (8) Whether it is a matter of argument?; (9) Whether it rightly employs metaphors and similes?; (10) Whether the Sacred Scripture of this doctrine may be expounded in different senses? Here is an example of how he argued his position:

Article 1: Whether, besides philosophy, any further doctrine is required?
Objection 1: It seems that, besides philosophical science, we have no need of any further knowledge. For man should not seek to know what is above reason: "Seek not the things that are too high for thee" (Sirach 3:22). But whatever is not above reason is fully treated of in philosophical science. Therefore any other knowledge besides philosophical science is superfluous.
Objection 2: Further, knowledge can be concerned only with being, for nothing can be known, save what is true; and all that is, is true. But everything that is, is treated of in philosophical science—even God Himself; so that there is a part of philosophy called theology, or the divine science, as Aristotle has proved (Metaph. vi). Therefore, besides philosophical science, there is no need of any further knowledge.
On the contrary, It is written (2 Timothy 3:16): "All Scripture, inspired of God is profitable to teach, to reprove, to correct, to instruct in justice." Now Scripture, inspired of God, is no part of philosophical science, which has been built up by human reason. Therefore it is useful that besides philosophical science, there should be other knowledge, i.e. inspired of God.

29. *ST* I, q.1, a.1.

I answer that, It was necessary for man's salvation that there should be a knowledge revealed by God besides philosophical science built up by human reason. Firstly, indeed, because man is directed to God, as to an end that surpasses the grasp of his reason: "The eye hath not seen, O God, besides Thee, what things Thou hast prepared for them that wait for Thee" (Isaiah 66:4). But the end must first be known by men who are to direct their thoughts and actions to the end. Hence it was necessary for the salvation of man that certain truths which exceed human reason should be made known to him by divine revelation. Even as regards those truths about God which human reason could have discovered, it was necessary that man should be taught by a divine revelation; because the truth about God such as reason could discover, would only be known by a few, and that after a long time, and with the admixture of many errors. Whereas man's whole salvation, which is in God, depends upon the knowledge of this truth. Therefore, in order that the salvation of men might be brought about more fitly and more surely, it was necessary that they should be taught divine truths by divine revelation. It was therefore necessary that besides philosophical science built up by reason, there should be a sacred science learned through revelation.

Reply to Objection 1: Although those things which are beyond man's knowledge may not be sought for by man through his reason, nevertheless, once they are revealed by God, they must be accepted by faith. Hence the sacred text continues, "For many things are shown to thee above the understanding of man" (Sirach 3:25). And in this, the sacred science consists.

Reply to Objection 2: Sciences are differentiated according to the various means through which knowledge is obtained. For the astronomer and the physicist both may prove the same conclusion: that the earth, for instance, is round: the astronomer by means of mathematics (i.e. abstracting from matter), but the physicist by means of matter itself. Hence there is no reason why those things which may be learned from philosophical science, so far as they can be known by natural reason, may not also be taught us by another science so far as they fall within revelation. Hence theology included in sacred doctrine differs in kind from that theology which is part of philosophy.

Late Scholastics and Reformation Thinkers

Aquinas' definition of theology as the "science of faith" was a groundbreaking definition at the time. It influenced other scholastics who saw the need to employ Aristotelian philosophy to improve on what Aquinas had begun. But with time abuses crept in and excessive use of Aristotelianism in theology, among other things, led to the demise of scholasticism. The sixteenth-century reformers presented a systematic argument against this dependence of theology on philosophy. One of Martin Luther's goals in the Reformation was to rid theology of philosophy. His program of *sola fide, sola scriptura* ("faith alone, Scripture alone") insisted on rejecting anything that was not scriptural, even if it meant renouncing all he had learned from the Church Fathers, including the learned Augustine, whom he revered. "At first, I devoured Augustine. But when the door was opened for me in Paul, so that I understood what justification by faith is, it was all over with Augustine. The books of his *Confessions* teach nothing; they only incite the reader; they are made up merely of examples, but do not instruct."[30] The attitude Luther had toward Augustine was the same attitude he had toward the church fathers in general. He had no use for their understanding of theology: "Jerome can be read for the sake of history, for he has nothing at all to say about faith and the teaching of true religion. I have no use for Chrysostom either, for he is only a gossip. Basil doesn't amount to a thing; he was a monk after all, and I wouldn't give a penny for him. Philip [Melanchthon]'s *Apology* is superior to all the doctors of the Church, even to Augustine himself."[31]

Luther's criticism of the church's doctrine and practices culminated in the sixteenth-century Protestant Reformation. In spite of its public condemnation of Luther, the Catholic Church had to reexamine some of its doctrine and practices. This reassessment led to the establishment of seminaries and divinity schools after the Council of Trent (held between 1545 and 1563) for the formal training of priests and pastors. Theology would no longer be taught in the universities, but in seminaries established specifically for that purpose. To help those trained in the seminaries receive a solid theological education, theology was divided into four main areas:

a. **Biblical theology**: a branch of theology that deals with the study of scripture. It concentrates on the Old Testament and the New Testament. It also pays attention to the study of the original languages, like Hebrew, Greek, Aramaic, Syriac, and Latin, in which the Bible was written.

b. **Historical theology**: a branch of theology that studies the history of Christian thought, ideas, and movements like the Reformation, Renaissance, and modernism, etc. It also pays special attention to patristic and historical figures like Augustine, Ambrose, Gregory the Great, and the Greek Church Fathers (Athanasius, Basil, Gregory of Nazianzus, and John Chrysostom).

c. **Systematic theology**: a branch of theology that studies Christian doctrine and dogma. It attempts a meaningful presentation of Christian beliefs, dealing also with the works and thought of systematic

30. Oakes, *Pattern of Redemption*, 107.
31. Oakes, *Pattern of Redemption*, 107–8.

theologians like Bernard Lonergan, Karl Rahner, Karl Barth, John Macquarie, Elizabeth Johnson, and Shawn Copeland.

d. Ethics, or moral theology: a branch of theology that deals with principles of Christian living and human conduct. It asks: How ought we to live as Christians?

Modern Era

In the modern period theology has become specialized and has moved from the seminaries back to the universities, where it originally took shape as an academic discipline. Today theology is taught both in seminaries and in universities that have departments of theology or religious studies. Modern theologians view theology somewhat differently from the way it was viewed in the past, as can be seen in the three modern definitions we shall examine: one by an Anglican theologian, another by a Catholic systematic theologian, and a third by an African-American womanist theologian.

a. John Macquarrie (1919–2007): John Macquarrie was a Scottish-born Reformed (Protestant) systematic theologian and an ordained priest in the Anglican Church. He was raised in a Calvinist environment, near Glasgow, Scotland, where he was born. His father was an elder in the Presbyterian Church. His desire to explore the influence of Martin Heidegger's philosophy on Rudolph Bultmann's theology led to the publication of his now famous work *An Existentialist Theology* (1960). Macquarrie taught systematic theology from 1962 to 1970 at the University of Oxford, where he served as Lady Margaret Professor of Divinity, a prestigious post he held until he retired in 1986. His works provide a broad methodology for investigating human nature. He analyzed human existence in light of scripture, tradition, and reason, understanding that reason plays a special role in human life. In another important work, *Principles of Christian Theology* (1966), he defined theology as "the study, which, through participation in and reflection upon a religious faith, seeks to express the content of this faith in the clearest and most coherent language available."[32]

b. Bernard Lonergan (1904–84): Bernard Lonergan was a Canadian Jesuit philosopher, economist, and theologian. He was born in Buckingham, Quebec, on December 17, 1904. At the age of thirteen he left for

---

32. Macquarie, *Principles of Christian Theology*, 1.

the prestigious Loyola College, a Jesuit high school and junior college in Montreal, and at seventeen he entered the Jesuit novitiate at Guelph, Ontario. After his novitiate and juniorate, he left for Heythrop College at Oxford for studies in philosophy. He also pursued a degree at the University of London and was ordained a priest in 1936 after the completion of his studies.

As a student, Lonergan devoted his free time to reading St. Augustine and Plato's early dialogues. He also read the *Summa* of Thomas Aquinas and was impressed by it. While doing his doctoral work at the Gregorian in Rome in 1938, Lonergan wrote his doctoral dissertation, *A History of St. Thomas' Thought on Operative Grace: A Study of the Development of St. Thomas' Notions of Grace and Human Freedom*. After his dissertation he moved to Montreal and served as professor of theology from 1940 to 1946 at the Collège de L' Immaculée-Conception. Lonergan has written numerous works in philosophy and theology. Two of his famous books are *Insight: A Study of Human Understanding* (which he began writing in the early 1950s while teaching in Toronto) and *Method in Theology* (1971), where he developed what has been termed a "general empirical method." In *Method in Theology* Lonergan articulates his understanding of the general empirical method (also known as the "cognitional method") and shows its application to religion, faith (Christian faith especially), and human cultures. He distinguishes between religion and theology. For him, any attempt to identify theology with religion would be "to revert to the earliest period of Christianity." Yet, while religion and theology are be separate, they still remain interdependent and should be integrated.

Integrating religion and theology, Lonergan defines religion as a mediation between religion and culture and theology as that which "mediates between a cultural matrix and the significance and role of religion in that matrix."[33] From this explanatory definition, we see that Lonergan conceives of theology as a reflection on religion. This means that we cannot speak of one theology or of theology as exclusively Christian. Rather, there are as many theologies as there religions— Hindu theologies, Buddhist theologies, Islamic theologies, Christian theologies, etc. Also, within Christian theology itself we can speak of liberation theology, African-American theology, Black theology, Latino/Latina theology, feminist theology, womanist theology, etc.

Theological reflection, for Lonergan, has two phases. In the first, the *mediating phase*, theological reflection ascertains the ideals, beliefs,

33. Lonergan, *Method in Theology*, xi.

and acts of the representatives of the religion under investigation. Here theological reflection encounters the past. In the second, the *mediated phase*, theological reflection is not just content to narrate the belief system of others and what they propose; it also pronounces which doctrines are true, how they can be reconciled with one another or with the findings of science, and also how they can be communicated appropriately to people of every race and culture. In this sense then, theology confronts the future. To accomplish these responsibilities, Lonergan lists eight distinct tasks that a theologian performs: research, interpretation, history, dialectic, foundations, doctrines, systematics and communications. He calls these eight tasks the "functional specialties." The functional specialties are interrelated, with one leading and yielding to the other. It is like a wheel whose parts, when set in motion, work cooperatively to get to the intended destination. A good theologian, for example, is one who engages in research and gathers available data. The data gathered is scrutinized and interpreted so that only what is relevant to the investigation is advanced. The material gathered is situated in its historical context. The pros and cons of the material are weighed. The outcome is subjected to further discussion and dialogue. After dialogue, there emerges a set of beliefs. This set of beliefs is articulated and explained. Finally, what is articulated and explained is communicated in ways that are relevant to everyday living. This is how the functional specialties, i.e., operations performed by the theologian, work in concert.

c. **M. Shawn Copeland** (b. 1947): M. Shawn Copeland is professor of systematic theology at Boston College. She is a former president of the Catholic Theological Society of America (CTSA). Her praxis-based theology engages the shifts in theological understanding of the human person, particularly as these play out in gender, class, race, and (female) body. Among her more than one hundred articles and books are *Enfleshing Freedom: Body, Race, and Being* (2010) and *The Subversive Power of Love* (2009). Copeland's political theology denounces "protracted intransigence toward Black and Womanist theologies" and what she deems the failure of mainstream theology to "interrogate the interaction of gender, race, and class." She suggests that European theological and philosophical sources are inadequate for dealing with "White America's intractable racism." She therefore calls for "a serious and exacting Black Catholic theology that goes well beyond historical retrieval." Copeland sees the need to uncover the particular, partial, and limited character of history. For her, theology should be used to contest and erase the distortions of Black men and women because, theology, strictly speaking, "clarifies how traditioning contributes to the constitution of cultural, social, and existential identity."[34] Copeland's understanding of theology follows that tradition (Black theology) that attempts to give hope to the suffering and oppressed of society by challenging societal structures and analyzing the meaning of hope in God. Thus, theology, for Copeland, must speak to the needs of the poor and oppressed.

34. Copeland, "Guest Editorial," 604–5.

2

Creation Accounts of the Abrahamic Religions

TODAY PHYSICISTS AND SCIENTISTS have a lot to say on the question of the origin of the universe. They suggest that an understanding of the physical laws that govern the universe and how these physical laws work hold the key to unlocking the mystery of the origin of the universe. Some physicists take a step further—that if we understand quantum mechanics (the branch of physics that studies atoms and tiny particles) and the theory of relativity (made famous by Albert Einstein), we will begin to understand how the universe came into existence. According to Quantum mechanics, there is no such thing as an empty space. What we assume to be a vacuum, according to Quantum mechanics, is not actually vacuous. Rather it contains tons of particles and antiparticles, which are capable of flaring into existence and fading back into nothingness. According to this theory (which seems unconvincing), the universe must have come into existence from these particles and antiparticles. Today some physicists are moving towards the idea that the universe may have begun with the Big Bang. The Big Bang theory is another cosmological attempt to explain the origin of the universe. There are different variations of the Big Bang theory, but the standard view is that the universe sprang into existence about 13.7 billion years ago. The theory suggests that the cosmic expansion of the universe led to the formation of subatomic particles that include protons, neutrons, and electrons, which, after some cooling-off stage, coalesced to form the stars and the galaxies as we know them today.

The question of the origin of the universe is a fundamental human question that religion also addresses. The three Abrahamic religions (Judaism, Christianity, and Islam) agree that the universe has a beginning. They differ with science on how the universe came into existence. For the three Abrahamic religions, the universe was created in time by God and this creation is not a natural event, but a supernatural act. We want to be clear that the Abrahamic religions were not the first to address the question of the origin of the universe in a religious way. From the beginning of human history the question of the origin of the universe, i.e., how the world as we know it came about, was a fundamental human question that ancient cultures addressed. It is part of the question of the meaning of life and ultimate significance that human beings, as religious persons, cannot escape. Every age and culture has its own constructed myths and stories aimed at answering this fundamental question. Many ancient cultures put the matter of the origin of the universe squarely in the hands of their gods. The great legacy of Mesopotamia, the site of several civilizations after 4000 BCE, was its creation myths.[1] Early civilizations that developed in Mesopotamia— the Sumerians, Akkadians, Chaldeans, Assyrians, and Babylonians—also used their creation myths to account for the plagues and natural disasters they experienced. These myths offered explanations for both the flood and drought that plagued the Tigris and Euphrates at various times. Ancient cultures, in general, cleverly devised myths as a way of explaining the flux and instability they experienced in their daily lives. What we find is a pattern in which civilizations that developed along rivers where the climate was unstable (like the Mesopotamians and Babylonians that developed along the Tigris and Euphrates) tend to have tons of creation myths, while those that developed along rivers where the climate was stable (like the Egyptian civilization along the Nile River) tend to have fewer creation myths. The myths serve both as an explanation to a problem and a possible solution.

JUDEO-CHRISTIAN ACCOUNTS

When we examine the canon of the Hebrew Scriptures we see that as the canon of Hebrew Scriptures was taking shape Greek or Hellenistic culture was becoming dominant throughout the Eastern Mediterranean basin. As more and more Jews spoke Greek the demand for Greek translations of the Hebrew Bible increased. We also see that each of the books of the Hebrew Bible, particularly the first five that Jews call the Torah (Christians call the Pentateuch), have different authors and translators. Part of the reason for

1. Carmody and Brink, *Ways to the Center*, 62–63.

difference in translators is that they were not all translated at the same time. Although controversy persists about the circumstances that led to the translations of these books, there was no doubt regarding the importance of the exercise itself. The first book of the Hebrew Bible, Genesis, was translated into Greek about the third century BCE in Alexandria, which was at the time a flourishing Greek-speaking Jewish community.[2]

The book of Genesis, like the various creation myths deriving from the civilizations that settled along rivers Tigris and Euphrates, attempts to tell its own creation story from an Israelite point of view, i.e., God's chosen people. The Hebrew title of the book, *Bereshit* ("In the beginning"), is the first phrase of the book. But in the Greek translation "Genesis" is a reference to the opening theme (i.e., creation) of the book.[3] The narrators creatively use the creation motifs of the ancient Near East to express their own experience of Yahweh's creative work.[4] The book, which divides naturally into two parts: the story of creation and human origins (Gen 1–11) and the story of the patriarchs, i.e., Abraham, Isaac, Jacob and Joseph, etc. (Gen 12–50), in theory spans about 2307 years. This number was derived "by combining the ages of the fathers of humanity at the birth of their successors with the years that elapsed between the birth of Abraham and the death of Joseph."[5] Genesis 1–11 is called the primeval story because it tries to tell the story of the origin of the universe, from the time Yahweh Elohim created the world to the time the earth was populated by human beings, i.e., the beginning of civilization. The remainder of the book (Gen 12–50) is an attempt by the narrators "to show that Yahweh had guided their ancestors in a way of promise up to the events of the exodus."[6]

It is helpful to keep in mind that the narrators of the Genesis story did not intend to give a scientific account of history as we know it today. Their story is rather a confessional statement about the origin of the universe, which they interpreted in light of Yahweh's mercy, kindness, and love. They narrated these stories with a good blend of myth and etiology (tales to explain a certain state of affairs). People sometimes tend to think of myth as contrary to facts. We pointed out in the last chapter that that is not necessarily true. Myth is a story about the past that is told and retold to express certain realities. Thus while myths do not pretend to have factual claims, they are told to express certain truths and values. Genesis 1–11 (primeval

2. Dines, "Imaging Creation," 439.

3. Cohn-Sherbok, *Hebrew Bible*, 12–13.

4. Landry and Penchansky, "Primeval Story," 20.

5. Cohn-Sherbok, *Hebrew Bible*, 13.

6. Boadt, *Reading the Old Testament*, 110.

history) then does not provide factual accounts of history in any scientific sense. In what way then are the stories historical?

> These stories are "historical" only in the sense that they plumb the depth of history's meaning and evince those fundamental experiences that have been common to human beings from the very dawn of history. The manner of presentation is poetic or pictorial, for the narrator is dealing with a subject that eludes the modern historian's investigation—namely, the ultimate source of the human drama in the initiative and purpose of God. Above all the narrative is written in the conviction that Israel's root experiences, Exodus and Sinai, provide the clue to the meaning of all human history, right back to the beginning.[7]

Two Creation Accounts

The primeval story begins with two accounts of creation. Apart from differences in style and vocabulary, the two stories differ significantly with respect to the order in which creation takes place, as well as in their portrayal of God. The traditions from which they drew their accounts probably had independent oral existences in the sense that people told the stories orally and passed them down to their descendants. In time they were written down and combined with other sources to assume the form in which they exist today.

Priestly "Elohim" Creation Story (Gen 1:1—2:4a)	Yahwist "YHWH ELOHIM" Creation Story (Gen 2:4b—3:24)
[1]In the beginning when God created the heavens and the earth, [2]the earth was a formless void and darkness covered the face of the deep, while a wind from God swept over the face of the waters. [3]Then God said, "Let there be light"; and there was light. [4]And God saw that the light was good; and God separated the light from the darkness. [5]God called the light Day, and the darkness he called Night. And there was evening and there was morning, the first day. [6]And God said, "Let there be a dome in the midst of the waters, and let it separate the waters from the	[4]These are the generations of the heavens and the earth when they were created. In the day that the Lord God made the earth and the heavens, [5]when no plant of the field was yet in the earth and no herb of the field had yet sprung up—for the Lord God had not caused it to rain upon the earth, and there was no one to till the ground; [6]but a stream would rise from the earth, and water the whole face of the ground—[7]then the Lord God formed man from the dust of the ground, and breathed into his nostrils the breath of life; and the man became a living being. [8]And

7. Anderson, *Understanding the Old Testament*, 160.

waters." [7]So God made the dome and separated the waters that were under the dome from the waters that were above the dome. And it was so. [8]God called the dome Sky. And there was evening and there was morning, the second day.

9And God said, "Let the waters under the sky be gathered together into one place, and let the dry land appear." And it was so. 10God called the dry land Earth, and the waters that were gathered together he called Seas. And God saw that it was good. 11Then God said, "Let the earth put forth vegetation: plants yielding seed, and fruit trees of every kind on earth that bear fruit with the seed in it." And it was so. 12The earth brought forth vegetation: plants yielding seed of every kind, and trees of every kind bearing fruit with the seed in it. And God saw that it was good. 13And there was evening and there was morning, the third day.

14And God said, "Let there be lights in the dome of the sky to separate the day from the night; and let them be for signs and for seasons and for days and years, 15and let them be lights in the dome of the sky to give light upon the earth." And it was so. 16God made the two great lights—the greater light to rule the day and the lesser light to rulethe night—and the stars. 17God set them in the dome of the sky to give light upon the earth, 18to rule over the day and over the night, and to separate the light from the darkness. And God saw that it was good. 19And there was evening and there was morning, the fourth day.

20And God said, "Let the waters bring forth swarms of living creatures, and let birds fly above the earth across the dome of the sky." 21So God created the great sea monsters and every living creature that moves, of every kind,

the Lord God planted a garden in Eden, in the east; and there he put the man whom he had formed. [9]Out of the ground the Lord God made to grow every tree that is pleasant to the sight and good for food, the tree of life also in the midst of the garden, and the tree of the knowledge of good and evil.

10A river flows out of Eden to water the garden, and from there it divides and becomes four branches. 11The name of the first is Pishon; it is the one that flows around the whole land of Havilah, where there is gold; 12 and the gold of that land is good; bdellium and onyx stone are there. 13The name of the second river is Gihon; it is the one that flows around the whole land of Cush. 14The name of the third river is Tigris, which flows east of Assyria. And the fourth river is the Euphrates.

15The Lord God took the man and put him in the garden of Eden to till it and keep it. 16And the Lord God commanded the man, "You may freely eat of every tree of the garden; 17but of the tree of the knowledge of good and evil you shall not eat, for in the day thatyou eat of it you shall die."

18Then the Lord God said, "It is not good that the man should be alone; I will make him a helper as his partner." 19So out of the ground the Lord God formed every animal of the field and every bird of the air, and brought them to the man to see what he would call them; and whatever the man called each living creature, that was its name. 20The man gave names to all cattle, and to the birds of the air, and to every animal of the field; but for the man there was not found a helper as his partner. 21So the Lord God caused a deep sleep to fall upon the man, and he slept; then he took one of his ribs and closed up its place with flesh. 22And the rib that the Lord God had taken from the man he made into a woman with which the waters swarm, and every winged bird of every kind. And God saw that it was good. 22God blessed them, saying, "Be fruitful and multixply and fill the waters in the seas, and let birds multiply on the earth." 23And there was evening and there was morning, the fifth day.

24And God said, "Let the earth bring forth living creatures of every kind: cattle and creeping things and wild animals of the earth of every kind." And it was so. 25God made the wild animals of the earth of every kind, and the cattle of every kind, and everything that creeps upon the ground of every kind. And God saw that it was good.

26Then God said, "Let us make humankind in our image, according to our likeness; and let them have dominion over the fish of the sea, and over the birds of the air, and over the cattle, and over all the wild animals of the earth, and over every creeping thing that creeps upon the earth." 27So God created humankind in his image, in the image of God he created them; male and female he created them. 28God blessed them, and God said to them, "Be fruitful and multiply, and fill the earth and subdue it; and have dominion over the fish of the sea and over the birds of the air and over every living thing that moves upon the earth."

29God said, "See, I have given you every plant yielding seed that is upon the face of all the earth, and every tree with seed in its fruit; you shall have them for food. 30And to every beast of the earth, and to every bird of the air, and to everything that creeps on the earth, everything that has the breath of life, I have given every green plant for food." And it was so.

and brought her to the man. 23Then the man said,

"This at last is bone of my bones
and flesh of my flesh;
this one shall be called Woman,
for out of Man this one was taken."

24Therefore a man leaves his father and his mother and clings to his wife, and they become one flesh. 25And the man and his wife were both naked, and were not ashamed.

1Now the serpent was more crafty than any other wild animal that the Lord God had made. He said to the woman, "Did God say, 'You shall not eat from any tree in the garden'?" 2The woman said to the serpent, "We may eat of the fruit of the trees in the garden; 3but God said, 'You shall not eat of the fruit of the tree that is in the middle of the garden, nor shall you touch it, or you shall die.'" 4But the serpent said to the woman, "You will not die; 5for God knows that when you eat of it your eyes will be opened, and you will be like God, knowing good and evil." 6So when the woman saw that the tree was good for food, and that it was a delight to the eyes, and that the tree was to be desired to make one wise, she took of its fruit and ate; and she also gave some to her husband, who was with her, and he ate. 7Then the eyes of both were opened, and they knew that they were naked; and they sewed fig leaves together and made loincloths for themselves.

8They heard the sound of the Lord God walking in the garden at the time of the evening breeze, and the man and his wife hid themselves from the presence of the Lord God among the trees of the garden. 9But the Lord God called to the man, and said to him, "Where are you?" 10He said, "I heard the sound of you in the garden, and I was afraid, because I was naked; and I

31God saw everything that he had made, and indeed, it was very good. And there was evening and there was morning, the sixth day.

1Thus the heavens and the earth were finished, and all their multitude. 2And on the seventh day God finished the work that he had done, and he rested on the seventh day from all the work that he had done. 3So God blessed the seventh day and hallowed it, because on it God rested from all the work that he had done in creation.

4These are the generations of the heavens and the earth when they were created. In the day that the Lord God made the earth and the heavens,

hid myself." 11He said, "Who told you that you were naked? Have you eaten from the tree of which I commanded you not to eat?" 12The man said, "The woman whom you gave to be with me, she gave me fruit from the tree, and I ate." 13Then the Lord God said to the woman, "What is this that you have done?" The woman said, "The serpent tricked me, and I ate." 14The Lord God said to the serpent,

"Because you have done this,
    cursed are you among all animals
    and among all wild creatures;
upon your belly you shall go,
    and dust you shall eat
    all the days of your life.
15I will put enmity between you and
    the woman,
    and between your offspring and
        hers;
he will strike your head,
    and you will strike his heel."

16To the woman he said,

"I will greatly increase your pangs in
    childbearing;
    in pain you shall bring forth
        children,
yet your desire shall be for your
    husband,
    and he shall rule over you."

17And to the man he said,

"Because you have listened to the
    voice of your wife,
    and have eaten of the tree
about which I commanded you,
    'You shall not eat of it,'
cursed is the ground because of you;
    in toil you shall eat of it all the days
        of your life;
18thorns and thistles it shall bring
    forth for you;
    and you shall eat the plants of the
        field.
19By the sweat of your face
    you shall eat bread
    until you return to the ground,

for out of it you were taken;
you are dust,
    and to dust you shall return."

20The man named his wife Eve, because she was the mother of all who live. 21And the Lord God made garments of skins for the man* and for his wife, and clothed them.

22Then the Lord God said, "See, the man has become like one of us, knowing good and evil; and now, he might reach out his hand and take also from the tree of life, and eat, and live forever"— 23therefore the Lord God sent him forth from the garden of Eden, to till the ground from which he was taken. 24He drove out the man; and at the east of the garden of Eden he placed the cherubim, and a sword flaming and turning to guard the way to the tree of life.

The first creation account, which was written at the time of the exile, comes from the Priestly writers who were in charge of cultic worship and whose duties as priests suggest that they were concerned with ritual matters. Their concern for rituals and worship was very evident in this creation account, which they framed in a seven-day structure, emphasizing how Yahweh imposed order on the watery chaos. In this (Priestly) account, which begins in Genesis 1:1—2:3, Yahweh created the world out of nothing and completed His work in six days. "The distribution of the separate creative acts into six twenty-four-hour days was a deliberate scheme utilized by the priestly writer. Organizing the activities in this way implies that God's design had rhythm and intentionality."[8] Human beings, made in the image of God, are the cream of Yahweh's creation. They are to assume leadership of created realities and take care of the earth. One of the goals of the Priestly account was to show creation as Yahweh's gift to humanity who in turn must worship Yahweh. The seventh day was given special status because it was the only day Yahweh blessed, a good reason to keep the Sabbath day holy.[9] The priestly writer deliberately emphasizes how the process of creation suggests

8. Bandstra, *Reading the Old Testament*, 53.
9. Bandstra, *Reading the Old Testament*, 60.

that order and structure are pleasing to Yahweh, thereby suggesting that order and structure must also be present in the religious activities of Israel.[10]

The second creation account, which begins in Genesis 2:4b—3:24, comes from the Yahwist source. This account, which predates the Priestly account, describes creation as having taken place in different sequence and time frame. Unlike the remote and abstract God of the Priestly tradition, here God is portrayed as humanlike. God even comes down at certain time of the day to enjoy the garden He has made and to commune with humans.[11] The Yahwist writers were concerned with the problem of evil and proliferation of sin. These concerns make them to tell their story in a four-part story plot of sin, divine punishment, divine mercy, and further sin.[12] Their account details how Yahweh created human beings out of clay. The first human being to be created was Adam. After fashioning him from clay God breathed into him the breath of life. Adam seemed so lonely that God had to create for him a partner. God caused him to fall into a deep sleep and from his ribs created a woman whom the man, after seeing her, liked. He named her Eve (meaning mother of all the living). The two were placed in the garden of Eden and were instructed to eat of all the trees in the garden, except for the tree in the middle of the garden—the tree of good and knowledge. The serpent tempted them and they ate of the tree God had commanded them not to eat. As punishment for their disobedience God cursed them and expelled them from the garden.

What Questions Does Genesis Try to Answer?

At the time the Genesis account was written the ancient world was dominated militarily by the Babylonians and later by the Persians. The text addresses the questions: what divine force is in control of the world, given that it has been dominated militarily by the Babylonians? How does Israel forge its identity in a world that tries to deprive her of her identity?[13] Genesis 1–11 in particular is primarily a document of faith, i.e., a community's faith in a God who acts in human history.[14] The two creation accounts of Genesis are part of this confession of religious faith meant "to strengthen the community's

---

10. Landry and Penchansky, "Primeval Story," 20.
11. Landry and Penchansky, "Primeval Story," 21.
12. Boadt, *Reading the Old Testament*, 111.
13. Bailey and Furnish, *Pentateuch*, 127.
14. Tuohey, "Gender Distinctions," 175–76.

faith in a God who acts in human history by grounding that activity in a story of God's acting in cosmic history."[15]

Genesis mounts a sustained attack on the polytheism of its neighbors. In contrast to the cosmic struggle of the Babylonian creation epic in which the national god, Marduk, subdues the primeval sea (Tiamat), Genesis reduces the "deep" sea to an impersonal matter, effortlessly shaped by a God who exists from the beginning. In contrast to the Sumerian epic in which the wind god, Enlil, brings order out of chaos, Genesis reduces the wind to an impersonal "thing" that does Yahweh's bidding.[16] "Light is created before the luminaries—before the sun god, in particular. Yahweh then separates light from darkness. They are not manifestations of the twin dualistic gods whom the Persians worshiped. The sun, the moon, and the stars also are objects created by Yahweh. They are not powerful gods, each with a sacred text, rituals, temple, and priesthood of its own, as in Mesopotamia and Canaan."[17] Some of Israel's neighbors were also attributing to certain animals divine power. Genesis shows that rather than bow down to the created order, humans are given dominion over these creatures.

The Priestly and Yahwist accounts of creation together "establish fundamental Hebrew truths about God in relation to the universe and humanity. God is sovereign and powerful, yet approachable and concerned."[18] The two stories complement each other. Both accounts tell us that the first human being, Adam, was made from the soil, *adamah*, and that he became a living being only after Yahweh had breathed into him the breath of life. Both accounts also deal with "the deeper question of why man and woman, God's creatures, refuse to acknowledge the sovereignty of their Creator, with the result that history is a tragic story of banishment from the life for which they were intended."[19] The garden of Eden story shows not only human rebellion against divine authority, but also human determination to assert independence by grasping for the fruit of the forbidden tree.[20]

CREATION ACCOUNTS IN THE QURAN

Like the Genesis creation story, the Quran speaks of God as creating the world in six days. "Indeed, your Lord is Allah, who created the heavens and

15. Tuohey, "Gender Distinctions," 176.

16. Bailey and Furnish, *Pentateuch*, 127–78.

17. Bailey and Furnish, *Pentateuch*, 127–78.

18. Bandstra, *Reading the Old Testament*, 69.

19. Anderson, *Understanding the Old Testament*, 161.

20. Anderson, *Understanding the Old Testament*, 162.

earth in six days and then established Himself above the Throne. He covers the night with the day, [another night] chasing it rapidly; and [He created] the sun, the moon, and the stars, subjected by His command. Unquestionably, His is the creation and the command; blessed is Allah, Lord of the worlds" (Quran 7:54) The Quran is also clear that six days here should be understood only metaphorically because, for God, a day is like one thousand years and one thousand years is like one day (Quran 32:5). The word used to describe the world is *alamin*. God is the creator of everything (Quran 39:62). But unlike Genesis, where the creation accounts occupy the first two chapters of the book, creation accounts in the Quran are not located in one place. They are intentionally scattered throughout the book, for example Quran 7:54, 10:3, 11:7, 25:59, 32:4, 50:38, and 57:4.

The biblical account suggests that God created out of nothing. According to John Kaltner, there is little support in the Quran for *creation ex nihilo* (creation out of nothing), as we have in Christian teaching. In each of the passages (like Quran 40:68) that speak of creation, "there is already some 'thing' or matter to which God is speaking, and so it is better to think of this as transformation or reordering rather than calling something into being out of nothing."[21] Unlike the biblical account, the Quran also does not specify what was created in each of the six days that God created the world. It is only in Quran 41:9–12 that a distinction is made "between the first four days, when the earth was formed, and the next two days, during which the heavens were created."[22] The manner of creation in the Quran, however, is like that of Genesis where God spoke and what God commanded happened. In the Quran God had to speak in order to create something. God says "'Be' and it is" (Quran 40:68; 2:117).

The creation of Adam in the Quran is also similar to the biblical story. Adam was created out of clay (Quran 6:2; 15:26). Reference is also made to Eve in the Quran, but no allusion to the biblical account where Eve was said to have been created out of Adam's rib. But some Muslim interpreters have no problem accepting the biblical account that Eve was created from Adam's ribs because the story is found in the hadith (Prophetic traditions), though not in the Quran.[23] What the Quran spells out is that Adam and Eve were instructed by God to reside in paradise and enjoy all the bounties God has placed in paradise for them, but with one exception, i.e., not to eat of the fruit of one of the trees. "Satan made them defy the divine commandment and they were ordered to descend to earth for a specified period of time (see

21. Kaltner, *Introducing the Qur'an*, 49.

22. Kaltner, *Introducing the Qur'an*, 48.

23. Nawaz, *Islam*, 427.

Quran 2:35–36). Adam repented for his transgressions and was forgiven by the Lord (see Quran 2:37)."[24] The Quran is always quick to point out that God is beneficent and merciful, always eager to forgive, if one repents of one's sins. That Adam repented and was forgiven by God is the Quran's way of showing Islam's disagreement with the Christian teaching of original sin (the sin of Adam and Eve, which in Christian teaching is inherited by everyone).

The Quran suggests that humanity is at the center of God's creation. God made them superior to other creatures. According to the Quran, the angels were with God when God created humans. The angels even protested when God wanted to create humans, telling God that human beings will bring nothing but trouble and mischief to God's creation. God ignored the angels' remonstration and created humans. After creating the first human being, Adam, God gives him a status higher than that of the angels by elevating him to the dignified position of *kalifa* or caliph (vicegerent or deputy of God). God teaches him the names of all the creatures but does not share the information with the angels, again showing God's predilection for humans.

> When your Lord said to the angels: "I am placing a caliph on earth," they replied: "Will You put there one that will do evil and shed blood, when we have for so long sung Your praises and sanctified Your name?" He said: "I know what you do not know." He taught Adam all the names and then set them before the angels, saying: "Tell me the names of these, if what you say be true." "Glory be unto You," they replied, "we have no knowledge except that which You have given us. You alone are wise and all-knowing." Then said He to Adam: "Tell them their names." And when Adam had named them, He said: "Did I not tell you that I know the secrets of heaven and earth, and all that you hide and all that you reveal?" (Al-Baqarah 2:30–33)

When God asks the angels for the name of the creatures none of them was able to name the creatures. Only Adam was able to name them. God then asks the angels to bow down and do obeisance to Adam. All the angels did except one, Iblis. God asks Iblis why he did not submit to Adam as he has been commanded. Iblis answered, "I am better than he; Thou has created me of fire, while him Thou didst create of dust" (Quran 7:12). God then banished Iblis from the Garden for his arrogance. Iblis (sometimes understood as Satan) promised to get even by exposing to Adam and Eve their nakedness. Iblis tricked them, telling them "Your Lord has forbidden you this tree, lest you become angels or become of the immortals" (Quran 7:20).

24. Nawaz, *Islam*, 426.

After he lured them and they ate of the forbidden tree their nakedness became exposed to them and they began to put together leaves to cover their nakedness. When they covered their nakedness God called out to them: "Did I not warn you that Satan was your sworn enemy?" They replied, "Our Lord, we have wronged our souls: if You do not forgive us and have mercy, we shall be lost" (Quran 7:23–24).

Unlike the Genesis creation story where God rested on the seventh day (Sabbath), the Quran does not specify that God rested on the seventh day. For the Quran, God "who created the heavens and the earth was not tired" (Quran 46:33).

Creation of Heaven and Earth (Quran 14:32–34)	Creation in Six Days (Quran 7:54)	Human Beings Created from Dust (Quran 3:20)	God gives Authority to Humans (Quran 7:11)
It is Allah who created the heavens and the earth and sent down rain from the sky and produced thereby some fruits as provision for you and subjected for you the ships to sail through the sea by His command and subjected for you the rivers. And he subjected for you the sun, and the moon, continuous [in orbit], and subjected for you the night and the day. And he gave you from all you asked of Him. And if you should count the favor of Allah, you could not enumerate them. Indeed, mankind is [generally] most unjust and ungrateful.	Indeed your Lord is Allah who created the heavens and earth in six days and then established Himself above the Throne. He covers the night with the day [another night], chasing it rapidly; and [He created] the sun, the moon, and the stars, subjected by His command. Unquestionably, His is the creation and the command; blessed is Allah, Lord of the worlds.	And of His signs is that He created you from dust; then, suddenly you were human beings dispersing [throughout the earth].	And we have certainly created you [O Mankind], and given you [human] form. Then we said to the angels, "Prostrate to Adam"; so they prostrated, except for Iblis. He was not of those who prostrated.

PROLIFERATION OF SIN IN THE BIBLE

According to the Genesis story, after Adam and Eve were expelled from the garden, they had conjugal relations, giving birth to their first son, Cain, and to another they named Abel. Cain was by profession a farmer. Abel was a shepherd. The two brothers offered sacrifice to God. God accepted Abel's offering but rejected that of Cain. Out of envy Cain slew his brother Abel, and by that singular act became the first murderer. The narrators of this story carefully show human belligerence and defiance even in the face of God's love and mercy. As punishment for his action, God cast a spell on Cain and he became a wanderer. After this incident Adam and Eve gave birth to their third son, Seth.

Human sinfulness and belligerence continue to get worse with successive generations. The sin of Cain continues in his lineage. Among his children were Enoch and Lamech. Genesis 4:17 speaks of Cain as being "the founder of a city, which he named after his son, Enoch." This narrative tells us how human culture got off to a bad start, since, ironically the first city was built by Cain, a murderer.[25] Genesis 4:17–24 also describes Lamech, Cain's other son, as a prototype of violent attackers. He even boasted to his wives about killing a man. Lamech also had three sons: Jabal, Jubal, and Tubal-Cain. Jabal was noted for domestication of animals, Jubal was famous for music, and Tubal-Cain famous for copper and iron industries. In spite of these achievements, sin continues to grow, as evident in Genesis 6:1–4, an account of human intransigence, the intermarriage between the sons of God and the daughters of men. The narrators of these accounts try to tell us "cultural advance was accompanied by violence, lust, and unbridled passion—a chain reaction of evil that proceeded from bad to worse. The last straw that broke the camel's back, according to this epic scheme, was the violence perpetrated by heavenly beings ('the sons of God') who espied beautiful human maidens and had intercourse with them (6:1–4)."[26] When God could not cope with human sinfulness God decided to destroy creation by sending the flood. But God spared Noah and his family whom God instructed to build an ark. The flood lasted forty days and forty nights. When the flood receded, God made a covenant with Noah and promised never again to destroy the earth with flood. "Despite the blessing to Noah and the great increase of nations seen in Genesis 10, the people again rebel in pride to challenge God's rule by building a tower to heaven. God punishes them by confusing human

---

25. Anderson, *Understanding the Old Testament*, 163.

26. Anderson, *Understanding the Old Testament*, 163.

languages, but again gives promise for the future in choosing Abraham."[27] The narrators tell us that even divine judgment could not check the evil impulses of the human heart because human culture was already infected by evil.[28] Anderson gives a good concluding remark to the primeval history:

> Primeval history, then, had a sad outcome, for humanity failed to find true wholeness—life in communion with God and in community with fellow human beings. From Cain to the Tower of Babel the human tragedy increased, despite advances in the arts and the sciences. History was urged on by "evil impulse" that polluted God's creation, leaving human beings estranged from their Creator and at odds with one another. Taken by itself, the story would be extremely pessimistic. But the primeval history is now part of the larger Israelite epic. In this narrative context, it serves as a prologue to what follows: the call of Abraham and his venture of faith.[29]

PROLIFERATION OF SIN IN THE QURAN

Islam accounts for the proliferation of sin in ways that are somewhat similar and somewhat different from the Genesis story. One of the Quran's central messages is that all created realities come from God, therefore everything in the heavens and the earth—sun, moon, stars, waters, and animals—are signs that point to God. "Time and again, the Quran repeats the theocentric message that everything was created by God and is controlled by God. Most of nature accepts that situation and does not try to rebel or deny God's authority. Only humanity attempts to wrestle control from God and assert its independence."[30] The Quran puts the fall squarely on both Adam and Eve who were tempted by Satan. According to one account of the event in the Quran, Satan made an evil suggestion to Adam and Eve so that he might reveal to them their shame that had remained hidden from them. He said to them, "Your Lord has forbidden you to approach this tree only to prevent you from becoming angels or immortals." (Quran 7:20). Upon hearing the sweet words of Satan, Adam and Eve thought too hard of the tree and they decided to eat of it. They were so preoccupied with the thoughts of the tree stemming from the whisperings of Satan that they forgot the decree of

27. Boadt, *Reading the Old Testament*, 113.

28. Anderson, *Understanding the Old Testament*, 164.

29. Anderson, *Understanding the Old Testament*, 166.

30. Kaltner, *Introducing the Qur'an*, 66.

Allah. Thus, both were tempted and both succumbed to the temptation of the devil. For Muslims, therefore,

- What happened in the garden was not "the fall" but a mistake or transgression.

- Satan may have deceived Adam and Eve into eating from the forbidden tree (Quran 2:24–36), but their transgression did not alienate them from God. In fact, Adam and Eve did acknowledge their transgression and repented. When they repented, God "turned toward them" because He is merciful and forgiving (2:37).

- Muslims believe it was God's plan from the beginning to put Adam and Eve on earth. God's plan was never to leave them in the garden permanently. The garden was only a temporary training ground to reveal God's continual need for guidance.

Muslims reject the Christian doctrine of original sin because the concept of original sin does not exist in Islam. Islam believes that because God is just, no one is held responsible for the sin of another unless they are responsible for it. Sin, therefore, is not hereditary. No one is born a sinner because it would be unjust for God who is just to punish all humanity because of the deeds of Adam and Eve. Islam, therefore, sees sin as a natural process built into creation. The human person whom Allah made from clot (clay) is destined to die (Quran 23:15) but will be raised up by Allah on the Day of Resurrection (Quran 23:16). Conversely, Muslims consider human nature at birth to be *fitrah*, i.e., a state of intrinsic goodness. Like Adam, everyone is born pure and sinless. This means that everyone is a Muslim by birth. If our state of *fitrah* (intrinsic innocence or goodness) does not last, it is only because of societal influences that make us deny our true nature. Satan's goal from the beginning is to make us forget God's guidance (Quran 58:19; 20:115). Disobedience is a result of forgetfulness; it is failure to remember God's instructions. Thus, it is because we are weak and forgetful that God sent prophets to remind us of the true path.

In sum, the act of submission to God, which is a central tenet of Islam, is performed naturally by all of God's creation, except humanity. Recall that in the Quran Adam and Eve repented for their disobedience and transgression and were forgiven by God (Quran 2:37). The Quran would further describe subsequent human sinfulness as part and parcel of this human failure to submit to the will of God. The rivalry between Cain and Abel (Quran 5:27–31) is described in terms of human belligerence, which became more obtuse in the story of Sodom and Gomorra. "Prophet Lot, a nephew of the prophet Abraham, settled among the people of Sodom and Gomorra and preached the divine message to them. Those were the people given to the abomination of homosexuality and were destroyed with an intense shower of brimstone and baked clay (Quran 7:80–84; 11:77–83; 15:58–77). The family of Lot was saved except his wife who betrayed her husband and denied the divine truth."[31]

Parallels in Ancient Near Eastern Texts

The two creation stories and the subsequent flood story in Genesis have parallels in the ancient Near East. Both the cosmic order and language of the Genesis creation story are similar to the cosmic order and language of the Egyptian creation story and the Babylonian creation myth. In the *Memphite Theology*, for instance, Ptah, the sun god, creates by speaking. By his spoken words the world comes to be and he declares it "good"; and in the Babylonian *Enuma Elish* a firm dome separates the waters of chaos from the waters of creation and Marduk achieves his creation by imposing cosmic order on this chaotic pre-existent cosmos.[32] There are also accounts of flood stories in the ancient Near East, like the Deluge Tablet, where the hero, Ziusudra, survived the flood by building a boat. In the Gilgamesh epic of ancient Mesopotamia, the hero, Utnapishtim, survived the flood sent by the gods, and in the Atrahasis epic, Atrahasis survived the flood. See the table below for echoes of the ancient pagan accounts in the creation stories of Genesis.

31. Nawaz, *Islam*, 428.
32. Landry and Penchansky, "Primeval Story," 20.

	Date	Setting	Cosmology	god who did creating	Manner they created	Things/people created	Other Information
Creation from Egypt	3rd Millenium B.C.E.	Egypt	Cosmos was dark, formless, watery void, encassed in darkness	Atum not only brought himself into being but also brought other creatures into being	Since he was male and had no mate he masturbated and brought lesser male and female deities into existence	"Lesser male" and female who populated the earth	Atum could also have created by naming his own body parts, from which came other separate beings.
Atrahasis Epic	19th Century B.C.E.	Mesopotamia	Heaven is ruled by the god Anu, earth by the god Enlil, and ocean by the god Enki.	pantheon of deities	The goddess Mami by mixing clay and saliva and shaping them	Human beings and all living creatures	Atrahasis epic includes both a creation and flood account. In its flood story, as the human population grew, they began to disturb Enlil's sleep. Enlil, after sending several warnings and plagues decided to destroy the earth by sending the flood. But he spared Atrahasis by giving him advanced warning to build a boat, loaded with animals and creatures of his choice.

	Date	Setting	Cosmology	god who did creating	Manner they created	Things/people created	Other Information
Enuma Elish	1700 B.C.E.	Babylonia	Before earth was created there were two vast bodies of water. The male fresh-water ocean was called Apsu and the female salt water ocean called Tiamat	Pantheon of gods came into being through the fusion of the male fresh water ocean Apsu and the female salt water ocean Tiamat	Younger gods came into being through sexual union	younger gods and human beings	Apsu wanted to dispose the younger gods. Ea found out and instead killed Apsu. Tiamat, in seeking revenge for the death of her husband Apsu, disposed the younger gods with the help of Kingu. Marduk decided to champion the cause of the younger gods. In the ensuing battle between Marduk and Tiamat, Marduk destroyed Tiamat and used her corpse to make the heavens. Marduk was enthroned as king of the gods by the lesser gods.
Genesis 1	The beginning of time	Israel	The earth was shapeless and void and darkness howvered over the face of the deep	Yahweh	He created by his spoken words. He made the heavens and the earth in six days, fashioned Adam from clay, and from his ribs made Eve.	He created human beings, the heavens and the earth, and all the living creatures.	Yahweh rested on the seventh day, which he blessed and made holy.

CHRISTIAN APPLICATION OF THE CREATION STORY

Christian tradition uses the Genesis creation story to answer some basic human questions: Where do we come from? What is our origin? And what is the goal of human life? Christian doctrine teaches that the creative act of God was creation *ex nihilo*, i.e., there was nothing in existence except the creator God, who fashioned everything out of nothing. "In Christian doctrine, it is not even possible to talk of 'before' creation, except metaphorically, for there was no time before creation; nor is it possible to talk of creation as an event occurring in place, for there was no space in existence previous to creation for creation to happen 'in.'"[33]

The Christian doctrine of original sin has its scriptural basis in the Genesis account of disobedience of Adam and Eve who, against the directive of Yahweh, ate of the tree of the knowledge of good and evil. This loss of innocence or original sin is about a state that we (humans) exist in and cannot escape.[34] The story accounts for "a condition we find in ourselves and in the world . . . It is precisely about something which has happened and cannot be undone."[35]

Human Dignity

In spite of the lost innocence of the Genesis creation account, Christian doctrine maintains that in human beings there is an imprint of the divine because man and woman are made in the image and likeness of God. In other words, there is some kind of resemblance between God and human beings that is not found between God and other animals.[36] In the narrative "humans are set off from all other creatures and are given power over them, immediately symbolized by Adam's naming of all the other creatures."[37]

The structure of the creation story suggests the special role assigned to humans in the whole narrative. Human beings were created last, meaning that they are the crown or apex of creation. Their being made in the image and likeness of God meant that Adam and Eve possessed some qualities that God possessed, qualities that distinguish human beings from other creatures. Medieval Christian theology used this to develop the idea that human

---

33. Smith, "Can Science Prove That God Exists?," 131.
34. Lowe, "Woman Oriented Hamartiologies," 128.
35. Lowe, "Woman Oriented Hamartiologies," 128.
36. Landry and Penchansky, "Primeval Story," 23.
37. Shannon, "Grounding Human Dignity," 114.

beings have a *potentia obedientialis*—the human capacity to be open to God in a personal way, i.e. what in the Christian tradition is known as grace.

James Cone, the African-American liberation theologian, points out that the human person is not a collection of properties to be scientifically analyzed, but a being-in-the-world-of-human-oppression. For Cone, to be human is to be free. "But on the other hand, human existence also discloses that the reality of evil is an ever-present possibility in our finite world, and to be (fully) human means to be identified with those who are enslaved as they fight against human evil. Being human means being against evil by joining sides with those who are the victims of evil."[38] Cone insists that the biblical notion of the human person as a being made in the image of God means that human beings are created in such a way that they cannot obey oppressive laws, for to be human is to be creative in ways that revolt against everything that is opposed to humanity.

38. Cone, *Black Theology of Liberation*, 87–88.

3

Judaism

JUDAISM IS THE PROPER name of the religious tradition of the people of Israel. Followers of this religious tradition began referring to themselves as Jews about the sixth century BCE, i.e., the same period the religion of Judaism gained currency. The term "Jew" serves as ethnic or national identity the same way a person might refer to one's self as an American, a German, Polish, Irish, an Indian or Togolese. One is considered a Jew if one is the son or daughter of a Jewish mother or a convert to Judaism.[1] The term "Jew" can be used in ways similar and yet different from "Israel" and "Hebrew." Jewish people trace their origin to their patriarchs (fathers), one of whom was Jacob whose name Yahweh changed to Israel. Jacob himself was the son of Isaac who in turn was the son of Abraham. All three: Jacob, Isaac, and Abraham were Hebrews by tribe. As Hebrews they also spoke the Hebrew language (the language of the Hebrew Scriptures). To properly understand Judaism, the religion of the Hebrew or Jewish people, a background knowledge of the second book (Exodus) of the Hebrew Bible is important.

The second book of the Hebrew Bible, Exodus, is so called because the Greek word from which it derives its name means "departure." As the second book of the Hebrew Bible or Tanak, Exodus occupies an important place in the Torah and the Hebrew scripture as a whole. It is through the exodus event that the Hebrew people came to understand themselves as a nation. The book derives its name from an important event that happened in Israel's history: after four hundred years of slavery and oppression in the hands of the Egyptians, Yahweh, through the able leadership of Moses, miraculously

---

1. Carmody and Brink, *Ways to the Center*, 123.

delivered Israel, and led them through the Red Sea to Mount Sinai on their way to the promised land. At Mount Sinai the people of Israel entered into a special covenant with Yahweh. The book not only recounts how Yahweh delivered the Israelites from slavery, but also tells the Israelites how to live lives of gratitude for the freedom that land and children bring.[2] From the moment of their deliverance, the people of Israel will interpret reality from their perspective of a wandering people who were delivered from bondage by Yahweh.[3] Some think Exodus is "Israel's Magna Carta, Declaration of Independence, and national constitution rolled into one."[4]

SOJOURN IN EGYPT

How did the Israelites end up in Egypt? The Yahwist who contributed one of the creation stories in Genesis inherited patriarchal material about generations that carried on the story of Abraham, i.e., the story of Joseph, the son of Rachel and Jacob (the son of Isaac).[5] Their goal in using the Joseph story was to show how Yahweh's grace prevailed to save a good man in the face of human plot of wickedness. The Yahwists also show that through human history and the actions of bad and good people the purpose of Yahweh is worked out and Yahweh's promises kept.[6] In the narrative they recount how the sons of Jacob, out of envy, sold their brother Joseph into slavery. They lied to their father (Jacob) by telling him that Joseph had been devoured by a wild beast. The irony here is that Jacob, who, as a young man, deceived his father, Isaac, and stole his brother's (Esau) blessing, was now being deceived by his own sons. "The Yahwist sees a line of guilt and suffering worked out in this family. And this inheritance of evil is used by God to bring about another phase in the history of the promise and its fulfillment."[7]

Meanwhile Joseph was brought to Egypt where he found himself in the house of Potiphar, an influential official of the court of Pharaoh. After some period of trials and tribulations, Joseph won the heart of Pharaoh and was entrusted with an important position in the royal court. As the story goes, after a series of events, Joseph soon reunited with his father Jacob (whose name had been changed to Israel) and his brothers, who came to Egypt to join him. According to Exodus 1:1–5, about seventy direct descendants of

2. Benjamin, *Old Testament Story*, 73.

3. Tuohey, "Gender Distinctions," 175.

4. Bandstra, *Reading the Old Testament*, 131.

5. Swanston, *Kings and the Covenant*, 80.

6. Swanston, *Kings and the Covenant*, 80.

7. Swanston, *Kings and the Covenant*, 80–81.

Jacob went with him to Egypt. Jacob and his children, because of the influence of Joseph who had risen to a high position of authority, prospered in Egypt where they and their descendants lived for centuries. The descendants of Jacob were called the Israelites. "The Israelites were fruitful and prolific. They became so numerous and strong that the land was filled with them" (Exod 1:7).

When Joseph died his descendants and the generation of Israelites were many. The prosperity of the Israelites soon landed them in trouble. "The Egyptians now regarded the Israelites as poor foreigners liable to be conscripted for the forced labor teams needed in the grandiose building schemes of Pharaohs. They had forgotten Joseph."[8] When a new king came to power, he decided to "deal shrewdly" with the Israelites "to stop their increase" (Exod 1:10).

> Accordingly, taskmasters were set over the Israelites to oppress them with forced labor. Thus they had to build for Pharaoh the supply cities of Pithom and Ramses. Yet the more they were oppressed, the more they multiplied and spread. The Egyptians, then, dreaded the Israelites and reduced them to cruel slavery, making life bitter for them with hard work in mortar and brick and all kinds of field work—the whole cruel fate of slaves. (Exod 1:11–14)

There has to be an explanation for the sudden reversal of the fortunes of Israelites in Egypt who went from being relatives of the chief minister to a slave population of a bitterly hostile country.[9] The narrators of this story used a technique called *chiasm* (derived from the Greek letter X, i.e., chi). Just as in chi (X) in which the top half of the letter is mirrored by the shape of its base, in *chiasm* the opening of a story is repeated at its closing. In the narrative of Exodus 1:7–12 the authors, in their use of chiasm, were careful to begin with the words: "the Israelites were fruitful and prolific; they multiplied and grew exceedingly" and end with similar words: "the more they were oppressed, the more they multiplied and spread."[10] Another possible explanation for this is that exodus as a whole was "not written to satisfy a demand for an historical narrative of Israel, at least not for that reason alone, but to show the men of the monarchy what Yahweh is like, how he always acts, and how men should respond in loyalty to Yahweh's providence."[11] It was written down, probably, after King David's time.

8. Swanston, *Kings and the Covenant*, 83.

9. Swanston, *Kings and the Covenant*, 83.

10. Benjamin, *Old Testament Story*, 75.

11. Swanston, *Kings and the Covenant*, 84.

Moses and the Burning Bush

The Yahwist shifts to the story of Moses' encounter with Yahweh at Mount Sinai. Some important events in Moses' life are carefully crafted to prefigure some major events in the life of the Israelites. "Moses goes into the Nile and is lifted up out of the Nile just as the Hebrews will go into the Red Sea and be lifted up out of it. He strikes down one Egyptian who was beating a Hebrew, just as Yahweh will strike down all the firstborn in Egypt. He goes into the desert and encounters Yahweh, just as the Hebrews will go into the desert and encounter Yahweh."[12] Exodus 2 narrates the story of the birth of Moses, in the face of Pharaoh's cruel decree to kill all male children of the Hebrews. To spare their son this cruel fate, Moses' mother put him in a basket and hides him on the bank of the Nile River. A puzzle is immediately introduced in the story: Pharaoh's daughter finds him and takes pity on him. She employs Moses' biological mother as his wet nurse and raises him in the courts of Pharaoh. "The birth of Moses shows that he was a miracle child destined by Yahweh from the very beginning of his life to fulfill a special role in Israel."[13]

Although Moses grew up in the court of Pharaoh, he never lost sight of his identity as a Hebrew. In fact, at one time he had to flee Egypt after killing an Egyptian taskmaster in defense of his Hebrew brother. Fearful for his life, he fled to the wilderness of Sinai. While there he married Zipporah. While tending the flock of his father in law, Jethro, Yahweh revealed Himself to Moses in a burning bush and told Moses that He has heard the afflictions of the Israelites in Egypt, and ordered Moses to go back to Egypt and negotiate their release. When Moses met Pharaoh, Pharaoh would not want the Israelites to be released. It was not until Yahweh afflicted the land of Egypt with series of plagues and natural disasters that Pharaoh acquiesced and allowed the Israelites to leave Egypt. The story of the plagues is found in Exodus 7–12.

The Passover Meal

The last plague was the plague of death. In this plague Yahweh slew the firstborn of the Egyptians, humans and beasts alike. The book of Exodus ties this story to the Passover feast.

---

12. Benjamin, *Old Testament Story*, 80.
13. Benjamin, *Old Testament Story*, 81.

The Lord said to Moses and Aaron in the land of Egypt, "This month shall stand at the head of your calendar. Tell the whole community of Israel: On the tenth of this month every one of your families must procure for itself a lamb, one apiece for each household. If a family is too small for a whole lamb, it shall join the nearest household in procuring one and shall share in the lamb in proportion to the number of persons who partake of it. The lamb must be a year-old male and without blemish. You may take it from either the sheep or the goats. You shall keep it until the fourteenth day of this month, and then, with the whole assembly of Israel present, it shall be slaughtered during the evening twilight. They shall take some of its blood and apply it to the two door-posts and the lintel of every house in which they partake of the lamb. That same night they shall eat its roasted flesh with unleavened bread and bitter herb. It shall not be eaten raw or boiled, but roasted whole, with its head and shanks and inner organs. None of it must be kept beyond the next morning; whatever is left over in the morning shall be burned up." (Exod 12:1–10)

At midnight, on the day of Passover, the Lord slew the firstborn of Pharaoh and every Egyptian. It was after the slaying that Pharaoh's heart softened and he gave the Israelites permission to leave the land. Even when he allowed the Israelites to leave Egypt, because of the hardness of his heart, Pharaoh and his army pursued the Israelites as they left the land of Egypt. With the Egyptian army in pursuit, Yahweh miraculously saved the Israelites as they crossed the Sea of Reeds (Red Sea). But he drowned Pharaoh and his army (Exod 14:10–31). This miraculous departure from Egypt is known as the "exodus." The Jews, to this day, still celebrate the exodus event, which they call the **Passover** or **Pesach**, because it is a story of their liberation and coming to birth as God's people. Today Passover is celebrated as a spring festival to commemorate this defining moment in Israelite history. Jews also celebrate **Shavuot**, a wheat harvest festival that takes place seven weeks after Passover. There is also another feast called the feast of **Booths** or **Sukkoth**, which is a fall harvest festival they celebrate by erecting straw booths or branch to commemorate the way God took care of them in the wilderness on their way to the promised land. Jews also have other feasts they celebrate throughout the year that is related to the Passover. One of these is **Yom Kippur** (Day of Atonement). This is somber and solemn ceremony in which Jews ask for forgiveness from their loved ones or anyone they have offended. There is also the feast of **Hanukkah** (festival of lights) in which Jews remember what God has done for them by liberating them through the hands of the Maccabees. The Maccabees led a successful revolt in 168 BCE against attempts to destroy traditional Judaism by Greek leaders who wanted to enthrone worship of Greek gods among the Jews.

THE COVENANT

Israel understands its existence as rooted in Yahweh's inescapable and unwavering commitment to its nationhood. In other words, Israel came to exist in the world of the Near East because of the decisive, sovereign, free, and initiatory action of Yahweh.[14] This inexplicable and irreversible commitment of Yahweh is rendered in the Sinai covenant narrative revolving around Moses, and also in the ancestor stories of Noah, Abraham, and the Patriarchs.[15] According to the terms of these covenants, Yahweh shows preferential treatment for the Israelites by promising to protect them, while the Israelites on their part would keep and observe Yahweh's laws. According to the story of the covenant in Exodus 24, after Moses entered the agreement with Yahweh, he related all the words and ordinances of Yahweh to the people who all answered in one voice, "we will do everything the Lord has told us" (24:3).

The word "covenant" (*berith* in Hebrew) is a biblical word for an agreement or treaty between Yahweh and Yahweh's people. The basis of the covenant, in Jewish understanding, is Yahweh's *hesed* (steadfast love). Aware of its divine predilection, Israel characteristically uses the verbs "love," "choose," and "set one's heart" to express its awareness that its existence is rooted only in Yahweh's commitment.[16] Yahweh is the one whose love for Israel causes Israel to be and in this act of love Yahweh assigns Israel a special role in the community of nations. "Yahweh's commitment to Israel is not simply a formal, political designation, but it is a personal commitment that has a dimension of affection and in which Yahweh is emotionally extended for the sake of Israel."[17]

Covenant can also be conceived as a treaty, like that found in the ancient world between kings and their vassals. Extra-biblical materials support the idea that the making of treaties in the ancient world predates Israel. The French archeologist, Jacques de Morgan (1857–1924), discovered the law stele of the Babylonian king Hammurabi (1901). The stele shows the

---

14. Brueggemann, *Theology of the Old Testament*, 414.

15. Brueggemann, *Theology of the Old Testament*, 414.

16. Brueggemann, *Theology of the Old Testament*, 414.

17. Brueggemann, *Theology of the Old Testament*, 417.

king receiving laws couched in casuistic form from the god Shamash.[18] This is akin to Moses receiving the laws from Yahweh. Since Morgan's discovery other ancient law codes have also been discovered. Reading the Israelite covenant law against "the background of this extensive corpus of cuneiform law reveals the extent to which early Israel appropriated an ancient and widespread legal tradition."[19]

The relationship between covenant and law in the ancient world was not always clear. While law was intended to be a social expression of the covenant bond, covenant was sometimes used for political treaty.[20] Scholars, while studying the relationship between covenant and law and analyzing international treatises of the late second millennium BCE, have been able to distinguish two types of treaties or covenants in the ancient world: (a) parity treaty: treaty between equals, and (b) suzerain treaty: treaty between a monarch and his vassals. "A parity covenant is reciprocal—that is, both parties, being equal in rank, bind themselves to each other by bilateral obligations. The suzerain covenant, on the other hand, is more unilateral, for it is made between a suzerain, a great king, and his vassal, the head of a subordinate state."[21]

In the Suzerain treaty found in the ancient world, there are six legal steps or procedures to be followed:

i.   Preamble: the suzerain or king identifies himself or herself, e.g., thus speaks Marduk the great king of the Hittites.

ii. Historical Prologue or Antecedent History: reference is made to what happened in the past, e.g., things (acts of kindness) the king had done for his vassal, implying that the proper response of the vassal ought to be gratitude.

iii. Stipulations: the purpose of the treaty is stated, and stipulations are imposed on the vassal, i.e., loyalty and obedience, especially in time of war.

iv. Deposition: legal document is signed. Copies of the document are preserved in the temples of both countries and they are expected to be read once a year, as a reminder to both parties of the agreement they had entered.

18. Blenkinsopp, *Pentateuch*, 201.
19. Blenkinsopp, *Pentateuch*, 201.
20. Anderson, *Understanding the Old Testament*, 98.
21. Anderson, *Understanding the Old Testament*, 98.

  v. List of Witnesses: gods of both countries are invoked but precedent is given to the gods of the king.

  vi. Curses/Blessings: violation attracts curse and faithfulness guarantees blessing.[22]

The covenant between Yahweh and Israel is patterned after the Suzerain treaty. Exodus 19:3–6, for instance, reflects a suzerain treaty. Here Yahweh is the Suzerain (King) whose all-seeing eyes and omnipotence are enough to protect Yahweh's client, Israel. Yahweh is portrayed as designating Israel as Yahweh's covenant partner and Israel is obligated to respond and meet Yahweh's expectations.[23] The relationship between the Israelites and Yahweh, and also the relationship between the Israelites, one to another, are governed by the terms of the covenant. The Decalogue or Ten Commandments become part of the terms of this agreement. This is why in the Ten Commandments found in Exodus 20 can be found prescriptions that guide the people's relationship to Yahweh ("Thou shall have no other god before me") and also prescriptions that govern interpersonal relationships ("Thou shall not covet thy neighbor's wife").

The Hebrew Bible has several other instances of Yahweh's covenant with people Yahweh has chosen:[24]

  1. Covenant with Noah: The first covenant Yahweh made is found in the primeval story of the flood. This is called the covenant of creation, the covenant Yahweh made with Noah in Genesis 9:1–17. This covenant prefigures the already effectuated covenant at Sinai as well as the covenant with David. In the flood story Noah was the hero whose life and that of his family was spared by Yahweh who later promised, after the flood, never again to destroy the earth with flood. The rainbow is traditionally assumed to be Yahweh's sign to Noah when Yahweh said to him, "I set my bow in the clouds to serve as a sign of the covenant between me and the earth" (Gen 9:13). Subsequent covenants are going to be modeled after the covenant with Noah. In Genesis 15 and 17 (covenant with Abraham) and Exodus 19 (covenant with Moses) we are reminded of Yahweh's words to Noah before and after the flood, but here the words have new meanings.[25]

---

22. Anderson, *Understanding the Old Testament*, 100.

23. Brueggemann, *Theology of the Old Testament*, 416.

24. See Dempsey, "2 Samuel 7," 7–10.

25. Goldingay, *Old Testament Theology*, 370.

2. The second covenant is Yahweh's covenant with Abraham (Gen 12 and 15). This covenant with Abraham and the ancestors is one of divine initiative and may be considered unconditional.[26] When Abraham heeded Yahweh's call to leave his father's land and proceed to a foreign land, Yahweh assured Abraham of land and posterity (Gen 17:1–21). According to the terms of this covenant, Yahweh promised to make Abraham "a great nation," and make the name of Abraham great (Gen 12:2–3). Yahweh changed his name from Abram to Abraham because he is to be the father of a host of nations. Yahweh continued this covenant with Abraham's son Isaac, and Isaac's son, Jacob, whose name Yahweh changed to Israel. "It is as "the God of Abraham, the God of Isaac, and the God of Jacob" that YHWH then appears to Moses (Exod 3:6; cf. 3:15–16). YHWH had gotten attached to Israel's ancestors, had come to love them and had chosen them."[27] Yahweh's covenant with Abraham is very important in Christian Scripture, the New Testament (covenant), and in Islam.

3. Then there is Yahweh's covenant with Moses at Mount Sinai (Exod 19–24). Yahweh's covenant with Moses is also a covenant between Yahweh and Israel. Here Moses acts as the representative of the people. "The Noah covenant neither required nor allowed for any human response. The Abram covenant required the mark of male circumcision and presupposed a broader commitment to a whole and open walk before God, but laid down no further specific expectations or requirements. The meeting at Sinai involves a renegotiating of these arrangements."[28]

    The basis of the covenant is Yahweh Himself, although a responsive reciprocal commitment to Yahweh on Israel's part is an absolute necessity.[29] As part of the covenant relationship between Yahweh and Israel, Yahweh devised a set of moral principles that will govern and guide relationship between Yahweh and Israel on the one hand, and the Israelites with one another, on the other. These moral principles or guidelines are called the Ten Commandments. Yahweh gave these commandments to Moses at Mount Sinai. The Torah gives two different accounts of the Ten Commandments. The first account is found in Exodus 20, while the second account is found in Deuteronomy 5. The latter account duplicates the former but with only minor variations.

---

26. Brueggemann, *Theology of the Old Testament*, 418.

27. Goldingay, *Old Testament Theology*, 302.

28. Goldingay, *Old Testament Theology*, 371.

29. Goldingay, *Old Testament Theology*, 372.

The Ten Commandments will form the backbone of Israel's law codes. Yahweh may punish the rebelliousness of Israel if they break the covenant, but that does not mean the covenant is annulled.[30]

4. At the time of the monarchy Yahweh also made a covenant with David (Ps 89:3–4, 19–37; Is 55:3–5). A detailed account of Yahweh's covenant with David is found in 2 Samuel. David, after becoming king, wanted to build a house for the Lord, a place of worship where the twelve tribes of Israel would gather to worship Yahweh. But David is told through the Prophet Nathan that he is not to build a house for the Lord but that the Lord will build a house for David. Yahweh promised David land and dynasty and assures him that his dynasty will last forever—that a descendant of David will always be on the throne. This is why the great Israelite kings always traced their lineage back to David. For Christians, the Lord's promise to David came to its full realization in Jesus Christ who was called "Son of David."

LAW CODES IN THE ANCIENT NEAR EAST

Law is an important cultural convention that counters that which threatens the social order.[31] "Ancient Near Eastern cultures produced many kinds of legal genres, including loans, leases, contracts, pledges, marriage agreements, adoptions, real-estate transactions, lawsuits, royal edicts, and law codes, among others."[32] Israel's traditions do not stand in isolation from the traditions of the legally ordered societies of the ancient Middle East. The law codes of the nation of Israel have many points of contact with ancient extrabiblical law codes. "Archeology has uncovered no less than seven ancient codes of law from Israel's neighbors. They range from the Sumerian code of Ur Nammu in the twenty-second century B.C. down to Babylonian codes of the sixth century B.C."[33] The seven famous law codes that have been found through the work of archaeologists are the Sumerian code of Ur-Nammu, the code of Lipit-Ishtar, the code of Eshnunna, Middle Assyrian laws, Hittite laws, Neo-Babylonian laws, and the code of Hammurabi.[34] Compare

---

30. Goldingay, *Old Testament Theology*, 372.
31. Sparks, *Ancient Texts*, 417.
32. Sparks, *Ancient Texts*, 417.
33. Boadt, *Reading the Old Testament*, 186.
34. Bandstra, *Reading the Old Testament*, 153–54.

the following law of retribution or *lex talionis* taken from the Code of Hammurabi with that taken from the Book of the Covenant:

Code of Hammurabi	Law of Moses (Exod 21:23–25)
"If a man has destroyed the eye of another man, they shall destroy his eye. If he has broken another man's bone, they shall break his bone."	"If any injury occurs, you shall take life for life, eye for eye, tooth for tooth, hand for hand, foot for foot, burn for burn, wound for wound, beating for beating."

Apodictic or Case Law

The example above is called "case law." Case laws are different from "apodictic laws," e.g., the Commandments in Exodus 20. Apodictic laws are laws that are couched in absolute terms and do not admit of conditions. These absolute laws that are stated in sharp, terse language seem "to be more characteristically Israelite and expresses the unconditional demands of the covenant."[35] Apodictic laws are infrequent in ancient Near East law codes but appear frequently in the Hebrew Bible.[36] In ancient Near East, the form of law was usually casuistic. A casuistic or case law specifies conditions and the consequences that will follow. A casuistic or case law is a "specific kind of legal article that states the facts of the case in the protasis ('when a person does X') and the legal consequences in the apodosis ('then Y follows')."[37] An example is found in Exodus 21:28–29: "If an ox gores a man or a woman to death, the ox must be stoned . . . but if the ox had the habit of goring in the past . . . then the owner must be put to death." This kind of law is also found in ancient law codes, especially the Code of Hammurabi.[38]

Jews are known for their adherence to the law. In fact, non-Jews tend to associate Jews with the Law or Torah. It is not only the Law that made Jews distinct and different from others. They also have dietary laws that are derived from their understanding of Torah. This dietary law or kosher has served as "a badge of Jewishness in many periods, serving to demarcate Jews from Gentiles and helping preserve the purity of the chosen people."[39] Jewish dietary laws were constructed or framed on the model of God as One, Complete, and Whole. To be holy is to be whole because holiness

35. Anderson, *Understanding the Old Testament*, 97.
36. Sparks, *Ancient Texts*, 417.
37. Blenkinsopp, *Pentateuch*, 204.
38. Anderson, *Understanding the Old Testament*, 97.
39. Carmody and Brink, *Ways to the Center*, 135.

is unity, integrity, and perfection.[40] The animals that the Jews considered unclean lacked completeness, unity, and perfection. In fact, they were not to be eaten because they were "imperfect members of their class."[41] These imperfect animals included "those that lived in the water but did not have fins and scales (eels, shellfish), birds of the air that at the same time lied in the water (gulls, pelicans). The pig was also unclean, for although it came within the category of cloven-hoofed animals, it did not chew grass like the edible goat and sheep."[42]

EXODUS: A CREATION STORY?

The book of Exodus can be understood as a creation story or the continuation of the creation story already begun in Genesis. The God who delivers Israel from Egypt is the same Yahweh-Elohim who created the world. The conviction that Yahweh did deliver Yahweh's people was older than the conviction that Yahweh had created the world, the former being the origin of the latter.[43] Israel hardly thought about itself as a people brought into being by God without linking it with the way the world itself was brought into being by the same deliverer God.[44]

> Further, even if its story once began with the ancestors or the exodus, Israel did not rest content with that, but came to preface it with an account of creation. Exodus is not the first book in the Bible and the story of Israel's deliverance is not the beginning of its gospel. Its gospel has a plot, and to start reading its story by beginning with its deliverance from Egypt is like coming into the theater when the play has already reached scene 3. For individuals too, deliverance is not people's first experience, even in the case of newborn babies. Before they are delivered from oppression, they were born into the humanity created by God.[45]

The language and structure of the deliverance story, especially of the death of the firstborn of the Egyptians in Exodus 1:7—13:6 and the privileged position of the firstborn of Israel in 13:17–20, are similar to the

40. Douglas, *Purity and Danger*, 64.

41. Douglas, *Purity and Danger*, 55.

42. See Arbuckle, *Culture, Inculturation, and Theologians*, 42, referencing Douglas, *Leviticus as Literature*.

43. Goldingay, *Old Testament Theology*, 288.

44. Goldingay, *Old Testament Theology*, 289.

45. Goldingay, *Old Testament Theology*, 289.

language of creation stories found in the ancient Near East.[46] These narratives, as creation stories, "follow the same basic pattern as the Enuma Elish Stories about Marduk who delivers Babylon from Tiamat and Kingu, and the Stories of Ea and Enki who deliver the household of Gilgamesh from Enlil, and the Stories of Baʿal and Anat who deliver Ugarit from Yam and Nahar."[47]

In the account of the firstborn of Egypt, Pharaoh is given a character similar to that of Enlil in the Atrahasis and Gilgamesh stories. Like Enlil, Pharaoh is perturbed by his slaves, and like Enlil he tries a number of strategies to control his fears. Enlil resorts to plague, drought, and floods. Pharaoh tries slave labor and the killing of new male born. In the same manner, the character of Yahweh is patterned after that of Enki in the Atrahasis epic and that of Ea in the Gilgamesh epic. "Like Ea and Enki, Yahweh is a friend to humans. Like Ea and Enki, Yahweh prevents the divine assembly from completely destroying humans with a flood, and like Ea and Enki, Yahweh requires the people to leave the land of their divine enemy."[48] Israel's history is then the foreground against which the people understood the origin of the universe and the primeval history.[49] The primeval history is at the same time a narrative that grounds the Exodus event by rooting it within the cosmic history.[50] "The fact that the deliverer is the creator might merely have meant YHWH was sovereign over the whole world and therefore capable of acting on Israel's behalf against other peoples, in bringing Israel out of Egypt and taking it into Canaan."[51]

Jewish people have several rites with which they commemorate Yahweh's sovereignty over their life and the whole of creation. They do this in their various rites of passage: **Bris**—infant circumcision on the eighth day of a person's birth. Its significance is to show that the male child has entered the covenant community of Israel; **Bar Mitzvah**—celebrates the coming of age; and **Kaddish**—funeral prayer requiring ten Jewish males. These celebrations reinforce the idea that life is good and that one should be committed to finding goodness in every stage of life, including death because death is not a final reality.[52]

46. Benjamin, *Old Testament Story*, 74.

47. Benjamin, *Old Testament Story*, 74.

48. Benjamin, *Old Testament Story*, 76.

49. Goldingay, *Old Testament Theology*, 290.

50. Tuohey, "Gender Distinctions," 175.

51. Goldingay, *Old Testament Theology*, 293.

52. Carmody and Brink, *Ways to the Center*, 138.

PROPHECY AND THE PROPHETIC BOOKS

Charlotte Buhler's (1893–1974) psychoanalytic theory speaks of the human person as a being with intentionality, meaning that human beings live with a purpose. The purpose of human life, according to this German developmental psychologist, is to create values and give meaning to life. The search for meaning is not the same as the search for pleasure. Viktor Frankl (1905–97) has also reminded us that the pleasure principle is self-defeating because the more one aims at pleasure the more one misses it. Pleasure-seeking, in Frankl's view, is responsible for the multi-layered sexual neurosis of our time. "Normally, pleasure is never the goal of human strivings but rather is, and must remain, an effect, more specifically, the side effect of attaining a goal. Attaining the goal constitutes a reason for being happy. In other words, if there is a reason for happiness, happiness ensures, automatically and spontaneously, as it were. And that is why one need not pursue happiness, one need not care for it once there is a reason for it."[53] In the ancient world of which Israel was a part, prophets were spiritually attuned people who, among other things, reminded their peers that the pursuit of happiness cannot be found in mundane or trivial pursuits.

Former Prophets and Latter Prophets

Ancient Israelite prophecy was a complex phenomenon that has been studied extensively by biblical scholars. Israelite prophets played a special role in the establishment of the Hebrew Covenant. The books of the prophets occupy an important place in the canon of Hebrew Scriptures. They are placed immediately after the Torah and before the Writings. The Prophetic books begin with six historical books (Joshua through Kings) that are sometimes called the Former Prophets. These historical books form a continuous history written according to the ideology of Deuteronomy, which scholars designate as Deuteronomist History.[54] "This history, which was composed toward the end of the monarchy, was probably revised and expanded upon during the exilic period, around the middle of the sixth century BCE.

The book of Joshua recounts the story of Israel under the able leadership of Joshua. It tells the story of how Israel conquered the land of Canaan and defeated so many enemies with the help of Yahweh. The book of Judges tells the story of the rise of Judges who ruled Israel in the period before the monarchy. The books of Samuel and Kings narrate the rise of monarchy

---

53. Frankl, *Will to Meaning*, 34.
54. Blenkinsopp, *History of Prophecy*, 11.

in Israel, with Saul as the first king. They recount the rise of kingship; the development and growth of the Israelite kingdom; and the division of Israel into two kingdoms, the Northern Kingdom and the Southern Kingdom. The story culminates in the eventual destruction of Judah by the Babylonians and their captivity and exile.

The Former Prophets give a detailed history of prophecy from Moses, who was considered the prophet par excellence, to Joshua, who received a share in his charisma, and those "servants of the Prophets" after Joshua who predicted the consequence of neglecting the Deuteronomic law.[55] Deuteronomy (18:15–19) specifically interprets prophecy as a way of continuing the work of Moses throughout history and urges the observance and transmission of the same message to posterity.[56] The two books of Kings were the first to mention explicitly the existence of a large band of prophets that were active in the two kingdoms of Israel, but not the first to make allusions to the existence of prophetic activity in Israel.[57] Numbers 23–24 tells the story of Balaam, a non-Israelite prophet who, though was hired to curse Israel, chose instead to offer a blessing. Samuel, one of the great judges in the days Judges ruled Israel, was considered a prophet. Even at the time of the great King David, prophecy also played a special role, for David had two court prophets, Nathan and Gad, who offered divine guidance, especially in royal policies.[58]

The Latter Prophets were like the supervisors of the covenant who indicated the shape of Israel's prophetic ministry.[59] A good number of the Latter Prophets emerged after the kingdom of Israel had been divided into two. Some also emerged either during the exile, when the people of Israel were forlorn and in despair because they had been taken out of their homeland. Other Latter Prophets emerged after the exile, when the nation was struggling to rebuild. The collected oracles of these prophets have come down to us in books that bear individual names like Isaiah, Jeremiah, Ezekiel, Hosea, and Amos.[60] The view of the Latter Prophets concerning Israel's inevitable dissolution did engender an eschatology, i.e., teaching about the final destination of God's people, to use Isaiah's vision (Isa 65–66) that looks toward a new beginning for a believing Israel and also toward a New Creation.[61] In

---

55. Blenkinsopp, *History of Prophecy*, 12.

56. Blenkinsopp, *History of Prophecy*, 12.

57. Boadt, *Reading the Old Testament*, 303.

58. Boadt, *Reading the Old Testament*, 303.

59. Dumbrell, *Faith of Israel*, 10.

60. Boadt, *Reading the Old Testament*, 303.

61. Dumbrell, *Faith of Israel*, 10.

order to understand the work of these prophets it is important that we first understand the meaning of biblical prophecy.

Former Prophets	Latter Prophets
Joshua	Isaiah
Judges	Jeremiah
1 Samuel	Ezekiel
2 Samuel	
1 Kings	*Minor Prophets:*
2 Kings	Hosea
	Joel
	Amos
	Obadiah
	Jonah
	Micah
	Nahum
	Habakkuk
	Zephaniah
	Haggai
	Zechariah
	Malachi

Prophecy in the Ancient Near East and Israel

The Hebrew Bible attests to the fact that prophecy was not confined to Israel.[62] To understand prophecy in Israel it is important to compare and contrast the nature of prophecy in the ancient Near East, of which Israel was a part. The ancient Near Eastern notion of prophecy is indispensable for the understanding of the prophetic phenomenon in general and also for the cultural and conceptual preconditions of prophecy in the Bible.[63] Although some contemporary scholars tend to reject the idea that Israelite prophecy was borrowed from one of the surrounding cultures,[64] Israelite prophecy was to a large degree dependent on the prophecies in ancient Near East, especially Mesopotamia, Egypt, Babylon, Assyria, and Canaanite societies. During the reign of Zedekiah, the last of the kings of independent Judah,

62. Blenkinsopp, *History of Prophecy*, 41.

63. Nissinen, "What Is Prophecy?," 28.

64. Wilson, *Prophecy and Society*, 90.

the prophet Jeremiah (27:1–15), was said to have urged rulers of the neighboring lands of Moab, Edom, and Phoenicia, not to give in to the demands of their prophets, divinizers, and the other intermediaries who were supporting a planned rebellion against Nebuchadnezzar. This has raised the question as to whether Israelite prophecy was one of several variations of a widespread cultural phenomenon. Were there special factors at work in Israel that dictated the direction in which prophecy developed?[65]

Archeological findings have also revealed that there existed in the ancient Near East a band of people called "seers" or "divinizers." In Babylonia, for instance, "divination was a highly technical job and the Babylonian priests have left many clay tablets of instructions on how to interpret such things as sheet livers. But beyond this type of seeking God's word, it was also recognized that God might speak directly to individuals in dreams or trances."[66] People went to these divinizers to discern either the mind of the gods or a particular life activity. They were like the astrologers or psychics of today. Even potentates and kings went to them for divinization, either of a particular political or social affair, or to find out the will of the gods. In Babylonian society for instance, *baru* (priest or prophet) often used a divinization method to deliver the message of the gods to the people.[67] Ancient Near Eastern religions made no formal distinction between prophets and priests. In Phoenicia the existence of ecstatic prophecy was already well-developed as far back as the eleventh century BCE. The priest-prophet performed cultic duties and also had a lot of magical powers, which enabled them to serve also as physicians. They were believed to be inspired and specifically chosen to speak to the people that which they heard from the gods. They were also actively engaged in the political life of the state, especially foreign policy. "This is evident especially from the second-millennium Mesopotamia texts from Mari, where prophets advise kings in time of war and warn them of impending military disasters."[68]

Prophecy in Israel did not emerge *ex nihilo* but was a development of and a reaction to previous prophetic activity throughout the ancient world. To the extent that Israel was dependent on its neighbors in the areas of politics, arts, and culture, the Israelite religion, and prophecy in particular, were dependent on ancient Near Eastern idea of prophecy. The idea of prophecy became ingrained in Jewish society. The Hebrew notion of the nature of God, however, was the unique basis of all prophetic activity in Israel. Since

65. Blenkinsopp, *History of Prophecy*, 41.

66. Boadt, *Reading the Old Testament*, 304.

67. For more on this see Miller, *Meet the Prophets*.

68. Barton, *Isaiah 1–39*, 28.

Yahweh is holy and righteous, Yahweh's people must also be holy and righteous. There is no area of life that the divine demands for righteousness and holiness do not penetrate.[69]

Prophets, who were known by various names, performed various functions. A prophet was a "Seer" who received the word of God (2 Sam 24:11) and could divinize and tell the future (1 Sam 9:6–11). They were sometimes hired to cast spells on the enemy as in the case of Balaam (Num 23–24). The prophetic insight of a Seer comes through some sort of "third eye" vision that is accompanied by words.[70] Some prophets were also isolated figures who lived alone (1 Sam 10); others lived with a band of prophets as in case of Elijah and Elisha (2 Kgs 2). While some prophets divined Yahweh's word and received their message through dreams and oracles, others spoke with Yahweh "face to face" (Num 12:8).

The Prophets of Israel were people who knew their environment and spoke about events that related to their world. They were spiritually attuned individuals living within a given period of time, whether at the time of Davidic dynasty, destruction of the kingdom, or at the time of Assyrian invasion, who tried to discern Yahweh's will. They spoke out against corruption and spiritual decline of their people and interpreted the events and catastrophes of their time in light of the people's rejection of the path of Yahweh. In some cases the prophets sought to give hope to a forlorn people.[71] If every social reformer has his or her utopia, then Hebrew prophets were not without their own idealized dreams of human society.[72]

In our day, owing to a misunderstanding of the Greek term *prophetes*, it is easy to assume that a prophet was one who told or predicted the future. But that is not the main idea of biblical prophecy. The word "prophet" is derived from the Greek *prophetes* (a combination of the verb *phemi*, "to speak," and the prefix *pro-*, "before" or "forth"), and it was usually given to a person connected with the oracles of Apollo and Zeus, and used to designate the one who "speaks forth" or "proclaims" the message of deity and interpret divine word for those seeking divine oracle.[73] But "because divine messages deal with future events, the *prophetes* later came to be seen as one who "speaks of the future," who "speaks before" events actually take place."[74] Predicting the future, however, is not the essential idea of biblical prophecy.

---

69. Francisco, "Moral Message," 435.

70. Boadt, *Reading the Old Testament*, 305.

71. Brown et al., *New Jerome Biblical Commentary*.

72. Francisco, "Moral Message," 441.

73. Fenton, "Israelite Prophecy," 131.

74. Fenton, "Israelite Prophecy," 22–23.

For if the ability to predict the future was the main aim of a prophet then meteorologists, psychic hotlines, and horoscopes will qualify as prophets. "Predicting the future was not the major component of the prophetic task in the Israelite world. The most basic function of biblical prophecy was to analyze political and social policies in light of Yahweh's demands of justice, loyalty, and faith in him."[75] No one denies that the prophets sometimes predicted the future. But that was not the purpose of the prophetic office:

> The purpose of God speaking through a prophet was not to communicate information about a timetable of events for the distant future. To be sure the prophets often made predictions, in the conviction that Yahweh was shaping the course of events leading from the present into the future. But these predictions, some of which came true and some of which did not, had reference to the immediate future, which impinged on the present. Just as a doctor's prediction that a patient has only a short time to live makes the patient's present moments more precious and serious, so the prophetic announcement of what God was about to do accented the urgency of the present. Their task was to communicate God's message for *now*, and to summon the people to respond *today*.[76]

The Hebrew word for prophet, *nabi*, derives from the Semitic verb "to call." A prophet then is either "one who is called" or "one who calls."[77] This indicates that the prophet does not speak his or her own words but the words of Yahweh, who does the calling.[78] Amos was a herdsman and a dresser of sycamore trees whom the Lord called to prophesy to Israel (Amos 7:14–15). Having received his divine mission, Amos called out (proclaimed) the word of God (Amos 8:4–14). A prophet, then, was someone who was simply called by God, to deliver a message, and he or she was concerned about the moral and religious principles that govern the corporate and personal lives of the people of God.[79] "This conviction that the words they spoke came directly from God was based on the prophetic experience of being summoned in some kind of a vision to hear God speak in the heavenly throne room."[80] Sometimes the message of the prophet was not palatable to the people who often sought to persecute them (Amos 7:10–13). The prophets of Israel were

75. Bandstra, *Reading the Old Testament*, 210.

76. Anderson, *Understanding the Old Testament*, 249.

77. Bandstra, *Reading the Old Testament*, 210.

78. Boadt, *Reading the Old Testament*, 306.

79. Bandstra, *Reading the Old Testament*, 210.

80. Boadt, *Reading the Old Testament*, 306.

not silent on the issues of just relationship between the people and the king. Wherever they found injustice they made their voices known.[81] But the prophets of Israel do not seek to overthrow the monarchy, but to restore justice, loyalty to the national deity, and an informed and sensible handling of the dangerous forces at work on the international scene.[82]

Patterns of Prophetic Speech

Like the prophetical books of the Bible and the other documents from the ancient Near East, the *ipsissima verba*, i.e., the actual spoken words of individual prophets, are difficult to find. "The development from oral performance to written record happened under material restrictions and linguistic constraints, and the path from the prophet to the recipient may have been a complicated one. Moreover, the ancient Near Eastern sources include quotations that may be purely literary imitations of prophetic language rather than actually proclaimed prophecies."[83] This kind of enigma would also be found in the study of Israelite prophecy. Some have attempted a distinction between ancient Hebrew prophecy and biblical prophecy. According to this distinction, ancient Hebrew prophecy refers to "the concrete transmission of the divine word in the Hebrew language in ancient Palestine by persons that qualify as prophets, that is a phenomenon belonging to the context of ancient Near Eastern prophecy," while biblical prophecy means "prophecy as interpreted by those who created the writings that gradually took the shape of what we call the Hebrew Bible."[84]

To the extent that Israel was a part of the Semitic world, its traditions, religious traditions especially, were indebted to the religious traditions of the ancient Near East. "The prophetic literature has been thoroughly analyzed, and the literary history of the prophetic corpus has been traced. Scholars have succeeded in delineating the characteristic patterns of the prophets' words and in some cases have been able to relate the various forms of prophetic speech to their original social settings."[85] In 1906, the biblical scholar, H. Gunkel, used the phrase *Sitz im Leben*, i.e., "setting in life," to develop the idea that all literary genres had a setting in the life of the people who used them. Since then "form critics have had a great deal to say about the literary genres of prophetic speech and about the original social matrix

81. Francisco, "Moral Message," 439.

82. Fenton, "Israelite Prophecy," 136.

83. Nissinen, "What Is Prophecy?," 29.

84. Nissinen, "What Is Prophecy?," 31.

85. Wilson, *Prophecy and Society*, 1.

of the language of those genres."[86] Biblical scholars, using **Form Criticism,** have attempted to situate the language of the Hebrew Bible in its original real-life situation. Form criticism or Form analysis, as a method used to examine the *Sitz im Leben* (original context) of biblical language, has been particularly productive especially in prophetic literature. Westermann has used such a method to demonstrate the origin of the phrase "thus says the Lord," which often prefaces the messages of Hebrew prophets. Westermann traced the phrase to the ancient Near Eastern kings' method of sending messages to vassals or client states. The messenger carrying the message of the king committed the king's message to memory. On arriving at his destination, the messenger would recite the king's message as if he were the king himself, prefacing the message with "Thus says the King." Hebrew prophets took over such a procedure, prefacing their message with "Thus says the Lord" to establish their words as a message from God and anchor them in divine authority.

The Prophetic Books

The prophetic books, as we noted earlier, consist of the Former Prophets (Joshua–Kings) and the Latter Prophets, comprised of the three Major Prophets (Isaiah, Jeremiah, and Ezekiel) and the twelve Minor Prophets. The latter prophets cover the period of Israelite history when the kingdom was divided into two: the north and the south, and continues into the ex-ilic and postexilic period. The influence of the prophets predominate the prophetic literature. We know a lot about some of the prophets and know little or nothing about others. In general, however, we know they knew their sense of mission and refused to compromise even in the face of persecution. Isaiah, for instance, described his divine commission: "In the year that King Uzziah died, I saw YHWH sitting on a throne, high and exalted. . . . Then I heard the voice of YHWH saying, 'Whom shall I send, and who will go for us?' And I said, 'Here I am, send me!'" (Isa 6:1–8). In spite of their wide diversity, characteristics, and wide range of activities, the one feature common to all the prophets is their commission to speak in the name of Yahweh, for divine revelation is a sine qua non of prophecy.[87]

The prophets did not speak in a vacuum. They all had a social loca-tion from which they spoke. They also had different cultural backgrounds, some agricultural, others urban. They also came from different regions: the

86. Wilson, *Prophecy and Society*, 11. See also Gunkel, "Fundamental Problems," 61–62.

87. Grabbe, *Priests, Prophets, Diviners, Sages*, 83.

Northern or Southern Kingdom. While Isaiah, for instance, directed his oracles and pronouncements against the ruling elites in Jerusalem (Southern Kingdom), Amos, a contemporary eighth-century BCE prophet, directed his pronouncements against the ruling class of Samaria (Northern Kingdom). The prophets also lived at different times: preexilic, exilic or postexilic. Some lived at the time before the Israelites were taken into captivity in Babylon. Others lived during the period of captivity. Still others lived and prophesied after the return to homeland. The concerns of the prophets also varied. While some were concerned with domestic issues or local politics, others were concerned with foreign affairs or international relations. There is also evidence that some of the prophets knew the prophetic oracles of either their contemporary prophets or the prophets before them. In some instances they even made use of the prophetic oracles of their predecessors. Isaiah, for instance, who lived in Jerusalem in the eighth century BCE (or at least those who compiled his sayings) knew of the prophetic oracles of Amos, Hosea, and Micah, and to some degree was influenced by them.[88] Thus, the prophets were dependent on the work of one another.

The final composition and editing of each of the prophetic books took a long period of time. It is essential to keep in mind that, when reading a prophetic book, we are not dealing with a prophetic person, but prophetic personalities that may be behind the final editing and shaping of the book. Though a prophetic book may bear the name of a named prophet, it is by no means an autobiography of the prophet in question. We should by no means confuse the modern notion of authorship with the biblical notion. For the most part prophetic books may contain the ideas of a band of disciples who align themselves to the named prophet. These disciples take the message of the prophet, rework them, and apply them to their new circumstance. These disciples sometimes are behind the final shaping and editing of the prophetic books, a point Boadt explains very well:

> The titles of books under individual names such as Amos or Hosea do not imply that they contain just the words of Amos and Hosea, but also words *about*, and in the *tradition of*, the prophet. Nor are the oracles sayings necessarily in the logical or chronological order that we would like. Ancient editors have collected and arranged words spoken by these prophets in an order that seemed important to them but often escapes us. Editors frequently added words taken from disciples of the prophet, or even unknown prophetic words that are similar in theme and which add to the thought of the prophet in whose book they

88. Bandstra, *Reading the Old Testament*, 302.

are included. Even more dramatically, later generations who cherished the words of an Amos or Micah occasionally added new applications and comments from their own centuries to the collected words of the long-dead prophet.[89]

Isaiah the Prophet

The story of Israel narrated in the book of Isaiah is, in a nutshell, a long account of Israel's life in the midst of a demanding sequence of imperial powers.[90] It was assumed until fairly recently that the story told in the book of Isaiah was the work of one single author, Isaiah of Jerusalem. This assumption was based on the fact that the book begins with the proclamation that it contains "the vision which Isaiah, son of Amoz, had concerning Judah and Jerusalem in the days of Uzziah, Jotham, Ahaz and Hezekiah, kings of Judah" (Isa 1:1). But far from being the work of a single author, scholars have discovered that the book contains prophetic materials and oracles that stretch over two centuries, "when Judah had fallen, when the people were in exile, and when Babylonia—then the superpower in the world—was about to fall before the rising empire of Persia."[91]

This discovery is largely due to the landmark work of Bernhard Duhm (1892) who, while building on the efforts of Doderlein (1775) and Eichhorn (1780–83), uncovered different thematic and historical interests.[92] The book of Isaiah is now believed to consist of three subcollections, each subcollection representing the oracle of a prophet who identified his/her name with Isaiah of Jerusalem. Only chapters 1–39 have been attributed to Isaiah of Jerusalem, the eighth-century BCE prophet who lived at a time when Israel was under threat from the Assyrian Empire. Due to differences in historical background, literary style, and theological emphasis, scholars believe that chapters 40–66 could have come from anonymous disciples, probably at the time of Cyrus of Persia (593 BCE), when the rising Persian Empire displaced the brutal and hated domination of Babylon.[93] In fact, chapters 40–55 have been attributed to a disciple of the prophet who lived during the time of the exile, suggesting that these chapters serve as prophetic interpretation and

---

89. Boadt, *Reading the Old Testament*, 313.

90. Brueggemann, *Isaiah 40–66*, 1.

91. Anderson, *Understanding the Old Testament*, 322.

92. Dumbrell, *Faith of Israel*, 107.

93. Brueggemann, *Isaiah 40–66*, 3.

elaboration of the traditions of Isaiah 1–39.[94] Finally chapters 56–66, assumed to have been written by a disciple of the disciple of the prophet who lived after the exile, elaborates and applies the message of Isaiah 40–55,[95] at a time "when Jews who had returned from exile went about the critical and difficult task of reshaping the community of faith after its long, exilic jeopardy."[96]

A Divided Kingdom

As we study Isaiah it is important to give a brief historical background of how the nation of Israel split into two kingdoms because such a background will help us better appreciate Isaiah when he makes references to places like Judah, Samaria, and even Israel as separate entities. For the prophetic activities of Isaiah Ben Amoz took place at a crucial time for both the Northern Kingdom (Israel) and the Southern Kingdom (Judah), i.e., it was a period of crises (national and international) and challenges in political as well as cultural life.[97]

Shortly after the death of Solomon, the son of David, during the reign of his son and successor, Rehoboam, the nation of Israel split into two kingdoms: the Northern Kingdom and the Southern Kingdom. As told in 1 Kings 12, after the death of Solomon, representatives of people in the north came to Rehoboam and put before him the request that their burdens be lightened. Rehoboam's father, Solomon, had imposed forced labor on the people, including high taxes and levies. Rehoboam sought the advice of his counselors (called Elders) who advised him to heed the people's request. But he went against the advice of his wise counselors, and arrogantly declared, "My father put on you a heavy yoke, but I will make it heavier. My father beat you with whips, but I will beat you with scorpions" (1 Kgs 12:14). This angered the northerners, who in mutiny exclaimed,

> What share have we in David?
> We have no heritage in the son of Jesse
> To your tents, O Israel!
> Now look to your own house, David. (1 Kgs 12:16)

Ten of the twelve tribes that seceded became known as the Northern Kingdom, while the South was left with two tribes: Benjamin and Judah.

94. Dumbrell, *Faith of Israel*, 108.

95. Dumbrell, *Faith of Israel*, 108.

96. Brueggemann, *Isaiah 40–66*, 3.

97. Widyapranawa, *Isaiah 1–39*, xiv.

Isaiah sometimes speaks of the Northern Kingdom as Israel and the Southern Kingdom as Judah or Jerusalem. This is akin to what we see in modern day politics where political pundits sometimes refer to the former Soviet Union as Russia, the United Kingdom as London, and the People's Republic of China as Beijing. Some prophets of the South (e.g. Amos), who were Isaiah's contemporaries, prophesied at Bethel, the great center of worship in the North. They, like Isaiah, sometimes referred to the South as Jerusalem or Judah, and the North as Israel, Ephraim or Samaria.

First Isaiah (Chapters 1–39)

The material in this collection has been attributed to Isaiah Ben Amoz, sometimes referred to as Isaiah of Jerusalem (eighth century BCE). First Isaiah contains preexilic materials, i.e., oracles or pronouncements that were delivered before the Israelites were taken into exile. Unlike some prophets of this period, we do know a little about the personal life of this prophet. From his own account we get to know that he was married to a woman whom he referred to as prophetess (Isa 8:3). He had two sons. One was called Shear-jashub, a name that means, "a remnant shall return" (Isa 7:3), and the other was called Maher-shalal-hash-baz, which means, "quick spoils, speedy plunder" (Isa 8:3).

Isaiah understands the symbolic meaning of his name and that of his two sons, which he applies to the nation of Israel: "Look at me and the sons the Lord has given me: we are signs and portents in Israel from the Lord of hosts who dwell on Mount Zion" (Isa 8:18). Isaiah is also vast in the traditions of Jerusalem. He is from Judea and knows a lot about the Davidic dynasty, a dynasty he reveres greatly. He accepts the idea of the election of the Davidic line and expands this to include the concept of the Davidic Messiah (Isa 16:5; 9:6).[98] He is also well educated and probably comes from an upper-class family. "The prophet seems to have known and had access to members of the royal court (Isa 8:2; 22:15–16), and he apparently had no difficulty gaining an unofficial audience with the king (Isa 7:3)."[99] He may also have been educated in the royal court or in the temple, based on the "wisdom" language he sometimes uses.[100] In all likelihood, he is familiar with the prophetic oracles of the other eighth-century prophets like Amos, Hosea, and Micah, and to some extent was influenced by them. While Amos

---

98. Wilson, *Prophecy and Society*, 270.

99. Wilson, *Prophecy and Society*, 271.

100. Wilson, *Prophecy and Society*, 271.

and Hosea prophesied in the north, Isaiah was active in Judah.[101] Some scholars have established literary and theological similarities between Isaiah and Amos based on some of the words and phrases used by Isaiah in his prophetic oracles, which are typical of Judean prophets.[102]

Isaiah Ben Amoz lived and prophesied at a time Israel and Judah were under the threat of the Assyrians.[103] Isaiah receives his divine commission in the context of these turbulent times and sees his service to the king of Judah as a divine call, a divine commission he vividly describes in chapter 6. His call took place "in the year king Uzziah died," when Yahweh was "seated on a high and lofty throne."

> Notice the time and the place. It was a critical time, heavy with urgency and foreboding. That is the meaning of the reference to Uzziah's death. Uzziah had been a strong king, and even while his son Jotham was acting as regent Uzziah remained a pillar of strength for the people. . . . Hence Uzziah's death was an event that touched the life of the people, especially in view of the weakness of his son Jotham and the menacing shadow of Assyria.[104]

Many of Isaiah's prophetic oracles relate to social justice. He cries out against the leaders and the people for social and cultic abuses, while still holding out the hope of salvation if they repent.[105] His cry for social justice is found in his famous Song of the Vineyard poem (Isa 5:1–7), where the prophet, with a play on words, declares Yahweh's indignant disappointment:

> He looked for justice [*mishpat*],
> and behold, bloodshed [*mispah*];
> for righteousness [*zedaqah*],
> but behold, a cry [*ze'aqah*].[106]

Isaiah prophesied during the reigns of Ahaz (735–715 BCE) and his son successor, Hezekiah (715–687 BCE), especially during the Assyrian crisis (701 BCE). The prophet may have witnessed the invasion of Judah by Israel and Syria in their attempt to force Judah to join the anti-Assyrian coalition. Assyria conquered Israel and forced Syria and Judah to become their client state. Some of Isaiah's prophetic oracles were pronounced at this

---

101. Boadt, *Reading the Old Testament*, 324.

102. Wilson, *Prophecy and Society*, 271.

103. Bandstra, *Reading the Old Testament*, 303.

104. Anderson, *Understanding the Old Testament*, 324.

105. Wilson, *Prophecy and Society*, 272.

106. See Anderson, *Understanding the Old Testament*, 328.

time. Isaiah was convinced of the majesty of God, "the Holy One of Israel" (Isa 6:1–13), who alone is King. The destiny of all nations, including the great ones, lies under the control of Yahweh. Isaiah made it clear that any kind of oppression against Yahweh's people offended Yahweh. Yahweh will redeem His own people at His own time. He then cautioned against the futility of Judah's attempt to control its own destiny by aligning with Assyria.

Immanuel Prophecy

First Isaiah has several themes: hope, restoration, and Davidic Promise. The Immanuel prophecy is one of the most important themes in this collection. Ahaz, the king of Judah, was faced with a serious political dilemma. Syria and Israel (sometimes referred to Ephraim in this book) were forming an anti-Assyrian coalition. Ahaz was not sure whether to join this anti-Assyrian coalition that the kings of Syria and Israel were pressuring him into. Isaiah felt compelled to tell Ahaz not to join the anti-Assyrian alliance and also to trust in Yahweh. But Ahaz, fearful of the consequences of not joining the alliance, was worried about Israel and Syria. Rather than join the coalition, he was inclined to seek the help of the Assyrians to ward off the threat from Israel and Syria. Isaiah advised Ahaz not to be afraid and guaranteed him Yahweh's assistance in the present situation. To assure Ahaz of Yahweh's help, Isaiah asked Ahaz to ask for a sign from Yahweh. But Ahaz would not ask for a sign because he did not want to "tempt the Lord." Isaiah then gave him a sign: "Therefore the Lord himself will give you this sign: the virgin shall be with child, and bear a son, and shall name him Immanuel" (Isa 7:14). One assumption is that the young woman Isaiah was referring to was the queen, i.e., the wife of Ahaz. Since the name Immanuel means, "God is with us," Isaiah was assuring Ahaz that the son whom the queen will give birth to will continue the Davidic dynasty, a sign that the Lord is still with Judah. The wife of Ahaz, in fulfillment of Isaiah's prophecy, gave birth to a son who was named Hezekiah. Isaiah saw the birth of Hezekiah as a sign of good things to come:

> The people who walked in darkness
> have seen a great light;
> upon those who dwelt in the land of gloom
> a light has shone.
> You have brought them abundant joy
> and great rejoicing,
> as they rejoice before you as at the harvest,
> as men make merry when dividing spoils.

> For the yoke that burdened them,
> the pole on their shoulder,
> and the rod of their taskmaster
> you have smashed. . . .
> For a child is born to us, a son is given us;
> upon his shoulder dominion rests.
> They name him Wonder-Counselor, God-Hero,
> Father-Forever, Prince of Peace.
> His dominion is vast
> and forever peaceful,
> from David's throne, and over his kingdom,
> which he confirms and sustains. (Isa 9:1–6)

Although Isaiah was not looking into the distant future, and although when Isaiah spoke of the "anointed one" he meant the reigning king, it is difficult to resist the conclusion that the child he meant, in this Immanuel prophecy, was to be a "messianic" figure, i.e., a deliverer.[107] But in spite of this Immanuel prophecy, Ahaz sought the help of Tiglath-Pileser III, the king of Assyria.[108] Tiglath-Pileser III helped Ahaz take care of the Syrian-Israelite threat. But the consequence of this was that Judah became an Assyrian client-state and remained so for about a century.[109] Upon the death of Ahaz, Hezekiah became the king of Judah. He began an expansionist policy that was to land him in trouble. He attacked some of his neighbors like Edom and Philistine and revolted against Assyria by aligning with Egypt to form an anti-Assyrian coalition. Prophet Isaiah warned him, without success, not to join this coalition. The result was that he was swiftly attacked by king Sennacherib of Assyria (see Isa 36–37). But Yahweh miraculously saved Judah from the invading Assyrians who had to retreat after suffering many casualties.[110]

Second Isaiah or Deutero-Isaiah (Chapters 40–55)

Israelite history is sometimes best told in the context of the fall and rise of foreign powers—Israelite neighbors. The Assyrian Empire, which was a great threat to Israel in the eight century BCE at the time of First Isaiah, had disintegrated by the seventh century BCE and its capital city, Nineveh, lay in

---

107. Anderson, *Understanding the Old Testament*, 334.

108. Assyria would be the modern-day Iraq, Babylon the modern-day Kuwait, and Persia the modern-day Iran.

109. Bandstra, *Reading the Old Testament*, 307.

110. Bandstra, *Reading the Old Testament*, 308.

ruins. In the vacuum left by the demise of Assyria, Babylon, led by Nabopol-assar (Nebuchadnezzar), became a formidable threat: "It is Nebuchadnezzar who enacts the devastation of Jerusalem in 587."[111]

Second or Deutero-Isaiah is an exilic material composed by a prophet who lived in the Babylonian exile, about the middle of the sixth century BCE. "As Isaiah 1–39 had ended with the prospect of exile before Jerusalem, so Isaiah 40 commences the second half of the prophecy on the comfort to be extended to Jerusalem and the exiles in Babylon."[112] Although the Isra-elites were exiled in Babylon, at this time Persia, under Cyrus, was increas-ingly becoming a dominant power. Cyrus practiced a benevolent imperial policy, which permitted exiles to return to their homeland.[113] Second Isaiah saw Persia under Cyrus as an agent of Yahweh's restorative justice in the same way Jeremiah thought of Babylon under Nebuchadnezzar as an agent of Yahweh's judgment.[114] Second Isaiah tries to show that Yahweh, in the form of the Persian army, will defeat Babylon and permit Judah to return in freedom to the beloved citadel of Zion.[115]

Unlike First Isaiah, we do not know the name of this prophet, since we have only scanty information about the prophet. "He has hidden his own identity behind that of the great prophet Isaiah so that those who hear or read his prophecies will see only the continuity of what God is doing from Isaiah's age to his own."[116] The anonymity of Second Isaiah may also be due to the common practice at the time of this prophet, i.e., the increase of pro-phetic anonymity resulting from concern over prophetic authority.[117]

> A number of the late prophetic writings are simply added on to earlier books, and in this way the anonymous author claims the authority of an earlier prophet who lived in a time when pro-phetic authority was still recognized. This device has been used by Second Isaiah, Third Isaiah, Second Zechariah, and Third Zechariah, among others. The tendency in this period to edit an existing prophetic book rather than create a new book may also reflect an attempt to gain support from the past.[118]

111. Brueggemann, *Isaiah 40–66*, 9.

112. Dumbrell, *Faith of Israel*, 115.

113. Brueggemann, *Hopeful Imagination*, 91.

114. Brueggemann, *Hopeful Imagination*, 91.

115. Brueggemann, *Isaiah 40–66*, 10–11.

116. Boadt, *Reading the Old Testament*, 417–18.

117. Wilson, *Prophecy and Society*, 291.

118. Wilson, *Prophecy and Society*, 291. Wilson notes some characteristics of late prophets: (i) the tendency to reuse earlier prophetic oracles to enhance their authority; (ii) they did not draw their earlier material from only one prophetic tradition; (iii)

In spite of the anonymity of Second Isaiah, this prophet has been described as "pensive" and "optimistic." In the prologue (40:6–7), the prophet describes his divine commission, telling us how he heard a voice summoning him to preach. His faith in Yahweh seems unflinching. It would seem that the prophet "regarded himself as the lineal descendant of the pre-exilic prophets. This is shown, first, by the fact that in substantiation of his message he adduces a call, and, second, that like Isaiah and Jeremiah, his first reaction is to shrink from it."[119] When he demurs at the summons to preach, his initial refusal is not an expression of his own personal lament, but of solidarity with his fellow exiles who think that the collapse of their nation is an expression of divine judgment.[120] "The thoughts of his fellow-exiles were his thoughts, too, and he had been every bit as flagging and weary as they. It was a word from outside himself, a command that made him a prophet, as it had done his predecessors."[121] The prophet stresses the culmination of historical events in God's plan. Yahweh is the Lord of all creation and every human event works according to His grand design.[122]

We also see the prophet's disappointment with some of the captives in Babylon who, it would seem, had rejected the prophet. Some of these captives had thought that the destruction of Jerusalem and the temple, and even their captivity, signaled the withdrawal of Yahweh and their abandonment. They thought Yahweh had perhaps withdrawn to the wilderness. The prophet denounced these people as being narrow-minded and prophesied a new Exodus: Yahweh will reveal Himself and bring His people once again to the promised land. This time it would not be through the Reed Sea but through the pathways of the Arabian Desert. The prophet, more than other prophets, stresses the power of the word of God and encouraged the people to have faith in God.[123] He also stresses the centrality of Jerusalem and its temple.

Second Isaiah is sometimes called the "Book of Comfort" or the "Book of Consolation" (Isa 40:1–2, 6, 8) because "the prophet offers no judgment and condemnation of Israel, but only a message of trust and confident hope

---

some of them used prophecy to advance their own views and oppose those of their opponents; and (iv) the tendency to overly use apocalyptic imagery, probably because they were becoming more and more isolated from the central social structure and so were beginning to formulate their own apocalyptic program.

119. Westermann, *Isaiah 40–66*, 7.

120. Westermann, *Isaiah 40–66*, 7.

121. Westermann, *Isaiah 40–66*, 7.

122. See Brown et al., *New Jerome Biblical Commentary*.

123. Bandstra, *Reading the Old Testament*, 311.

that God is about to end the exile."[124] These other main features of Second Isaiah should also be noted:

- Encourages Israel to have faith in the new exodus (Isa 43:16–19).

- Full of promises of hope and restoration. The prophet stresses that there will be a new creation because everything, including the wicked schemes of the nations, fall under the saving plan of God (Isa 40:12–31; 48:13–14).

- Second Isaiah has the Songs of the Servant passages: 42:1–4; 49:1–6; 50:4–11; 52:13—53:12. In these passages Israel is described as the "servant of God" in whom God's predilection rests.

- Feminine imagery of God: compares God to a mother (Isa 42:14; 45:10; 49:10).

- While other prophets had implicitly allowed the idea of the existence of other gods, Deutero-Isaiah was the first to stress explicitly that there is no other God but Yahweh.[125]

Third or Trito-Isaiah (Chapters 56–66)

Third or Trito-Isaiah is a late sixth-century postexilic prophetic oracle about Judah. The viewpoint of the prophet is no longer that of someone in Babylon, but of one already back in the promised land.[126] In 538 Cyrus the king of Persia allowed the exiles to return home and issued an edict to rebuild the Jerusalem temple (see Ezra 6:3–11). He also gave back the temple vessels that were carted off when Jerusalem was captured.[127] Situated within this context, Trito-Isaiah falls within the period between 537 and 455 BCE.[128]

Trito-Isaiah must have been an anonymous disciple of Second Isaiah. Where Second Isaiah mocks foreign idols and believes they have no power over Israel, Third Isaiah berates Israel for falling into idolatry (Isa 57:1–13), and while Second Isaiah never accuses Israel of sin but assures them that their sins have been doubly forgiven, Third Isaiah is full of condemnation of Israel's sins (Isa 58:1–9; 65:1–7).[129] The prophet is confronted with a Jew-

124. Boadt, *Reading the Old Testament*, 416.
125. See Laurance, *Introduction to Theology.*
126. Boadt, *Reading the Old Testament*, 443.
127. Westermann, *Isaiah 40–66*, 295.
128. Westermann, *Isaiah 40–66*, 296.
129. Boadt, *Reading the Old Testament*, 443–44.

ish community in crisis and struggling to rebuild itself. There seemed to have been conflicts between the returnees from exile and the remnants of Israel, i.e., those who never left the land. The problem could be both cultural and religious. The prophet continues the theme of Second Isaiah with prophetic messages meant to sustain the returnees from exile, and messages meant to reconcile the division in the community. The prophet feels he has been "anointed to bring good news to the afflicted . . . shore up the broken hearted, proclaim freedom to the captives and freedom to those in bondage" (Isa 61:1–2). Third Isaiah has messages or themes of hope, consolation, and restoration that were addressed to those who just returned from exile.

Christian Metaphors in Isaiah

The book of Isaiah has deep significance for New Testament writers. No prophetic book is quoted in the New Testament as often as the book of Isaiah. For the early Christians, Isaiah, together with Genesis and Psalms, form the core of the Old Testament.[130] In the Christian New Testament Matthew 1:23 is seen as the fulfillment of the promise of Isaiah 7:14. Yahweh's promise to deliver Judah is seen as a metaphor for the coming Messiah, Jesus Christ, whose virgin birth would be seen as a fulfillment of Yahweh's promise to deliver the whole world. Second Isaiah's image of highway for return of the exiles also becomes a powerful metaphor for Christians whose gospel accounts employ this image of Isaiah to show how the ministry of Jesus is good news for all downtrodden people of the earth.[131]

---

130. Barton, *Isaiah 1–39*, 13.

131. Brueggemann, *Isaiah 40–66*, 19.

4

The Canon of the Hebrew Bible
and the Christian Old Testament

IN OUR DEFINITION OF theology in chapter 1 we saw how the sixteenth-century Protestant reformation radically altered the way Christian theology was conceived. We also saw how the Catholic Church responded to Protestant criticism of some Church practices by establishing seminaries and divinity schools for the training of priests and pastors. It was after this shift that theology was divided into the four broad areas of Biblical, historical, systematic theology, and ethics. The Hebrew Bible (Christian Old Testament) needs to be studied in the context of the history of the peoples of ancient civilization of which the people of Israel were a part.

ANCIENT CIVILIZATION AND ISRAELITE HISTORY

In the past two centuries the science of archeology has revolutionized our understanding of human origins. We have learned a lot about the history of the human race, ancient civilizations, Israel's predecessors and neighbors, and the Bible.[1] One of the many things these archeological findings reveal is that the history of the people of Israel ought to be studied in relationship to that of their neighbors, whose history, compared to that of Israel, was politically, economically, and socially larger. This means that Israel's history is "a minor sideshow in the larger history of the ancient Near East, and its

---

1. Wright et al., "History of Israel," 1220.

81

culture is overshadowed by the more brilliant cultures of antiquity."[2] Among Israel's neighbors were the Sumerians, creators of civilization in Lower Mesopotamia in the Copper-stone Age (4500–3200 BCE) who introduced the pictographic (cuneiform) system of writing.[3] There were also the Mesopotamians who built strong civilization, and the Egyptians whose civilization was concentrated along the Nile River and who made great strides in the development of agriculture and irrigation and invented the hieroglyphic script. For more than two thousand years Egypt was a dominant power in the Middle East. But its rise to power and fame was checked in succession by the rise of the Persians, Assyrians, and Babylonians.

In trying to help us understand the different stages of human existence on earth, archeologists distinguish various stages according to the material commonly used as tools and weapons. There is the Old Stone Age or Paleolithic period, which was a period in time when people were hunters and gatherers and moved from cave to cave for food and shelter. This period was followed by the Middle Stone Age or Mesolithic Period (18,000–8000 BCE) when people made strides from hunter gatherers to domesticators of animals. Then there was the New Stone Age or Neolithic Period (8000–4500 BCE) when people lived more sedentary life and became food producers. In the Chalcolithic or Copper-stone Period (4500–3200 BCE) that followed, agriculture was vastly improved and expanded. The Bronze Ages are divided into the Early Bronze Age (3200–2000 BCE), Middle Bronze Age (2000–1550 BCE), and Later Bronze Age. The Bronze Ages ended what is known as prehistory and ushered in a new era—history properly speaking.

The rise of the Israelite nation cannot be separated from the social upheavals of the Late Bronze Age.[4] The Hebrew Bible did not set out to tell an all-out scientific story. It did not set out to tell a secular history of Israel either. The story the Hebrew Bible tries to tell is one of sacred history, namely that the God of Israel played a role in a very real human history.[5] The events covered by the Hebrew Bible, i.e., the time of Abraham and the patriarchs (the period from Abraham to Joseph) to the Maccabean revolt, span about two thousand years of history. Both Jews and Christians alike accept these narratives as sacred history—that in these historical experiences, as seen through the eyes of faith, the ultimate meaning of human life is disclosed.[6] As a story of Israel's testimony of faith encounter with God,

2. Anderson, *Understanding the Old Testament*, 8.

3. Wright et al., "History of Israel," 1221.

4. Lemche, "Hebrew," 95.

5. Lonergan, *Method in Theology*, 306.

6. Anderson, *Understanding the Old Testament*, 8.

both the Hebrew and Christian Bible have a lot in common. They share the conviction that God has revealed God's self to the people of Israel.[7] But there are also significant differences—the arrangement of the books, the terminologies used to describe them, and the fact that the Christian Bible has the New Testament. The Hebrew Bible does not have the New Testament because Jews do not share the Christian idea of Jesus Christ as the final and definitive revelation of God in human history.

THE NATURE OF THE BIBLE

The Bible is the word of God in human language. As the word of God, expressed in human language, the Bible has two authors: divine and human. The church understands this to mean that God chose certain people and made use of their powers and abilities, so that with God acting in them and through them "they, as true authors, consigned to writing everything and only those things which [God] wanted."[8] The divine author is technically then the Holy Spirit who reveals to the human author what God wants them to write. God's first act of self-disclosure is through creation. After creation God reveals God's self through events in human history. God always wants "to manifest and communicate both himself and the eternal decrees of his will concerning the salvation of humankind."[9] The Bible is understood to be the place where God definitively reveals God's self to humankind. This process of God's self-disclosure to the human person is called **Revelation**.

The human author writes under the promptings of the Holy Spirit. The Holy Spirit breathes on this person who has been specially chosen, telling him or her to write what God wants and only what God wants. This is called **Inspiration**. According to the church's understanding therefore, "the books of both the Old and New Testaments in their entirety, with all their parts, are sacred and canonical because written under the inspiration of the Holy Spirit, they have God as their author and have been handed on as such to the Church herself.[10] Since the human author communicates only the truth of God and under the guidance of the Holy Spirit the Bible is said to be without error. This idea that the Bible is free from error is called **Inerrancy** (see 2 Tim 3:16). "Therefore, since everything asserted by the inspired authors or sacred writers must be held to be asserted by the Holy Spirit, it follows that the books of Scripture must be acknowledged as teaching solidly,

7. Boadt, *Reading the Old Testament*, 14.

8. Paul VI, *Dei Verbum*, 11.

9. Paul VI, *Dei Verbum*, 6.

10. Paul VI, *Dei Verbum*, 11.

faithfully and without error that truth which God wanted put into sacred writings."[11] If the Bible is inspired and is written by human authors under the guidance of the Holy Spirit, how do we determine which of the human authors wrote under the promptings of the Holy Spirit? Who adjudicates? The process of determining which books should be among the collections of the Bible and which should not is called **Canonicity** or **Canon**. "Canon" means "measurement," "rule," or "standard." We shall return to the question of canonicity later because of the difference between Catholic canon and Protestant canon.

THE HEBREW BIBLE

The Hebrew Bible, sometimes referred to as **Tanak**, has three main divisions: the Law (Torah), Prophets (Nevi'im), and Writings (Ketuvim). The word "Tanak" is derived from the first consonants of these three parts of the Hebrew Bible: **T** from Torah, **N** from Nevi'im, and **K** from Ketuvim = TNK. The Jews added vowels to make for the easy acronym "Tanak." The Torah or Law, which Jewish tradition holds was written by Moses, is at the heart of the Tanak. It consists of the first five books in the Hebrew arrangement of the Bible: Genesis, Exodus, Leviticus, Numbers, and Deuteronomy. The traditional division of the Hebrew Bible into Torah, Prophets, and Writings reflects the Jewish understanding that each division or block forms a unit. Observant Jews commit them to memory, especially the Torah, because of the belief that the Torah contains Yahweh's instruction for the people of Israel.

The second part of the Hebrew Bible, the Prophets or the Nevi'im, has three main subdivisions:

(a). The first block consists of the historical books of Joshua, Judges, 1 and 2 Samuel, and 1 and 2 Kings. These are sometimes referred to as the **Former Prophets**.

(b). The second block consists of the three Major Prophets of the Hebrews: Isaiah, Jeremiah, and Ezekiel.

(c). The third block consists of the Book of the Twelve, what in Hebrew tradition is known as the Minor Prophets: Hosea, Joel, Amos, Obadiah, Jonah, Micah, Nahum, Habakkuk, Zephaniah, Haggai, Zechariah and Malachi. The last two subdivisions, i.e., the Major and Minor Prophets, are sometimes collectively referred to as the **Latter Prophets**. "The

11. Paul VI, *Dei Verbum*, 11.

titles Former and Latter are unfortunate because they foster the perception that the Latter Prophets are later than the historical books."[12] The distinction that has been made between the Former and the Latter Prophets does not refer to the chronology of the books but simply their placement in the Bible.[13] The prophetic books generally re-interpret some events in Israelite life and redact some of these events in light of the covenant—that faithfulness to the covenant leads to prosperity and violation of tenets of the covenant brings curses, like the removal of many leaders of the Israelite community and their deportation to Babylon in the sixth century BCE.[14]

The Writings or Ketuvim include books like Psalms, Job, Proverbs, Ruth, Song of Songs, Ecclesiastes, Lamentations, Esther, Daniel, Ezra, Nehemiah, 1 Chronicles, and 2 Chronicles. Though the Ketuvim has less status than the Torah or the Prophets, this collection includes later and disparate materials that have been considered authoritative interpretations of relevance to the existence of Israel.[15]

In light of these three broad divisions, the suggestion here is that the three divisions of the Hebrew Bible be understood as a scheme of three concentric circles. "The inner circle, the Torah, presents the basic story of the people and includes the laws which are to guide them in living. The next circle, the Prophets, is a critical commentary on the life of the people to whom the Torah is given. The outer circle, the Writings, a diverse and open-ended collection, broadens out from Israel's worship and festal celebration to wisdom reflections."[16] Not included in the official list of the Hebrew Bible are seven books that Catholics and Protestants "disputed" (Apocryphal books) but which made their way into the official collection of Catholic Bible (Tobit, Judith, I and II Maccabees, Wisdom, Ecclesiasticus, and Baruch). The Jews consider them sacred but do not include them in their official list or canon.

---

12. Bandstra, *Reading the Old Testament*, 204.

13. Bandstra, *Reading the Old Testament*, 205.

14. Carmody and Brink, *Ways to the Center*, 124.

15. Carmody and Brink, *Ways to the Center*, 125–26.

16. Anderson, *Understanding the Old Testament*, 3. See also Brueggemann, *Creative Word*, 170.

THE CHRISTIAN OLD TESTAMENT

The entire Hebrew Bible, the Tanak, is what Christians traditionally call the Old Testament. "Old" here implies a Christian reading of the Hebrew Bible. The use of the term "Old Testament" probably derives from a passage in Jeremiah that speaks of both the old covenant and a new covenant to be established:

> The days are coming, says the Lord, when I will make a covenant with the house of Israel and the house of Judah. It will not be the covenant I made with their fathers the day I took them by the hand to lead them forth from the land of Egypt, for they broke my covenant and I had to show myself their master, says the Lord. But this is the covenant which I will make with the house of Israel after those days, says the Lord. I will place my law within them, and write it upon their hearts; I will be their God, and they shall be my people. (Jer 31:31–34)

To call the Tanak "Old Testament" can be somewhat misleading if by "old" one understands something antiquated or something no longer relevant. In fact, Christianity rejected that idea when it was first expounded by Marcion in the second century CE. Marcion erroneously taught that the Old Testament has been rendered void because of the New Testament. Orthodox Christianity considers the Old Testament to be "an indispensable part of Sacred Scripture" because its books are divinely inspired.[17] In the eyes of the Christian church, even though the Old Testament may contain "matters imperfect and provisional" they were deliberately designed to "prepare for and declare in prophecy the coming of Christ." Since the Old Testament bears witness to the "whole pedagogy of God's saving love," in these same books the "mystery of our salvation is present in a hidden way."

The first five books of the Christian Old Testament are properly called the **Pentateuch**, a term derived from the Greek *pentateuchos*, meaning "five scrolls or containers." Origen Adamantius (182–254 CE), an early Christian theologian from Alexandria, was said to have been the first to refer to these books as Pentateuch. The early Christian Church was a Greek-speaking community and they read the scriptures in Greek, especially the more authoritative Septuagint (Greek translation of Hebrew Scriptures) that was begun in Alexandria, Egypt, in the third century BCE.[18] The second set of books is the Writings, which include the Psalms, Proverbs, Ecclesiasticus, etc. Here we see another difference between the Hebrew Bible and the

17. See *Catechism of the Catholic Church* (hereafter CCC), no. 121.
18. Anderson, *Understanding the Old Testament*, 125–26.

Christian Old Testament. In the Tanak, for example, Daniel and Lamentations are grouped with the Ketuvim (Writings). But in the Christian Old Testament Daniel and Lamentations are considered prophetic books. The third part of the Christian Old Testament is the Prophets. The basic difference here between the Christian and the Hebrew arrangement of these Prophetic books pertains to Baruch, which is a canonical book in the Christian Old Testament but did not make it to the Hebrew canon. There is also the case, as we pointed out earlier, with Daniel and Lamentations, which in the Christian Old Testament are prophetic books, but in the Hebrew Bible are grouped with the Writings. The Christian placement of the prophetic books as the last block of materials of the Old Testament is meant to convey the idea that the prophets of the Old Testament stand as a bridge between the Old Covenant and the New Testament, and that the events prophesied in the Old have found fulfillment in the New. In the standard version of the Bible, for instance, the book of the Prophet Malachi is the last book of the Old Testament. Malachi uses expressions like "my Messenger" and "sacrifice." The Catholic placement of this book as the last book of the Old Testament is to give the idea that John the Baptist, the last of the Old Testament prophets and the forerunner of Christ, is that "Messenger" Malachi spoke about and that the sacrifice of Jesus stands as the "sacrifice" foretold by the prophet. It is for this reason that the Christian reading of the Old Testament is often referred to as allegorical or typological readings, i.e., Christians read the Old Testament "in light of Christ crucified and risen," with the understanding that such typological reading "discloses the inexhaustible content of the Old Testament."[19]

CATHOLIC AND PROTESTANT CANONS

The Bible is not a single unified work, but a collection of books written by different authors spanning about seven centuries. Each author wrote for a different audience, using different styles and modes of communication that appealed to their audience. Most of the books of the Old Testament were written in Hebrew, except for parts of the books of Daniel (2:4—7:28), Ezra (4:6–6; 7:12–26), and Jeremiah (10 and 11) that were written in Aramaic. The whole of the New Testament, on the other hand, was written in Greek. The process of gathering and putting together these various books into a single collection was a long and arduous process. During this long and difficult process some books were accepted and others were thrown out. Those books that were accepted as meeting all the criteria to be included in the

19. CCC, no. 129.

official list of the Bible are said to have made the "canon." The word "canon" is from the Greek meaning "rule" or "measurement." The Jews made a decision about which books to be included in their canon toward the end of first century CE, at the Council of Jamnia (90 CE), which officially accepted only thirty-nine books (mentioned above). The Catholic decision about which books to be included in the canon did not come until the Council of Trent in the sixteenth century.

Catholic and Protestant Canons of the Old Testament

Christians, like the Jews, had a long deliberation about which books were to be included in the canon of the Old Testament and the canon of the New Testament. They must have followed criteria such as (i) the content of the book, (ii) the author of the book, and (iii) how often the book was used in the Church's liturgy and teachings. At the end of the deliberations there was no unanimity between Protestants and Catholics regarding the canon of the Old Testament. Both Catholics and Protestants accept the division of the Bible into the Old and the New Testament, but differ on the issue of the number of books to be included in the Old Testament. The Catholic Church accepts forty-six canonical books of the Old Testament while the Protestants, strictly following the Jewish canon, accepts only thirty-nine books of the Old Testament. The canonical books of the Old Testament in the Catholic Bible are as follows: Genesis, Exodus, Leviticus, Numbers, Deuteronomy, Joshua, Judges, Ruth, 1 and 2 Samuel, 1 and 2 Kings, 1 and 2 Chronicles, Ezra and Nehemiah, Tobit, Judith, Esther, 1 and 2 Maccabees, Job, Psalms, Proverbs, Ecclesiastes, the Song of Songs, Wisdom, Sirach (Ecclesiasticus), Isaiah, Jeremiah, Lamentations, Baruch, Ezekiel, Daniel, Hosea, Joel, Amos, Obadiah, Jonah, Micah, Nahum, Habakkuk, Zephaniah, Haggai, Zechariah, and Malachi. Most Protestant Churches accept these books as canonical except for the following seven: Wisdom, Ecclesiasticus, Baruch, Tobit, Judith, and 1 and 2 Maccabees. These seven disputed books are called the Apocrypha.

Why the difference between Catholic and Protestant Bible? Early Christians "used an ancient Greek translation of the Old Testament (the Septuagint). This Greek version of the Bible had forty-six books. Since most of the early Christians were Greek-speaking, the Septuagint was their preferred version. But when Judaism officially set out to determine its canon at the end of the first century, it drew up a shorter list of thirty-nine books, mainly written in Hebrew. In the Reformation period, Protestants went back to this shorter Hebrew canon, considering it more authentic.[20] This difference aside, Protestants and Catholics accept twenty-seven books of the New Testament: the four Gospels—Matthew, Mark, Luke and John—the Acts of the Apostles, the Letters of St. Paul to the Romans, 1 and 2 Corinthians, Galatians, Ephesians, Philippians, Colossians, 1 and 2 Thessalonians, 1 and 2 Timothy, Titus, Philemon, the Letter to the Hebrews, the Letters of James, 1 and 2 Peter, 1, 2, and 3 John, Jude, and Revelation or the Apocalypse.

DEUTERONOMIST HISTORY (DH)

What in the Hebrew Bible are referred to as the Torah and Former Prophets are sometimes collectively called **Primary History** because together these books give a complete account of the history of Israel, starting from the beginning of time in Genesis, when Yahweh-Elohim created the universe, to the days of Israel's development as a nation ruled by judges and kings, and even up to the Israelites' exile. In this narrative the book of Deuteronomy is pivotal. Deuteronomy also occupies a central position in the Tanak as a whole, especially for two reasons: first, Deuteronomy concludes the Torah, and second, it opens the door to the Former Prophets.

The Former Prophets are also called the **Deuteronomist History (DH)**. This is because the historical and theological perspective of the Former Prophets was shaped, by and large, by the book of Deuteronomy.[21] DH should by no means be confused with Deuteronomic material. While Deuteronomic material refers to the materials found in the book of Deuteronomy (Deut 5–28), DH refers to those writings that were "influenced by the Deuteronomic torah, that comprise the so-called Deuteronomist History that extends from Joshua through II Kings."[22]

There is a neat pattern in the history that the Deuteronomist historian tells: that Israel's vitality and solidarity lay, not only in a united, exclusive loyalty to Yahweh, but also that obedience to Yahweh's Torah leads to welfare and peace and disobedience results in hardship and defeat. The composition of DH is very complex, in particular because of its multiple themes. Martin Noth (1943), who was the first scholar to develop a theory of DH, has argued that DH was composed to explain why Yahweh allowed the nation of Israel to be destroyed by the Babylonians in the sixth century BCE. DH was, for Noth, a book of judgment, for the reason that Yahweh allowed

20. See the general introduction to *The Catholic Study Bible*, RG 3.

21. Bandstra, *Reading the Old Testament*, 205.

22. Anderson, *Understanding the Old Testament*, 183.

the nation of Israel to be destroyed because of their idolatry.[23] Building on the suggestions of Noth, Gerhard von Rad (1962) suggested that in addition to the theme of judgment, DH was composed to show the Israelites that hope for the future was based on a total return to the covenant Yahweh made with the House of David.[24] Wolff (1982), who also developed a theory regarding the composition of DH, added that DH was composed as a call to repentance, i.e., to show the nation of Israel that if they repent and return to the covenant Yahweh would restore them to their preexilic state.[25]

In studying the Torah and the development of DH, the importance of Deuteronomy to the Torah and the Former Prophets cannot be disputed. But as more and more theories are developed, scholars seem to work with more or less than the Pentateuch.[26] For example, Noth have suggested that the first four books of the Tanak (Genesis, Exodus, Leviticus and Numbers) should be read as a unit. His suggestion yields what is known as **Tetrateuch**. Still others like von Rad suggest that the book of Joshua be added to the first five books of the Tanak, because Joshua continues the story already began in Deuteronomy. This suggestion that the Torah and Joshua be read as a unit yields a **Hexateuch**. These terms are significant because they "express a particular understanding of the formation and relationship of the books concerned."[27]

THEMES IN THE PENTATEUCH

In the first five books of the Bible (the Pentateuch) can be found multiple themes: (i) Genesis 1–11 details primeval history; (ii) Genesis 12–50 recounts the story of Abraham and the ancestors and ancestresses; (iii) Exodus 1–18 gives a detailed account of the exodus or the escape from Egypt; (iv) Exodus 19 through Leviticus and through Numbers 10 give an account of the Law and the Wilderness sojourn; and (v) Numbers 11–36 gives a detailed account of the entrance into the promised land. Who put these stories together? In other words, who is the author of the Pentateuch?

---

23. Bandstra, *Reading the Old Testament*, 206.
24. Bandstra, *Reading the Old Testament*, 206.
25. Bandstra, *Reading the Old Testament*, 206.
26. Murphy, "Introduction to the Pentateuch," 3.
27. Murphy, "Introduction to the Pentateuch," 3.

THE PENTATEUCH AND THE HISTORICAL-CRITICAL METHOD

For a long time both Jewish and Christian traditions assumed that Moses was the author of the Pentateuch. As far back as the postexilic period (after 539 BCE), Moses was explicitly identified as the author of the Pentateuch.[28] Even renowned historians like Titus Flavius Josephus (37–ca. 100 CE) and the distinguished scholar and Jewish philosopher, Philo of Alexandria (25 BCE–50 CE), took it for granted that Moses authored these books.[29] This assumption was based on the Jewish understanding of passages in the Hebrew Bible where references were made to Moses and the Law. The New Testament simply continues this Jewish view. In Mark 10:3–12 and Matthew 19:7–12. Jesus is said to have made reference to "the hardness of your hearts," because of which Moses allowed, in the Law, "a bill of divorce." Acts 15:5 also makes reference to those Christians who wanted Gentile converts to be circumcised and be made to observe "the law of Moses." In the Tanak, we read that "Joshua inscribed upon the stones a copy of the law written by Moses" (Josh 9:32). The argument for Mosaic authorship of the Pentateuch went unchallenged for centuries. It was not until the early Middle Ages that people began to examine more closely some passages in the Tanak that seem to cast doubt, not only on the Mosaic authorship, but also on the theory of one single author of the Pentateuch. One of such passages was Deuteronomy 34:5–6, which gives an account of the death and burial of Moses: "So there, in the land of Moab, Moses, the servant of the Lord, died as the Lord had said, and he was buried in the ravine opposite Beth-peor in the land of Moab, but to this day no one knows the place of his burial." How could Moses have written about his own death?

A thorough examination of passages that cast doubt on the Mosaic authorship, coupled with an examination of the language and style of the Pentateuch, led to the realization that the authorship of the Pentateuch was more complex than originally thought. The groundbreaking work of Richard Simon (1638–1712) and the milestone work of Jean Astruc (1684–1766) brought to an end the view that Moses was the single author of the Pentateuch. Simon and the Dutch philosopher Baruch Spinoza (1632–77) found in the Pentateuch "repetitions and contradictions," which led them to conclude that these books "seemed to lack the style of a single author."[30] Simon developed a theory that the Pentateuch was derived from a compilation of

28. Boadt, *Reading the Old Testament*, 90.

29. Boadt, *Reading the Old Testament*, 90.

30. Boadt, *Reading the Old Testament*, 90.

a number of sources beginning from the time of Moses to the time of Ezra (fifth-century BCE postexilic material). Astruc discovered that the Pentateuch derives from a compilation of two major materials and several minor materials especially in the way the texts refer to God either as Elohim or Yahweh, but still thought that it was Moses who compiled these materials.[31]

The work of Simon and Astruc have led scholars, using **source analysis** or **literary analysis**, to argue not only for multiple authorship of the Pentateuch but also for a complex process of compiling and editing, of which Moses was not a part. Through the pioneering work of these men, scholars have come to understand that the purpose of the Pentateuch was not necessarily to give a historical account of the people of Israel, but to express faith in Yahweh. In expressing this faith, the narrators told their stories in songs, epics, proverbs and various traditions available to them at the time. Through source analysis, scholars have also come to the conclusion that at least four different sources were used in the compilation of the Pentateuch: the Yahwist source (known as J), the Elohist source (known as E), the Priestly source (P), and the Deuteronomist source (D). This idea that the Pentateuch was a compilation of four main sources is called the **Documentary Hypothesis**. Julius Wellhausen worked out this schema in its complete form and published it in his *Prolegomena to the History of Israel* (1878). According to documentary hypothesis, the composition and final editing of the Pentateuch evolved over a long period of time.

DOCUMENTARY HYPOTHESIS

The Torah, as we have seen, is a very complex book. The complexity of these books calls for recognition of various strands and units. The pioneering effort of Simon and Astruc was synthesized by Julius Wellhausen (1844–1918), giving us what we now know as the documentary hypothesis. Despite modifications that have been made since the synthesis of Wellhausen, biblical scholars still speak of these four documents: J (eighth century BCE), E (eighth century), D (seventh century), and P (postexilic, sixth century BCE). These four main sources, probably written, were eventually merged together in the postexilic period by the P tradition and another redactor. Five literary identifiers are used to distinguish the sources: (a) duplications and repetitions of material; (b) different ways of referring to God; (c) contrasting geographical and political perspectives; (d) variation in vocabulary and literary style; and (e) evidence of editorial activity.[32]

31. Bandstra, *Reading the Old Testament*, 39–40.
32. Bandstra, *Reading the Old Testament*, 40.

J/Yahwistic Source

- Dates back to the time of Davidic monarchy (1000 BCE).

- Uses the name YHWH for God.

- Uses anthropomorphism (i.e., speaks of God as if God were a man).

- Vivid storytelling and theological vision.

- Recounts traditions of the Davidic monarchy.

- Speaks of Jerusalem as the one center of worship.

- Tells the story of Israel as that of a people under the special guidance of Yahweh.

- This material was probably written or preserved in the Southern Kingdom, Judah (ca. eighth century BCE).

E/Elohistic Source

- Dates back to the Davidic monarchy.

- Uses the name Elohim for God.

- Emphasizes morality.

- Does not necessarily recount Davidic monarchy, but references tribal traditions of the conquest of the land.

- Recounts covenant traditions.

- Has flare for worship, but locates worship centers outside of Jerusalem. Probably originated in the Northern Kingdom (perhaps earlier than J), before the establishment of the monarchy (like J, dated ca. eighth century BCE).

D/Deuteronomist Source

- Recognized by style of the book of Deuteronomy—highlighting role of the law of Moses.

- Exhortatory in style.

- It was understood to be instructional or preaching material that used language, concepts, and theological perspectives similar to that found in the book of Deuteronomy.

- Stresses the faithfulness of God as found in covenant traditions.

- Stresses obedience as the proper response to God.

- Thought to have influenced some of the liturgical traditions of the books of Samuel and Kings as well as prophetical books.

- Scholars contend that there are two distinct phases in the editing or redaction of D materials. Some believe that an early form of the D document existed during the reign of Josiah (ca. 621 BCE), which Josiah used as a basis for reform. After the exile, a later version of this material was reedited to apply the theology of Moses to the crisis of exile.

P/Priestly Source

- Understood to be priestly material and focused on the concerns of priests serving in the Jerusalem temple.

- Concerned with cult and rituals (book of Leviticus).

- Concerns itself with record-keeping and legal traditions concerning the proper functioning of the temple.

- Concerns itself with ordering events into sequence, genealogies, and keeping of religious laws.

- Concerned about atonement for sins.

- Like D, P contains traditions from all previous periods of Israel's history.

- Final shaping of P traditions is considered late in the development of the final form of the Pentateuch, since the priests emerged as leaders and wielders of power after the exile. Most P materials are postexilic (fifth century BCE or later.)

5

The Christian New Testament

IN ITS EARLY BEGINNINGS Christianity was thought to have begun as a sect within Judaism by the ruling Roman authorities. What was thought to be a sect quickly gained ground and became, not only the official religion of the Holy Roman Empire, but also the most dominant religion in the whole of the Western world. What was responsible for the growth of this religion? How did it start? And how did it spread and become dominant? New Testament scholars like to make a distinction between Jesus, the early church, and the author of the Gospels (evangelist).[1] This distinction assumes that there is an interconnection between these terms and that the words and deeds of Jesus and the early Christian understandings of them were what was put into writing by the evangelists. The prevailing idea the Gospel writers tried to communicate was that the God once understood in the Israelite tradition as an ethnic God (Yahweh) for a few "chosen people" has been revealed in the resurrection of Jesus of Nazareth as the God of all humanity and that everyone is now potentially a member of God's chosen people.[2]

THE GOSPELS

The Greek word for Gospel, *euangelion*, and its Latin form *evangelium*, literally means Good News. The term "gospel," as used in the New Testament, refers primarily to the oral proclamation of the Good News of salvation whose core is usually the death and resurrection of Jesus Christ or the

1. Swartley, *Israel's Scripture Traditions*, 9.
2. Malina and Rohrbaugh, *Social Science Commentary*, 427.

salvation message proclaimed by Him.[3] All four Gospel writers give an account of the Good News of Jesus Christ, even though only Mark begins his narrative with reference to the "gospel" of Jesus Christ. The different Gospel accounts about Jesus were written by and for third-generation followers of Jesus who wanted to know more about the first-generation experience and about what Jesus said and did in ways that would be relevant to them, since second-generation followers like Paul wrote almost nothing about what Jesus said and did.[4]

The Gospels were not the earliest Christian writings of the New Testament. But they occupy a central place in the New Testament and in the life of the church. Some second-generation writings, like the Pauline letters, which were thought to have been written ca. 50–70 CE, predate the Gospels, which were estimated to have been written between 65 and 100 CE. During this time, i.e., the period between Jesus' death and the first canonical Gospel, information about Jesus' life and death was transmitted orally.[5] It was not until much later that some of the circulating oral information was committed to writing in the canonical Gospels. The first generation of Jesus' followers were dying and memories of life and teachings of Jesus were fast fading. Then there arose the need to record information about Jesus that had initially been transmitted orally.[6]

The order of arrangement of the Christian Gospels—Matthew, Mark, Luke, and John—is not necessarily the order of composition. Earliest Christian reflections on Jesus appealed to the Old Testament to interpret the meaning of faith in Jesus Christ,[7] for the early church understood the meaning of Jesus' life, death, and resurrection through the lens of the Old Testament.

Survey of the New Testament

The Christian church existed before there was ever such a thing as a New Testament writing. In the first and second century, there was no such thing as the New Testament, since none of the books we now call New Testament scriptures existed then. The Christian communities at the time only read the Hebrew Scriptures. What is now today the New Testament were themselves crystallizations of the different documents and traditions of the early

---

3. Duling and Perrin, *New Testament*, 295.

4. Malina and Rohrbaugh, *Social Science Commentary*, 16–17.

5. Freed, *New Testament*, 38.

6. Freed, *New Testament*, 40.

7. Swartley, *Israel's Scripture Traditions*, 9.

Christian communities who engaged the Hebrew Bible and interpreted the events of the Tanak in light of their understandings of God's new revelation in the man Jesus. What we now call the Gospels first circulated as stories that emerged from the preaching, worship, and teachings of the early Christian communities, while the Epistles "bear fragments of, and make allusions to, liturgical formulae, hymns, ritual practices, and prophecies."[8] The collection of books that came to be known as the New Testament developed gradually over the course of several centuries and attained the form in which we know them in the fourth century.[9] The earliest Christian writings of the New Testament were composed by credible leaders of these communities as exhortations, admonitions, and encouragement for suffering Christian communities. These letters were read publicly by the communities to whom they were addressed and these communities sometimes shared them with other Christian communities. For example, Paul's letters to the Christian communities he founded (the first Christian writings of the New Testament) were "used by churches other than the ones for whom they were originally written, and indeed were regarded as having a special authority."[10] The church recognized these books as scriptures because they proved more helpful to the Christian communities than the available Jewish Scriptures.

The final and definitive canon of the New Testament was agreed upon after a lengthy and laborious process. Catholics and Protestants did not initially agree on the books of the New Testament mainly because of the event of the Reformation. Luther had insisted on scripture alone as the authoritative guiding principle of the Christian Church. But the Catholic Church, while not fundamentally disagreeing with Luther, insisted on Scripture and Tradition (Magisterium) as authoritative norms of the Christian life.

The Four Gospels and Criteria for Canonicity

The Catholic Church, as we pointed out in our treatment of the Hebrew Bible, accepts forty-six books of the Old Testament as divinely inspired, while the Protestant Church accepts only thirty-nine books. They saw these books as foreshadowing the new covenant to be inaugurated by the man Jesus Christ. It is still not clear why the early Christian Church accepted only four Gospels out of the many "gospels" in circulation at the time, just as we are not sure when the events of the life of Jesus were committed to

8. Johnson, *Writings of the New Testament*, 596–97.

9. Gamble, *New Testament Canon*, 12.

10. Johnson, *Writings of the New Testament*, 598.

writing. For example, among the gospels that were known and used by the early Christian communities were the gospel of Thomas, the gospel of Peter, the Dialogue of the Savior, the gospel of the Hebrews, and the gospel of the Egyptians. The circulation of multiple gospels created some difficulties. "Just as each Gospel was composed in the first place with the aim of providing a sufficient and self-contained account, it was not easy for Christian communities to see why there should be more than one: a plurality of Gospels cast doubt on the adequacy of any."[11] With this came the need to reassert the authority of the Gospels by authoritatively recognizing some as authentic accounts of the history of the life of Jesus. As early as 180 CE, evidence from the writings of St. Irenaeus (130–202 CE), bishop of Lyon, suggested that the Christian Church had recognized only four Gospels out of the many in circulation. Another second/third-century fragment, the Muratorian canon, also attested to the existence of four Gospels. What criteria were used in this selection? We shall return to this later. But one thing is clear: the four canonical Gospels were widely accepted and used by the early Christians. These Gospels, before their compilation, were written for individual Christian communities and for a specific purpose.

When the idea of devising scripture emerged, five main criteria were used:

(1) Apostolicity—writings that had direct or indirect connection to the apostles were more likely to be recognized as authentic.

(2) Catholicity—the ideal of catholicity means that a document must have a wider appeal, i.e., it must be considered relevant to the whole church, and not just a specific local community.

(3) Orthodoxy—the document must be orthodox in the sense of being in agreement with the faith of the universal church.

(4) Usage in Christian worship—a document must conform to the traditional practices of the church to be considered authentic, i.e., it must have expressed the faith of the church in a way that must have called for its use in Christian liturgy and worship.

(5) Inspiration—since the church is led by the Spirit, to the extent that a document conforms to the first four criteria and were so designated by the church, the document was said to be inspired.

---

11. Gamble, *New Testament Canon*, 30.

The Centrality of Mark

A good number of New Testament scholars hold the view that the Gospels were written by anonymous authors and that the present titles were probably a second-century addition. "Because the form of the title is the same for every gospel, a title was probably given to each only after the gospels had been collected as a group of four. Then the name of a well-known person was included in the superscription of each gospel."[12] Second-century Christians, "possessing anonymous manuscripts and eager to give names to them, fastened upon four historical figures—the Apostles Matthew and John, Luke the 'beloved physician' of Paul (Col. 4:14), and John Mark of Jerusalem, the 'son' of Peter (Acts 12:12; 1 Peter 5:13)."[13]

Viewed in this light, the issue of the authorship of the Gospel of Mark is still problematic. While some assume that an anonymous Hellenistic Christian who lived in Syria wrote the Gospel, tradition assigns it to John Mark whom Papias (135 CE), bishop of Hierapolis in Phrygia, Asia Minor, describes as "an interpreter of Peter," and whom Peter described as "Mark, my son" (1 Pet 5:13). A tradition from Clement of Alexandria (ca. 150–220) also associates Mark with Peter in Rome, which means that Peter was thought to be the authority behind Mark's Gospel.[14] Thus, in the second century it was thought that the author of the Gospel of Mark was not an eyewitness of Jesus, but a personal associate of someone (Peter) who was.[15]

"Mark" probably was not his real name.[16] There are quite a few references to John Mark in the New Testament. Colossians 4:10 identifies him as "the cousin of Barnabas," and Acts 12:25 identifies him as the one who accompanied Paul and Barnabas in one of their missionary journeys. Second Timothy 4:11 describes him as someone Paul wanted to meet because he was "helpful in the ministry." His mother's name was Mary, according to the account in Acts 12:12, and she was thought to be a devoted Christian because the Christian community sometimes gathered at her house for prayer. Eusebius of Caesarea (263–339 CE), the famous church historian of the fourth century, in his *Ecclesiastical History*, credits Papias (ca. 140 CE) with the following, regarding Mark:

> Mark became Peter's interpreter and wrote accurately all that he remembered, not indeed, in order, of the things said or done

---

12. Freed, *New Testament*, 97.
13. Helms, *Who Wrote the Gospels?*, i.
14. Freed, *New Testament*, 98.
15. Helms, *Who Wrote the Gospels?*, 2.
16. Anderson and Moore, "Introduction," 2.

by the Lord. For he had not heard the Lord, nor had he followed him, but later on, as I said, followed Peter, who used to
give teaching as necessity demanded but not making, as it were,
an arrangement of the Lord's oracles, so that Mark did nothing
wrong in thus writing down single points as he remembered
them. For to one thing he gave attention, to leave out nothing
of what he had heard and to make no false statements in them.[17]

Just as not much information was available regarding the author of
the Gospel of Mark, not much information was available regarding its audience as well. "The Gospel was unsigned and undated and contains nothing
that attests explicitly either to its geographical location or to the specific
circumstances of its writings or even to the gender of its author."[18] But it
is projected that the Gospel could have been written in Rome, sometime
between 65 and 70 CE. "The reason for the date A.D. 70 is that chapter 13
suggests Mark knew about the Jewish insurrection against Rome and the
resulting destruction of the temple in Jerusalem in A.D. 70."[19] Some place
Mark's origin in Syria, where Greek was the common language.[20] This is
based on the argument that Mark wrote in koine Greek, a not-very-literate
Greek, and he also knew Jesus' language of Aramaic and quotes several
sayings of Jesus transliterated from Aramaic into Greek. With this kind of
bilingualism some place the origin of the Gospel in Syria, "where a substra-
tum of Aramaic seems to have survived."[21]

There is a general agreement, however, that the Gospel was addressed
to Gentile Christians who were facing rejection and persecution,[22] at a
time the city of Jerusalem and the Jewish temple were under siege. Perhaps
"a Greek-speaking non-Jewish Christian wrote about Jesus for an audience like himself of non-Jewish Christians who mistakenly expected that
the destruction of Jerusalem was the beginning of the end of the age."[23]
The persecution of these Christians came from both Judean and Roman
authorities.[24] These Gentile Christians did not know a lot about Jewish laws
and customs. The period was particularly a difficult time for Christians because the Romans regarded them as Jews while the Jews regarded them as

17. Anderson and Moore, "Introduction," 3.

18. Rhoads et al., *Mark as Story*, 1.

19. Davies, *New Testament*, 90.

20. Helms, *Who Wrote the Gospels?*, 9.

21. Helms, *Who Wrote the Gospels?*, 9.

22. Rhoads et al., *Mark as Story*, 2.

23. Helms, *Who Wrote the Gospels?*, 9.

24. Rhoads et al., *Mark as Story*, 2.

outcasts. Moreover, their apocalyptic and eschatological expectations were intensified and Christians living in Rome, Syria, and Galilee would have been greatly affected by the tumultuous times.[25] The author of this Gospel tries to explain some Jewish customs, emphasizes Christ's passion, and encourages the community to stand steadfast in the midst of persecution. The author seems to tell the Gentile Christians that membership in the family of Jesus is not so much by blood as it is by faith. Only those who acknowledge him, as did the Gentile Centurion who acclaimed him as the "Son of God" (Mark 15:39), can lay claim to the family of Jesus.

The Gospel of Mark is "a collection of what had previously been unconnected fragments about Jesus, units of oral tradition, and brief written stories and sayings that reveal a long history of transmission before they reached Mark; the collection looks nothing like the 'reminiscences' of Peter, though its lack of a clear chronology accounts for Papias' sense that it is 'not in order.'"[26] Mark is the shortest of the four Gospels. St. Augustine thought Mark copied and summarized Matthew "like a slave,"[27] an idea that has since been discarded, since it is now generally believed that Matthew expanded upon Mark. This Gospel has a literary device called the "Messianic Secret," according to which the identity of Jesus is not known by his family and friends, who thought he was either "possessed by Beelzebul" (Mark 3:22) or "out of his mind" (Mark 3:21). Even though his family and friends do not know him, the demons knew who he was and called him "Jesus of Nazareth, the Holy One of God" (Mark 1:24).

The discovery of the "Messianic Secret" in the Gospel of Mark was largely due to the efforts of William Wrede, whose book *Das Messiasgeheimnis in den Evangelien* (The Messianic Mystery in the Gospels [1901]) noted a pattern in Mark, especially in Mark 9:9, where Jesus specifically directs his disciples not to tell anyone what they have seen until he rises from the dead. On many occasions Jesus tries to keep his identity secret. In Mark 1:34 he refuses to let the demons speak "because they knew him." In Mark 1:43 he heals a leper and commands him to "say nothing to anyone." In Mark 5:43 he raises a young girl from the dead and strictly orders that "no one know about this." Even in discussing with his disciples in Mark 8 he refuses to speak openly about his identity and commands silence when someone recognizes that he is the messiah (i.e. the "anointed one" like Israel's Kings).[28] Mark wanted the truth about Jesus to be proclaimed at the moment of his

25. Freed, *New Testament*, 98.

26. Helms, *Who Wrote the Gospels?*, 3.

27. Anderson and Moore, "Introduction," 3.

28. Ehrman, *New Testament*, 75.

death, even if all the disciples had fled.[29] Wrede notes that the "messianic secret is not a historical fact so much as a theological idea, the idea that Jesus became Messiah through his resurrection."[30]

The "Messianic Secret" is Mark's invention, and not part of the stories of the Christian tradition Mark inherited.[31] It is the "central theological idea pervading the entire Gospel and which concretely determines its structure."[32] By using this device Mark wants to show that "contrary to the popular understanding, the job of the Messiah is not to rule at first, but first to suffer and die before returning to rule."[33] Mark depicts the content of Jesus' preaching as proclaiming that the kingdom of God is at hand and that there is need for repentance and faith in God. The Gospel begins with the story of John the Baptist, the precursor and baptizer, who baptized Jesus and preached this need for repentance. The death of John the Baptist is going to prefigure the death of Jesus. Jesus taught his disciples by parables. He also performed miracles. The greatest of all miracles was his death and resurrection. In Mark (16:8) even the resurrection is part of the Messianic Secret, for only the three women at the tomb are told about it and, because they were afraid, they said nothing to anybody.[34]

Mark emphasizes the passion of Jesus, stressing the necessity of His suffering and death. The German philosopher-theologian, M. Kahler (1835–1912) observed in this Gospel the pattern of "the passion narratives with extended introductions."[35] Mark's interest in the passion of Jesus is both to convey the significance of the person and work of Jesus and also to stress the meaning of true discipleship. The structure of Jesus' prediction of His passion is always the same: Jesus' prediction, the disciples' misunderstanding, and Jesus' sayings about what is required of those who follow him.[36]

The Synoptic Problem

The Gospel of Mark has a lot in common with the Gospels of Matthew and Luke. These three Gospels have so much in common that they are

29. Davis, "Mark's Christological Paradox," 177.

30. Anderson and Moore, "Introduction," 3. See also Wrede, *Messianic Secret*, 129.

31. Helms, *Who Wrote the Gospels?*, 12.

32. Helms, *Who Wrote the Gospels?*, 13; quoting Conzelmann and Lindemann, *Interpreting the New Testament*, 219.

33. Helms, *Who Wrote the Gospels?*, 12.

34. Helms, *Who Wrote the Gospels?*, 13.

35. Freed, *New Testament*, 101.

36. Freed, *New Testament*, 101–2.

significantly different from John. In the eighteenth century the first three Gospels came to be called the Synoptic Gospels. The German biblical scholar, J. J. Griesbach, was the first to label these gospels Synoptic Gospels.[37] When placed side by side (synoptically) these three Gospels have a lot in common. Griesbach's choice of the word was influenced by the high degree of similarity he found in these Gospels' presentations of the ministry of Jesus, particularly similarities in structure, content, and tone.[38] It is enlightening to view them (-*optic*) with (*syn-*) one another, alongside one another.

Example 1.

Matt 8:16–17	Mark 1:32–34	Luke 4:40–41
When it was evening, they brought him many who were possessed by demons, and he drove out the spirits by a word and cured all the sick, to fulfill what had been said by Isaiah the prophet: "He took away our infirmities and bore our diseases."	When it was evening, after sunset, they brought to him all who were ill or possessed by demons. The whole town was gathered at the door. He cured many who were sick with various diseases, and he drove out many demons, not permitting them to speak because they knew him.	At sunset, all who had people sick with various diseases brought them to him. He laid his hands on each of them and cured them. And demons also came out from many, shouting, "You are the Son of God." But he rebuked them and did not allow them to speak because they knew that he was the Messiah.

Matthew, Mark, and Luke, in ways significantly different from John, structure the ministry of Jesus according to a general geographic sequence, i.e., Jesus' Galilean ministry, ministry in Judea, and final ministry in Jerusalem. In content, in ways significantly different from John, they relate many of the same events, i.e., Jesus' teaching and healing ministry. In tone, contrary to the more mellow and meditative tone of John, Matthew, Mark, and Luke convey a tone of intense, rapid-fire action by juxtaposing Jesus' constant movement and teaching with miracles.[39]

---

37. Carson et al., *Introduction to the New Testament*, 19.

38. Carson et al., *Introduction to the New Testament*, 19.

39. Carson et al., *Introduction to the New Testament*, 19.

Example 2: Triple Tradition

Mark 2:10–11	Luke 5:25	Matthew 9:6
"But that you may know that the Son of Man has authority to forgive sins on earth"—he said to the paralytic, "I say to you, rise, pick up your mat, and go home."	"But that you may know that the Son of Man has authority on earth to forgive sins"—he said to the man who was paralyzed, "I say to you, rise, pick up your stretcher, and go home."	"But that you may know that the Son of Man has authority on earth to forgive sins"—he then said to the paralytic, "Rise, pick up your stretcher, and go home." He rose and went home.

According to *The New Jerome Biblical Commentary*, Mark has 661 verses, Matthew has 1068 verses, and Luke has 1149 verses. About 80 percent of Mark is found in Matthew, and about 65 percent of Mark is found in Luke. (Material found in Mark that are in Matthew and Luke is known as the **Triple Tradition**.) But in spite of these similarities we still see some significant differences between these Gospels (materials that Matthew and Luke have in common, about 220 verses, that are not found in Mark is known as the **Double Tradition**). How could one account for the similarities and differences without recourse to the Holy Spirit?[40] The problem of determining the similarities and differences between these three Gospels is what is known as the synoptic problem.[41] In other words, synoptic problem is the study of the similarities and differences of the first three Gospels in an attempt to explain their literary relationship.[42]

How then do we solve the synoptic problem, since we are dealing with three known documents (Matthew, Mark, and Luke) plus unknown hidden factors, such as the possibility of written fragments and oral traditions?[43] There seems to be an agreement in language and order of narratives among these Gospels. Is it possible that any of the evangelists had access to one or more Gospel accounts? J. A. Fitzmyer has observed that the history of the synoptic research has shown that the synoptic problem is practically insoluble.[44] What Fitzmyer means is that the argument that Matthew and Luke used a second source in addition to Mark is no longer guaranteed, nor can the priority of Matthew or proto-Luke hypothesis resolve the synoptic problem.[45] But given that there seems to be direct literary dependence

40. Anderson and Moore, "Introduction," 5.

41. See Brown et al., *New Jerome Biblical Commentary*.

42. Goodacre, *Synoptic Problem*, 16.

43. Fee, "Text-Critical Look," 164.

44. Fee, "Text-Critical Look," 163.

45. Lührmann, "Q: Sayings of Jesus or Logia?," 97.

among the Gospels, "that Gospel is to be preferred as having priority which best explains how the others came into existence."[46] In other words, what hypothesis best accounts for the combination of exact agreement and the divergence that characterizes Matthew, Mark, and Luke?[47]

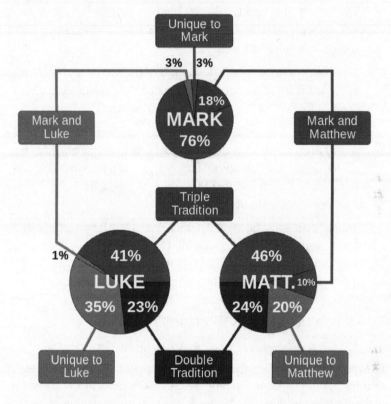

The relationships between the three synoptic Gospels by A. M. Honoré[48]

Solutions to the Synoptic Problem?

Different theories have been offered as solutions to the synoptic problem:

---

46. Fee, "Text-Critical Look," 164.

47. Carson et al., *Introduction to the New Testament*, 27.

48. This graph by A. M. Honoré is licensed under the Creative Commons Attribution-Share Alike 3.0 Unported license. See https://commons.wikimedia.org/wiki/File:Relationship_between_synoptic_gospels-en.svg.

1. In 1771 the German literary critic G. E. Lessing propounded the idea of an "Ur Gospel," an original gospel written in Hebrew or Aramaic that the synoptics relied on. In Lessing's view, this common dependence on one original Gospel accounts for the relationship among the synoptics.[49] Some scholars, like Eichhorn, have adopted and modified this theory, postulating the existence of several lost Gospels as the sources of Synoptic Gospels.[50]

2. Some who disagreed with Lessing, like the German J. G. Herder, suggested that the interdependence among the synoptics can be accounted for by their dependence on some common oral sources.[51]

3. The German theologian Friedrich Schleiermacher came up with a theory of common dependence on gradually developing written fragments, suggesting that "several fragments of the gospel tradition exited in the early church and that these gradually grew until they became incorporated into the Synoptic Gospels."[52]

4. Finally, there is the theory of interdependence; that two of the evangelists have used one or more of other Gospels.[53] There are several variants of this theory, as we shall explain below.

Two-Source Theory or Two-Document Hypothesis

There are two facets of the two-source theory: the Priority of Mark and the Q hypothesis.[54] This hypothesis which was postulated in the eighteenth century and developed in the nineteenth century states that Mark was the first written gospel and that Matthew and Luke depended on Mark. This hypothesis explains the pattern of divergence by proposing that although Matthew and Luke used Mark as a common source, they diverge from Mark at certain points because they wrote their accounts independently.[55] Investigation of parallel units of these three Gospels "reveals that where Matthew deviates from Mark, Luke usually doesn't, and that where Luke

49. Carson et al., *Introduction to the New Testament*, 27.

50. Carson et al., *Introduction to the New Testament*, 27.

51. Carson et al., *Introduction to the New Testament*, 28.

52. Carson et al., *Introduction to the New Testament*, 29.

53. Carson et al., *Introduction to the New Testament*, 29.

54. Goodacre, *Synoptic Problem*, 20.

55. Masson, *Charmed Circle*, 118.

deviates from Mark, Matthew usually doesn't."[56] How then does one account for the Double tradition, i.e. the non-Marcan materials that are in Matthew and Luke? One posits the existence of a lost writing, the "Q" source. The Q, which derives from the German word *Quelle* ("source"), was understood to be a written work that contained "Sayings" of Jesus from which Matthew and Luke each drew. Thus the Q hypothesis holds that both Matthew and Luke, independently of each other, besides Mark, used a second source.[57] In the earliest phase of this hypothesis it was generally assumed that Q was a written document.[58] But in the light of the understanding that in "the early years of Christian history, there seems to have been a great deal of freedom to move back and forth between written and oral tradition,"[59] scholars are willing to allow "some influence of the oral tradition between the time of its crystallization and its use by the two Synoptists."[60] Although the original language of written Q was thought to be Aramaic, it is safe to assume "that Q was a Greek document with only pre-literary connexion [*sic*] with Aramaic."[61] Thus, at the time the Q document was used by Matthew and Luke, Q was in a fixed written form, although "some sayings might have undergone slight alterations due to the influence of the oral traditions."[62]

Two Source Hypothesis

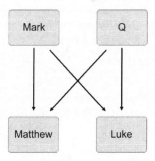

The priority of Mark does not sufficiently resolve the synoptic problem. What about the materials unique to Matthew that are not found in

56. Masson, *Charmed Circle*, 118.

57. Vassiliadis, "Nature and Extent of the Q-Document," 138.

58. Vassiliadis, "Nature and Extent of the Q-Document," 139.

59. See Beardslee, *Literary Criticism of the New Testament*, 73; cited in Vassiliadis, "Nature and Extent of the Q-Document," 143.

60. Vassiliadis, "Nature and Extent of the Q-Document," 143.

61. Vassiliadis, "Nature and Extent of the Q-Document," 146.

62. Vassiliadis, "Nature and Extent of the Q-Document," 160.

Luke and materials unique to Luke that are not found in Matthew? How do we resolve these? Scholars acknowledge the existence of a hypothetical "M" for materials found only in Matthew but not found in Mark or Luke and hypothetical "L" for materials found in Luke but not in Matthew or Mark.[63] It is not clear whether M or L is only one source or group of sources, or whether it was written or oral. What it suggests is only that it represents a single or multiple documents available to the author of Matthew or Luke and most likely stories that had been transmitted orally.[64]

A. M. Honoré of Oxford, in his statistical study of the synoptic problem, arrived at the following conclusion:

> Mark is the main link between Matthew and Luke.
> Matthew and Luke used Mark.
> Matthew did not use Luke.
> Luke did not use Matthew.
> Matthew and Luke used sources other than Mark (i.e., Q).
> Q is not a single document.[65]

Those who reject the Two-Source theory posit the **Priority of Matthew**, also known as the **Griesbach Hypothesis**. This hypothesis, which goes back to the time of Augustine (fourth century) and was reformulated by J. J. Griesbach (1789), states that Matthew was the first written Gospel and that Luke depended on Matthew, and Mark then abbreviated Matthew and Luke. This theory was revived in 1964 by William Farmer[66] who dispenses with the two facets of the Two-Source Theory, assigning the order of composition as Matthew, Luke, and Mark.[67]

Griesbach hypothesis

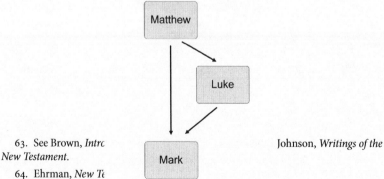

63. See Brown, *Intro*   Johnson, *Writings of the*
New Testament.

64. Ehrman, *New Te*

65. Honoré, "Statistical Study of the Synoptic Problem," 110.

66. See Farmer, *Synoptic Problem.*

67. Goodacre, *Synoptic Problem*, 22.

CRITICAL RECONSTRUCTION OF THE LIFE OF JESUS

The Christian religion is anchored on the events surrounding the life of Jesus of Nazareth. As a historical person who lived and walked among us, Jesus had a history, a history that changed the course of world events. Some have sought to understand this history beyond the events narrated in the canonical Gospels. But research into Jesus himself has long been controversial.[68] Many wonder if there is still something new to be said about Jesus and if the attempt to say something new is not a denial of Christian tradition and the sufficiency of Scripture.[69] Those who want to reconstruct the life of Jesus argue that "even in a human relationship of knowledge and love there can be misunderstandings, false impressions, wrong assumptions, which need to be teased out and dealt with, how much more when the one to whom we are relating is Jesus himself."[70] To reach Jesus himself, the argument continues, there is the need to go beyond the four canonical Gospels, the New Testament information about Jesus, and even the Greco-Roman Christian sources. This critical probing or attempt to reconstruct the life of Jesus is known as the Quest for the Historical Jesus.

The Quest for the Historical Jesus

The Gospels are confessional statements about Jesus, the Christ. Unlike other New Testament writings, the Gospels make their confession by going back to tell the story of Jesus' earthly life and ministry. With their backward glance the Gospels present us with a challenge of faith in Jesus and with a problem about Jesus.[71] In addition, when read with the intent of finding information about the life of Jesus, the Gospels pose a particular historical problem, stemming from their conspicuously different images of Jesus presented by the Synoptic Gospels on the one hand and John on the other. Moreover, these sources, i.e., the Synoptics and John, "exhibit, each within itself, a striking contradiction. They assert that Jesus felt himself to be the Messiah; and yet from their presentation of his life it does not appear that he ever publicly claimed to be so. They attribute to him, that is, an attitude which has absolutely no connection with the consciousness which they assume that he possessed."[72] Related to this is the lack of connecting thread

---

68. Wright, *Challenge of Jesus*, 13.
69. Wright, *Challenge of Jesus*, 13.
70. Wright, *Challenge of Jesus*, 14.
71. Tatum, *In Quest of Jesus*, 87.
72. Schweitzer, *Quest of the Historical Jesus*, 9.

in the materials they offer. While the Synoptics seem to be mere collections of anecdotes, John seems selective in his account of events and discourses.[73] "Not only do the events lack historical connection; we have no indication of a connecting thread in the actions and discourses of Jesus, because the sources give no hint of the character of his self-consciousness.... All that we know of the development of Jesus and of his messianic self-consciousness has been arrived at by a series of working hypothesis."[74]

These and similar difficulties have led to the question as to whether the Jesus portrayed in the Gospels is the same Jesus that lived and walked in Galilee. In other words, is Jesus of faith the same as Jesus of history? The critical investigation of the life of Jesus is one of the greatest achievements of German theology,[75] an investigation carried out in opposition to the "tyranny of dogma."[76] The issue, as Schweitzer posed it a century ago, is this:

> Is it possible to explain the contradiction between the messianic consciousness of Jesus and his non-messianic discourses and actions by means of a conception of his messianic consciousness which will make it appear that he could not have acted otherwise than as the evangelist describe; or must we endeavor to explain the contradiction by taking the non-messianic discourses and actions as our fixed point, denying the reality of Jesus' messianic self-consciousness and regarding it as a later interpolation of the beliefs of the Christian community into his life?[77]

Since Albert Schweitzer's groundbreaking work, *The Quest for the Historical Jesus* (1906), it has become customary to attribute the origin of the "Quest for Historical Jesus" to Hermann Samuel Reimarus (1694–1768) in the eighteenth century.[78] Reimarus, whose *Fragments* were posthumously published in 1778 by G. E. Lessing, was out to prove that the traditional European idea of Jesus was based on historical distortion or fantasy.[79] When the *Fragments* made their appearance in Germany they created an intellectual excitement.[80] Influenced by deism and the liberal enlightenment views, Reimarus argued that Jesus was no more than a Jewish revolutionary.[81] He

---

73. Schweitzer, *Quest of the Historical Jesus*, 8.

74. Schweitzer, *Quest of the Historical Jesus*, 8.

75. Schweitzer, *Quest of the Historical Jesus*, 3.

76. Schweitzer, *Quest of the Historical Jesus*, 5.

77. Schweitzer, *Quest of the Historical Jesus*, 11.

78. Wright, *Contemporary Quest for Jesus*, 1.

79. Wright, *Contemporary Quest for Jesus*, 6.

80. Talbert, *Reimarus*, 1.

81. Wright, *Contemporary Quest for Jesus*, 7.

saw the Gospels' story of Jesus' death and resurrection as "a creation of the disciples of Jesus after their disappointment over Jesus' crucifixion."[82]

Reimarus' view of the Christian religion was conditioned by the prevailing liberal Enlightenment environment that saw history and faith as antithetical,[83] splitting history and faith, facts and values, religion and politics, and nature and super nature.[84] The liberal view of early Christianity rested on four assumptions:[85]

1. The life of Jesus can be neatly divided into two periods: an earlier, successful period of ministry and a later journey to Jerusalem characterized by hostility and eventual death.

2. The passion narratives have been influenced by the Pauline notion of atonement.

3. The kingdom of God, a theme that dominates the passion narrative, is conceived as an ethical society of service to humanity and

4. The success of the passion depended on the disciples' understanding of the kingdom.[86]

David Friedrich Strauss (1808–74), in *The Life of Jesus: Critically Examined*, presented a different reconstruction of the life of Jesus.[87] Although Strauss did not share Reimarus' desire to discredit Christianity, he found in Reimarus "a valuable ally in his fight for a mythical view of the miracle tradition in the Gospels."[88] Strauss first portrayed Jesus as a disciple of John the Baptist who regarded himself as the messiah and had premonitions about his own death; and later under the influence of Hegelian philosophy "omitted the apocalyptic aspects of his earlier portrait of Jesus and presented him as a man with an intense consciousness of the sacred."[89] Strauss' goal was in part to show that while Christianity may not have resulted from a fraud as Reimarus thought, neither was it supernatural as his nineteenth-century contemporaries thought.[90]

---

82. McKnight, *Jesus Christ in History and Scripture*, 8.

83. Wright, *Challenge of Jesus*, 15.

84. Wright, *Challenge of Jesus*, 21.

85. Weaver, *Historical Jesus*, 28.

86. Weaver, *Historical Jesus*, 28.

87. McKnight, *Jesus Christ in History and Scripture*, 8.

88. Talbert, *Reimarus*, 36.

89. McKnight, *Jesus Christ in History and Scripture*, 8.

90. Talbert, *Reimarus*, 36.

The last truly significant effort along these lines was Schweitzer's 1906 study.[91] "His survey of prior attempts to retrieve the 'real' Jesus illustrated the obvious difficulty. Each interpreter found a different Jesus. Moreover, each found his own ideals embodied in Jesus."[92] Schweitzer objected to some liberal views by pointing out that while Reimarus was right to see Jesus in the context of first-century Judaism, he was wrong to see him as a revolutionary.[93] "Jesus shared the first century apocalyptic expectation of the end of all things, and though he died without it having come about, he started the eschatological movement that became Christianity."[94] For Schweitzer, "there never was a Jesus who cavorted around Galilee happily winning converts with his message about an ethical kingdom of human service; the service of which he spoke was the necessary repentance providing moral renewal as preparation for the supernatural kingdom."[95] For him, the Christian faith stands by the question of Jesus' messianic consciousness, for if Jesus did not know himself as the messiah then the judgment of the early church is not binding on us.[96]

Although the quest for the historical Jesus continues to this day, thanks to Ernst Kaseman's 1953 lecture, "The Problem of the Historical Jesus," which revived the quest in the modern time, the historical investigation of the real Jesus beyond the confines of dogma continues to prove difficult. In fact, some have tagged the attempt a complete failure. "The quest for the historical Jesus did not fail because the gospels are unreliable sources. The quest failed because interpreters like Reimarus misunderstood what kind of sources the gospels were and so asked the wrong sorts of questions."[97]

Non-scriptural Sources of the Life of Jesus

Although the canonical Gospels of Matthew, Mark, Luke, and John remain "the most complete sources for a study of Jesus," they are not the only sources.[98] Some New Testament writings give information about Jesus and even some early Christian writers whose work did not make the canon of the New Testament give some information about Jesus, just as there were some

91. Masson, *Charmed Circle*, 116.

92. Masson, *Charmed Circle*, 116.

93. Wright, *Contemporary Quest for Jesus*, 10.

94. Wright, *Challenge of Jesus*, 28.

95. Weaver, *Historical Jesus*, 29.

96. Weaver, *Historical Jesus*, 30.

97. Masson, *Charmed Circle*, 117–18.

98. McKnight, *Jesus Christ in History and Scripture*, 28.

writers in the first century CE who, in interpreting Jewish traditions and recording Roman history, make references to Jesus:[99]

1. Talmud: Jesus is sometimes mentioned in Jewish literature, especially "in the Jewish materials that came into fixed form in the Talmud, the repository of Jewish interpretation of the Law from the time of Ezra to the middle of the sixth century CE."[100] Some Talmudic references to Jesus contradict the Christian account. One possible explanation might be because some Talmudic traditions "attempt to destroy the validity of Christian truth by altering and interpreting the Christian tradition."[101] But even in doing so they do not destroy the basis of Christian truth.

2. Flavius Josephus: Some information about Jesus is found in the work of the Jewish historian Josephus. His work, *Antiquities*, references James as "the brother of Jesus, who was called the Christ."

3. Pliny: In a second-century CE correspondence between Pliny the Younger, the governor of Bithynia, and Trajan, the Roman emperor, there were specific references to Christians and what they believe and references were made to Christ in the context of the existing hot political climate. In a letter to the emperor, Pliny notes how Christians "were in the habit of meeting before dawn on fixed days and singing hymns to Christ as to a god."[102]

4. Tacitus: The Roman historian Tacitus, in two celebrated works, *Histories* and *Annals*, gave information about the Christian religion and the man called Christ, who was crucified under Pontius Pilate.

5. Suetonius: Suetonius, a friend of Pliny's, while acting as secretary to Emperor Hadrian, published *The Lives of the Twelve Caesars*, mentions the persecution of Christians and the expulsion of those Jews from Rome who made disturbances at the instigation of "Chrestus."[103]

6. Agrapha: There are documents, Agrapha (meaning "unwritten things"), that contain words ascribed to Jesus. They probably were words of Jesus that were first circulated orally by his followers before they were eventually written down. "Some of these sayings of Jesus are

---

99. McKnight, *Jesus Christ in History and Scripture*, 28.

100. McKnight, *Jesus Christ in History and Scripture*, 28–29.

101. McKnight, *Jesus Christ in History and Scripture*, 29.

102. Amiot, "Jesus, an Historical Person," 8.

103. McKnight, *Jesus Christ in History and Scripture*, 33–34.

found in New Testament writings outside the Gospels. First Corinthians 11:23–25 and Acts 20:35 contain sayings that are clearly attributed to Jesus."[104]

7. Apocryphal Gospels: Some information about Jesus is found in the non-canonical or apocryphal gospels.

THE STAGES IN-SETTING OF THE GOSPEL

On October 30, 1902, Leo XIII established the Pontifical Biblical Commission (PBC) because he was worried that Catholics were giving in to the opinions of "heterodox writers" and seeking understanding of Sacred Scripture "in the researches which the erudition of unbelievers has arrived at."[105] The pope charged the PBC to give a "thorough interpretation" of the text of Sacred Scripture and shield it "from every breath of error . . . [and] temerarious opinion."[106] In 1979, however, the PBC ceased from being an official organ of the Catholic Church, in matters of scriptural interpretation. It is now a consultative body of scholars whose conclusions are revered and esteemed in the Church.

The PBC has issued some helpful documents regarding the methods of interpretation of Scripture. One such document was *On the Historical Truth of the Gospels* (1964),[107] in which the PBC sets some guidelines for Catholic exegetes. The Catholic exegete, the PBC admonishes, must make use of all the resources for the interpretation of the sacred text, which the church has provided, such as the writings of the Fathers and Doctors of the Church.

> In order to bring out with fullest clarity the enduring truth and authority of the Gospels he must, while carefully observing the rules of rational and of Catholic hermeneutics, make skillful use of the new aids to exegesis, especially those which the historical method, taken it its widest sense, has provided; that method, namely, which minutely investigates sources, determining their nature and bearing, and availing itself of the findings of textual criticism, literary criticism, and linguistic studies. The interpreter must be alert to the reminder given him by Pope Pius XII of happy memory when he charged him "to make judicious

104. McKnight, *Jesus Christ in History and Scripture*, 34.

105. See *Enchiridion Biblicum*, 141.

106. *Enchiridion Biblicum*, 139.

107. Pontifical Biblical Commission, "Instruction on the Historical Truth of the Gospels," 299–312.

inquiry as to how far the form of expression or the type of literature adopted by the sacred writer may help towards the true
and genuine interpretation, and to remain convinced that this
part of his task cannot be neglected without great detriment to
Catholic exegesis."[108]

While encouraging the use of historical method, the PBC also urges
caution because "the method in question is often found alloyed with principles of a philosophical or theological nature which are quite inadmissible,
and which not infrequently vitiate both the method itself and the conclusions arrived at regarding literary questions."[109] The PBC hinges its caution
on the following areas of concern: (a) Some who have used the method have
not only been led astray by "rationalistic prejudices," which made them not
only to deny the existence of the supernatural order, but also to deny the
reality of prophecies and miracles. (b) Some with erroneous view of faith
advance the view that "faith is indifferent to historical truth, and is indeed
incompatible with it." (c) Some deny the historical value and character of
the documents of revelation. And, finally, (d) some underestimate the authority of the apostles as eyewitnesses of Christ and their influence in early
Christian community.[110]

In order to guard against these errors, the PBC endorsed the following
three stages of the development of the Gospel tradition and asked the interpreter to take careful note of these "stages of tradition by which the teaching
and life of Jesus have come down to us."

(a). First Stage, **the Public Ministry**: Jesus chose disciples who worked
with him and were firsthand eyewitnesses of His life and teaching. Jesus
proclaimed His message orally and accommodated His teaching to the
mentality of his audience and disciples. The disciples correctly understood the teachings, miracles, and other events in the life of Jesus. The
disciples "grasped correctly the idea that the miracles and other events
of the life of Jesus were things purposely performed or arranged by
Him in such a way that men would thereby be led to believe in Christ
and to accept by faith the doctrine of salvation."[111] Raymond Brown,

108. Pontifical Biblical Commission, "Instruction on the Historical Truth of the
Gospels," 306.

109. Pontifical Biblical Commission, "Instruction on the Historical Truth of the
Gospels," 306.

110. Pontifical Biblical Commission, "Instruction on the Historical Truth of the
Gospels," 306–7.

111. Pontifical Biblical Commission, "Instruction on the Historical Truth of the
Gospels," 307.

commenting on this, asserts, "It is important for modern readers to keep reminding themselves that these were memories of what was said and done by a Jew who lived in Galilee and Jerusalem in the 20s. Jesus' manner of speaking, the problems he faced, his vocabulary and outlook were those of that specific time and place."[112]

(b). Second Stage, **the apostles**: The apostles were witnesses to Jesus. His resurrection was the key turning point. They proclaimed His death and resurrection, and preached the events of His life, taking into account the circumstances of their hearers. Jesus was a Galilean, who spoke Aramaic. His message was proclaimed in Greek, a language he never or rarely spoke. Raymond Brown comments that this "change of language involved translation in the broadest sense of that term, i.e., rephrasing in vocabulary and patterns that would make the message intelligible and alive for new audiences."[113] The PBC continues that after Jesus "had risen from the dead, and when His divinity was clearly perceived, the faith of the disciples, far from blotting out the remembrance of the events that had happened, rather consolidated it, since their faith was based on what Jesus had done and taught."[114] The disciples did not turn Jesus into a "mythical" personage, nor did they distort His teaching. Rather they handed on faithfully their understanding of the words and deeds of Jesus and interpreted them according to the "mentality of their hearers." The disciples illumined their own faith by their post-resurrection kerygma. They understood their mission as people sent forth to bring others to faith by proclaiming the risen Lord.[115]

(c). Third Stage, **the Sacred Writers**: The sacred authors, for the benefit of the church, took what was first transmitted orally, and later written down, and drew up a narrative that resulted in the four Gospels. "They selected certain things out of the many which had been handed on; some they synthesized, some they explained with an eye to the situation of the churches, painstakingly using every means of bringing

---

112. Brown, *Introduction to the New Testament*, 107.

113. Brown, *Introduction to the New Testament*, 108.

114. Pontifical Biblical Commission, "Instruction on the Historical Truth of the Gospels," 307.

115. Pontifical Biblical Commission, "Instruction on the Historical Truth of the Gospels," 307.

home to the readers the solid truth of the things in which they had been instructed."[116] The PBC continues:

> For, out of the material which they had received, the sacred authors selected especially those items which were adapted to the varied circumstances of the faithful as well as to the end which they themselves wished to attain; these they recounted in a manner consonant with those circumstances and with that end. And since the meaning of a statement depends, amongst other things, on the place which it has in a given sequence, the Evangelists, in handing on the words or the deeds of our Savior, explained them, one Evangelist in one context, another in another. For this reason, the exegete must ask himself what the Evangelist intended by recounting a saying or a fact in a certain way, or by placing it in a certain context. For the truth of the narrative is not affected in the slightest by the fact that the Evangelists report the sayings or the doings of our Lord in a different order, and that they use different words to express what He said, not keeping to the very letter, but nevertheless preserving the sense.[117]

The exegete must consider these factors, which have a bearing on the origin and composition of the Gospels, if the exegete is to ascertain the true intentions of the sacred writers. The teachings and life of Jesus, according to the PBC, were not recounted just to be kept in remembrance, but were "preached" to furnish "the Church with the foundation on which to build up faith and morals."[118] The PBC then called on the exegete to "cherish a spirit of ready obedience to the Church's teaching authority,"[119] bearing in mind that the apostles who proclaimed the Good News were filled with the Holy Spirit who preserved them from error when they committed the Good News to writing.

The three stages noted by the PBC are commonly referred to as three "settings-in-life": (1) in the life of Jesus before his resurrection, (2) in the life of the church, i.e., of early Christians before the Gospels were written, and (3) the setting in the context of the Gospel writers and their shaping of

116. Pontifical Biblical Commission, "Instruction on the Historical Truth of the Gospels," 308.

117. Pontifical Biblical Commission, "Instruction on the Historical Truth of the Gospels," 309.

118. Pontifical Biblical Commission, "Instruction on the Historical Truth of the Gospels," 309.

119. Pontifical Biblical Commission, "Instruction on the Historical Truth of the Gospels," 309–10.

the written Gospels, i.e., Jewish setting, Jewish-Hellenistic setting, and the purpose of the evangelists.

THE FOUR SENSES OF SCRIPTURE

The Christian Church venerates the scriptures as the word of God in human language. Earlier we saw that there are two authors of the sacred text, human and divine—that God is the author of Sacred Scripture in the sense that God revealed God's divine word to human beings who committed them to writing under the inspiration of the Holy Spirit. God chose certain men, whom he inspired, made full use of their own faculties and powers, and guided them through the power of the Holy Spirit to write down only whatever God wanted. We also saw that sacred Scripture is inerrant (without error)—that God inspired the human authors of sacred scripture and they committed to writing only what God intended. The sacred scriptures firmly, faithfully, and without error teach the truth God wanted to convey to human beings for our salvation.

There are two senses of scripture, according to ancient tradition: the literal sense and spiritual sense. The spiritual sense has three subdivisions: allegorical, moral, and anagogical senses.

- Literal sense: This is the meaning conveyed by the human author. All other senses of Scripture are based on the literal sense.

- Allegorical sense: This is the profound understanding of the text by recognizing its significance in Christ. When the Hebrews crossed the Sea of Reeds for instance, the crossing of this sea is a type of baptism in Christ.

- Moral sense: This is the ethical interpretation of the text of sacred Scripture such that it helps us lead a good or moral Christian life.

- Anagogical sense: Viewing the text of the sacred Scripture in terms of their eternal significance, such that it leads us to our eternal home, heaven.

HERMENEUTICS AND THE NEW TESTAMENT

The English word *hermeneutics* is derived from the Greek verb *hermeneuin*, which means "to make known" or "to translate." Greek mythology depicts "Hermes" as the god whose duty it is to communicate to human beings the message of the gods. Later Hermes came to be known as the patron of communication and understanding. Hermeneutics, deriving from this mythic god-messenger, Hermes, means the art or science of interpretation. As Hermes bridged the gap between two realms: the divine and human realm, hermeneutics examines the relationship between two realms: the realm of the text and the realm of those who wish to understand the text.[120] In classical Greek literature, especially that beginning from Plato, hermeneutics "referred to the interpretation of divine signs and oracles as they related to the fate and destiny of people or individuals."[121] Properly speaking, hermeneutics is a branch of philosophy that is concerned with human understanding and interpretation of a written text. It examines the way one understands a text or a work of art.[122] Hermeneutics seeks to answer the question: how can a text that originates in a particular historical context be unfolded in a different (later) cultural setting? In their study and analysis of literature, the ancient Greeks looked for coherence and consistency in grammar, style, and logic. Later Hebrew also responded to the need to interpret Hebrew Scripture.

The Need for Hermeneutics

Christians venerate the Bible as the revealed Word of God and are challenged to be obedient to God's Word. But "it can be daunting to face a voluminous Bible full of alien genealogies, barbaric practices, strange prophecies, and eccentric epistles."[123] There is also the fact of linguistic, historical, social, and cultural gaps between the ancient world of the scriptural writer and the modern world that needs to be bridged.[124] This then calls for a proper method of interpretation—hermeneutics. To properly understand the revealed word of God "we need an approach and methods that are appropriate to the task. Hermeneutics provides the means for acquiring an understanding of the Scriptures" in ways that avoid arbitrary and erroneous interpretation that suits our whims.[125]

A written or oral communication involves three layers of meaning: what the speaker or writer intends to convey, what the listener or recipient actually understands, and what meaning is actually encoded in the text or

---

120. Jeanrond, *Theological Hermeneutics*, 1.

121. Houtepen, "Hermeneutics and Ecumenism," 1.

122. Henn, "Hermeneutics and Ecumenical Dialogue," 47.

123. Klein et al., *Introduction to Biblical Interpretation*, xxv.

124. Klein et al., *Introduction to Biblical Interpretation*, 5–6.

125. Klein et al., *Introduction to Biblical Interpretation*, 5.

utterance itself.[126] "Authors may occasionally unconsciously convey more than they intended, but the point is that they normally determine what they will say, how they will encode their message, and what results they hope to achieve."[127] Since the biblical author is not available to make these known to us, it is only by means of biblical texts that we can reconstruct what the authors intend to convey and what their audiences understood.[128]

The Jews recognized the importance of scriptural interpretation very early in their history. Scholars allude to 2 Chronicles 35:13, which attempts to reconcile the paschal prescriptions of Exodus 12:9 and Deuteronomy 16:7, as proof that what was later called rabbinic exegesis had long existed in the Jewish reading of Scripture.[129] In the late sixth century BCE, when the Jews started returning home from exile, the Levites were said to have helped Ezra the scribe interpret the Mosaic Law. The Jews who returned from exile did not speak Hebrew. They spoke a Babylonian version of Aramaic. According to the story attested in Nehemiah (8:7–8), whenever Ezra proclaimed the Mosaic law during solemn assembly, it was the Levites who, in addition to explaining to the people what Ezra was reading, translated and interpreted the text. This practice led to what was later known as the *Targum*, the translation and interpretation of biblical texts in the period known as the intertestamental period. They interpreted the text in ways that explain obscure words and reconcile conflicting passages, and also found ways to apply the text to the daily life of the people.[130]

There was also the widespread use of the Midrashim in Hellenistic Judaism, when Greek culture and influence predominated in the period that followed the inauguration of worldwide transnational culture due to the conquest of the civilized world by Alexander the Great in about 333 BCE. Midrash is a Hebrew word that denotes "a method of reading details" into the biblical text. It is essentially a way of searching for the meaning of a biblical text. In the Hellenistic period, especially in the cultural center, Alexandria, hermeneutics assumed a more scientific style. Hellenistic scholars sought the origin and meaning of a given work by attending carefully to the logic, style, and grammar of the text. The method proved so useful that the Church Fathers applied it to the study of the New Testament. They favored allegorical reading of scriptural text over its literal meaning and found, in

126. Klein et al., *Introduction to Biblical Interpretation*, 8; paraphrasing Caird, *Language and Imagery*, 32–61.

127. Klein et al., *Introduction to Biblical Interpretation*, 8.

128. Klein et al., *Introduction to Biblical Interpretation*, 9.

129. Halivni, "Aspects of Classical Jewish Hermeneutics," 77.

130. Klein et al., *Introduction to Biblical Interpretation*, 24.

reading the Old Testament, a "hidden" meaning. They saw the Old Testament as prefiguration of the New Testament.

The teaching office of the Catholic Church, the Magisterium, favors proper interpretation of the biblical text and sees this as essential to its duties of preserving the Christian faith and tradition. In its concern for correct scriptural interpretation, the Magisterium sometimes intervenes in cases where they believe individuals or schools of thought are misrepresenting a scriptural text. The Magisterium's intervention in scriptural matters has been well documented, especially since the last century, beginning with Leo XIII, who in 1902 established the Pontifical Biblical Commission to oversee issues of scriptural interpretation. Pius X, following Leo's lead, founded the Biblical Institute in 1909. In 1920 Benedict XV issued an encyclical on the interpretation of the Bible to celebrate the 1500th anniversary of the death of St. Jerome, the patron of Catholic biblical scholarship, and in 1965, the Second Vatican's Council's document, Dei Verbum, gave another boost to Catholic biblical studies. The involvement of the Catholic Church in Biblical studies, however, has been defined mainly by two encyclicals, Leo XIII's *Providentissimus Deus* (November 18, 1893) and Pius XII's *Divino Afflante Spiritu* (September 30, 1943)

On April 23, 1993, the centenary anniversary of *Providentissimus Deus*, the Catholic Church released another landmark document for biblical studies prepared by the Pontifical Biblical Commission (PBC), titled *The Interpretation of the Bible in the Church*. The PBC "is not an organ of the teaching office, but rather a commission of scholars who, in their scientific and ecclesial responsibility as believing exegetes, take positions on important problems of Scriptural Interpretation and know that for this task they enjoy the confidence of the teaching office."[131] This PBC document examines modern approaches to biblical interpretation, its advantages and disadvantages, and outlines ways of knowing (interpreting) the meaning of a text. In this document, PBC notes that its intention is "to indicate the paths most appropriate for arriving at an interpretation of the Bible as faithful as possible to its character both human and divine."[132] In laying this path for correct interpretation of biblical texts, the document begins with a cautionary note, denouncing the hermeneutics of some rationalist philosophers.

---

131. Pontifical Biblical Commission, *Interpretation of the Bible*, 28.
132. Pontifical Biblical Commission, *Interpretation of the Bible*, 34.

Does Philosophical Hermeneutics Have a Place in Biblical Interpretation?

Hermeneutics or the theory of interpretation of texts has "provided occasion for the elaboration of the impressive epistemological and metaphysical constructions associated with names such as Schleiermacher, Dilthey, Heidegger, Gadamer, Habermas and Ricoeur."[133] It was against their involvement in matters of hermeneutics that the PBC directed its cautionary note because they "stressed the involvement of the knowing subject in human understanding, especially as regards historical knowledge."[134] In the assessment of the PBC, however, if this involvement of the knowing subject is seen in terms of rationalistic philosophical thought, especially that of the eighteenth-century German philosopher Immanuel Kant (1784–1804), it undercuts true interpretation. Kant had denied metaphysical knowledge since, for him, we cannot know the metaphysical world, the world of "noumena," as he calls it. In their concern, the PBC notes,

> In its recent course exegesis has been challenged to some rethinking in the light of contemporary philosophical hermeneutics, which has stressed the involvement of the knowing subject in human understanding, especially as regards historical knowledge. Hermeneutical reflection took new life with the publication of the works of Friedrich Schleiermacher, Wilhelm Dilthey and, above all, Martin Heidegger. In the footsteps of these philosophers, but also to some extent moving away from them, various authors have more deeply developed contemporary hermeneutical theory and its applications to Scripture. Among them we will mention especially Rudolph Bultmann, Hans Georg Gadamer and Paul Ricoeur. It is not possible to give a complete summary of their thought here. It will be enough to indicate certain central ideas of their philosophies which have had their impact on the interpretation of biblical texts.[135]

1. Friedrich Daniel Ernst Schleiermacher (1768–1834): a German philosopher/theologian who became deeply involved in the Romantic movement in Berlin. Romanticists believed in individualism and expression of individual freedom. Schleiermacher was sympathetic to the French Revolution.

---

133. Henn, "Hermeneutics and Ecumenical Dialogue," 47–48.
134. Pontifical Biblical Commission, *Interpretation of the Bible*, 76.
135. Pontifical Biblical Commission, *Interpretation of the Bible*, 76.

2. Hans Georg Gadamer (1900–2002): a German philosopher/theologian, and a student of Heidegger. His most famous work was *Wahrheit und Methode* (Truth and Method) in which he argues that the element of effective history is operative in all understanding of tradition. Gadamer stressed the historical distance between the text and its interpreter.

> That the text is the object of interpretation means that it presents a question to the interpreter. To understand the text is to understand the question of the text. Whoever wishes to understand the text must see it as the answer to the question. But the interpreter does not come as an empty vessel; the interpreter comes with a horizon of meaning that is broadened so as to become fused with that of the text.[136]

3. Paul Ricoeur (1913–2005): a French philosopher who was influenced by the work of Gabriel Marcel. Ricoeur was preoccupied with what has been known as the hermeneutic of the self, i.e., need to make one's life intelligible to oneself. He refers to a principle approach in his hermeneutic method as **hermeneutic of suspicion**, because every discourse both reveals and conceals something about the nature of being. Hermeneutic of suspicion has been appropriated by Liberation theologians, especially Latin American liberation theology, feminism, and Black theology. Feminist theologians and Black theologians alike look at such texts as these with suspicion:

- "Wives should be subordinate to their husbands as to the Lord. For the husband is the head of his wife just as Christ is the head of the Church." (Eph 5:22–24)
- "Slaves be obedient to your human masters with fear and trembling, in sincerity of heart, as to Christ . . ." (Eph 6:5–6)

136. McKnight, *Jesus Christ in History and Scripture*, 150.

THE HISTORICAL-CRITICAL METHOD AND BIBLICAL ANALYSIS

The PBC considers the historical-critical method an "indispensable method for the scientific study of the meaning of ancient texts,"[137] inasmuch as the sacred scripture is the word of God in human language. The historical-critical method makes it possible to understand more accurately the intention of the authors and editors of the Bible. The origin of the method goes back to antiquity, to Greek commentators of classical literature, and to the Patristic period (Origen, Jerome, Augustine, etc.). At this time the method was still in its infancy and less developed.

The PBC traces the modern form of the method to the refinements of the humanists of the Renaissance who called for *recursus ad fontes* (return to the sources). The work of Richard Simon (seventeenth century), who drew attention to the doublets, discrepancies in content and style of the Pentateuch ushered in the beginning of literary criticism. His discoveries disproved the notion of Moses as the single author of the Pentateuch. Literary criticism was further developed and in the nineteenth century there developed from it the **Documentary Hypothesis,** which posits that four documents have been woven together to produce the Pentateuch. These four documents, as we have seen, are the Yahwist (J), the Elohist (E) the Deuteronomist (D) and the Priestly (P). Literary criticism has also been applied to the Gospels, yielding, for instance, the **Two-Source Theory or Two-Source Hypothesis**, which states that the synoptics, Matthew and Luke, in composing their Gospels, relied on Mark and a collection of the Sayings of Jesus called Q.

The PBC, however, maintains that this kind of literary criticism, in its desire to establish chronology of the biblical text, restricts "itself to the task of dissecting and dismantling the text in order to identify the various sources,"[138] and as such does not pay sufficient attention to the final form of the biblical text, i.e., the work of the final editor. The PBC also notes the insufficiency of textual criticism and the form criticism, which Martin Dibelius and Rudolph Bultmann applied to the synoptic Gospels, and also the insufficiency of redaction criticism. What this means, according to the PBC, is that the historical-critical method sometimes dissolves and destroys the text. But it still "opens up to the modern reader a path to the meaning of the biblical text."[139]

137. Pontifical Biblical Commission, *Interpretation of the Bible*, 35.
138. Pontifical Biblical Commission, *Interpretation of the Bible*, 36.
139. Pontifical Biblical Commission, *Interpretation of the Bible*, 42.

The Pontifical Biblical Commission, far from endorsing any particular method of biblical analysis, states that no method of biblical analysis, no matter how scientific, is adequate enough to comprehend the richness of the biblical text. In this respect, then, the historical-critical method is necessary but not altogether sufficient for grasping the richness of the biblical text. The PBC also examined other methods of literary analysis, such as rhetorical analysis, narrative analysis, and semiotic analysis, pointing out their usefulness as well as their limitations.

Rhetorical analysis is a systematic way of studying the biblical text by analyzing its rhetoric or pattern of speech. Rhetoric is the art of persuasion. Classical rhetoric distinguished between three modes of discourse or three different modes of public speaking:

- Deliberative rhetoric that was used in political assembly;

- Judicial rhetoric that was used in the court of law; and

- Demonstrative rhetoric that was used in festivities or occasions that called for celebration.

In classical Greco-Roman literature, in every discourse (whether deliberative, judicial, or demonstrative discourse) were present three basic elements: the speaker, the discourse or speech, and the audience. The quality of the speech is determined by three factors: (i) ethos, i.e., the authority of the speaker; (ii) logos, i.e., the force of the argument; and (iii) pathos, i.e., the feelings or emotions aroused in the audience.

Biblical scholars, recognizing the influence of rhetoric in Hellenistic culture, now pay attention to the rhetorical features of scripture. The PBC acknowledges that the Bible is not simply a statement of truths and that its message carries within it a function of communication within a particular context. Insofar as rhetorical analysis recognizes the power of argument and rhetorical structure of the Bible, the PBC says of rhetorical analysis, "Because of the enrichment it brings to the critical study of the text, such rhetorical analysis is worthy of high regard. . . . It makes up for negligence of long standing and can lead to the rediscovery or clarification of original perspectives that had been lost or obscured."[140] PBC also points out the limitations of rhetorical analysis: (i) rhetorical analysis sometimes remains on the level of description and therefore concerns itself only with style; and (ii) rhetorical analysis cannot claim to be an independent method which would be sufficient in itself. Thus its application to the biblical text raises several questions, which cast doubts on the use of the method.

---

140. Pontifical Biblical Commission, *Interpretation of the Bible*, 45.

Narrative analysis attempts to understand the biblical message in form of story and personal testimony. The Hebrew Scriptures, for instance, according to this analysis, presents the story of salvation which finds expression in the profession of faith and liturgy of the Hebrew people, and the Christian New Testament presents a sequence of telling the story of the life, death, and resurrection of Jesus Christ. Narrative analysis often makes distinction between "real author" (the person who actually composed the story) and "implied author" (image of the person or author the text progressively creates) and "real reader" (the one who has access to the text from those who first read it) and "implied reader" (the reader the text progressively creates). The PBC says of narrative analysis that it is well suited to the narrative character, which so many biblical texts display. But its distinction between "real author" and "implied author" makes the problems of interpretation more complex.

Semiotic analysis used to be called structural analysis or structuralism and is traceable to the work of Swiss linguist Ferdinand de Saussure, whose theory claimed that language is a system of relationships that obey fixed laws. One of the prominent biblical scholars who have refined the method and applied it to the Bible was Algirdas Greimas. In the way Greimas used it, semiotic analysis is based on three principles or presuppositions: (a) the principle of immanence, in which a text forms a unit of meaning complete in itself; (b) the principle of the structure of meaning, in which the analysis of the text consists in establishing network of relationships between the various elements of the text; and (c) the principle of the grammar of the text, in which every text follows a "grammar" or certain number of rules or structures.

According to the PBC, "by directing greater attention to the fact that each biblical text is a coherent whole, obedient to a precise linguistic mechanic of operation, semiotics contributes to our understanding of the Bible as the Word of God expressed in human language."[141] But the PBC also cautions that the semiotic approach must be open to history, i.e., history of those who play a part in the texts, history of the authors and readers. "The great risk run by those who employ semiotic analysis is that of remaining at the level of a formal study of the content of texts, failing to draw out the message."[142]

---

141. Pontifical Biblical Commission, *Interpretation of the Bible*, 51.
142. Pontifical Biblical Commission, *Interpretation of the Bible*, 51.

CHARACTERISTICS OF CATHOLIC EXEGESIS

The first interpreters of scripture in the Christian church were the church fathers. The fathers made sure that their exegesis was relevant to the needs of the Christians of their day. According to the PBC, what the Bible and the history of its interpretation show is that there is a need for a hermeneutics, an interpretation that addresses the peculiar needs of our time. But the fundamental question remains: which hermeneutical theory or combination of methods best leads to the profound reality of which scripture speaks and its meaningful expression for people today? In light of this question, the PBC states that one must admit that some hermeneutical theories are inadequate for scripture. The PBC lists Bultmann's existentialist interpretation and its excessive "demythologization" of Scripture as an instance of an inadequate hermeneutic.

The Pontifical Biblical Commission lists the following as the characteristics of Catholic exegesis:

- Catholic exegesis is not tied to any particular scientific method but recognizes that the biblical text is the word of God expressed in human language by the human author who expressed this message in the social context of his time.

- Catholic exegesis makes use of scientific methods and approaches that allow for a better grasp of the meaning of the text in its linguistic, literary, sociocultural, religious, and historical contexts.

- Catholic exegesis is situated within the living tradition of the church and concerns itself with fidelity to the revelation attested by the Bible.

6

Two Great Influences

CHRISTIANITY—THE SECT WITHIN JUDAISM in the mind of the Roman authorities—had become well established in the empire by the end of the fourth century CE. The growth continued at a very fast pace that by the Middle Ages Christianity had become entrenched and synonymous with Western civilization. Among the many factors responsible for this were the influences of two great theologians: Augustine of Hippo in the fourth century and Thomas Aquinas in the thirteenth century. Their writings, which were formative and influential for the church, will ironically become the key reference points for the sixteenth-century reformers. Luther and some of the churches of the reformation that severed relations with Rome will appeal to Augustine's doctrine of grace to validate one of their key positions, i.e., human depravity and inability of human free-will to bring about salvation. The Roman Catholic Church will counter by appealing to Thomism (theology of Thomas Aquinas) and seeking a synthesis of faith and reason.

Fourth-century CE Christian communities were organized along the Mediterranean coastlands, from modern Egypt and Libya through Tunisia, Algebra, Morocco, and Mauritania. But the fourth century was also a time of crisis for the church because of the Diocletian (284–305 CE) persecution. Nero (Roman emperor from 54 to 68 CE) began the era of formal persecution of Christians and Diocletian brought it to an art form. Making matters worse for the Christian communities scattered all over the Mediterranean coastlands, the proconsul of Africa, Anullinus, "exceeded the requirements of the Diocletian edicts and directed the persecution not only at the hierarchy, in order to discredit it, but also at the laity."[1] The persecution made the Christian communities in North Africa (or North African Church) the hot bed of martyrdom. North African church produced many martyrs, like Perpetua (a twenty-two-year-old woman from a noble family in Carthage) and her slave girl Felicitas. The two women and their companions were thrown to the lions. There were also other witnesses like Cyprian, the bishop of Carthage (ca. 200–258 CE).

AURELIUS AUGUSTINUS (354–430)

It was into this church community of martyrs that Augustine of Hippo, the most well-known Christian theologian of antiquity, was born. Rome had destroyed Carthage and annexed it about five hundred years before. Ancient Carthaginians spoke Latin (the language of Rome) as well as their own Berber and Punic languages. We know a lot about Augustine's early life from his own detailed account in *The Confessions*, which he wrote when he was about forty-three years old. Augustine was almost certainly a Berber (a tribe in present-day Libya). He was born in Thagaste, an insignificant town in Numidia, a center of Berber culture. His name, Augustine, is "a typical version of a Berber honorific name."[2] His other name, Aurelius, suggests that his family was among those who were made Roman citizens, thanks to the edict of Caracalla. Roman citizenship was a prized possession that granted privileges to anyone that had it. The Edict of Caracalla (212 CE), promulgated by Emperor Caracalla, granted Roman citizenship to all free-born inhabitants of the empire. It conferred the same privileges enjoyed by male Roman citizens to any free-born male in the empire and conferred the same privileges enjoyed by female Roman citizens as well to all females in the empire. Before the edict Roman privileges were enjoyed only by those living in Italy. They were not extended to anyone in the provinces controlled by Rome.

Augustine was born of a pagan father, Patricius, a name that indicates that he must have been wealthy and well-to-do, and a Christian mother, Monica, a name that derives from the Berber deity Mon. Augustine was attached to his mother, but alienated from his father. He moved to Carthage in search of education. In Carthage he lived a licentious life and had a mistress who bore him a son, Adeodatus (God-given). Augustine does not mention the mother of his mistress who bore him Adeodatus in *The Confessions*.

---

1. See Bright, "Church, North African," 185.
2. Thompson and Ferguson, *Africa in Classical Antiquity*, 184.

Augustine was interested in learning. He was also drawn to literature, rhetoric, and philosophy, particularly the philosophy of Plato. This desire for learning led him to Manicheanism (sometimes rendered Manichaeism), a religious sect in North Africa. He spent nine years as a member of this sect. Manichaeism was dualistic. It taught that matter or flesh was bad and spirit was good. Manichaeism condemned all sexual unions. The Manicheans considered it a crime to birth children because matter was thought to be evil. Giving birth to children would be to needlessly imprison their soul in the body. The Manicheans proposed a mythical explanation for the problem of evil (theodicy) and suggested that there was a perpetual struggle between coeternal principles of light and darkness. Manicheanism also denied liberty. It offered a scientific explanation of nature that contradicted sacred Scripture. Augustine was fascinated by the teaching of the problem of conflict between two forces, matter and spirit.

The sect was hierarchically structured. According to their degrees of membership, priest or "elect" was the highest and "auditor" was the lowest. Members of this sect go through initiation rite to become an "elect." The "elect" performed rigorous ascetical practices. But auditors were permitted to engage in sexual relations, though they were forbidden to reproduce. Augustine never attained the degree of "priest" or "elect" and probably never went beyond "auditor." In the end, Manicheanism did not satisfy his quest for knowledge and he left the sect after nine years. Later as a Christian Augustine would counter the Manichean idea that sexual union and procreation are bad. Augustine the Christian would see marriage as ordained by God and sexual union as having its place only in marriage.

Augustine's spiritual yearning led him to Neo-Platonism, a teaching that derived from Plotinus (207–70 CE). Augustine learned Neo-Platonism through the Latin translations of Victorinus. Plotinus himself was an Egyptian by birth. He taught that humans participate in divine activity through the mind and that a person should reject material things as a way of purifying the soul and unifying oneself with what he called the One. Augustine was fascinated by the Neo-Platonic teaching that evil was a privation of the good. But again, in the end Neo-Platonism did not completely satisfy Augustine's spiritual quest. In fact, his confidence in Neo-Platonism "was shaken by the discovery that the Neo-Platonist Victorinus had joined the Church and made a public confession."[3] Later as a Christian Augustine would see aspects of Neo-Platonism to be in harmony with Christian teaching. In fact, when he became a Christian Augustine and some other early Christian thinkers used the neo-Platonic theme of emanation (the doctrine

3. Bainton, *Christianity*, 118.

that the Mind or "Nous" and the Soul or "Psyche" derive from the One) to explain the Christian teaching of *exitus et reditus* (that God is the beginning and final end of human life). Augustine would also realize much later, as a Christian, that evil is not merely an absence of the good, as the Neo-Platonists taught, but a rebellion against God. Augustine turned to the New Testament upon the urging of his mother.

Augustine went to Rome in 383 CE and accepted a teaching position in Milan in 384 CE. Milan at the time was an important cultural and intellectual center in all of the Roman Empire. The see of Milan was overseen by an influential bishop, St. Ambrose of Milan (339–97 CE). Ambrose was a scholar, a powerful orator, and preacher. His preaching made great impressions on Augustine who became a catechumen. After eight months of studying and reflecting in solitude at Cassiciacum, near Milan, Augustine was baptized in 387 CE on Easter eve. Augustine tells us in *The Confessions* that apart from the preaching of Ambrose, two other factors were responsible for his about face: his mother Monica who prayed for thirty years for his conversion and his reading of *The Life of St. Anthony of Egypt* by St. Athanasius. Augustine was impressed by the way the holy monks were able to control their passions. When he became a Christian and accepted baptism Augustine was baptized alongside his son, Adeodatus, and his friend Alypus.

Augustine returned to Africa immediately after his baptism and was hit by tragedy soon after. His mother died on the way to Africa, in Ostia in 387 CE. His son Adeodatus also died in 390 CE upon arrival. Augustine never again left the African soil. His reputation as a Christian grew and he was consulted by many on various topics and subjects. At this time "the power of Rome was then rapidly declining and Christianity was still a minority religion, with many of the wealthiest citizens and officials still attached to the old religions or to a degenerate Neo-Platonic philosophy with its hedonistic culture."[4] Severed from all family ties, Augustine established a semi-monastic community in Thagaste to help him and other Christians live ascetic life. He studied for the priesthood and was ordained in 391 CE. When Valerius, the bishop of Hippo, died in 396 CE Augustine was appointed to succeed him. He became the bishop of Hippo at the age of forty-two and held the position for thirty-four years.

The Donatist Controversy

As bishop, Augustine was beset by many problems. One of these was the Donatist controversy. Diocletian persecution forcefully removed Christians

4. Sanneh, *West African Christianity*, 12.

from their places of worship. Christians were also made to renounce their faith and hand over sacred Scripture and holy church artifacts to the Roman authorities. Those who refused to comply suffered martyrdom while those who did were spared. In the eyes of the church those who recanted were apostates, guilty of sin of apostasy (denial of faith). Those who surrendered church property for destruction were called the *dies traditores*. Their crime was considered by some Christians to be more heinous than those of the apostates because they handed church property to the Romans.

As persecutions wane, questions arose regarding what the church should do with the traditores. Some Christians in North Africa came up with the idea that neither the traditores nor anyone associated with them can get to heaven. They also adopted a policy to exclude the traditores and everyone associated with them from the church. These Christians who wanted the traditores excluded from the church adopted a strict and austere lifestyle. It became a standard insult to associate a Christian or Catholic bishop with traditores.[5] Even when martyrdom ceased and Christianity became a legal and accepted religion in the Roman Empire, these people who wanted the traditores excluded from the church still continued their austere lifestyle and sought other forms of martyrdom, such as mortification (denial of self from pleasure).

In 321 CE a Christian man named Caecilian was consecrated bishop of Carthage. One of those who consecrated him bishop, Felix of Aptuca, had been a traditores. The bishops from all areas of Numidia protested and refused to recognize the consecration of Caecilian as valid. They chose instead Donatus. When Donatus was appointed bishop of Carthage he identified Carthage as the "church of the martyrs" and soon after Carthage became the center of activity of those Christians who wanted a strict and austere church. "Donatus gave his name to the church community that was galvanized by his presence, and then by his memory for more than a century."[6] This singular act distinguished the Donatist from orthodox Christianity.

There were also socio-economic differences between the Donatists and the rest of the church. Many of the Donatists were pagan converts and a whole lot came from the Berber people of North Africa who were usually poor and rural. Donatism became for these Berbers a vehicle of Berber patriotism and socio-economic protest "against a Church increasingly closely identified with the landowning classes and imperial authority."[7] But this is not to suggest that Donatism was limited only to the rural areas or

---

5. See Bright, "Church, North African," 185.

6. Bright, "Church, North African," 185.

7. Isichei, *History of Christianity in Africa*, 37.

that Donatism was just an African phenomenon. Donatism was as much an urban phenomenon as it was rural. The phenomenon extended from North Africa to Spain and Gaul (France). In the main, what distinguished the Donatists was their ideology—their concept of the church as a small body of the chosen.[8] They wanted the church to remain holy and demanded the highest moral standard. As far as they were concerned, the validity of the sacraments depended on the worthiness of the priest or minister. The Donatists thought they were the true church and demanded a rebaptism of lapsed Christians and clergy. The Donatists also had their own peculiar way of interpreting the Scripture. Given their African root, "they cherished texts that could be construed to mean God's special predilection for Africa, such as a version of the Song of Solomon 1:6 ('my beloved is from the South')."[9]

Augustine defended the Catholic Church against what he saw as the Donatists' attack. To Augustine who was more interested in the unity of the church, it was bizarre to suggest, as the Donatists did, that God's church was primarily located in Africa.[10] Augustine compared the Donatists to "frogs in a pond, who thought that they were the universal church."[11] Augustine also stressed that church contains both good and bad because the church is at one and the same time holy and sinful. He also argued that the validity of the sacraments does not depend on the worthiness of the minister (*ex opere operantis*), as the Donatists suggested, but on the fact that the sacraments have their own validity (*ex opere operato*) on the correct celebration by the church.[12]

The Pelagian Controversy

After the Donatist controversy Augustine was embroiled in another huge argument—the Pelagian controversy. A British monk by the name Pelagius propounded a teaching that denied original sin. The human person, according to Pelagius, is born without the stain of sin. Adam's sin, therefore, was a personal sin and does not extend to his offsprings. A person, according to Pelagius, can also attain salvation unaided by God's grace. A person can choose good over evil without divine help. Augustine denounced the Pelagian teaching and reiterated the church's teaching that everyone inherits the guilt of original sin (see Romans 5:12), meaning that everyone is deserving

8. Isichei, *History of Christianity in Africa*, 38.

9. Isichei, *History of Christianity in Africa*, 38.

10. Isichei, *History of Christianity in Africa*, 38.

11. Isichei, *History of Christianity in Africa*, 38.

12. Holmes and Bickers, *Short History*, 41.

of hell. But baptism cleanses original sin. Augustine also taught that human nature is seriously flawed because it has been corrupted by original sin. Because of our fallen nature the human person needs God's grace to attain salvation. Even though the human person is free, God predestines us to salvation. Grace is irresistible for those whom God has predestined. This teaching, sometimes called Predestination, will be at the center of controversy much later in the sixteenth-century church. Towards the end of Augustine's life, a moderate teaching of Pelagian teaching (known as Semi-Pelagianism) resurfaced again. It was propagated by those who misunderstood the role of human cooperation in the process of human salvation.[13] Augustine responded "that even the initial desire to change one's life or to accept the Christian faith was the work of God's transforming power of love and grace."[14]

Augustine's Writings

Augustine was a true pastor and theologian who had genuine concern for the salvation of his flock.[15] He composed a vast body of literature, totally over twelve hundred, on a variety of subjects, as a response to the many theological questions and sociopolitical problems facing the church.[16] Augustine started writing *The Confessions* shortly after becoming a Christian. *The Confessions* is not an autobiography but Augustine's own illustration of a human person's capacity for corruption, imperfection, and redemption.[17] It is divided into thirteen books. Each book is in turn divided into chapters. Augustine's other well-known works are *The City of God* and the *Enchiridion* (handbook on the grace of God).

Conclusion

Augustine spent his whole life trying to answer the questions: Who am I? How does one find true happiness? What is salvation? And what is the role of one's neighbor or community in the search for true happiness and salvation?[18] Augustine gathered together strands from Christian thought, as

13. McGonigle and Quigley, *History of Christian Tradition*, 114.

14. McGonigle and Quigley, *History of Christian Tradition*, 114.

15. McGonigle and Quigley, *History of Christian Tradition*, 112.

16. McGonigle and Quigley, *History of Christian Tradition*, 112.

17. Bainton, *Christianity*, 116.

18. McGonigle and Quigley, *History of Christian Tradition*, 111.

well as strands from classical philosophy, and creatively wove them into a new fabric that would profoundly influence Christian thought until it would be surpassed in the Middle Ages by the genius of Thomas Aquinas.[19]

Augustine was a controversialist. Many of his works were written in the heat of debate with his opponents. Because of this his writings are sometimes difficult to follow as he moves from one subject to another. "In the midst of controversy an author often overstates his case and emphasizes certain factors that would be more carefully balanced in a less intense situation."[20] Augustine has also been criticized for some of his theological views. Some have wondered how much of his theological views (e.g., transmission of original sin and his views on marriage) were influenced by Manichean piety. When he was preparing for baptism in Cassisiacum as a catechumen Augustine wrote some works like "Dialogues," "Contra Academicos," "Providential Order of the World and the Problem of Evil," and "God and the Soul." Some have questioned whether he wrote these works as a Christian or as a non-Christian. The importance of Augustine, however, cannot be diminished, His life "coincides with the end of classical era and the beginning of the Middle Ages. He was a man who looked back to the past as well as one who predicted the future, and his life would become a paradigm for subsequent Christian understanding of the individual's journey to salvation."[21]

THE MIDDLE AGES AND CHRISTIANITY

Some Christian theologians see the historical study of the Middle Ages as a gift to our century.[22] It was in the Middle Ages that some discovered that the study of theology was useful for the understanding of God, the human person, and the world at large. Christian faith flourished in the Middle Ages, particularly the thirteenth century that has been considered the golden age of Church intellectual history. What might be called Catholic conservatives or traditionalists in the likes of Hilaire Belloc (1870–1953) and G. K. Chesterton (1874–1936) look to the thirteenth century as the "greatest of centuries" and point to it as the high point from which all later history has been mostly a dismal decline.[23] But some more contemporary theologians, like the Swiss Hans Urs von Balthasar (1905–88), thought the decline of

19. Bainton, *Christianity*, 115.

20. McGonigle and Quigley, *History of Christian Tradition*, 113.

21. McGonigle and Quigley, *History of Christian Tradition*, 111.

22. O'Meara, *Thomas Aquinas Theologian*, xii.

23. Oakes, *Pattern of Redemption*, 160–64.

modern theology began in the thirteenth century because of scholasticism, a system of philosophy we shall explain later.

What is it that makes the Middle Ages significant and contentious at the same time? Three important developments took place in the thirteenth century. First, there was the founding and flourishing of universities and centers of learning—Bologna, Paris, and Oxford. These centers became places where the study of theology and rigorous intellectual activities took place. Second, there was the establishment of mendicant orders—Dominic de Guzmán (1170–1221) and Francis of Assisi (d. 1226), for example. The mendicant orders brought to a church in need of reform a new spirit of evangelical poverty that appealed to the laity that was sick and tired of corruption and abuses by clergy. Dominic founded the Order of Friars Preachers (Dominicans) in 1216, stressing apostolic preaching and assiduous study. Francis founded the Franciscans in 1210, stressing evangelical poverty and the imitation of Christ. Both Dominic and Francis are now canonized saints. The third great development of the thirteenth century was the discovery in the Latin West translations of Aristotle's works, a discovery made possible by Jewish and Arabic philosophers, such as Moses Maimonides (1138–1204), Ib'n Cina or Avicenna (980–1037), Avicebron (1021–58), and Averroes (1126–98). The discovery of Aristotle supplanted the influence of Plato's philosophy hitherto employed by neo-Platonic Christians

When the Latin West first discovered Aristotle it was not without skepticism and suspicion, mainly because the works in question were mediated by Arabs and Jewish scholars who translated and commented on them. These two groups were at the time considered archenemies of Christians. There was also the problematic of Aristotle's own teaching on the eternity of the universe. Aristotle taught that the universe was eternal and uncreated. This teaching and his other thoughts on the immortality of the soul seemed to contradict Christian teaching of creation of the universe. These difficulties led to three major reactions or responses to Aristotle. One group, known as the Augustinian group, refused to accept anything that contradicted the teachings of St. Augustine. They were led by the Franciscans, particularly Bonaventure (1221–74). Bonaventure himself "was skeptical of the ability of the human mind, unaided by God, to reach the truth. He maintained that any philosophical propositions which were contrary to faith must be dismissed, and he reminded people that, in his opinion, philosophy was very much at the service of theology."[24] The second group, the Averroists, championed by Siger of Brabant (1240–ca. 1281), accepted Aristotle's teachings, but tried to find a middle ground whenever Aristotle contradicted

24. Holmes and Bickers, *Short History*, 94.

Christian teaching. "When Aristotle contradicted Christian teaching the Averroists tried to overcome the difficulty by what was called the 'theory of double truth.' According to this, as philosophers they accepted the teaching of Aristotle and as Christians the teaching of the church. In other words, they claimed that the conclusions of theology and philosophy could contradict each other while both remained valid."[25] The third and final group attempted a synthesis or harmony of Aristotelianism with Christian teaching. They tried to show that Augustine and Aristotle were not in any way opposed to each other, that what was needed was a correct interpretation of Aristotle. To this group belonged Thomas Aquinas, a key figure we shall examine later.

The Middle Ages was also the age of Dante Alighieri (1265–1321) and Albert the Great (1193–1280), among many others. It was, among other things, the age of the Schoolmen, affectionately called scholastics. The Schoolmen were idealized by Pope Leo XIII as the "Doctors of the Middle Ages" who set out to do a work of very great magnitude by diligently gathering for their use and convenience of those who came after them the "rich and fruitful crops of doctrine scattered everywhere in the mighty volumes of the Holy Fathers."[26] The schoolmen or scholastics were "teachers" of the "new period' after the barbarian invasions of Rome. The ideal they embodied found expressions in the works of two great saints of the period: the Dominican Thomas Aquinas and the Franciscan Bonaventure. Both men saw ancient wisdom in the teaching of the Church Fathers and found ways to make them relevant to their time by employing Aristotelian and Platonic philosophies. Leo XIII spoke lovingly of "the angelic St. Thomas, and the seraphic St. Bonaventure" as "two glorious Doctors" who brilliantly unfolded the scholastic method.

The Catholic Church relies greatly on their method, particularly St. Thomas, for correct interpretation and understanding of Scripture, for reading and expounding the fathers with clarity, and for answering different errors and heresies. Although Aquinas to this day "still fashions ways in which Roman Catholics think,"[27] not everyone agrees with St. Thomas and his ways of thinking. It was precisely his style of thinking and the undue influence of scholasticism on Christian theology that Protestant theology opposed during the Reformation. Thomas and scholasticism were, for some of the reformers, the epitome of the stagnancy of the medieval church. Protestant theology viewed "Thomas and his times as just what they were trying

---

25. Holmes and Bickers, *Short History*, 94.

26. Leo XIII, "*Aeterni Patris*," xiv.

27. O'Meara, *Thomas Aquinas Theologian*, xiv.

to escape" and the Middle Ages as "a great backwater into which the river of history poured for centuries before finally, in the sixteenth century, making a new start."[28]

THOMAS AQUINAS (1224/5–74)

Thomas was born to a noble family in Roccasecca, near Aquino, north of Naples, in Southern Italy. His father, Landulph, was the Count of Aquino, and his mother, Theodora, the Countess of Teano.[29] The exact date of his birth is still disputed. Catholic hagiographers approximate the date of his birth on the basis of the date of his death. The consensus is that he died in 1274, on his way to the Council of Lyons, although some still contend that he died in 1276 or 1277. What is more probable in all these conjectures is that Thomas "had completed forty-nine years and begun his fiftieth year" before he died. On the basis of this calculation, 1224/25 has been suggested as the probable year of his birth. His father had at least nine children (four boys and five girls). As the youngest of the sons, Thomas was destined, according to the custom of the time, for an ecclesiastical position. His father offered him as an oblate to the Benedictine monastery of Monte Cassino, hoping that someday he would become an abbot.

At age five Thomas was enrolled in the school run by the Benedictine monks of Monte Cassino where he had his elementary education and was exposed to the Benedictine religious life of prayer, scriptural reading, and manual labor. Even at this tender age he was said to have shown signs of a future scholar. One of the monks of Monte Cassino who noticed his talent and passion for learning advised Landulph (Thomas' father) to send him to Naples to study at the prestigious University of Naples. The University of Naples was founded by the emperor of the Holy Roman Empire, Frederick II, for the education of his court functionaries. At the time Naples was the only university to be teaching Aristotelian logic that was then beginning to infiltrate the borders of Christendom by way of Islamic scholars in Spain.[30] Thomas proceeded to this university in 1236, at the age of fourteen, and received training in the liberal arts.

At Naples Thomas was fascinated by the lifestyle of a new religious Order of Preachers that was founded a decade earlier. This newly formed mendicant Order that went by the name Dominicans was quite popular in the city because of their commitment to the evangelical vows of chastity,

---

28. McDermott, preface to *Summa Theologiae: A Concise Translation*, xvii.

29. Torrell, *St. Thomas Aquinas*, 1:1–9.

30. McDermott, preface to *Summa Theologiae: A Concise Translation*, xviii–xix.

poverty, and obedience and also because of their dedication to the preaching apostolate. They based their life on the Gospel mandate (Luke 9: 1–6) to go out and preach, two by two, taking nothing for the journey. "If Aristotle represented a new current in secular thinking, the friars were the most radical representatives of the new spirit of reform within the church." Their life of preaching and austere poverty made a great impression on the young Thomas who decided to join their ranks.

In 1244, against the wish of his family, Thomas made the official move to join the Dominicans. The Dominicans at this time were beginning to devote their attention to preaching in the universities and committed to exploring the newly translated works of Aristotle that were seen by some to be a threat to the Catholic faith. Theodora, his mother, was particularly distressed by her son's decision to join this brand of preachers. Thomas joining the Order of Preachers would jeopardize her grand plan for him to become the abbot of the Benedictine monastery of Monte Cassino and so she did all she could to stop him. At her instigation Thomas was kidnapped by two of his brothers who kept him in solitary confinement for two years, hoping to dissuade him from joining the Friars. But rather than be discouraged, Thomas' time in captivity reinforced his decision to fully commit himself to the order whose preaching apostolate he had come to love so much.

After Thomas was released by his family in the summer of 1245, the Dominicans in Naples, fearing another kidnap plan, thought it unsafe to keep him around. They sent him to Rome from where he would proceed to Paris to begin studies at the University of Paris, under the famous German Dominican friar, Albert the Great. Albert, at this time, was just beginning his encyclopedic commentaries on Aristotle. Three years after this turn of events, Albert was sent to Cologne on a mission to begin a Dominican study house. Thomas went with him to Cologne and taught as a Bachelor under Albert the Great.[31] For some reason his peers there nicknamed him the "dumb ox." Albert was so impressed with the talent of Thomas that he remarked that one day this "dumb ox" would make a great impression on the world.

Under the tutelage of Albert, Thomas was excited when he discovered the works of Aristotle whom he called "the Philosopher." Thomas' friend and confrere, William of Moerbeke, helped him translate the works of Aristotle from Greek into Latin. While many at that time saw Aristotle's work as "pagan" and incompatible with the Christian message, Thomas saw in the works of this great philosopher a gold mine and found ways to harmonize

---

31. Bachelors are like today's teaching assistants. They assisted the Masters or Scholastics who taught in the universities.

them with Christian doctrine. It was not only the work of Aristotle that Thomas examined, he also studied the works of some prominent Greek, Latin, and Arab philosophers of the time (chief among whom were Averroes and Avicenna) and acknowledged coming to know more about Aristotle through them.

Thomas was sent to Paris in 1252, at the recommendation of Albert the Great, to fill a vacant position of Bachelor at the Dominican center for studies. This event proved to be the turning point of Thomas' illustrious career. While in Paris, he lectured and commented on *The Sentences* of Peter Lombard (1100–1160), the most referenced theology textbook of the time. Upon completion of his formal studies he received his master's degree and at the age of thirty-two occupied the chair of theology Albert once held. After three years in Paris as professor of sacred theology he was sent to Italy where he spent six years at the papal court in Orvieto. He also spent another two years at the Dominican study center in Rome and one year at another papal court in Viterbo before returning to Paris 1269. After three years in Paris he finally returned to Naples in late 1273. Thomas had a mystical experience in Naples on December 6, 1273, an experience that made him abandon all teaching and writing. The force of his mystical experience was so great that Thomas had to declare that all he wrote was "mere straw" compared to the divine revelation that was revealed to him. He died shortly after this revelation.

Authority of Thomas Aquinas

Thomas Aquinas was the most influential Christian philosopher of the Middle Ages. He ranks as one of the most outstanding Christian thinkers in the history of Western civilization. His work was seminal in the formulation of Catholic teaching and doctrine. His authority is so revered in Catholic circles that the Code of Canon Law legislates that the clergy receive their philosophical and theological formation according to the methods, doctrine, and principles of the Angelic Doctor. Pope Leo XIII glowingly paid tribute to the authority of Thomas in his 1879 encyclical *Aeterni Patris*, in which he called for the revival of Thomism. As the pope recalled it, "in the midst of the Council of Trent, the assembled Fathers so willing it, the Summa of Thomas Aquinas lay open on the altar, with the Holy Scriptures and the decrees of the Supreme Pontiffs, that from it might be sought counsel and reasons and answers."[32]

---

32. Leo XIII, "*Aeterni Patris*," xvi.

Thomas was canonized on July 18, 1323, by Pope John XXII who extolled Thomas' devotion to study and prayer and pronounced him a model of fidelity to the Roman Church. His canonization paved way for other titles his disciples and admirers had adjudged for him. Even as far back as 1317, he was already called *doctor communis* by the faithful at the University of Paris. The title *doctor Angelicus* was attributed to him in the second half of the fifteenth century, and a hundred years later, on April 15, 1567, Pope Pius V, a Dominican pope, proclaimed him *doctor ecclesiae* (Teacher of the Church). On August 4, 1880, Pope Leo XIII declared him patron of all Catholic schools and institutions.

Although the title *doctor ecclesiae* was not exclusively applied to St. Thomas, it was still a significant achievement when he received this encomium, especially when one considers the fact that there were only four Doctors of the Church when he was given the title (St. Ambrose, St. Jerome, St. Augustine, and St. Gregory the Great). *Doctor ecclesiae* is a special title the Church reserves for distinguished saints whose writings and teachings have been adjudged useful in the formulation of Christian doctrine. In addition, the universal church is invited to honor them and celebrate their feasts in the Church's liturgy. When Pius V accorded the honor to St. Thomas, he also announced four other great Doctors of the Eastern Church: St. Athanasius (ca. 293–373), St. Basil the Great (ca. 329–79), St. Gregory of Nazianzus (ca. 325–89), and St. John Chrysostom (ca. 347–407).

The Works of Thomas Aquinas

Thomas wrote for various occasions and lectured on different subjects. Some of these have been collected and edited by his disciples. There is, for example, edited commentary on *The Sentences* of his Parisian days. There are also collections of his lectures on Matthew's Gospel, Isaiah's Prophecies, the books of Job and Jeremiah, and the epistles of Paul. Some of his debates on theological questions of his own choosing have also been collected in the *Quaestiones Disputatae de Veritate*, his Rome public debates in *de Potentia*, *de Malo*, and *de Spiritualibus Creaturis* and questions thrown at him by his audience have been collected in *Quaestiones Quodilibetales*.[33]

Thomas began writing a comprehensive theology manual in 1266 and left it unfinished before his death. Some of his writings give us his insight into some contemporary controversies. He wrote volumes on the theology of angels. No wonder he was called "Doctor Angelicus." He also has commentaries on well-known traditional texts, which speaks to why

33. McDermott, preface to *Summa Theologiae: A Concise Translation*, xx.

he was called "Doctor Communis," i.e., common teacher of all Christians. His four major works in theology are: *A Commentary on the Sentences of Peter Lombard* (1256), *A Compendium Theologiae* (an incomplete work that has not been satisfactorily dated), the *Summa Theologiae*, and the *Summa Contra Gentiles* (1264). Of the four, the last two are well-known and widely used. The *Summa Theologiae* (Summary of Theology) is regarded as the most comprehensive treatment of the relation of philosophy and theology. Thomas was dissatisfied with the then-existing manual of instruction and intended this work to be a systematic introduction to theology for Dominican novices. The *Summa Contra Gentiles* (Summary against the Gentiles) was also designed to be an apologetic work. Thomas again intended it as an aid to his brother (Dominican) missionaries in their efforts to convert Muslims in Spain and North Africa. He probably composed the *Summa Contra Gentiles* at the request of his religious superior, Raymond of Penafort, who would have asked Thomas to equip the Dominican missionaries working in the Muslim world, particularly Spain, with the necessary intellectual tools. But the *Contra Gentiles* today is more than a missionary manual.

In these works Thomas shows inclination towards apophatic theology, that there is nothing to know about God except to know that which God is not. Apophatic theology attempts to distinguish God from all that is not God, moving from negation to negation to arrive at the knowledge that God is distinct from everything. In addition to apophatic theology, Thomas also shows in these works how Christian theology is the sum and summit of all sciences. He establishes revelation as a source of knowledge because (i) it aids us in comprehending truths already known by reason and (ii) it is the absolute source of knowledge of Christian mysteries. Consistent with his apophatic approach, Aquinas built his system around two sources of knowledge: revelation and human reason. Revelation is not scripture alone but scripture and tradition. Reason is not just individual human reason, but collective reason, the foundation of natural truth (philosophy), as in the philosophies of Aristotle and Plato. For Aquinas, reason alone is not a sufficient guide for human actions. Reason has to be aided by revelation, for faith and reason are not opposed to each other.

The Plan of the *Summa*

The *Summa Theologiae* is today the most widely used work of Aquinas and without doubt the central source for a discussion of his theology and the climax of his life work and synthetic masterpiece.[34] But it was not widely

34. O'Meara, *Thomas Aquinas Theologian*, xv.

received in Aquinas' lifetime. His ideas so frightened authorities during and immediately after his lifetime that his work faced ecclesiastical censorship. He was even denounced as a heretic because of the Aristotelian influences in his work. Aristotelian philosophy was then considered a "pagan" philosophy. In 1276, for instance, Albert the Great, Thomas' mentor, reported knowing certain bishops who lumped together all who used Aristotle in theology, calling them "Averroists," which means that they were more Muslim than Christian. Thomas was among those branded "Averroists." The Bishop of Paris, at the decree of Pope John XXI, ordered an investigation of theologians who employed Aristotelianism. On March 7, 1277, the third anniversary of the death of Aquinas, as many as two hundred propositions, some of which were found in the work of Aquinas, were condemned and those who taught them excommunicated. It was only through the insistence of his Order and Dominican confreres who vigorously defended him and promoted his course that the ecclesiastical censorship against his work was lifted and it was gradually brought back into the mainstream of Catholic theology.

Between 1286 and 1405, after Aquinas' work had been rehabilitated, although *The Sentences* of Peter Lombard and Sacred Scripture were the normal text of the universities, the leadership of the Dominican Order insisted that Aquinas' writings be part of their school curriculum. With much insistence and maneuvering the *Summa* in time became the accepted textbook of Catholic theology, supplanting even *The Sentences* of Peter Lombard as a symbol of Catholic orthodoxy. Many find the originality and style of the summa appealing. "The greatness and originality of a philosophical or theological work," remarked M. D. Chenu of the *Summa*, "are not measured primarily by the amplitude of its conclusions, but by the order of its construction in the light of principles which determine logically and spiritually the conception and the arrangement of its parts."[35]

St. Thomas' unique style sometimes makes him difficult to read, especially for beginners not familiar with the scholastic method. If great minds are difficult because they write in a kind of code, the "code" in which Aquinas wrote his *Summa* is decipherable in the context of medieval debate, an expression of the thought-form of his culture. Here is a description of the format of medieval debate:

---

35. Chenu and Bremner, "Plan of St. Thomas' Summa Theologiae," 67.

At the beginning of the disputation the master would announce the "Article" or subject to be debated, which was itself a subdivision of a broader "Question" being discussed. This was followed by a number of objections which were put forward by the audience, to which preliminary responses were made by "bachelors" (in present-day terms, teaching assistants) who were working with the master (professor), possibly also referring to authorities who held views contrary to the objections. The next day the master would give his response ("I answer that") to the basic issue or issues posed and would follow this with formal replies to each of the initial objections. The disputation was sometimes taken down by a secretary and later edited by the master for publication. The oral disputation thus gave rise to the formal structure used by the scholastics to analyze philosophical and theological problems—a statement of an issue, alternative opinions or objections, contrary quotations from recognized authorities, the author's response to the problem, followed by answers to each of the initial objections.[36]

Following this conventional method of debate, a medieval text, when printed, is divided into hundreds of topics called questions. Each topic consists of a sequence of dilemmas called articles. In a dilemma are three short arguments, i.e., objections, against some traditional position called the *sed contra*. They are resolved by an argued point of view called *responsio* which are applied to each objection in answers to the objections.

The *Summa Theologiae* is patterned after this medieval method of debate. The *Summa* is composed of series of questions or discussion topics, each question further divided into articles. Since the intent is to dialogue with an imaginary dialogue partner, Aquinas always gives an alternative view after stating the question. He will give a *Sed Contra* (on the Contrary), which would contradict the alternative view he has stated, and often close to Aquinas' own view. Then at the end, he gives a *Responsio* (response of formal replies), where he offers explanation for rejecting the alternative views and even discusses why reasons given for the rejection of the alternative views may not be adequate.

Traditionally the *Summa Theologiae* is divided into three parts.

(I.) The First Part: The first part is called the *Prima Pars* (**Ia** pars). Here Aquinas takes up the Neo-Platonic theme of emanation and shows how God is the First Principle of human life. He also discusses the basis of theology and issues like Sacred Doctrine, God, Trinity, Providence, Predestination, creation, angels, and human beings.

(II.) The Second Part: Theology for Aquinas and the scholastics is the science of God. Here Aquinas discusses all things in their relation to God, *exitus reditus*, i.e., either God as their origin or final end, which

---

36. See Sigmund, *Aquinas on Politics and Ethics*, xvii.

was Aquinas' intelligible way of explaining everything and human action in light of God. Due to the wide range of topics treated here, the second part of the Summa is divided into two parts. The first part is called *Prima Secundae* (**Ia IIae** pars), i.e., First part of the Second part. It deals with the goal of human existence, human acts, passions, character development, virtues, vices, sin, law, and divine grace. The second part is called *Secunda Secundae* (**IIa IIae** pars), i.e., second part of the Second part. It deals with the theological virtues, the cardinal virtues, and the vices opposed to these virtues.

(III.) The Third Part: The third part is called the *Tertia Pars* (**IIIa** pars) and is also divided into two parts, though not by design. Aquinas died before he could complete the *tertia pars* and so his disciples added this sequel, known under the name of Supplement. The first part of the tertia pars contains some of the original thought of Aquinas. Since the *exitus et reditus* (the going forth from and the return to God), according to Aquinas, is accomplished in Christ, here Aquinas discusses the Life of Christ, Sacraments (Baptism and Eucharist), and the Christian conditions for that return. The second part of the tertia pars is called *Supplementum Tertia Pars*. It deals with Penance, Extreme Unction (now called Anointing of the Sick), Holy Orders, Matrimony, Resurrection, and Appendices.

Content of the *Summa*

In spite of its abrupt ending, i.e., because of the mystical experience and untimely death of the angelic doctor, it was the intention of St. Thomas to divide the *Summa* into three parts. He begins the *Summa* with this prologue, which gives the intent and context of his work:

> Because the Master of Catholic Truth ought not only to teach the proficient, but also to instruct beginners, we purpose this book to treat of whatever belongs to the Christian Religion, in such a way as may tend to the instruction of beginners. We have considered that students in this Science have not seldom been hampered by what they have found written by other authors, partly on account of the multiplication of useless questions, articles, and arguments; partly also because those things that are needed for them to know are not taught according to the order of the subject matter, but according to the plan of the book

might require, or the occasion of the argument offer; partly too, because frequent repetition brought weariness and confusion to the minds of the readers. Endeavoring to avoid these and other like faults, we shall try, by God's help, to set forth whatever is included in this sacred science as briefly and clearly as the matter itself may allow.[37]

Thomas begins by speaking about God in the Prima Pars, the movement of rational creature toward God in the Secunda Pars, and finally in the Tertia Pars about Christ who, according to his humanity, is for us the way that leads towards God.[38]

1. Prima Pars: Q.1 treats the nature and extent of sacred Doctrine. QQ.2–26 treat those things that belong to the divine essence and QQ.27–43 those that belong to the distinction of persons. Since God is the beginning and the end of all things, QQ.44–46 treats creation in general, QQ.48–49 the distinction and cause of evil, QQ.50–64 regarding angels, QQ.65–74 regarding the six-day creation story, QQ.75–102 treats the human person as a creature made in the image of God, and QQ.103–19 treats the way God governs creation through the mediation of secondary causes.[39]

2. Secunda Pars: The second part has two subdivisions. Aquinas devotes these to the orientation or movement or return of rational creatures to God who is the goal or end of human life. He begins the prologue of the treatise on the last end with the statement: "Now that we have treated of the exemplar, i.e., God, and of those things which came forth from the power of God in accordance with His will; it remains for us to treat of His image, i.e., man, inasmuch as he too is the principle of his actions, as having free-will and control of his actions."[40] QQ.1–5 treats this end of human life as consisting in beatitude. QQ.6–48 begin Aquinas' treatment of means of arriving at this end, beginning with voluntary and free acts of the will and the passions of the soul. QQ.48–49 deal with virtues and vices, QQ.90–108 with law as exterior principles influencing human activity, and QQ.109–14 concludes the Prima Secundae with Aquinas' treatment of grace.[41]

37. ST I, Prologue.
38. Torrell, Saint Thomas Aquinas, 1:148.
39. Torrell, Saint Thomas Aquinas, 1:149.
40. ST I-II, Prologue.
41. Torrell, Saint Thomas Aquinas, 1:149.

Secunda Secundae continues Aquinas' theme of the return of rational creature to God. QQ.1–46 probes how this return can be achieved by dedication to the theological virtues of faith, hope, and charity. QQ.47–170 analyzes the cardinal virtues of prudence, justice, temperance, and fortitude, specifying both their proper acts and contrary sins. QQ.171–89 concludes the Secunda Secundae with a treatment of charism and ecclesial diversity that ends with the contemplative life.[42]

3. Tertia Pars: Aquinas begins his treatment of Jesus Christ as the savior who brings salvation to human race. In the prologue he states: "It is necessary in order to complete the work of theology that after considering the last end of human life, and the virtues and vices, there should follow the consideration of the savior of all, and of the benefits bestowed by Him on the human race."[43] QQ.1–26 treats the mystery of the incarnation and QQ.27–59 examines the mystery of the suffering of Christ and the salvation he brings to the human family. The second section of the Tertia Pars, beginning with QQ.60–90, examines the sacraments of the church as means of arriving at this salvation. The third part, which Thomas was not able to write, was to "consist of a detailed reflection on the end to which we are called, eternal life, into which we enter by being raised through Christ."[44]

REVIVAL OF THOMISM

Although the philosophy of St. Thomas was not properly received in the fourteenth and fifteenth centuries, the significance of the *Summa Theologiae* as a symbol of Catholic orthodoxy has not been disputed since his philosophy (Thomism) became the official Catholic philosophy. At the Council of Trent, the *Summa*, in a symbolic gesture, was laid on the altar alongside the Scriptures and decrees of the popes. While for Catholics that may have been a symbol of Catholic orthodoxy, for Protestants it was a metaphor for adulteration of the pure word of God. The limitations of Thomism were of course the reasons for its decline and rejection, not only among Protestants but in Catholic circles as well. For example, "one can notice in lines of

42. Torrell, *Saint Thomas Aquinas*, 1:149–50.

43. *ST* III, Prologue.

44. Torrell, *Saint Thomas Aquinas*, 1:150.

Aquinas some naïve exegesis, some limits of past science, and a sparse view of history. Some moderns have been distracted by the un-modern pattern of centering all on God or by the teleological dynamic."[45] Another reason for the collapse of Thomism stemmed from its identification as perennial philosophy. "This encomium, hastily imposed by anxious theologians and church authorities, presumed that time and culture had little impact on human consciousness, and implied that one philosophical theology could serve all people. By claiming too much it rendered Thomism bland and arrogant."[46]

Learned Catholics have on several occasions attempted a revival of Thomism as a good representation of official Catholic teaching. The most recent and authoritative attempt was Leo XIII's 1879 encyclical, Aeterni Patris, which called for the revival of scholasticism and gave official support for the study of Thomism as the best means of realizing scholastic thought. Leo extolled the virtues of St. Thomas:

> There is no part of philosophy which he did not handle with acuteness and solidity. He wrote about the laws of reasoning; about God and incorporeal substances; about man and other things of sense; and about human acts and their principles. What is more, he wrote on these subjects in such a way that in him not one of the following perfections is wanting: a full selection of subjects; the best method of treating them; certainty of principles; strength of argument; perspicuity and propriety in language; and the power of explaining deep mysteries.[47]

Leo concluded with the exhortation that Thomism be considered a perennial philosophy and itemized four reasons why modern youths should engage in the study of the Angelic Doctor. First, young men and women are faced with a world besieged by "the wiles and craft of a certain deceitful kind of wisdom." Therefore those growing up "ought to be fed with healthful and strong food of doctrine."[48] Second, there are those who, "with minds alienated from the Faith," hold that reason alone is their teacher and guide. "To heal these men of their unbelief and to bring them to grace and the Catholic Faith, We think that nothing, after the supernatural help of God, can be more useful in these days than the solid doctrine of the Fathers and the Scholastics." Third, family life and civil society are greatly threatened by "pestilence of perverse opinions." A doctrine more in unison with the

---

45. O'Meara, *Thomas Aquinas Theologian*, xiv.

46. O'Meara, *Thomas Aquinas Theologian*, 156.

47. Leo XIII, *Aeterni Patris*, xv.

48. Leo XIII, *Aeterni Patris*, xvii.

perpetual teaching office (Magisterium) of the church, as found in the works of Thomas Aquinas, would be more suitable for the universities and schools. Lastly, the pope reasoned that it is a proven fact that the liberal arts have been most flourishing when the honor of philosophy has stood inviolate and neglected and almost obliterated when declining philosophy has been enveloped in errors and absurdities. Hence the pope called for the restoration of philosophy according to the ancient wisdom of "Thomas, and Blessed Albert the Great, and other princes of the Scholastics [who] did not so give themselves up to the study of philosophy, as to have little care for the knowledge of natural things," as part of the process of rehabilitating and restoring the dignity of the liberal arts.

CRITIQUE OF THOMAS AQUINAS

In spite of his creative genius, the work of St. Thomas contains "some naïve exegesis, some limits of past science, and a sparse view of history."[49] The contemporary person who takes seriously the issues of race, gender, and class will find some of Aquinas' work a little troubling. Liberation theologians are quick to remind us that the problem of human suffering is inextricably tied to race, class, and gender, issues that St. Thomas did not give considerable attention. Thomas accepted the world order of his time, which makes his views on women and slaves completely unacceptable to the modern person.

On the issue of women, Thomas followed Aristotle who described the female as a male manqué, meaning that females are conceived from a "weak seed." Thomas used this to support his argument on "the natural inequality and subordination of women to men, who are by nature more reasonable and discerning." In the *Summa Theologiae* Thomas reiterates his argument that the production of woman comes from "defect in the active force or from some material indisposition," that nature's intention for the woman is only for "generation," and that the woman was not made to be man's helpmate but man's "helper." Thomas held a view of women as "an occasion of sin to man" and follows Paul's literary injunction that women not be allowed to teach in public.[50]

Black people also find St. Thomas' view on slavery a little disturbing because some of his views have been used historically to justify the subordination of people of color. Thomas did not challenge prevailing views on slavery. Although slavery at the time of Thomas was not the same as the trans-Atlantic slave trade that dehumanized Africans that were brought to

49. O'Meara, *Thomas Aquinas Theologian*, xiv.

50. *ST* I, q. 91, a. 1.

the Americas, Thomas accepted slavery as a human institution or contrivances designed for the good of society. He took for granted that some people are meant to be subordinate to others. Aquinas took it for granted that this kind of subordination would have existed in the state of innocence. The reason for this, according to him, is because human beings are by nature a social animal. Therefore, people living together in an organized socio-political community need some form of single authority, if they are to achieve the common good. He, therefore, reasoned that if some men are more gifted in knowledge and also more just (pious) than others, it would be the right thing to use those gifts for the benefit of the community.

7

The Church, Christology, and Salvation

THE PSYCHOTHERAPIST VIKTOR FRANKL always began his therapy sessions by asking his patients why they have not committed suicide. He discovered astonishingly that for every patient there was a different answer to the question, why have you not attempted suicide? People's motivations and will to meaning in life differ. For one it may be the love of children, for another it may be the love for a talent yet to be used, still for another it may be a lingering memory worth preserving. The human will to survive in the face of inexplicable odds is what Frankl captures in his book about his prison camp experience. He relates how his parents, brother, and wife were gassed to death in Nazi gas chambers. As Gordon Allport sums it up in the preface to Frankl's book, "To live is to suffer, to survive is to find meaning in the suffering. If there is a purpose in life at all, there must be a purpose in suffering and dying. But no man can tell another what this purpose is. Each must find out for himself, and must accept the responsibility that his answer prescribes."[1]

THE PROBLEM OF EVIL

As human beings we are always confronted with the reality of evil. We experience natural disasters, like hurricanes, tornados, and earthquakes. We are aware of moral evils, like the holocaust, slavery, and the extermination of Native Americans. We also know of structural evils, like abuse of women and the oppression of the poor and minorities. We experience evil as a fact

1. Frankl, *Man's Search for Meaning*, 11.

and a reality. In June 2001, America woke up to one of these such realities that shocked the moral fibers of our nation. A woman in Houston, Texas, Andrea Yates, confessed to drowning her five children in the bathtub. As details of the tragedy emerged, we came to discover that Andrea Yates had been suffering from postpartum psychosis. Although the jury later convicted Yates for killing her five children, many believed that she was a victim of forces beyond her control. Andrea Yates was not evil. But in her actions many experienced the troublesome problem of evil. To cite one more example, in the last couple of years the world's attention has turned to the rising incidence of anti-Semitism in Europe. In March 2012 a gunman went to a Jewish school in Toulouse, France, and killed a rabbi and three Jewish children. In 2014 French authorities reported that a nineteen-year-old girl that was raped in Paris was targeted and raped because she was Jewish. These are just a tip of the iceberg of the rising wave of anti-Semitism in Europe (and France especially) that has led to about seven thousand French Jews emigrating to the state of Israel in 2014 alone.

This brings us to the complex problem of suffering and the age-old question: what is evil? What forces, if any, are responsible for evil? Where is God in relation to this pervasive problem? Jews who have been victims of anti-Semitism have a cultural connection to Judaism. Their cultural connection to the sufferings of their fellow Jews during the holocaust and sufferings of Jewish people throughout history may help them pull through. Believing in a hopeful future promised by God in the Torah, some Jews use the tragedy of the past as lessons towards realizing the promise. In theological terms, the attempt to articulate the problem of evil is known as **theodicy**. Christianity, like Judaism and Islam, recons with the fact of evil. These religious traditions take a hopeful view that a person can transcend his or her predicament and that in the face of suffering one can discover meaning in life. Viktor Frankl tells of a promise he made to himself the first day he arrived at the concentration camp in Auschwitz. The camp in Auschwitz was surrounded by electric wires to prevent prisoners from escaping. If prisoners touched the electric wires they were electrocuted instantly. Prisoners who could not tolerate the horrors of prison camp took to suicide as an escape. One popular method of suicide was to run into the wire and touch the electrically charged fence. The phrase "run into the wire" became a common phrase among prisoners. Frankl made himself a promise not to "run into the wire."[2] In his work on Logotherapy, Frankl distinguishes between different forms of neurosis "and traces some of them (the noogenic neuroses)

2. Frankl, *Man's Search for Meaning*, 37.

to the failure of the sufferer to find meaning and a sense of responsibility in his existence."[3]

The practical problem is not whether evil exists, but what can be done about it? Life holds a potential meaning under any circumstances, especially the most miserable ones.[4] Since God is the ground of all human endeavors, the question is also about what God is and what God has been doing about the fact of evil. The question of what God is doing about the fact of evil is what is known as **special transcendent knowledge—that God must be doing something about evil, if God truly loves humanity**.[5] For Christians, God explicitly addressed the problem of evil by sending Jesus to die on the cross. We shall examine the meaning of the church in the next section, but not before examining the causes of evil.

Causes of Evil

When we speak of human evil we are talking of the human person who in freedom chooses to do this as opposed to that or refrains from doing this as opposed to that. Human existence comes with freedom and responsibility. In freedom we give determinate validity to our life. Given this human ability to choose and make determinations for one's life, there is an extent to which human beings are responsible for the evil in the world. Some evil are brought about by our excessive desires and lusts for power, which sometimes lead to war. Some evils are as a result of the pollution of the environment and lack of adequate care of our natural resources. Ignorance, i.e., wrong or erroneous belief, is also to some degree responsible for evil. An example of this may be the issue of global warming. For a long time it was erroneously thought that we humans had nothing to do with the changing climate. But scientists are now discovering that we can do a lot to help reduce global warming. Among the many evils that afflict the human person and the human community at large there is none worse than the erroneous beliefs that distort a person's mind and make systematic aberrations of their conduct.[6] The September 11th terrorist attack in New York is a good example. The terrorists who hijacked planes and crashed them into the Pentagon and the World Trade Center, we are told, were convinced of their cause, "martyrdom," but their belief was erroneous. Something can be also be said of athletes who knowingly take drugs and unintentionally cause bodily harm

3. Frankl, *Man's Search for Meaning*, 10.

4. Frankl, *Man's Search for Meaning*, 16.

5. Lonergan, *Insight*, 709.

6. Lonergan, *Insight*, 709.

to themselves because of the erroneous belief that taking drugs can make them better athletes. The course of action that people choose reflect either their ignorance or their bad will or even their ineffectual self-control. This is called sin in Christian theology.[7]

The reality of sin is at times evident in the way societies are configured. Some societies have structures that are in themselves unjust and sinful. In many countries, especially developing countries of Africa and Latin America, the structures of society are such that the rich get richer and the poor get poorer. Nowhere is this more evident than in Latin America where Liberation theologians have spent a great deal of time challenging structural injustice. One of the prominent voices in this regard is the Peruvian-born theologian Gustavo Gutiérrez, who insists that the situation of the poor in Latin America calls for a revolutionary transformation of the very basis of society. Gutiérrez calls for a theology that addresses this need (liberation theology), insisting that true liberation has three main dimensions: (1) it involves political and social liberation that eliminates the immediate causes of poverty and injustice; (2) it involves the emancipation of the poor and marginalized from those things that inhibit their capacity to develop themselves freely and with dignity; and finally, (3) true liberation involves liberation from selfishness and sin and a reestablishment of right relationship between God and God's creatures. Liberation theology has been continued in Latin America by theologians like the Brazilians Clodovis and Leonardo Boff, Juan Luis Segundo of Uruguay, Ignacio Ellacuria of El Salvador, Dom Helder Camara, the Catholic Archbishop of Olinda and Recife (Brazil), and the Brazilian educator Paulo Freire.

Are We Responsible for Evil?

We know that greed, avarice, and insatiable human appetite are at the root of human pain. Buddhism suggests the doctrine of the Four Noble Truths as panacea for human suffering. The Four Noble Truths teach that (1) all life is suffering; (2) the cause of suffering is desire; (3) stopping desire will stop suffering; and (4) the Eightfold Path (i.e., right views, right intention, right speech, right action, right livelihood, right effort, right mindfulness, and right concentration) is the best way to stop desire.[8] Some Christian theologians are beginning to adopt positions similar to the Buddhist notion that ignorance or erroneous beliefs are responsible for some of our bad actions. According to Bernard Lonergan, as a person advances in

7. Lonergan, *Insight*, 711.
8. See Carmody and Brink, *Ways to the Center*, 224–25.

truth he or she begins to acquire the capacity to correct his or her errors. "Our advance in understanding is also the elimination of oversights and misunderstandings."[9] If ignorance is in part responsible for erroneous belief, which in turn leads to concrete act of evil, it is necessary to take steps to free oneself from false beliefs. If there are erroneous beliefs that make evil possible, it also means that there must be opposite intelligible good choices that lead to good acts. To make good choices is to be attentive, intelligent, reasonable, and responsible. While rational and responsible decision-making processes do not completely eliminate evil, they significantly reduce them. People who are attentive, intelligent, reasonable, and responsible may still have to suffer from the evil of those who are not as intelligent and reasonable. This is one of the reasons why Viktor Frankl speaks of suffering as what one may sometimes be required to accept, i.e., an act of fate or even a cross to be borne. "When a man finds that its his destiny to suffer, he will have to accept his suffering as his task; his single and unique task. He will have to acknowledge the fact that even in suffering he is unique and alone in the universe. No one can relieve him of his suffering or suffer in his place. His unique opportunity lies in the way in which he bears his burden."[10] But why do the just have to suffer?

The problem of evil raises for us the question of God whose all-knowing and almighty power can remedy all evils. Since God is good and wills the goodness of all of God's creatures, it is meaningless to speak of a problem of which there is no solution.[11] The fact of evil means that God is doing something about it. The reality of God must have meaning and value for us. The Bible is very clear about God's participation in human events, a reason for which God intervened in human affairs by sending Jesus as the savior who would deliver God's children from sin and evil. The promise of a savior was realized in the man Jesus Christ who was miraculously born of the Virgin Mary. The story of Jesus is preserved by the church. What is the church? Who was Jesus Christ? In what way was he a savior? If he was a savior, was he a savior for a select few or savior of the whole world?

THE CHURCH

The church is identified with the person and work of Jesus. While on earth Jesus knew himself to be the "absolute mediator of salvation."[12] The Bible

9. Lonergan, *Method in Theology*, 110.

10. Frankl, *Man's Search for Meaning*, 99.

11. Lonergan *Insight*, 716.

12. Rahner, *Foundations of Christian Faith*, 322.

describes him as "the Lamb of God who takes away the sin of the world" (John 1:29). In carrying out his mission on earth, Jesus did not found an institution or a large cathedral church, like the ones we see in major metropolis. Rather, he went about preaching the good news, healing the sick, and forgiving sins. "He did take a stand and gathered people around himself as disciples and called them to stand with him. He defined this stance in terms of symbols like the Kingdom of God and the 'twelve' (representative of the tribes of Israel) and in terms of a call for a qualitatively radical conversion."[13] Jesus shared his healing powers with the disciples who took a stand with him. On the eve of his death he shared a special meal with his disciples (the Last Supper) and commanded them to do this often "in memory of me" (1 Cor 11:24). The followers of Jesus, after his death, called themselves *ekklesia*, the Greek term for "assembly" or "gathering" of a people set apart. They considered themselves to be an assembly or community that was different from the existing Jewish community and the rest of society. At Pentecost the followers of Jesus received the power of the Holy Spirit (Acts 1:18) and were emboldened to proclaim the coming of the kingdom of God. The power they received on Pentecost empowered them to scatter all over Palestine where they founded more communities. The different Christian communities founded by the apostles met regularly to celebrate the Eucharist as Jesus had directed them. They also had a governmental structure—bishops, presbyters, and deacons. Thus, it is this line of continuation of Christ through the believing community who profess faith in him and knew him to be the savior of the world that we call "church."[14]

Because of the sixteenth-century reformation that led to division in Christian unity today we have different ecclesial communities that call themselves "church." This sometimes lead people to wonder which one of these different ecclesial communities is the true church of Christ. According to Karl Rahner, "the question of the church which was really intended and founded by Christ" is one of the most difficult questions in church history.[15] What we mean by "church," therefore, is best spoken in terms of models. Speaking of the church in terms of models leaves space for different ecclesial communities to identify with any of the models. People throughout Christian history have come up with different models. The American Jesuit Avery Dulles (1918–2008) has offered six good models that can help our discussion.[16]

---

13. Masson, *Charmed Circle*, 221.

14. Rahner, *Foundations of Christian Faith*, 322.

15. Rahner, *Foundations of Christian Faith*, 324.

16. See Dulles, *Models of the Church*.

1. Church as institution: Today the word "structure" carries negative connotations because of the awareness of the dangers structures can pose and how structures of society can be institutionalized to legitimize oppression. Often when we speak of institution we think of unjust structures, like those that marginalize women and ethnic minorities. Applying the metaphor to the church may seem problematic. But when we speak of the church as an institution it is intended to mean that the church teaches and rules with the authority of Christ (Matt 16:18). It also intended to highlight the fact that the church has a governmental structure (pope, bishops, priests, and deacons) responsible for administering the sacraments and clarifying doctrines.

2. Church as community: the church is the Body of Christ or a fellowship of love where members reflect in their relationship to one another the love between God the Father, the Son, and Holy Spirit (Rom 12; 1 Cor 12). The Catholic Church emphasizes two aspects of the community that are related to each other: the local church and the universal church. The local church is where the believing Christians in a given locale gather for worship. A local church is related to all other sister churches. The church then is a place where everyone is truly welcomed and becomes part of a community. "One of the great human paradoxes" of the church community as Dennis Doyle observed, "is how we can all be so different and yet so similar."[17]

3. Church as sacrament: the church is a visible manifestation of God's grace in human community. The church manifests grace in the way it witnesses and in the way it worships (1 Pet 2:9; Eph 5:32). The Belgian Catholic theologian Edward Schillebeeckx (1914–2009) was one of the chief proponents of the typology of church as sacrament. Traditionally, a sacrament is "an outward sign instituted by Christ to confer grace." The Catholic Church teaches that there are seven sacraments and that they all confer grace. Schillebeeckx was concerned about some misunderstandings in the way grace is conferred. He thought that some Catholics were beginning to treat the sacraments of the church like magical rituals and therefore saw the need to reshape the church's teaching on the sacrament. In his book *Christ the Sacrament of the Encounter with God* (1963), Schillebeeckx pointed out that Jesus Christ is the proto-sacrament in whom God's love for humanity became visible and irrevocable. He also pointed out that insofar as the mission

17. Doyle, *Communion Ecclesiology*, 7.

of the church is to make visible the love God has shown us in Jesus Christ that the church is equally a sacrament. Before his death in 2009, Schillebeeckx took his typology of church as sacrament a step further, emphasizing how our encounter with the poor and the marginalized provide us an opportunity to encounter God.

4. Church as herald: the church is God's faithful people who hear God's word and keep it alive (Matt 28; Acts 2). This model places emphasis on the mission of the church to proclaim the Good News of the coming of God's kingdom.

5. Church as servant: the church is an instrument by which God brings justice and peace on earth (John 13:34). This model emphasizes the mission of the church to reach out to the poor and marginalized people of the earth.

6. Church as discipleship: the church is a group of people who follow Christ and learn from him. According to this model, the church, as followers of Christ, learn from Christ and try to live out the life of Christ in the world.

CHRISTOLOGY

Christology is an attempt to understand Jesus Christ. Was Jesus human or divine? Or was he human and divine? If he was human, we have a fairly accurate knowledge of the point in time in which he became man, since we know of his virgin birth. But if he was divine, when did he become divine? Was he always divine? As a man did he know he was divine? If he was aware of his divine nature at what point did he know it? Was he fully conscious of his mission as divine redeemer? If he was, why did he not explicitly say so?

The Gospel of John answers some of these questions. The author of this Gospel, sometimes referred to as the Fourth Gospel, begins the prologue by asserting the divinity of Jesus: "In the beginning was the Word, and the Word was with God, and the Word was God" (John 1:1). The author immediately tells us that it was because of God's kindness to give to the human race "grace upon grace," that Jesus became man like us: When he "became flesh and made his dwelling among us" (John 1:14), Jesus, as it were, identified with our frail human nature. He did not identify with us just to sympathize with us. Rather, he identified with us so he could do something about it, something he accomplished through suffering, death, and resurrection.

The resurrection of Christ is for the New Testament writers the cornerstone of the Christian faith. It is a testimony that God, at a particular moment in history, decided to do something about human sinfulness. Faith in God's decision to act was based on faith in the Lord Jesus. The apostle Paul states that if Christ had not risen from the dead we (Christians) are the most pitiable of people. The word "Christ" is a Greek translation of the Hebrew word Messiah, meaning an "anointed one." For Christians, Jesus' death and resurrection prove that He was the "anointed" One chosen by God to redeem God's people from the evil of sin and death. Jesus was the messiah prophesied in Old Testament scriptures. In him the messianic hope long awaited by the people of Israel was fulfilled.

Early Christological Controversies

Faith in the Lord Jesus was not always a given. The contemporaries of Jesus did not all accept him as the promised messiah. Worse still, the early Christian church did not always understand his divinity. The church was for a long time embroiled in controversies regarding the person of Jesus and his mission. These led to heated debates—the Christological controversies. The first seven ecumenical councils of the church dealt with these controversies. The first problem had to do with the human and divine natures of Christ. Subsequent Christological controversies dealt with the question of how Jesus Christ can at one and the same time be human and divine.

In the early church there were three patriarchates (theological centers): the two rival schools of Alexandria and Antioch, and Rome, which enjoyed the special privilege as "overseer" of the church. The theological center of Alexandria boasted of eminent theologians like Clement of Alexandria (150–215 CE) and Origen (182–254 CE) and was noted for its allegorical interpretation of Scripture. Allegorical interpretation is a method of interpretation that assigns contemporary meanings to Old Testament passages and words. The Alexandrian emphasis was on the unity of the human and divine natures of Christ. The rival school of Antioch, on the other hand, preferred literal interpretation of scripture. Their emphasis was on the humanity of Christ. The Christological controversies unfolded in this arena, i.e., the two contrasting styles or starting points of theology. The first Council of Nicaea (325 CE) was convened in response to the Arian problem. Arius (256–336 CE), a priest from Alexandria had claimed that Jesus was a creature and not God as God the Father is God. After much deliberation and heated arguments, Nicaea affirmed that Jesus was one in "being (essence) with the Father," "begotten not made," and "homoousios (consubstantial) with the Father." Constantinople (381 CE) affirmed the decisions of Nicaea and added that the Holy Spirit is "the Lord the Giver of Life who proceeds from the Father [and] together with the Father and the Son is to be adored and glorified." A more refined definition of the relationship of the human and divine natures of Christ was given at Chalcedon (451 CE). According to the decree of the Council, the two natures of Christ were "unmixed and unchanged, undivided and unseparated," and the qualities of each nature were by no means destroyed in this union, but preserved and united in one person (*prosopon*) and one *hypostasis*. The word "hypostasis" signifies that there is a real distinction between the Father, the Son, and the Holy Spirit, all of them being unto themselves supreme reality in divine substance, essence, and nature. We will discuss the ecumenical councils more fully in the next chapter in the context of heresies and the church's responses to them. These responses led to the development of Christian doctrine and spirituality.

Church as Sign of God's Desire to Save Humanity

God's universal salvific will is continued in the church, an institution, if you like, established by Jesus. Insofar as the church is a continuation of the work of Christ, the church is a sign of salvation or what Karl Rahner calls "the basic sacrament of salvation." As sacrament of salvation, the church is not only for those who profess to be Christians, but for all of God's people. God's desire to save humanity (salvation history) "has entered into its final, eschatological and irreversible phase."[18] The church is not the salvation, but a sign of that salvation that comes from Christ. Christ established within the church means of attaining salvation—sacraments. The Catholic Church speaks of seven of these sacraments. The origin or institution of these sacraments "can be understood in a way which is analogous to the institution of the church itself by Jesus."[19] The seven sacraments are baptism, eucharist, confirmation, anointing of the sick, holy order, penance, and matrimony.

Baptism, confirmation, and Eucharist are called sacraments of Christian initiation. Baptism is the sacrament that washes away original sin and makes a person a member of the Church. "Membership in the church and belonging to the church is the first and most immediate effect of this sacrament of initiation which every Christian receives, and which for every Christian is the foundation of his Christian existence."[20] Confirmation is the sacrament that perfects the grace of baptism in that one receives the Holy

18. Rahner, *Foundations of Christian Faith*, 412.

19. Rahner, *Foundations of Christian Faith*, 413.

20. Rahner, *Foundations of Christian Faith*, 415.

Spirit and becomes an adult member of the church. It is the sacrament that strengthens a person's faith "against the powers and forces of this world, the powers of untruth and of disbelief, and of the demonic hybris to want to redeem oneself."[21] The Eucharist is at the center of the church's liturgical life. It is a memorial sacrifice that is offered for the nourishment of the Christian and reparation of sin. Rahner calls the Eucharist the sacrament of the church in "a very radical sense" because of this sacrament's "decisive importance for the founding of the church and for the self-understanding of Jesus as the mediator of salvation."[22]

The sacraments of penance and anointing of the sick are called the sacraments of healing because they take away sins that are committed after baptism and reconcile the sinner to God. The last two sacraments: Holy orders and matrimony are called the sacraments of Christian vocation because they are geared towards the service of others. Matrimony is a sacrament of marriage while Holy orders is the sacrament of consecration of priests by which the apostolic mission of the church is continued.

CATHOLIC AND CATHOLICISM

We need to distinguish between two words that are related but nonetheless not synonymous: "catholic" and "Catholicism." The word "catholic" is from the Greek *kat'holou*, meaning "to be whole" or "to be complete." The word "catholic" is usually used in contrast to sects or schismatic groups, like the Donatists or the Arians that were sectarian or provincial, as we saw earlier. "Catholic" is usually used as an adjective or a noun to denote universal. St. Augustine used the term "catholic" exactly this way in his dealings with the Donatists. He spoke of the church of Christ as "catholic," meaning universal, as against the Donatists who were sectarian (incomplete) and parochial (limited). The Donatists wrongly taught that the church was the church of the few, not for everyone. In the way Augustine used the term, the word "catholic" denotes something that is complete or a faith that is unified and orthodox. The Council of Nicaea (325 CE) and Council of Constantinople (381 CE) also used the word "catholic" as a rallying point for unity of faith. In fact, the first person to use the word "catholic" was St. Ignatius of Antioch (50–117 CE), who stated, "Wherever the bishop is to be seen, there let all his people be, just as wherever Jesus Christ is present, we have the Catholic Church." The bishop represents, for Ignatius and the fathers of the church, a symbol of orthodoxy.

21. Rahner, *Foundations of Christian Faith*, 417.
22. Rahner, *Foundations of Christian Faith*, 425.

The word "catholic" became problematic and took a new twist in the eleventh century when the Eastern Church (Orthodox Christianity), for political and theological reasons, separated and severed ties with Rome (Western Church). The Western Church held on to the title "Catholic Church," while the Eastern Church became the Orthodox or Byzantine Church. It was called Byzantine because it had its capital in Byzantium. The meaning of the word "catholic" got even more complicated in the sixteenth century when those Western Christians who severed relations with Rome during the Protestant Reformation took the name Protestants. Those who retained ties with Rome were called Catholics, as a way of distinguishing them from the Protestants. Thus, as a result of the eleventh century split between the East and West and the subsequent sixteenth-century Protestant Reformation, the meaning and understanding of the word "catholic" became severely distorted from its original meaning. Today it is not only the Roman Catholic Church that calls itself "catholic." There are several other ecclesial communions, like the Armenian, Byzantine, Coptic, Ethiopian, East Syrian, and Maronites, that call themselves "catholic."[23] Therefore, we may say that to be Catholic "is to be a kind of human being, a kind of religious person, and a kind of Christian belonging to a specific Eucharistic faith-community within the worldwide, or ecumenical, Body of Christ."[24]

We see from our analysis of the word "catholic" that the church is composed of many churches, which means the noun "church" can refer to the Catholic Church, the Orthodox Church, the Baptist Church, the Lutheran Church, the Presbyterian Church, etc.[25] If, as we said in our earlier chapter, to be religious is to be human in a unique way, then we might also say that to be Catholic is an instance of this unique or specific way of being human. Catholicism (as used to mean the Roman Catholic Church) is a particular understanding, affirmation, and expression of this unique affirmation of human existence.[26] Catholicism in this sense is also a religious perspective that offers an understanding of God, an understanding that is "the foundation and context for tis understanding of creation, redemption, incarnation, grace, the Church, moral responsibility, eternal life, and each of the other great mysteries and doctrines of Christian faith."[27]

23. See McBrien, *Catholicism*, 5.

24. McBrien, *Catholicism*, 6.

25. McBrien, *Catholicism*, 7.

26. McBrien, *Catholicism*, 6.

27. McBrien, *Catholicism*, 7.

Characteristics of Catholicism

Christians generally affirm the uniqueness of Jesus and how God, in Jesus, actualized God's desire to save humanity. Be that as it may, many Christians also admit that there is no one way of talking about how Jesus affects our lives and for this reason think that we should be open to developing new images that can help us understand how his mission of salvation affects our lives.[28] The Catholic approach to Christian life is different from non-Catholic, particularly the Protestant approaches to Christian life, in many ways. These differences are what characterize Catholicism.

Characteristics of Catholicism

1. Sacramentality: Catholicism has a practical commitment to the principle of sacramentality. Catholicism sees all reality as sacred. It does not make sharp distinction between nature and grace (divine presence). It sees human nature as already from the beginning graced; that the world is good, even though sin is in the world. This Catholic approach of nature-grace harmony differs from the approaches of the ecclesial communions deriving from the Reformation. Take the example of Jehovah's Witnesses who generally believe that a blood transfusion from one person to another violates God's law against ingesting blood. Jehovah's Witnesses believe that a person who accepts blood transfusion from another human being risks losing eternal salvation because the act violates biblical prohibition against ingesting blood. For this reason parents who are Jehovah's Witnesses do everything in their power to prevent their children from receiving blood transfusions. They would not want to preserve human life of their children at the expense of their eternal life. But the Catholic sacramental principle accepts genuine advancement in human medicine as an instance of graced nature. The spiritual is in the material because God plays an active part in human history and God has a hand in modern medicine. Thus, the Catholic sacramental principle affirms that God is already present in human life and history. This sacramental vision sees God in all things, in the whole cosmos, and in all human events.[29] "The great sacrament of our encounter with God, and of God's encounter with us, is Jesus Christ. The church, in turn, is the fundamental sacrament

28. See Knitter, "Uniqueness of Jesus," 4.
29. McBrien, *Catholicism*, 10.

of our encounter with Christ, and of Christ with us."[30] Catholicism, in a nutshell, does not follow a grace or nature, but a graced-nature approach.

2. Mediation: Catholicism holds that the human encounter with God is mediated through persons or created realities. "Catholicism's commitment to the principle of mediation is evident especially in the importance it has placed on the ordained ministry of the priest. . . . The function of the priest as mediator is not to limit the encounter between God and the human person, but to focus it more clearly for the sake of the person and ultimately for the sake of the community of faith."[31] Catholicism's principle of mediation is seen in the emphasis it places on the role of Mary, the mother of Jesus, in salvation history, as well as emphasis it places on intercession of the saints. Catholicism "engages in the veneration (not worship) of Mary and asks her to intercede for us, not because Catholicism perceives Mary as some kind of goddess or super creature or rival of the Lord himself, but because she is a symbol, image, and instrument of God."[32] Mary and the saints, like sacraments do, signify and cause grace.[33] But the churches deriving from the Reformation differ from Catholicism in this regard and de-emphasize any mediatory or intercessory roles for Mary or the saints for that matter. Their emphasis is only on Jesus, the one mediator.

3. Communion: In some cultures, particularly "the dominant European culture of the United States, ultimate significance is often placed on the individual, on personal rights and freedoms, sometimes even to the extent that the relationship of the individual with the social groups to which he or she belongs gets overlooked."[34] But Catholicism affirms that our way to God is not only mediated but is also communal because God's encounter with individuals is always mediated through the community of faith. This means that for Catholicism "there is no relationship with God, however profound or intense, that dispenses entirely with the communal context of every relationship with God."[35] Catholicism, for this reason, speaks of the communion of saints and

---

30. McBrien, *Catholicism*, 10.
31. McBrien, *Catholicism*, 12.
32. McBrien, *Catholicism*, 12.
33. McBrien, *Catholicism*, 12.
34. Huff and Wetherilt, *Religion*, 11.
35. McBrien, *Catholicism*, 13.

the church as a community where the human person encounters God through the sacraments and the various ministries and gifts God has endowed the church. Take the example of what happened in 1992 in New York City when the Ancient Order of Hibernians organized St. Patrick's Day Parade but refused to allow gays and lesbians of Irish descent to join the parade. The exclusion of gays and lesbians from the march, as would be expected, was controversial. The city of New York took legal action, accusing the Hibernians of violating the city's law against discrimination. In their defense, the Hibernians argued that they belonged to the Roman Catholic communion and that they were following their charter, which following Roman Catholic teachings considers homosexuality objectionable. The following year, 1993, the city of New York denied the Hibernians permit to hold their annual parade in so far as they cannot hold a more inclusive parade. The Hibernians sued the city for denying them permit, an act they thought violated their own First Amendment rights. The Hibernians won the case on the argument that their parade was designed "to honor the patron saint of Ireland and to proclaim their allegiance to the Roman Catholic Church and its teachings."[36] Although the surface issue in this case is discrimination, the underlying issue was religious autonomy.[37] The Hibernians demonstrated that they belonged to a religious community and that though they respect the laws of the state, their primary allegiance was to a community of faith to which they belong. This Catholic idea of communion is also found in the ecclesial communions that separated themselves from Rome, but in a different way.

4. Sacred Tradition: Catholicism places great emphasis, not only on Scripture, but also on sacred tradition. Catholicism sees "a close connection and communication between sacred tradition and Sacred Scripture. For both of them, flowing from the same divine wellspring, in a certain way merge into a unity and tend toward the same end."[38] Catholicism recognizes that even the Bible itself is a product of many traditions that have come down to us through the church. It therefore sees the history of the church as part and parcel of divine revelation.[39] Unlike many of the ecclesial communions deriving from the Reformation

36. See Carter, *Culture of Disbelief*, 34.
37. Carter, *Culture of Disbelief*, 34.
38. Paul VI, *Dei Verbum*, 9.
39. McBrien, *Catholicism*, 14.

that adopt a Scripture-alone approach, Catholicism adopts Scripture nourished by tradition approach. For "Sacred Scripture is the word of God inasmuch as it is consigned to writing under the inspiration of the divine Spirit, while sacred tradition takes the word of God entrusted by Christ the Lord and the Holy Spirit to the Apostles, and hands it on to their successors in its full purity."[40] Thus, the Catholicism teaches that since it is not from Scripture alone that the Church draws its certainty, but Scripture nourished by sacred tradition, "both sacred tradition and Sacred Scripture are to be accepted and venerated with the same sense of loyalty and reverence."[41]

5. Reason: Because Catholicism recognizes that all created reality is a graced reality, it places emphasis on the use of reason in the understanding of faith. Fideism (naïve faith) cannot grasp the mysteries of God. Faith needs reason.[42] Back to our earlier example of Jehovah's Witnesses who refuse blood transfusion on the argument that it violates Sacred Scriptures prohibition against ingestion of blood, the US courts have in many cases forcibly ordered blood transfusions to save the lives of Jehovah's Witnesses. Even some hospitals require doctors to refer protesting Jehovah's Witnesses to psychiatrists because they suspect "the patient was not acting rationally in rejecting medical advice for religious reasons."[43] Catholicism does not follow an either faith or reason or law or gospel approach, but reason illumined by faith and law inspired by the gospel approach.

6. Analogy: Catholicism affirms that we come to our knowledge of God through our knowledge of created realities and therefore that God can be known analogically. In other words, we come to a knowledge of God through our own human experience. The Catholic analogical thinking is a way of thinking about God and understanding our encounter with God by seeking "'similarity in difference,' in contrast to a more typically Protestant way of thinking that is dialectical—emphasizing always what is unique in God and, therefore, the radical dissimilarities that exist between the divine and the human."[44]

---

40. Paul VI, *Dei Verbum*, 9.
41. Paul VI, *Dei Verbum*, 9.
42. See Orji, *Catholic University and the Search for Truth*, particularly chapter 7.
43. Carter, *Culture of Disbelief*, 14.
44. McBrien, *Catholicism*, 15.

7. Universality: Catholicism prides itself in being at one and the same time a church universal and local. Catholicism is not a church that is tied to one culture. It can find expression in any culture that accepts the Gospel. Catholicism reflects on questions like: How do we reevaluate the Christian message in a world of cultural pluralism in such a way that it does not become disruptive to other people's cultural identities? How is an African or Asian, for example, to live and express his or her faith in such a way "that the Christian faith does not become an alienating reflection of a foreign world behaving aggressively towards indigenous African customs and beliefs?"[45] The Catholic universal principle makes it to be radically open to anything that has truth and value.[46] Catholicism is not about unity or diversity but unity in diversity.

45. Orji, *Semiotic Approach to the Theology of Inculturation*, 31.
46. McBrien, *Catholicism*, 15.

8

Development of Christian Doctrine and Spirituality

CHRISTIAN DOCTRINES DEVELOPED, NOT in abstract, but in historical contexts. In some cases these doctrines developed simultaneously with the church's attempt to define itself and shape its identity in a culture that already had its own religion and socio-political structures. To understand Christian doctrine, therefore, is to understand how the church evolved over time, beginning from its Jewish roots to its foray in a Hellenized Roman world. "All History, that of the Church included," writes Glenn Olsen, "has taken place under the sign of contradiction and has been full of irony, tragedy, success that breeds failure, failure unexpectedly successful, roads not taken, and roads taken that should not have been taken."[1]

It is easy to assume today that Christianity was from the very beginning different from Judaism. But the difference between the two religions was not always clear, at least in the eyes of the Roman authorities. One of the first steps taken by the early Christians was to assert their autonomy from Judaism. When the distinction between Christianity and Judaism did become clear to the Roman authorities, it was not without bloodshed. The birth of Jesus in Bethlehem and his upbringing in Nazareth essentially made him a Jew in the true sense of the term. According to the Gospel account of Luke 2, Jesus was born during the reign of Augustus Caesar, at the time Herod the Great was king of Judea, and Quirinius the governor of Syria. As a devout Jew, Jesus read and knew the Hebrew Scriptures. He also received

---

1. Olsen, *Beginning at Jerusalem*, 13.

rabbinical education. Called like a prophet to communicate God's message to his fellow Jews, Jesus began his public ministry at the age of thirty. He went to the temple and synagogues where he taught his followers and gathered disciples. His main message was that "the kingdom of God has come near! Repent and believe in the good news" (Mark 1:15). After his death and resurrection, his disciples continued to worship in the temple and synagogues, proclaiming Jesus Lord and the promised Messiah.

The Roman conflict with the people of North Africa, the Carthaginians, with whom the Romans fought three Punic wars, began as far back as the middle of the third century BCE and came to an end when Rome became the undisputed power of the western world. Roman control of North Africa and the Mediterranean world meant that such a huge empire would be ethnically and religiously diverse. The policy of religious freedom or toleration, which the Roman rulers introduced for practical reasons, had some political risks because the policy also threatened the unity of the empire. The Roman authorities decided, in the interest of the unity of the empire, to have a uniform religion and mandated one public religion for everyone, i.e., the worship of Roman gods (which later evolved into worship of Roman emperors). "This was not so much a religious obligation as a political one. The acceptance of the Roman gods was an acceptance of Roman governmental authority."[2] But the Jews on their part were not going to compromise the worship of the one true God. Through some political negotiations they were able to gain some religious concession from the emperor. Respect for the antiquity of their monotheistic tradition was a rationale for this exception, at least in the Roman view. Even those Jews who had settled in other cities (Jews of the Diaspora) benefited from this concession, "which safeguarded their freedom of worship, gave them exemption from the Cult of the Emperor and allowed them to be judged by their own civil law, a law which assumed enormous importance in their lives."[3] Christians enjoyed these same benefits as long as they were thought to be members of the Jewish people. But when it was clear that Christians were different from Jews and that Christianity was different from Judaism this Christian self-assertion led to conflicts with the Roman authorities, conflicts that produced both martyrs (people who shed their blood for the Christian faith) and apologists (people who vigorously defended the Christian faith by their writings).

2. Hogan, *Dissent from the Creed*, 17–18.
3. Holmes and Bickers, *Short History*, 11.

CHRISTIAN COMMUNITIES IN ASIA MINOR

Acts of the Apostles, the New Testament book that takes up the story where the Gospel of Luke left off, gives a detailed account of the development of the church from its humble beginnings in Jerusalem to its growth in parts of the Mediterranean basin. The story in Acts is a story of how Christianity defined and distinguished itself from Judaism and Jewish traditions. The first Christian community, according to the story in Acts, was in Jerusalem where the disciples, together with some women and Mary the mother of Jesus, devoted themselves to prayer and fasting. These disciples, under the leadership of Peter, saw the need to choose a replacement for Judas, who had committed suicide after betraying Jesus. They cast lots to choose a successor. The lot fell on Matthias, who then became one of the Twelve (Acts 1:15–26).

The city of Jerusalem was important for early Christians. Jesus had commanded them not to leave the city until they had received "power from on high." Acts 2 tells the story of how the disciples received the gift of the Holy Spirit on Pentecost, which in effect signaled the beginning of the Christian church, as we know it today. The Pentecost experience emboldened the disciples who began to preach and witness to Jesus, even in the face of persecution. This preaching and the persecution that followed it took them to cities other than Jerusalem where Jews had taken up residences. From there they founded Christian communities all over Asia Minor.

One of the early Christian converts was Saul of Tarsus, a zealous Pharisee, who was christened Paul after his conversion, and who proclaimed himself an apostle to the Gentiles. "Paul was certain that he too was an apostle, although he went up to Jerusalem to meet with Peter three years after his conversion (Gal 1:18)."[4] His newfound vocation impelled him to embark on three great missionary journeys between 46–58 CE. He founded Christian communities in many of the cities he preached. Some of his communities included Corinth, Philippi, Galatia, Thessalonica, Ephesus, and Rome. He was also associated with the community at Antioch, where Gentiles were first admitted to the Christian faith.[5] Acts tells us that it was at Antioch that the disciples of Christ were for the first time called Christians (11:26). Paul himself preached first to Jews wherever he went, then to "God-fearing" Gentiles, admirers of Jewish monotheism.

There were also other Christian communities founded by disciples other than Paul. Philip, for example, founded the community at Samaria. Christian tradition also links Mark the Evangelist to Alexandria, the

---

4. McEnhill and Newlands, *Fifty Key Christian Thinkers*, 215.
5. McEnhill and Newlands, *Fifty Key Christian Thinkers*, 216.

commercial capital of Egypt and one of the early centers of Christianity. Christian tradition also links Andrew, the brother of Simon Peter, to the community in Constantinople, and Peter with Rome, not as its founder, but as its leader.[6] These Christian communities had one thing in common: they had to deal with two tough issues: the Roman authorities that barely tolerated them, and Jewish authorities whose hostility towards Christians was clearly obvious.[7]

THE FIRST MINISTERIAL POSITION: THE DIACONATE

While the early Christian community was dealing with the external threats of Roman authorities and Jewish hostilities on the one hand, it was also barraged with hosts of internal conflicts on the other hand. The internal conflict, which had ethnic and cultural undertones, had to do with the Hellenists (Greek-speaking Jews) question. The first recorded account of this problem is found in Acts 6:1–7. The Hellenists had complained against the Hebrews that their widows were being neglected in the daily distribution of food. The issue was brought to the attention of the apostles who wisely discerned that it was not right for them as apostles to neglect the word of God for the distribution of food. They asked the community to choose from among them "reputable men, filled with the Holy Spirit and wisdom," to help in this task. After some prayer and discernment, the community chose seven men, all with Greek names: Stephen, Philip, Prochorus, Nicanor, Timon, Parmenas, and Nicholaus of Antioch. The Greek name of these diaspora-born Jews was a testimony of the attraction of the Gospel to people other than Jews. They became the first seven deacons of the Christian church. According to the story in Acts, the Jewish authorities stoned to death Stephen, the best-known of the seven deacons. Following Stephen's death, more persecutions followed under Herod Agrippa (ca. 42 CE), who made a calculated risk that by harassing followers of Jesus he would win the support of the Jewish authorities.

The Council of Jerusalem

The election of the seven deacons did not put an end to rift in the Christian community. Soon after they settled the Hellenist problem, the community at Antioch was faced with another problem: the question of whether it was

---

6. Holmes and Bickers, *Short History*, 13.

7. Holmes and Bickers, *Short History*, 13.

proper for Gentile Christians to undergo circumcision. Unable to resolve this, the community sent Paul to Jerusalem to consult with Peter, James, and the other apostles. Paul met with the apostles in Jerusalem (ca. 50 CE), at a meeting popularly referred to as the **Council of Jerusalem**. The Council resolved the Gentile question by insisting that Gentile Christians not be forced to go through the Jewish rite of circumcision. While that momentous decision may have temporarily resolved the tension between Jewish Christians and non-Jewish Christians, it did nothing to alleviate the wider problem between Judaism and Christianity. The hostility between the two religious groups reached its climax sometime between 66–70 CE, when a Jewish political group, the Zealots, orchestrated a revolt against the Roman authorities.[8] The Romans, led by a commander, Vespasian, who later became emperor, attacked Judea in 67 CE and conquered Jerusalem in 70 CE, destroying the temple, except the Western or the Wailing Wall.[9] In the period following this revolt, Jewish Christians emigrated to Pella, an act that was regarded as treachery by those Orthodox Jews who remained to fight, in spite of the destruction of the city.[10] The destruction of the temple around this period played a significant role in the growing distinction between Christianity and Judaism.

Era of Formal Persecution of Christians

Attempts by the Roman authorities to unify the empire, as we pointed out earlier, led to the imposition of one state-sanctioned religion, the Cult of the Emperor. Refusal to partake in this cult (except for the Jews who gained religious exemption) was considered treasonous, a crime punishable by death. The era of formal persecution began with Nero who ruled from 54 to 68 CE. The apostles Peter and Paul died under Nero. Some accounts of this persecution come from the Roman historian Tacitus (ca. 55–120 CE), who recorded in his *Annals* that Christians were made a scapegoat for everything that went wrong. According to the report of Tacitus, who was himself a non-Christian, when fire gutted the city of Rome in 64 CE Nero accused Christians of setting the blaze. Tacitus also reports that Christians were charged with crimes of atheism, immorality, and cannibalism.[11] The Christian writer Tertullian (ca. 160–225), in corroborating Tacitus' account of how Christians were made scapegoats for everything that went wrong,

---

8. Holmes and Bickers, *Short History*, 12–13.

9. Hogan, *Dissent from the Creed*, 18–19.

10. Holmes and Bickers, *Short History of the Catholic Church*, 13.

11. Holmes and Bickers, *Short History of the Catholic Church*, 15.

reported "that if the Tiber flooded its banks or the Nile failed to flood, or if the stars stood still or the earth trembled, the cry in the streets was always the same: 'Christians to the lions!'"[12] Christians were made to suffer the humiliation of social and legal legislation: they were forbidden access to public places; those who did not recant their faith were tortured and put in prison. Those who survived the prison experience were sent to the amphitheater as baits for the wild animals.[13]

In the second century other prominent Christians, like Ignatius of Antioch (d. 107 CE), Justin Martyr (100–165 CE), and Polycarp of Smyrna (69–155 CE), died as a result of the draconian policy of Emperor Trajan (98–117 CE). The general policy and severity of persecution at times depended on local circumstances and individual emperors. During the reign of Decius (249–51 CE), for instance, the Roman Empire was under severe threats from its neighbors. It was threatened by the Visigoths who attacked from the western Mediterranean and by the other Barbarian tribes who attacked from the Roman borders of Gaul, Spain, and Asia Minor. Decius ordered every citizen to offer sacrifices to the Roman gods, as a symbol of solidarity and as an invocation of help from the Roman gods.[14] According to the terms of this edict, all the inhabitants of the empire who offer public sacrifice to the Roman gods were to be supervised by an elected official who in turn will issue a *libellus* (certificate) stating that one had offered the desired sacrifice. Some Christians refused to partake in this sacrifice and their refusal made the Roman authorities to view Christianity as a dangerous sect and a threat to the security of the state. Christianity, for them, violated the Roman pietas, i.e., the virtue by which citizens showed their love and respect for the state. This virtue of Roman pietas was outwardly expressed through the rites and usages by which the gods of Rome were honored such that refusal to participate in this common expression of pietas was considered criminal, blasphemous, and treasonous.[15]

In all, apart from the persecution initiated by Nero, there were at least nine other recorded formal persecutions of Christians in the Roman Empire: Domitian (ca. 80 CE), Trajan (ca. 108 CE), Marcus Aurelius (ca. 161 CE), Severus Septimus (ca. 192 CE), Maximus (ca. 235 CE), Decius (ca. 249 CE), Valerian (ca. 257 CE), followed by the Aurelian persecution (ca. 274 CE) and Diocletian persecution (ca. 303 CE). The Diocletian persecution, sometimes called "the Great Persecution," lasted from 303 to 312

---

12. Cunningham, *Catholic Heritage*, 11.

13. Cunningham, *Catholic Heritage*, 11–12.

14. Cunningham, *Catholic Heritage*, 12–13.

15. Cunningham, *Catholic Heritage*, 10–11.

CE and was the last of the formal persecutions in the Roman Empire.[16] All the emperors adopted a policy that allowed for treating as criminals those Christians who refused to sacrifice to idols.

The persecution of Christians, which increased significantly during the reign of Marcus Aurelius (ca. 161–80 CE), went hand in hand with literary polemics against the church. One of those who attacked Christians with his writings was Celsus, whose book, *True Discourse*, painted a grim picture of Christians and attacked them on the level of both doctrine and practice.[17] These literary attacks gave a false picture of the church and left Christians more vulnerable in a society that was ever ready to increase its hostility towards those who would not abide by the Roman pietas. There emerged, in about the second century CE, a group of church leaders called the **Apologists** who devoted time and energy defending the church against offensive literary attacks. Christians were accused of acts of immorality and spreading teachings that made no sense. The Apologists "wrote a series of works with the double purpose of denying the false rumors regarding Christian practice and of showing that Christianity was more than mere nonsense."[18] Thus, in providing the intellectual basis of Christian doctrine, the Apologists wrote literary works, "Apologies," i.e., legal briefs, in defense of the church's doctrine and practice. The most famous of the Apologists and one who gave the strongest argument in defense of the Christian faith was Justin Martyr (100–165 CE). Justin suffered martyrdom during the reign of Marcus Aurelius. Justin was born of pagan parents. After his baptism he moved to Rome where he opened a philosophical/theological school. His best-known work was the *Dialogue with Trypho the Jew*. Among Justin's teachings was that in Jesus Christ the prophecies of the Old Testament had been fulfilled and that life in Christ is initiated by baptism and sustained in the Eucharist. He also argued that Jesus was the "Logos" or Word of God. Justin suggested that since Jesus is the "Logos" of God, the "Logos" or Word of God illumines everything that came before and after the incarnation. On the basis of this argument Justin accepted anything of value in pagan philosophy.[19] His teaching that anything of value in pagan philosophy can illuminate the Christian faith would later have significant impact on Christian theology. Other notable apologists were Melito of Sardis (d. 180 CE); Quadratus (d. 129 CE) and Aristides (d. 133 or 134 CE), both of Athens; Athenagoras of Athens (133–90 CE); Theophilus of Antioch (d.

---

16. Cunningham, *Catholic Heritage*, 13.

17. Holmes and Bickers, *Short History*, 19.

18. González, *Church History*, 27.

19. González, *Church History*, 27.

181 CE); and Tatian (120–80 CE). Tatian was later forced out of the church because he wrote the controversial work *Diatesseron*, "a highly influential harmony of all four Gospels"[20] that tried to create a single Gospel narrative out of the many existing ones. After the apologists there followed a list of great teachers of the faith, among whom were Tertullian, Clement of Alexandria, Origen, and Cyprian of Carthage. We shall discuss their impact and contribution to development of church doctrine in the next section. The conversion of Constantine brought Christians a much-needed reprieve. In 313 CE Constantine promulgated the edict of religious toleration, **Edict of Milan**, which gave Christians right to freedom of worship. With the Edict, Christianity was at first tolerated and later flourished under Constantine (ca. 380 CE) to become the official state religion. "In consequence, the church, which until then was composed mostly of people from the lower echelons of society, made headway among the aristocracy."[21]

CHURCH LEADERSHIP AND ORGANIZATION

Conversion of Constantine to Christianity radically changed things for Christians. Transitioning from outlawed religion to one officially recognized as the state religion was not easy for some Christians who were used to persecution. Their response to the new situation varied significantly, depending on the social location. "Some were so grateful for the new situation that it was difficult for them to take a critical stance before the government and society. Others fled to the desert or to remote places and took up the monastic life. Still others simply broke away from the majority church, insisting that they were the true church."[22] This means that the church could only survive the new situation with true leadership and guidance. Thankfully the church was blessed with a new crop of church leaders in the second century CE. These new leaders came after the apologists and wrote works of great significance. They thought of themselves as following apostolic succession—in the footsteps of church leadership of which Peter the apostle was the first in line.

From the time Jesus called Simon and changed his name to Peter, meaning rock (Luke 5: 1–11), it was clear that Peter was the uncontested head of the apostles and he assumed this leadership role until his death. After Peter's death, and death of the other apostles, the leadership of the church fell on a group of people who were themselves disciples of the apostles. These were

---

20. Anderson and Moore, "Introduction," 1–2.

21. González, *Church History*, 12.

22. González, *Church History*, 12–13.

known as the **Apostolic Fathers**. Prominent among them were Clement of Rome (d. 99 CE), Ignatius of Antioch (d. 107 CE), Polycarp of Smyrna (69–155 CE), and the Shepherd of Hermas (second-century CE valuable Christian work). The Apostolic Fathers provided the church with much-needed leadership at a time when the church was struggling for survival in the Roman Empire. There was also the leadership provided by late second-century CE Christians such as Quintus Tertullian (160–220 CE), Irenaeus (130–202 CE), Clement of Alexandria (150–215 CE), Cyprian of Carthage (d. 258 CE), and Origen (182–254 CE). Apostolic succession and leadership became a fortress that held the church together.

Tertullian was from Carthage in North Africa. "He wrote in defense of the faith against pagans, and also against several heresies. He was the first to use the formula 'one substance, three persons' to refer to the Trinity, and also the first to speak in terms of 'one person, two substances' in Jesus Christ."[23] Irenaeus was from Smyrna, a town in Asia Minor, but spent most of his adult life in Lyon (modern day France). He devoted a great deal of time defending and strengthening the faith of Christians under his care against the threat of heresy. Clement of Alexandria preoccupied himself with the issue of how to adapt Greek philosophy and make it relevant to the Christian faith. Cyprian was a church leader and bishop of Carthage who died in 258 CE during the persecution of Christians. Origen was also "a prolific writer, much inclined to philosophical speculation. Although after his death many of his more extreme doctrines were rejected and condemned by the church, for a long time the vast majority of Greek-speaking theologians were his followers in one way or another."[24] In all, these late-second-century CE group of church leaders wrote great theological works and treatises that answered questions on various subjects. The theological works they produced before Christianity became the official state religion to a great extent helped Christians struggling to adapt to their new situation as members of the only recognized state religion until the sacking of Rome in 410 CE by the Visigoths and the Germanic peoples, a sacking that finally led to the last of the Western Emperor, Romulus Augustus, being deposed in 476 CE.[25]

Internal Problems: Heresies

Although the sacking of Romulus Augustus by the Visigoths in 476 CE, as well as the Barbarian invasion of Rome, greatly devastated the power and

23. González, *Church History*, 30.

24. González, *Church History*, 30.

25. González, *Church History*, 13.

influence of Rome, it did not decimate the rising influence of Christianity. Before the invasion of Rome, for administrative reasons the Roman Empire was divided into two parts: the Western half, which spoke Latin, with its capital in Rome, and the Eastern half, which spoke Greek, with its capital in Byzantium. The invasion of Rome by the Visigoths and Barbarians "had a much deeper impact on the Latin-speaking Western church than on the Eastern and Greek-speaking branch of Christianity."[26] Church doctrines that developed around this time developed mostly as a response to heresies (false teachings) that the church had to correct. It is difficult to put a time-line on some of these heresies because some predate the sacking of Rome. The expansion and growth of the church brought to it "people of various religious backgrounds, and this in turn gave rise to diverse interpretations of Christianity."[27] Some of these interpretations, which bothered on what the church would later consider heresies (false teachings) represent internal threats to the church. There were, for example, Gnosticism, Marcionism, and Montanism, etc. All threatened to tear Christians apart even before Christianity became the official state religion of Rome. These heresies merit some attention because of their significance in the development of church doctrine.

(a) Gnosticism: There are different variations of Gnosticism. But in general terms, Gnosticism is derived from the Greek *gnosis* (knowledge) and *gnostikos* (good at knowing). The Gnostics were an elitist group that taught that one could be redeemed only through knowledge (cosmic redemption through knowledge). As an elitist group, they separated themselves from other people, i.e., people who in their interpretation lacked knowledge. The Gnostics had a dualistic view of reality: spirit and matter. Spirit was good and matter evil. Matter was considered evil because it is a deterioration of spirit. Gnostics denied creation, holding that the created world was the work of a lesser god, demiurge. Human beings, according to their teaching, are prisoners in this world of mat-ter. The ultimate goal of human existence is union with the Supreme God, not the lesser god. This, according to them, can be achieved only through *gnosis*, knowledge, which only a few people possess. They considered the vast majority of human beings to be doomed.

The Gnostic doctrine was essentially in conflict with the Christian doctrine. One implication of their teaching was that Christ could not

---

26. González, *Church History*, 13.

27. González, *Church History*, 28.

have been human, since anything human or material was evil. They, in fact, taught that Christ came to bring gnosis to effect a union with Supreme God. Though no one can tell precisely the origin of Gnosticism, its origin is generally held to have predated Christianity. Its rise was mainly due to the influence of Greek philosophy.

(b) Marcionism: Marcion of Sinope (85–160 CE), an influential early Christian writer, was a native of Asia Minor who was influenced by the gnostic doctrine. Like gnostics, Marcion denied that the material world was the work of the good God. Denying the goodness of creation, Marcion took the gnostic position further, formulating a doctrine that made a sharp distinction between the God of the New Testament and the God of the Old Testament. For Marcion, the God of the Old Testament was a God of Law and the God of the New Testament the God of Love. Marcion considered the God of the Old Testament to be inferior to the God of the New Testament. He also rejected the Old Testament and drew his own canon of scripture. His canon consisted mainly of selected letters of St. Paul's writings and selected parts of the Gospel of Luke. Like the Gnostics, Marcion promoted austere lifestyle.

(c) Montanism: Montanus (ca. second/third century CE), the founder of this sect, claimed to be a prophet called to speak on behalf of the Holy Spirit. He taught the need for austere lifestyle and perpetual fasting. His followers were called Montanists. They promoted a doctrine of the imminence of the Second Coming of Christ. They also taught their followers not to avoid martyrdom, but to seek it and embrace it.

The church responded in various ways to threats posed by heresies. Against the gnostic distinction between supreme (good) God and evil god (demiurge), the Christian church insisted that there is only one good God. It also rejected the gnostic dualism of spirit (good) and material (evil) universe, insisting on the goodness of the whole created universe. Against Marcionism, the church formulated its own canon of scripture (i.e., books officially recognized as part of Christian Scripture). Individual church leaders like Justin, Tertullian, and Irenaeus also refuted Marcion's teaching by insisting on a church with greater organization and well-defined doctrines and practices. We shall discuss other heresies, particularly Arianism and other Christological controversies, in the context of the ecumenical councils since it was these councils that clarified the Christological problems and authoritatively defined the church's creed. But key to the unity of the Christian churches scattered throughout the Roman Empire was the institution of Roman primacy whose origin goes back to the primacy conferred on Peter by Jesus. We already saw how the city of Antioch was very important for early Christians, since it was there that the disciples of Jesus were for the first time called Christians. Two other cities, in addition to Antioch, emerged as an important center of Christian activity: Rome and Constantinople. Each of these cities or centers of Christian activity had its own leader to whom the local Christian faithful looked up for leadership. But the bishop of Rome enjoyed enormous power and influence over the whole church. "The primacy conferred by Christ on Peter was in no way a temporary, circumstantial affair, fated to disappear when Peter died. It was a permanent institution, an earnest of the permanence of the Church, something that would be valid for all times."[28] There were also other reasons for the esteemed position of the bishop of Rome. First, Rome was the capital of the Roman Empire before Constantine moved it to Byzantium in 324 CE. Second, the apostolic witness of Peter (the first bishop of Rome) and Paul, who were both martyred in Rome under Nero, helped raise the status of Rome. Third, the relocation of the capital of the empire to Constantinople helped consolidate Rome's position for this reason: in the separation of East and West that followed, the emperor became the major power in the East, while the bishop of Rome emerged as the major rival power in the West. Speaking of the esteemed position the bishop of Rome enjoyed over the whole church, Ignatius of Antioch spoke of Rome as the "bond of love" uniting the whole church. Damasus, who was the Bishop of Rome from 366–84 CE, not only referred to Rome as the "Apostolic See," but also referred to other bishops as "sons." He claimed that the primal place of Rome was due to divine will. Siricius, who became the bishop of Rome from 384 to 399 CE, was believed to be the first to use the title "pope" (father). He was also the one that began a tradition later popes would follow, i.e., meddling and giving decisions in cases of dispute, something referred to as the decretals.[29] The eminent position of the bishop of Rome assumed great importance during the pontificate of Leo the Great (440–61) who championed the theory that the Bishop of Rome was the successor of the apostle Peter.

---

28. Orlandis, *Short History of the Catholic Church*, 20.
29. Holmes and Bickers, *Short History of the Catholic Church*, 39.

ORIGIN AND RISE OF MONASTICISM

Constantine's conversion to Christianity left a remarkable imprint on Christianity. By the time he died Christianity was not yet the official state religion of Rome. But "his policies and those of his successors left their mark in the religious life of the Roman Empire"[30] that by the time Christianity became the official state religion in the late fourth century "the church, which until then was composed mostly of people from the lower echelons of society, made headway among the aristocracy."[31] Constantine, before his death, supported the Christian faith with the power of the state, building churches in Byzantium (which he changed to Constantinopolis, meaning the City of Constantine).[32] Some of the net result of Constantine's conversion was codification of Christian worship. "Christian worship became ever more formal, in part imitating the usage of the court. There also began to develop a typically Christian architecture, whose most common expression was the type of church known as 'basilica.'"[33]

The support the church got from the state as the official state religion was a mixed bag. "The change was not easy, and Christians responded in many different ways. Some were so grateful for the new situation that it was difficult for them to take a critical stance before the government and society."[34] Some who were fed up with the level of corruption or the level of "worldliness" Christianity had degenerated in the empire began to flee to the desert, particularly the desert of Egypt, to practice what in Greek was known as *askesis* (athletic training), i.e., asceticism. These people lived a life of total self-denial, which they saw as a new form of martyrdom. They were described as "athletes for Christ."[35] Their goal, which was to attain *apatheia* (a state of inner peace), was achieved in a two-step process: *apotasis*, i.e., total renunciation of the world, and *enkrateia*, subduing one's passions by living a life of poverty, chastity, and obedience.[36] This became the origin of monasticism. Athanasius, the bishop of Alexandria (ca. 297–373), writes in his biography, *The Life of Anthony*, that the first person to practice this kind of life was Anthony of Egypt. Anthony withdrew to the deserts of Egypt in 271 CE to live a life of hermit (solitary life). He sought perfection in prayer,

---

30. González, *Church History*, 33.
31. González, *Church History*, 33.
32. González, *Church History*, 33.
33. González, *Church History*, 34.
34. González, *Church History*, 34.
35. Cunningham, *Catholic Heritage*, 28.
36. Cunningham, *Catholic Heritage*, 29.

fasting, and penance. He began a lifestyle known as the eremitical tradition of asceticism. Eremitical tradition of asceticism is a solitary lifestyle in which a hermit seeks perfection by waging spiritual war against his own demons. A second form of asceticism was begun by Pachomius (290–346 CE) who practiced cenobitical lifestyle (life in common or community). This was communal-based—a group of like-minded people lived together in search of perfection. This kind of monastic life is known as cenobitical tradition of asceticism. Like hermits, cenobites (monks who live in common) pursued a life of prayer, fasting, and self-denial. The cenobitical lifestyle soon became popular throughout the Christian world, thanks to the efforts of men like Basil the Great (ca. 329–79). Basil wrote a Rule to guide the day-to-day life of the monk. He also put great effort into organizing cenobitical style of monasticism. There was also Benedict of Nursia (ca. 480–547 CE), whose monastic Rule was adopted in the West. Another great advocate of monasticism was Augustine, one of the most important figures of Western (Latin) Christianity whose life journeys and encounter with Christianity we discussed at length in another chapter.

EARLY ECUMENICAL COUNCILS

We have seen some of the internal threats that plagued the Christian church in the early years of its existence. We also saw how the church dealt with these threats that came in the form of heresies (false teachings), particularly Gnosticism, Montanism, and Marcionism. But as debilitating as these threats were, they pale in comparison to the controversies surrounding Arianism, a theological problem that began in Alexandria that would later spread to the whole of the Christian world. The controversies led to the first ecumenical Council that authoritatively defined the Christian creed (statement of faith about God, church, and human salvation).

The Council of Nicaea (325 CE)

The conversion of Constantine that helped the church politically did not put an end to the church's internal conflicts. A priest in Alexandria, Arius, became the focus of a theological dispute that threatened to split the church. By the fourth century, as we pointed out earlier, there had developed in the early church two important theological centers that rivaled each other and tried to outdo the other. One was the theological school of Antioch in Syria and the other was the theological school of Alexandria in Egypt. Arius, who grew up in Libya, was a product of the school of Antioch.[37] In his interpretation of the Logos in John 1:1 and the relationship of this Logos to the Father, Arius argued that the Logos was God's first creature, but a created being nevertheless. This teaching, which subordinates the Son to the Father and which gained popular appeal among the followers of Arius, is sometimes known as subordinationism. Arianism or subordinationism led to a big theological controversy that forced Constantine to convoke a council to settle the dispute. This council, which was attended by as many as three hundred bishops from Asia Minor, opened in Nicaea on May 20, 325 CE.

Constantine convoked the Council by virtue of his position both as the emperor and the pontifex maximus (chief priest or "bridge builder"), a title he assumed after his victorious battle over his rival Maxentius, which made him believe he was put on the throne by God to be the chief defender of the Christian faith.[38] Although Nicaea was the first official ecumenical gathering of the church, there is no official record of the proceedings of the Council.[39] But we do know that those in attendance were unanimous in their condemnation of Arius. They affirmed the divinity of the Son, Jesus, and produced a creedal formula, the **Nicene Creed**, which proclaimed the Son as being *homoousios* (consubstantial) with the Father. But this nonscriptural Greek word, *homoousios*, which some of the bishops felt had its origin in gnostic literature, would later become another contentious issue for the church to deal with.

The Council of Constantinople (381 CE)

The condemnation of Arius by the Council of Nicaea did not fully resolve the Arian controversy, especially for three reasons. First, there was the contentious issue of *homoousios*. Second, Arianism resurfaced in different forms, taking different variations: the *Anomeans* who stressed the difference between the Father and the Son, the Semi-Arians who stressed the likeness between the Father and the Son, and the *Homeans* who thought there was (only) a similarity between the Father and the Son. Third, the death of Constantine in 337 CE. At Constantine's death the empire was divided between his three sons, each one favoring a different theological position, further fueling the theological divide in the empire. There were, however, those like Athanasius who continued to champion the Nicene orthodoxy. When Athanasius died in 373 CE the Cappadocian Fathers (Gregory Nazianzus, Basil

---

37. Hogan, *Dissent from the Creed*, 79.

38. Hogan, *Dissent from the Creed*, 82.

39. Jones, *Constantine and the Conversion of Europe*, 129.

of Caesarea and his brother Gregory of Nyssa) emerged as the leaders of the Nicene orthodoxy and laid the groundwork for the impending Council of Constantinople.

The Cappadocian Fathers, realizing that the Western part of the empire and the Eastern half of the empire were drifting more and more apart because of cultural, linguistic, and theological differences, saw "no solution to the continuing theological difficulties unless the West and East could talk with each other and understand what the other was trying to say. Further, they understood that some solution to the question of the Holy Spirit had to be found."[40] They sought imperial cooperation which they thought was needed to settle the divisive question of the relationship of the Holy Spirit to the Father and the Son.

In May 381 emperor Theodosius saw the need for a council of the church in Constantinople. Appolinarius (ca. 310–95 CE) taught that Christ was not fully human, that in Christ the human spirit was replaced by the divine logos. Apollinarius went on to affirm the divinity of Christ while denying his humanity. The Council of Constantinople that met in 381 CE condemned Apollinarius, reaffirmed the decisions of Nicaea and added a statement about the Holy Spirit to the creed. This statement states that the Holy Spirit "proceeds from the Father," and is not, therefore, created, but strictly speaking divine like the Son. Thus the additions of the Council of Constantinople to the Nicene Creed gave birth to the Nicaea-Constantinople creed. Although the Council of Constantinople was the second ecumenical council of the church, it was not until the fourth ecumenical council at Chalcedon in 451 (seventy years later) that the 381 Council of Constantinople was officially recognized as the ecumenical council of the whole church.[41] We should point out that in the ninth century CE the West added the phrase "and the Son" to Constantinople's statement about the procession of the Holy Spirit. This changed the text to read, at least in the West, that the Holy Spirit "proceeds from the Father and the Son." This addition, which in Latin was known as the *Filioque*, had no Greek equivalent. It became a source of more argument and misunderstanding and (unwarranted) mutual condemnations between the East and the West.

The Council of Ephesus (431 CE)

The Christological controversies soon took a new twist. The church had struggled with how best to respond to people who denied the divinity of

40. Hogan, *Dissent from the Creed*, 97.
41. Hogan, *Dissent from the Creed*, 98.

Christ (Arianists) and those who denied the humanity of Christ (Apollinarians). Since there was no precise terminology to express the union of these two natures in Christ, it seemed to some that there were two persons in Christ.[42] Related to this was the popular piety that emerged very early in the church's liturgical life in which Mary, the mother of Jesus, was venerated and honored as "Theotokos," i.e., God bearer. The origin of this title goes back to the struggle against Apollinarius who had been condemned for propounding a doctrine that questioned the humanity of Christ. The opponents of Apollinarius countered by affirming the divinity of Jesus. If Jesus is God and Mary is the mother of Jesus then Mary must be the mother of God, they reasoned. But such an honorific title did not go down well with Emperor Theodosius II and the bishop of Constantinople, Nestorius (ca. 428 CE), who decided to clamp down on those promoting the Marian title because of its negative link with the heretic, Apollinarius. But what the emperor and the bishop did not realize was that in spite of its connection with Apollinarius, the Marian title, *theotokos*, had assumed a position of orthodoxy and was now championed by such eminent personality as Cyril of Alexandria who had earlier been involved in other controversies with Nestorius. The conflict between Cyril and Nestorius "was partly a clash of strong personalities. In addition to the personality clash, there was also the rivalry between Antioch, represented by Nestorius, and Alexandria, represented by Cyril . . . Alexandria emphasized the divinity of Christ, while Antioch was more concerned (but not exclusively so) with Christ's humanity."[43]

The Christological issue now turned into a conflict between Cyril of Alexandria and Nestorius who saw an opportunity to charge Cyril with heresy. For Nestorius, Mary could not be properly called the "Mother of God" but the "Mother of the Christ." Nestorius offered two good reasons for his argument. First, if Mary is the mother of God it would imply that the divine nature was born, suffered, and died. Second, since God is unchangeable one can never impute to God the changing process of birth, suffering, and death.[44] Cyril denounced Nestorius' view, charging that Nestorius denied the divinity of Christ and offended the dignity of Mary by refusing to apply to Mary the title "Theotokos." A general council was convened in Ephesus in 431 CE to settle this Christological question. Nestorius refused to attend and was charged with heresy by the council which deposed him and sided with Cyril. They affirmed the Nicene and Constantinople creed and declared "Theotokos" orthodox Christian doctrine.

42. Hogan, *Dissent from the Creed*, 123.
43. Hogan, *Dissent from the Creed*, 127.
44. Hogan, *Dissent from the Creed*, 124.

The Council of Chalcedon (451 CE)

Another controversy broke out in 446 CE, this time regarding a leader of a large monastery in Constantinople, Eutyches, who denied the two natures of Christ. This heresy, known as monophysitism, emphasized the divinity of Christ while denying his humanity. It was popular among local Christians in Egypt. The council of Chalcedon met in 451 CE, condemned monophysitism, and declared: "We believe and we teach one and the same Christ in two natures, unmixed and unchanged, undivided and unseparated." The union of the two natures of Christ, according to the Council, is preserved in one hypostasis (person). Some Christians, especially Egyptian Christians, refused to accept the declaration of Chalcedon and held on to Monophysite doctrine and later formed their own Coptic church.

CHRISTIANITY IN AFRICA

Africa is the ancient home of the Christian religion. It is common today to hear some Christian antagonists call Christianity a "white man's religion." In our chapter on Islam we shall discuss Islam as a religion, beginning from its early beginnings in Arabian Peninsula to its development in non-Middle Eastern cultures, like the United States. We shall see how Black Muslims in the United States, i.e., Muslims who belong to the Nation of Islam, refer to Christianity as a "white man's religion," as part of their effort to show Black Americans why they should discard Christianity and embrace Islam. But Jesus was, from the very beginning, connected to Africa. The Gospel narratives relate how Jesus was born in Bethlehem at a time the whole civilized world was under the rule of Roman Empire. The greatness of Rome, apart from its military might, was evidenced in how it united and brought distant provinces under its control by a unified administration with an efficient communication and transport system. Jesus' parents, according to the Gospel narratives, out of concern for the safety of the infant Jesus, had to flee Bethlehem in a hurry for Egypt because of threat from Herod, the district governor of the Romans. The flight to Egypt was in effect the first tradition connecting the Christian story to the African continent.[45]

Apart from refuting the mistaken notion that Christianity is a "white man's religion," the history of Christianity cannot be complete without situating it in its African context. From the very beginning "Africans played a prominent role in the life and expansion of the early Church."[46] Some of the

45. Sanneh, *West African Christianity*, 1.
46. Sanneh, *West African Christianity*, 1

best and prominent theologians of the early church came from Africa. A famous early center of Christian activity was the ancient city of Alexandria, Egypt, the other two being Rome and Antioch. As part of the Roman Empire, Alexandria also had some sizeable Jewish population. Jews had been attracted to Egypt when Egypt became part of the Roman Empire in 30 BCE. Many of them took part in the research and scholarship that was going on in Alexandria and some were converted to Christianity. One of such men was Philo of Alexandria who attempted a synthesis of the Christian faith using Greek philosophy. As far back as 280 BCE what is known as the Septuagint, the Greek translation of the Old Testament, was carried out in Alexandria: "the first translation of any part of the Bible into a foreign language. It was later used by Christians who, in response to Jewish taunts that they had no access to the Hebrew original, developed a myth that the Septuagint was divinely inspired, the work of seventy translators in seventy days, working independently and producing miraculously identical texts."[47]

The Catechetical school of Alexandria, which was famous for its great learning and allegorical interpretation of scripture, was led by Clement of Alexandria. Although Clement was not a native of Alexandria (he was born in Greece and migrated to Alexandria in 180 CE), Alexandria produced some famous second-century figures like Origen and Athanasius, and the fourth-century dominant figure, Cyril of Alexandria. By the seventh century BCE Greeks had populated the ancient city of Alexandria that was in 331 BCE named after one of the foremost rulers in Greek history, Alexandria the Great.

There were several prominent church theologians of African origin in North Africa, like Tertullian of Carthage who in the third century became the first Christian theologian to use Latin in his writings instead of the customary Greek, and the great Augustine of Hippo of the fourth and early fifth centuries.[48] Tertullian brought vitality and vigor to early Christianity. "He is regarded as the father of Latin Christianity in the sense of having created a Latin vocabulary for Christian theology. He was the first to formulate and coin the term 'Trinity,' marshalling reasons as to its central place in the Church's teachings."[49] Pope John Paul II did not mince words in recalling the glorious splendor of Africa's Christian past: "We think of the Christian Churches of Africa whose origins go back to the times of the Apostles and are traditionally associated with the name and teaching of Mark the Evangelist. We think of their countless Saints, Martyrs, Confessors, and Virgins,

47. Isichei, *History of Christianity in Africa*, 16.

48. Schwarz, *Theology in a Global Context*, 501.

49. Sanneh, *West African Christianity*, 8.

and recall the fact that from the second to the fourth centuries, Christian life in the North of Africa was most vigorous and had a leading place in theological study and literary production."[50]

Asceticism and the African Origins of Monasticism

Christian monasticism began in Africa. Its origin is traceable to Anthony of Egypt (251–356 CE) who fled to the desert of Egypt to seek communion with God. Anthony began the eremitical tradition of monasticism, living alone as a hermit. There was also Pachomius (290–345 CE), the man from Upper Egypt who was born of pagan parents. He converted to Christianity and began the cenobitical tradition of monasticism. The cenobitical tradition stressed communal life and ascetical practices under the leadership of an elected leader called the abbot. Anthony and Pachomius were the first founders of the monastic life that later spread and further developed in the East and West. According to John Paul II, it was because of the examples of these saintly men that Africa produced some saintly (African) Popes in the likes of Victor I, Melchiades, and Gelasius I whose noble examples enrich the common heritage of the Christian church. There were also, in the first-century church of Africa, saintly African Christian women like St. Perpetua, St. Felicitas, St. Monica, and St. Thelca.[51] Perpetua was an African woman mystic. She was married with a son. She and her slave Felicity and their other companions were martyred in Carthage in 203 CE. Their martyrdom and sacrifice was symbolic of the sacrifices of early African Christians who gave their lives for the faith at the time of great persecution.

Arab Conquest of North Africa

Islam came to Africa in the seventh century when an Arab force invaded Egypt seven years after the death of the Holy prophet Muhammad. The invading Muslims surrounded Egypt and the whole of North Africa, re-naming it the "Maghrib," an Arabic word for "West." Before the Arab conquest Christianity had concentrated mainly in North Africa. "The Sahara and the difficult terrain of the mountain Berbers sealed off the church from active contact with sub-Saharan peoples, whom Christianity was to reach mainly by way of the sea."[52] The Arab conquest further prevented the spread

50. John Paul II, *Ecclesia in Africa*, 31; quoting Pope Paul VI.

51. John Paul II, *Ecclesia in Africa*, 31.

52. Sanneh, *West African Christianity*, 13.

of Christianity to the southern interior. Even North Africa that had been Christianized before the conquest, Christianity completely disappeared in several places with the exception of Egypt where the Orthodox Coptic Church remained powerful. The people known as the Copts were ancient Egyptians who lived mostly in the rural areas and practiced the old religions of the Pharaohs before the advent of Christianity. In the middle of the third century many Coptic villages and towns along the Nile embraced Christianity.[53] The Copts were noted for their rich liturgical and sacramental practices. Even when Islam took over North Africa the Copts still kept their Christian traditions. The Muslim conquerors must have been lenient with Copts who paid their poll tax in return for religious toleration. The Arabs appreciated the Copts as taxpayers and even sometimes intermarried with them and allowed them to keep their language and traditions. By the end of the tenth century most Egyptian Christians spoke Coptic. But by the end of the twelfth century most spoke Arabic and thereafter Christian literature was translated into Arabic.[54]

By the beginning of the eleventh century there was hardly any trace of Christianity in that region of Africa known as the Maghrib. Islam had predominated and Christian churches and cathedrals had been converted into mosques. The Portuguese who explored the coast of Africa in the fifteenth and sixteenth century attempted a re-evangelization of the African continent, setting up posts in present-day Benin, Sao-Tome, Angola, Mozambique, and Madagascar. The Portuguese did not only come for evangelization, they also came for commerce, dealing with the export of slaves from Africa to Europe and the New World which they monopolized between 1440 and 1640.

In 1491 Christian missionaries from Europe sailed into Pinda, the mouth of the Zaire River and with the help of the great king of Congo, Nzinga-a-Nkuwu, set up Christian missions and erected Episcopal Sees. The result of this mission was the consecration in 1518 by Pope Leo X of Don Henrique, the son of Don Alfonso I, King of Congo, as Titular Bishop of Utica. Don Henrique went on to become the first native bishop of Black Africa.[55]

The second phase of the evangelization of Africa came to an abrupt end in the eighteenth century, making way for the third phase, which began in the nineteenth century with the European exploration of the African interior. European powers established colonies throughout Africa, ushering

53. Sanneh, *West African Christianity*, 8.

54. Isichei, *History of Christianity in Africa*, 43.

55. John Paul II, *Ecclesia in Africa*, 32.

in the era of colonialism. It is in this colonial context that Christianity was re-introduced to Africa. This is why we have "predominantly Roman Catholic-Christianity in the former Belgian Congo region, British (Anglican) Christianity in Kenya, and a strong Lutheran church in Namibia. South Africa was settled in the seventeenth century by Dutch immigrants and later conquered by the British, so Anglican and Dutch Reformed churches prevail there."[56]

In the Roman Catholic context, the list of saints that Africa gives to the church continues to grow: Blessed Clementine Anwarite, a virgin and martyr of Zaire was beatified in 1985 by Pope John Paul II; Blessed Victoria Rasoamanarivo of Madagascar and Blessed Josephine Bakhita of Sudan were also beatified by John Paul II, Blessed Isidore Bakanja, martyr of Zaire, there were also the Martyrs of Uganda and Blessed Cyprian Tansi of Nigeria, to mention a few.

56. Schwarz, *Theology in a Global Context*, 501.

9

Schism and Reformation

C. S. Lewis famously likened the history of the church to the layers of an onion—that each period is like a new layer. Using this metaphor, Glenn Olson notes: "If, under the assumption that the best was at the beginning, one attempts to peel through the accrued layers in search of the purported pure and perfect beginnings beyond which all development was distortion or decline, one ends up destroying the onion."[1] History of the Christian Reformation has been written from different viewpoints. But like an onion with different layers, some of its layers are pleasant and joyful and others not so pleasant. Far from being completely peeled off and consigned to the annals of the past, the effects of the unpleasant (layer) division of the Body of Christ, which is the Church, linger to this day. "Our pasts have made us whatever we are and on that capital we have to live or else we must begin afresh."[2] Is it possible to retrieve and correct the past? If so, how easy or difficult is the task? The difficulty of such an endeavor was captured by the famous twentieth-century Jesuit theologian Bernard Lonergan, whose work has been influential in Catholic re-imagination. "Suppose a man suffers total amnesia," Lonergan writes. "He no longer knows who he is, fails to recognize relatives and friends, does not recall his commitments or his lawful expectations, does not know where he works or how he makes his living, and has lost even the information needed to perform his once customary tasks. Obviously, if he is to live, either the amnesia has to be cured, or else

---

1. Olsen, *Beginning at Jerusalem*, 39.
2. Lonergan, *Method in Theology*, 181.

he must start all over."[3] It is erroneous to think that the Reformation was caused by a single act. The events that led to the Reformation were the result of many factors—economic, social, political, and religious—some of which the participants at the time may have been oblivious of.

THE GREAT WESTERN SCHISM AND CONCILIAR MOVEMENT

A movement known as **Conciliarism** emerged in the Middle Ages. Conciliarism taught the doctrine of supremacy of general councils over the Pope in matters pertaining to the well-being of the whole church and in matters of faith. The conciliar movement gained momentum because of the failure of the popes to provide leadership to a fragmented church in need of reform. Conciliarism was also impelled by the Great Western Schism. Both of these factors, particularly the Great Western Schism that ranks as one of the most difficult problems of late medieval church history,[4] combined to create a degenerate condition that later sixteenth-century reformers would capitalize on.

The Great Western Schism (not to be confused with the Great Schism of 1054 that separated the Eastern Church from the Western Church) produced two popes, Urban VI (1378–89) in Rome and Clement VII in Avignon (1378–94), each one claiming to be the legitimate pope and denouncing the other as schismatic heretic. This rivalry led to a divided loyalty, not only among the hierarchy but especially among the faithful. Italy, England, Hungary, most of the German empires, and the Nordic countries, for example, recognized Urban as the true pope, while France, Naples, Savoy, Scotland, Aragon, and Castile pledged allegiance to Clement.[5] The situation got messy when Urban was succeeded by Boniface IX (1389–1404) and Clement was succeeded by Benedict XIII (1394–1423). Boniface died in Rome and was himself succeeded by Innocent VII. Innocent died within two years and was succeeded by Gregory XII (1406–15).

The rival claimants to the papacy before it was finally resolved were Pope Gregory in Rome and Pope Benedict in Avignon. When the schism finally ended, thanks to the Council at Pisa (March 1409–August 7, 1409), which declared (June 5, 1409) the Roman see vacant and the two rival popes "notorious schismatics and obdurate heretics," the schism had lasted for

3. Lonergan, *Method in Theology*, 181.

4. Beck et al., *History of the Church*, 4:402. See also La Due, *Chair of Saint Peter*, 157.

5. La Due, *Chair of Saint Peter*, 157.

more than thirty years.[6] In the interest of peace the cardinals of the two rival camps united and elected a neutral pope, the archbishop of Milan, who took the name Pope Alexander V (1409–10). Although the election of Alexander V brought temporary relief, the damage had been done. The schism severely impaired the church and the "division of allegiance to the 'heads' of Christianity greatly accelerated the break-up of Western Christendom in the sixteenth century."[7]

The relief brought by the election of Alexander V did not last long. "Benedict XIII (Avignon) and Gregory XII (Rome) still had their faithful followers, so the crisis in many ways became more pressing than ever. Now the Christian people had to deal with three papal claimants."[8] Since the schismatic popes did not provide the kind of leadership the church needed, some learned men (conciliar theorists) suggested that only a general council of the church could carry out the much-needed sweeping reforms. Also men, like Pierre d'Ailly (1351–1420) and Jean Gerson (1363–1429) of France, and Nicholas of Cusa (1401–64) of Germany, advanced the argument that "only a general council represented the will of the entire Church and could end the schism, reform the church, and put an end to heresy."[9] There were also some teachers of cannon law who suggested that the cardinals have a right to call a council and that when such councils convene the popes should be bound by the decisions of the council. These canonists, or decretists (commentators on the Decretum of Gratian, 1140), as they were called, argued that although the church itself could not err in declaring the faith, the Pope alone did not enjoy that prerogative, since previous pontiffs had fallen into error.[10]

To return to the Council that met at Pisa in 1409 to settle the issue of rightful claimant to the papacy, it would seem that the cardinal representatives who gathered at the Council acted too hastily and made matters worse by electing a new pope. They made matters worse because they elected a new pope without compelling the other two claimants to the papacy to resign. So by electing a new pope, in practice it seemed as though there were now three popes. In fact, the Council that actually ended the Great Western Schism as such was the Council of Constance (1414–18). This Council was convened by Emperor Sigismund. Where the Council at Pisa had acted

6. La Due, *Chair of Saint Peter*, 157–58.

7. Ullmann, *Origins of the Great Schism*, 96. See also La Due, *Chair of Saint Peter*, 157.

8. La Due, *Chair of Saint Peter*, 158.

9. Grimm, *Reformation Era*, 45.

10. La Due, *Chair of Saint Peter*, 158.

hastily, the Council of Constance proceeded with caution and finally ended the papal schism. However, the Council of Constance did not make much progress with respect to reforms in the church. But it did enact two decrees that were considered revolutionary at the time. The first decree, called *Sacro sancta* (1415), stated that the general council had its authority directly from Christ and that therefore the entire church was bound by the decisions of the general council. The second decree, called *Frequens* (1417), encouraged regular meetings of the general council.[11]

The Council of Constance may have ended the Great Western Schism, at least temporarily. But the problem persisted when the Fathers of the Council elected Martin V pope, and the long-awaited reform failed to materialize.[12] The French clergy, dissatisfied about the inability of the church to carry out reforms, took advantage of the weakness of the hierarchy during this Great Western Schism and appealed to Charles VII to convene an assembly of his clergy at Bourges for the purpose of carrying out reforms in the French church. At Bourges (1438) the French church not only reaffirmed the conciliar theory of the supremacy of the council over the pope but also laid down some basic liberties ("Gallican liberties"):

- the right of the French church to elect its own clergy without papal interference;

- the prohibition of the payment of *annates* (taxes on inferior benefices and tithes) to the papacy; and

- the limitation of the number of appeals from the French courts to the Roman Curia.[13]

Tensions between the papacy and the conciliarists continued even after the "Gallican liberties." The Council of Basel (1431–49) attempted to resolve this problem, as well as the issue of reform and heresy. The conciliarists continued to stress the supremacy of the council over the papacy and the role of the council as the supreme authority in the church. Though at the close of the Council of Basel in 1449 there emerged the recognition of papal power as the supreme authority, the tension between papalism and conciliarism was to be one of the battleground issues of the reformation. Sadly, some of the popes preoccupied themselves with temporal (secular) matters,

11. Grimm, *Reformation Era*, 46–47.

12. Kapr, *Johann Gutenberg*, 59.

13. Grimm, *Reformation Era*, 46.

concerning themselves less with religious affairs. Much of their time and energy were devoted to politics, a trend that was resented by many.[14]

Growth of Humanism

Although humanism was by no means identical with the Reformation, it did much to prepare the way.[15] The beginning of the humanist movement is traceable to one of the famous poets of the fourteenth century, Francesco Petrarch (1307–74), who, drawing his inspiration from ancient writings, particularly Greek and Roman literature, emphasized the importance of education.[16] Petrarch's love for ancient wisdom inspired him to learn Greek. He was struck by the works of Homer, which he translated into Latin for the benefit of his contemporaries who could not read Greek. Petrarch was able to express in his poetry the beauty of nature and the uniqueness of each individual human person.[17]

The work of Petrarch sparked interest in education and the study of languages. Other humanists soon emerged and began to concentrate their energy on literature, biblical exegesis, and general education, their priority being to reform the church. They saw education as the only effective means of achieving this goal. Like Petrarch, the humanists saw good in the human person. The human person, for them, is not just a rational being, but a sentient rational being who can appreciate music, literature, and the arts. The impact of the humanist ideals was felt in Rome. Though some popes seemed hostile to the humanist ideals, others embraced their devotion to music and the arts. During the reign of Sixtus IV (1471–84), for instance, a lot of renovations were carried out in the Palace Chapel of the Vatican.[18] The famous Sistine Chapel was built at this time. Julius II (1503–13) commissioned the building of St. Peter's basilica and the re-painting of the Sistine Chapel by Michelangelo. All these were largely due to the influence of the humanists whose love for music and the arts was unparalleled.[19]

The humanist movement paved the way for what would become the Renaissance (fourteenth to seventeenth centuries). Renaissance is from the Italian *rinascuta*, meaning "rebirth." It was used in reference to the rebirth of the styles of ancient Rome and Greece in the spheres of literature and

14. Holmes and Bickers, *Short History*, 118.
15. Grimm, *Reformation Era*, 85.
16. Holmes and Bickers, *Short History*, 119.
17. Holmes and Bickers, *Short History*, 119.
18. Holmes and Bickers, *Short History*, 121.
19. Holmes and Bickers, *Short History*, 121.

art.[20] Towards the end of the Middle Ages, some Italian cities, Venice and Florence especially, spurred by economic prosperity, on the one hand, and the desire to free themselves from excessive church control (papal domination), on the other, strove for independence from the Holy Roman Empire.[21] They saw no reason why the church should interfere in the secular affairs of the city-states. The humanists turned to the work of Cicero to propound their theory of city-state. "Just as Thomas Aquinas previously had turned to Aristotelian theory to develop the concept of the state, the early civic humanists turned to Cicero."[22] They emphasized the Ciceronian concept of virtues (that virtue which unites wisdom with eloquence) and sharply contrasted it with the Thomistic-Augustinian Christian view of human nature.[23] "Whereas Augustinians saw only human depravity and sin, the humanists believed people, as citizens, could achieve excellence in political and civil society."[24] It was in this new context that the notion of "the Middle Ages' arose. The period between classical culture and the Renaissance now was seen as a sort of cultural depression between two creative periods.

The humanist ideals were expressed in the Renaissance and led to the theory of separation of church and state, separation of temporal and spiritual powers. The most renowned humanist whose work embodied the call for separation between the two powers was the sixteenth-century political writer Niccolò Machiavelli (1469–1527), who believed that the preservation and liberty of the republic are the highest values (common good) that every citizen should do whatever it takes to uphold. He argued that Christianity undermines the citizen's devotion to liberty because it renders people humble and feeble, making them too willing to submit to tyranny. He saw Christianity as something inimical to the preservation of the republic.[25] Machiavelli further opened the conceptual gap between church and state, arguing in *The Prince* (1513)[26] that the state would do better without religion because Christianity corrupted political affairs.[27]

20. Holmes and Bickers, *Short History*, 119.

21. Feldman, *Merry Christmas*, 50.

22. Feldman, *Merry Christmas*, 50.

23. Feldman, *Merry Christmas*, 50.

24. Feldman, *Merry Christmas*, 50.

25. Feldman, *Merry Christmas*, 52.

26. See Machiavelli, *Prince*.

27. Feldman, *Merry Christmas*, 52.

Johann Gutenberg and William Caxton

The birth of Johann Gutenberg (1396–1468) was to be an added impetus to the cause of the humanist movement in the fifteenth century. Gutenberg was born in Mainz (anywhere between 1394 and 1404) where he also went to school and developed a bent for research and discovery.[28] Gutenberg discovered the first printing press in 1450 when he invented a typecasting machine and in 1455 printed the "Gutenberg Bible," also known as the "42-line Bible" because it had forty-two lines to each column.[29] The cause of the humanists, in general, was helped by the discovery of printing, a discovery that was to play a pivotal role during the reformation.

The Englishman William Caxton (1422–91) was another key figure in the printing field. Caxton did not invent printing; he merely introduced it to England.[30] In 1474 he printed, in Cologne, the first book in English, The Histories of Troy. He also established a printing press in Westminster, the place that printed in 1476 The Indulgence of Sixtus IV, the first book printed in England, and in 1484 printed Chaucer's Canterbury Tales.

Erasmus and Thomas More

Most of the fifteenth-century humanists were what was considered then as ordinary non-ordained people. Since they were not ordained members of the church they were virtually free from any kind of censorship that could come from the church. They devoted their time to scholarship and were, for the most part, critical of the church, bringing to light the weaknesses and abuses in the church. They were irked by what was perceived as the ignorance of the clergy and their lack of education. They also spoke out against over-clericalization of the church and some of the popular piety of the time, which in their view, bordered on superstition. Two of the famous humanists of this period were Erasmus, who incidentally was an ordained clergyman, and Thomas More, a lawyer and statesman. These two spoke out against the abuses in the church, called for reform, but refused to be part of the reform movement that severed ties with Rome. One of More's main works was Utopia (1516), a work in which he satirically presented the dilemma of the Christian religion in a world subject to fools as leaders and followers.

Erasmus (1466–1536) was concerned with Christian history. His conception of history was Christocentric. For him, all history was, in a sense,

28. Kapr, Johann Gutenberg, 25.
29. Holmes and Bickers, Short History, 122.
30. Blake, Caxton and His World, 13.

Christian history. He saw Christian history as proceeding in the wrong direction. "In the Middle Ages, especially in the last few centuries, faith had grown cold, and humanity had become distracted by care for mere outward things. Erasmus saw it as his task, at least in his mature years, to direct the process and to lay the foundations for liberation of the soul."[31] In his view, sacred and cultural history were inextricably intertwined and he saw in the study of ancient literature, i.e., Greek and Latin classics and the Bible, the restoration of cultural, intellectual, moral, and spiritual standards of the society that had hitherto been in decline because of the neglect of these studies.[32] Erasmus blamed the intellectual decline of the high Middle Ages on the moral degeneration of the Christian world of the time and criticized the clergy and religious for what he perceived as their ignorance, pride, idleness, luxury, and superstition.[33]

The Rise of Mysticism

The medieval church, especially the fourteenth- and fifteenth-century church, witnessed a spiritual revival that blossomed into a mystical piety. Not all popular piety, which the humanists criticized for its superstition, bordered on superstition in the true sense of the word. There was some real genuine piety that led to the rise of mysticism. Mysticism was a natural product of the flourishing monastic life of the period. There were, at least, at the time, two general preconditions for mysticism. The first was the quest for an ascetic life. Ascetic life allows a person to overcome the cravings of the flesh. The second was the quest for a life devoted more to prayer, meditation, and contemplation. Although this interior life is open to everyone, including lay people, it was perceived to be a life that was more easily attained by nuns, monks, anchoresses, and hermits. These could devote more time to prayer, meditation, and contemplation, unlike the lay people whose lives would be dominated more by the affairs of daily life and the needs of the body—food, drink, shelter, children.[34] Though most of the well-known mystics lived in the fourteenth century, their influence was all the more felt in the fifteenth century and greatly impacted the Reformation.

Mystics did not usually attack or criticize the church openly. Most of the mystics that emerged in the Middle Ages "were quiet and scholarly persons, who devoted themselves to study, meditation, and contemplation,

31. Bejczy, *Erasmus and the Middle Ages*, xiii.
32. Bejczy, *Erasmus and the Middle Ages*, xiv.
33. Bejczy, *Erasmus and the Middle Ages*, 96–97.
34. Fanning, *Mystics of the Christian Tradition*, 75.

but who did not set out to convert the entire church to their understanding of the Christian life. Nevertheless, their mere existence and their exemplary lives, coupled with the fact that many of them made little of the ecclesiastical hierarchy, made many wonder whether this was not an alternative way of being Christian."[35]

(a) Brethren of the Common Life

The origin of this group goes back to Gerard Groote (1340–84 CE), who devoted himself to a life of simplicity. Groote studied in Paris and taught briefly in Cologne before he turned to asceticism. His preaching won him a band of followers who adopted a semi-monastic lifestyle known as the Brethren of Common Life.[36] Groote's preaching brought him in conflict with the diocesan clergy and the Mendicants who were bitter about his criticism of their way of life. He was accused of heresy and banned from preaching. His movement, however, continued. His followers spent time in prayer, devotion, and manual labor. They contributed to the mass production of manuscripts and the creation of schools where the best available education of the time was made available to the youth.[37]

The most famous student of the Brethren of the Common life was **Thomas à Kempis** (1380–1471), who was a student in Deventer, in the Netherlands. Though Thomas did not remain a member of the Brethren, he was partly responsible for one of the most famous spiritual classics of the time, *The Imitation of Christ*, a book that invites the reader to seek perfection through an assiduous following of Christ.[38] The book has four main divisions or sections: The first section stresses the need for self-control and aims to help the reader gain inner peace of mind by helping the reader to become humble. The second section deals with the need to persevere through suffering. The third section stresses God's power in aiding us through God's gift of grace. The fourth section deals with the sacrament of Holy Communion and gives the reader three practical exercises to help the reader appreciate the power of God's love.[39]

---

35. González, *History of Christian Thought*, 19.
36. Holmes and Bickers, *Short History*, 124.
37. González, *History of Christian Thought*, 19.
38. Holmes and Bickers, *Short History*, 125.
39. Holmes and Bickers, *Short History*, 125.

(b) German Mysticism

The origin of German mysticism goes back to **Meister Eckhart** (1260–1327/8). Eckhart was born Johannes Eckhart in Tübingen, Germany. He joined the Dominican Order at the age of fifteen and took up studies in Cologne, Germany, where he also taught and was given the title "Meister." Eckhart was a powerful preacher and spiritual director and wrote his works in German and Latin.[40] He later became the Dominican provincial of Saxony and was active in the administration of the Order. His mystical writings emphasized union with God through a mystical union of the soul. His mystical ideas were thought to have had much in common with Eastern thoughts, especially Vedantic Hinduism and Zen Buddhism.[41] The Archbishop of Cologne later accused him of heresy and Pope John XXII condemned several propositions found in his works. This condemnation prevented many from embracing his teaching. His disciples, however, felt that he was not treated fairly and some took up his cause.

One of Eckhart's most famous disciples was **John Tauler** (1300–1361). Tauler did not know Eckhart personally. He only came to know him through his writings. Tauler was born into a wealthy family in Strasbourg, at the time a German city and part of the Roman Empire. He joined the Dominican Order in 1314 and became famous for his preaching and spiritual directions.[42] Tauler, like Eckhart, stressed union with God through mystical union of the soul. He ensured the survival of the core of Meister Eckhart's apophatic mystical theology, admonishing that Christians shun vices, cultivate the virtues, and detach themselves from anything that is not God.[43] For Tauler, union with God is achieved through practical Christian charity.

Another disciple of Eckhart's and contemporary of Tauler's was the highly influential **Henry Suso** (1295–1366) who was born to a noble family in Constance, Switzerland. His real name was Henry von Berg, but he adopted the family name Sus (Latinized into Suso) to honor his mother.[44] Suso joined the Dominican Order in Constance at the tender age of thirteen. He went to Cologne for studies and there encountered Eckhart. He fell in love with the Meister's teaching and

40. Fanning, *Mystics of the Christian Tradition*, 103.

41. Fanning, *Mystics of the Christian Tradition*, 103; see also Eckhart, *Selected Writings*.

42. Fanning, *Mystics of the Christian Tradition*, 104.

43. Fanning, *Mystics of the Christian Tradition*, 104–5.

44. Fanning, *Mystics of the Christian Tradition*, 105.

soon became a loyal disciple. Suso greatly defended the teachings of Eckhart, a defense that brought him in conflict with his Dominican superiors. He wrote a practical book of meditation called *The Little Book of Eternal Wisdom*.[45]

(C) English Mystics

One of the famous English mystics was **Richard Rolle** (1300–1349), a hermit from Yorkshire, who wrote most of his works in English and Latin. He went to school in Oxford but had to drop out because of what he perceived as the "aridity of the curriculum."[46] He considered what was taught at the universities "an arid and barren tower of truth" and turned to true prayer, which he claimed could never be found in another false tower, i.e., the monastery.[47] He became a hermit in Yorkshire where he sought mystical experience with God. He expressed his experience with God with three words: "heat," "sweetness," and "song" (*calor, dulcor, canor*). Rolle was also a prolific writer. Some of his works include *The Fire of Love* and *The Emending of Life*. He also wrote several mystical works and scriptural commentaries.[48] He served as spiritual advisor and counselor to many Christians at the time. He extolled the solitary life as the surest way of experiencing God. He died in 1349, during the Black Death.[49]

There was a popular book at the time that was very much in the tradition of Richard Rolle, but not written by him: *The Cloud of Unknowing*. Though the author of the book is still unknown, it stresses the need to know God, not by reason, but by God's self-revelation, stressing also the need for contemplation and prayer.[50] The author of this work must have known the mystical theology of Pseudo-Dionysius because he or she refers to Dionysius by name. The author must have also been familiar with the apophatic approach of Pseudo-Dionysius who denied that God could be found through intellect and reason. Rather, "the Cloud of unknowing," that surrounds God, the author insists, can be penetrated only by love.[51] The author insists that true prayer means

45. Holmes and Bickers, *Short History*, 123–24.

46. Ward, "English Mystics," 50.

47. Ward, "English Mystics," 51. See Rolle, *Fire of Love*, and Rolle, "Form of Living."

48. Holmes and Bickers, *Short History*, 125–26.

49. Fanning, *Mystics of the Christian Tradition*, 119.

50. Holmes and Bickers, *Short History*, 126.

51. Fanning, *Mystics of the Christian Tradition*, 124.

an increase in love, a love that goes beyond knowledge, leading to a new way of understanding or responding to God's call of love.[52]

Another influential English mystic was the lady **Julian of Norwich** (1342–1413). Her actual name is unknown. She is referred to as Julian only because of her association with the church of St. Julian in Norwich.[53] She told the story of how she became ill at the age of thirty and during her illness fell into a trance lasting about five hours during which she received fifteen revelations. She received another vision the following day and after years of reflecting on her visions wrote *The Revelation of Divine Love*. Her book stresses belief in the passion and cross of Christ and the eventual triumph of love as seen in the final expulsion of evil.[54] Julian may have had a single, near-death mystical experience, an experience that completely changed her life, making her to become an anchoress in a single-room cell attached to the church of St. Julian.[55] Julian was noted for having popularized the feminine imagery of God. She constantly referred to God as mother, a maternal imagery that goes back to Paul and the Hebrew Scriptures. But Julian emphasized it more frequently that she became associated with it.

Popular Piety

Due in part to the influence of the mystics and the spiritual classics that were circulating in the fifteenth century, two major themes dominated the preaching manuals of the time: Death and Judgment. The preachers of the gospel were primarily concerned with preparing people for death. They encouraged the dying person not to despair at the moment of death, but to look at the crucifix and remind themselves of the death of Christ. They also reminded people the judgment that follows death and stressed in graphic pictures the fate of those who go to heaven and the fate of those who go to hell.[56] In emphasizing the passion and death of Christ they hardly mentioned the resurrection, thereby portraying God, not as a loving Father, but a judge. Even the story of the prodigal son and the good shepherd, which portray God as a loving Father, was hardly ever mentioned. Instead the

52. Ward, "English Mystics," 55. See also Walsh, *Cloud of Unknowing*.

53. Fanning, *Mystics of the Christian Tradition*, 124.

54. Holmes and Bickers, *Short History*, 126.

55. Fanning, *Mystics of the Christian Tradition*, 125.

56. Holmes and Bickers, *Short History*, 127.

people got a good dose of the parable of the last judgment, i.e., the separation of the sheep and goats. This kind of preaching gave the people an image of a distant God, even Christ, the sole mediator between God and his people seemed distant.[57]

Such a terrifying image of God led to a popular piety in which people approached God through the help of mediators. Mary was seen as a person who could help in averting the anger and judgment of this distant and angry God. The Dominicans and Franciscans championed this cause of seeking intercessions through Mary. They stressed the recitation of the rosary. From this Marian devotion also emerged the cult of the saints. "In the Middle Ages its growth was luxuriant, and few valleys, territories, diseases, or professions lacked their specific saint, at once a protector and refuge in difficult times and an embodiment of some aspect of God's truth to be emulated."[58] The saints were seen as friends the people could turn to for help, so much so that with time some saints began to be associated with some specific skills. The early venerated saints were largely martyrs, except for St. Martin of Tours who was born about four years after the conversion of Constantine and who died in 397 CE.[59] People turned to these saints for different favors. For instance, people turned to St. Dennis when they had headache because he was known for averting headaches, St. Vitus was for people suffering from epilepsy, St. Barbara for people afraid of lightning, St. Christopher for those in need of safe journey, and St. Margaret for people suffering from insanity.[60] Superstition aside, there were those who genuinely saw the saints as God's continuing revelation, each saint's life revealing something universal in something particular.[61]

Although the material remains of martyrs (relics) were accorded great respect in the early church by Christians who celebrated the Eucharist over the tombs of the martyrs, devotion to the saints in the medieval church increased the importance attached to relics. There was increase in the demand for relics and in some cases some dismembered the saints' bodies and transferred them from place to place just to meet the demand for relics. People who went to Rome for pilgrimage often came back with bones and other objects of the saints. It was often not easy to verify such claims. Some saints were associated with particular shrines to which people made pilgrimages. Relics and pilgrimages were connected with indulgences. People believed

57. Holmes and Bickers, *Short History*, 127.

58. Olsen, *Beginning at Jerusalem*, 49.

59. Olsen, *Beginning at Jerusalem*, 50–51.

60. Holmes and Bickers, *Short History*, 127–28.

61. Olsen, *Beginning at Jerusalem*, 51.

they could be released from their temporary punishment from sin if they had particular relics or made particular pilgrimages. The reformers were quick to point out the abuses of such practice.[62]

In the early church the Eucharist was the center of the church's liturgical life. It was primarily community worship, the whole community gathered around the local bishop as a sign of this unity. The fifteenth-century church seemed to depart from this practice. There was a fundamental change in the way the Eucharist was celebrated and also notable abuses. One of the abuses was the rise of "Private Mass," where the priest alone celebrated the mass in private. There was also the barrier that came from the use of Latin as the sole language of the liturgy. The bread used for mass was replaced with a thin wafer. The priest stopped offering the chalice to the laity. The laity was discouraged from receiving communion on a regular basis lest they receive it unworthily. There was also the fact of language. Given that the language of worship was Latin, people no longer understood what was going on at mass and depended on the priest for their understanding.

There were also some architectural changes: the priest now said mass with his back towards the people because altars were placed against the East Wall, side altars were built to facilitate private masses, communion rails were introduced, which mandated that the people kneel to receive communion in their tongue, "rood screens" were erected, which heightened the sense of awe, but also further increased the distance between the people and the priest. Emphasis was shifted from receiving communion to "seeing" the host. In an attempt to accommodate this, elevations of the consecrated host now lasted longer and bells were rung to remind people that elevation was going on. When bells rang, people rushed to catch a glimpse of the host in the belief that their fortunes would change for the better. In spite of the good intentions of these practices, a great deal of superstition crept into the Mass.[63] There was, to say the least, a great deal of change in the liturgy in the fourteenth/fifteenth century. Some were positive changes, but a great deal bordered on superstition and abuses. The humanists and the reformers were quick to highlight these deficiencies but their call for change was stymied by the papacy.

SOCIAL CHANGES IN EUROPE

Remarkable change took place in the social structure of Europe at the end of the fifteenth century. The population of western Europe that was hitherto

---

62. Holmes and Bickers, *Short History*, 128.

63. Holmes and Bickers, *Short History*, 128–29.

fifty-three million in 1350 had risen to about seventy million in the 1500s. There was an uneven distribution of wealth. Most wealth was concentrated in the hands of a few. For the poor and underprivileged, the standard of living took a turn for the worse. This led to a lot of disaffection among the poor and underprivileged.[64] Much of the dissatisfaction among Europeans at the end of the fifteenth century and the beginning of the sixteenth century centered on economic changes. The economic prosperity that was achieved in the thirteenth century was giving way to a prolonged period of economic depression, caused largely by plagues and farming, and even wars, which greatly decreased the population and hampered trade.[65] While the majority of the people were suffering from deprivation, the rich landowners and traders were amassing more and more wealth. This further enlarged the gulf between the rich and the poor, the lower class and the aristocracy. "The peasants, who had retrogressed rather than advanced in status since the thirteenth century, joined the malcontented groups whenever the opportunity to register protests presented itself."[66]

On the positive side, important discoveries took place at this time as well. These were phenomenal discoveries of new lands led and championed by Spain and Portugal. The discoveries led to a Commercial Revolution—rapid increase in commercial activities in Europe and the new found lands.[67] Portugal established trading posts in Africa, thanks to people like Bartolomeu Dias (1450–1500), who sailed around the coast of Africa and established the Cape of Good Hope in 1487. In 1488 Vasco da Gama (d. 1524) discovered India by sailing off the eastern coast of Africa, and Pedro Cabral (1467–1520) discovered the coast of Brazil and South America in 1500. The Italian explorers and navigators Christopher Columbus (1451–1506) and John Cabot (d. 1498) circumnavigated the world. Columbus made four voyages from 1492 to 1502 and sailed to places like the West Indies, Panama, Trinidad, and the northern coast of South America. The discoveries of Columbus were to be followed by the discovery of other Spanish explorers of such places as Yucatan, Mexico, Florida, and the lands along the Rio Grande and Colorado rivers of North America, as well as some South American countries.[68] These voyages gave Spain much control of the New World.[69] Although the English did not follow the discoveries

---

64. Holmes and Bickers, *Short History*, 130.

65. Grimm, *Reformation Era*, 6.

66. Grimm, *Reformation Era*, 6.

67. Grimm, *Reformation Era*, 6.

68. Grimm, *Reformation Era*, 8.

69. Grimm, *Reformation Era*, 8.

of Cabot with territorial claims in the New World or the Far East until the middle of the sixteenth century, the discoveries and expansions themselves increased trade and commerce, leading to the emergence of a strong middle class. A strong middle class deeply altered the existing social order.

In 1493 Pope Alexander VI divided the discovered lands between Spain and Portugal.[70] National consciousness or the spirit of nationalism now reigned supreme. In Spain the marriage between Ferdinand of Aragon and Isabella of Castile not only united the two most powerful families in Spain, but also heightened national pride, especially when Spain controlled almost the whole of the Iberian Peninsula.[71] This enabled Spain to follow the lead of Portugal in establishing colonial empire in places like Africa. England at this time was still reeling from Henry Tudor's success in the 1485 War of the Roses. The twenty-four-year rule of Henry Tudor gave England a new spirit of national consciousness. The landscape of Europe was changing and the world was changing socially, economically and politically.[72] All these changes also paved way for a church in need of change.

The social position of the clergy also added impetus to the reform movement. There was in the sixteenth century a big gulf between the clergy and the laity. "By means of a number of election decrees, the laity had been excluded from the administrative affairs of the church, which consequently became in personnel, cult, and culture intrinsically a church of priests."[73] Lay people were further and further distanced from the mass, their role became more of onlookers than that of worthy participants. A good number of the clergy had enriched themselves and their attention focused more on secular matters. "It is no wonder that many townsmen looked upon the clergy as hoarders of wealth who drained their cities and lands of gold and silver. The poorer classes also often resented the wealth, as well as the tremendous power which the clergy exercised over them 'from the cradle to the grave.'"[74] The situation with the hierarch was far worse, a situation into which Martin Luther was born:

> The pope, as the absolute ruler over the clergy and all the church lands, ranked among the highest monarchs of Christendom, while his magnificent court in Rome became the envy of the most powerful kings. The cardinals, the high officials in the papal Curia, the archbishops, bishops, and abbots, and all the

70. Holmes and Bickers, *Short History*, 131.

71. Holmes and Bickers, *Short History*, 131.

72. Holmes and Bickers, *Short History*, 131.

73. Grimm, *Reformation Era*, 17.

74. Grimm, *Reformation Era*, 18.

higher clergy throughout Europe lived on a relatively high social plane. Usually men of noble birth who had obtained their positions through political influence or by the expenditure of large sums of money, they lived on a par with kings and princes. This was particularly true in western Germany, where, for example, the archbishops of Mainz, Trier, and Cologne were also electors in the Holy Roman Empire and ruled their territories like kings.[75]

Martin Luther (1483–1546)

Martin Luther was born in the town of Mansfeld, in Saxony, Germany, on November 10, 1483, at a time when the wind of change was blowing. It was a time when national consciousness was gaining ground and central authority of Christendom with its concentration of power on the pope was seriously challenged.[76] Luther was baptized a day after his birth and named after St. Martin of Tours. His parents gave him a very strict, conservative, and puritanical religious upbringing. As a child, Luther feared God whom he saw as a judge. His family moved to Mansfeld where he went to school. At the age of fourteen Luther moved to Magdeburg to continue his education and attended a school run by the Brethren of the Common Life. He went to the University of Erfurt where he came under the influence of Ockhamism. There he got his bachelor's and master's degrees. Luther entered the Reformed Monastery of the Augustinians at Erfurt, in spite of his father's objections.[77] His father wanted him to pursue a career in law but Luther instead chose to become a monk after a frightening experience during a thunderstorm in which he feared he would die without receiving the sacraments.[78] Erfurt was at the time a leading center of monastic ideal among Augustinians, an institution that stresses the fact of human sinfulness and the need of salvation effected only by the intervention of grace in Christ Jesus.[79] Luther made his religious profession in 1506 and in 1507 was ordained a priest. He was haunted by his fears and scruples and was convinced of his own unworthiness.

As a monk, Luther was pious and faithful to his monastic vocation. He was, however, haunted by what he recognized to be his sinfulness. Luther

75. Grimm, *Reformation Era*, 18.

76. Holmes and Bickers, *Short History*, 132.

77. Holmes and Bickers, *Short History*, 132–33.

78. McEnhill and Newlands, *Fifty Key Christian Thinkers*, 180.

79. McEnhill and Newlands, *Fifty Key Christian Thinkers*, 180.

meticulously followed the church's prescribed penitential rites but was never satisfied because he thought his sins were still with him. He always felt he was not good enough and that no matter how contrite he was or how faithful he adhered to the rules of his order that his sins were still with him. Luther feared for his salvation because he felt that he was not contrite enough and that even when he confessed his sins there was always something he omitted. He seemed to have been troubled by what was known in the theology manuals of the time as scrupulous conscience. He "could not understand how he, a sinner, could make an act of sufficient contrition or penance that would satisfy a righteous and just God. The righteousness of God was a fearsome concept that hung over Luther like a cloud, for he believed that he could do nothing that could please such a God. If God was truly righteous and just and judged everyone impartially then surely God could only condemn the sinner that Luther knew himself to be."[80]

Luther acknowledged the enormous influence Johann Staupitz, the Vicar-General of the Augustinians and professor of Scripture at Wittenberg University, had on him during his formative years. Staupitz tried to help Luther overcome his fears. In 1508 Luther became professor of moral theology at Wittenberg. In 1510 he was sent to Rome to represent Erfurt at a conference of Augustinians. Luther recounts how in Rome he was shocked by the "abomination of the papacy," which he saw firsthand. Luther received his doctorate in theology in 1512 and succeeded Staupitz as professor of Scripture at Wittenberg University. Luther became more convinced that faith alone justified a person and nothing could alter that fact. He stressed the primacy of the Word of God over anything else.

Luther had a revelation experience, the famous "Tower Experience," while studying in the tower of the monastery in Wittenberg. His experience taught him that it is God who justifies one by God's gift of faith. This changed, in his mind, the picture of God whom he had feared as a judge from his youth. Now salvation, he realized, was a free gift of God; faith alone, not a person's works, brought justification before God. This realization gave him the courage to speak out against the so called "Indulgence Preachers." In 1505 Pope Julius II (1503–13) in rebuilding St. Peter's Basilica in Rome announced the issuance of indulgences (granting of "spiritual" benefits) to help finance the cost. In 1514 Albert of Magdeburg paid a huge amount of money to the curia to become the archbishop of Mainz. Part of his deal with the curia was to allow preachers to come to his diocese and preach indulgences. Tetzel, the Dominican priest, preached indulgences to help build the Basilica of St. Peter, and many flocked to hear him. Luther took

80. McEnhill and Newlands, *Fifty Key Christian Thinkers*, 181.

exception to the indulgences. He wrote the Archbishop of Mainz criticizing the way indulgences were being preached. He also sent to the Archbishop a copy of the Ninety-Five Theses, which he wrote to clarify the teaching on indulgences. The Archbishop failed to act and Tetzel dismissed Luther's objection as heretical. Legend has it that Luther nailed his famous Ninety-Five Theses to the door of the church in Wittenberg with the hope that it would encourage academic and scholarly discussion, especially regarding the sale of indulgences.[81]

Luther was ordered to Rome on August 7, 1518 after attempts to silence him failed. He openly challenged the authority of the Pope and some church practices. These forced him into a series of debates with prominent church members—the Heidelberg Disputation of 1518, the Leipzig Disputation of 1519 in which he debated John Eck, and the debate with Erasmus on the Freedom of the Will, which led to the publication in 1524 of *De Servo Arbitrio*.[82] Pope Leo X sent Cardinal Cajetan to Germany to try Luther in Germany. Luther and Cajetan met in Augsburg and the meeting ended inconclusively. "The meeting in Augsburg was a disappointment, because Cajetan did not allow Luther to debate the issues, but only gave him an opportunity to recant. When the interview was finished rumor reached Luther that the Cardinal was empowered to arrest him, so by night Luther escaped from Augsburg."[83] Cajetan asked the secular ruler of Saxony, Frederick the Wise, to extradite Luther to Rome. Frederick the Wise rejected the appeal of Cardinal Cajetan to either extradite Luther or banish him from his territory. Frederick the Wise held Luther in protective custody. "The Roman curia now tried diplomatic means to settle the affair. A series of negotiations and debates followed, culminating in Luther's hearing before the German Diet (or Parliament) in the town of Worms in 1521."[84] But Rome had already pre-judged the issue without waiting for the hearing, and in 1520 sent a papal bull to Luther declaring that he was a heretic and was excommunicated from the church.[85] In the same year (1520) Luther wrote "An Open Letter to German Nobility" in which he claimed that the Roman church had erected three 'walls,' which had effectively blocked all attempts to reform. These three 'walls' were (i) the claim that spiritual jurisdiction was superior to the secular (ii) that the pope was the sole interpreter of scripture and (iii) that the pope alone could summon a general council. In October of the

---

81. McEnhill and Newlands, *Fifty Key Christian Thinkers*, 184.

82. McEnhill and Newlands, *Fifty Key Christian Thinkers*, 184.

83. Grosshans, *Luther*, 6.

84. Grosshans, *Luther*, 7.

85. Grosshans, *Luther*, 7.

same year Luther published *The Babylonian Captivity of the Church* where he denied the seven sacraments and charged that the Roman church had "shackled" the Eucharist by refusing the chalice to the laity, maintaining the doctrine of transubstantiation, and reducing the Mass to a "good work."[86]

The June 1520 the bull *Exsurge Domine*, which Leo X issued, condemned forty-one of Luther's theses as heretical. Luther responded by making a last attempt to come to peace with Rome and wrote "The Freedom of a Christian," a kind of diplomatic letter that summarizes his theology. In it he stressed his three major doctrines: primacy of scripture, justification by faith alone, and priesthood of all believers. On January 3, 1521, Luther was formally excommunicated and he severed himself from the church in 1524 when he married ex-Cistercian nun, Katherine von Bora. Luther assumed leadership of the Reformation in Wittenberg and the whole of Germany.[87] His books were burnt in some cities in Germany, while he remained under the protective custody of Frederick the Wise in Saxony. His excommunication was to be "the beginning of the division in the church which was to lead to the formation of the new Protestant Churches, and was to influence dramatically the political history of Europe and beyond."[88]

Ulrich Zwingli (1484–1531)

Ulrich Zwingli was born in 1484 in Wildhaus, a village high in the Alps of the Toggenburg, a duchy allied with the Swiss Confederacy.[89] He was educated at the universities of Basle and Vienna where he was introduced to the scholastic style education and the newly emerging humanist approach to faith and learning.[90] He was ordained to the priesthood in 1506 and served as chaplain to the Swiss mercenary forces that fought at the battles of Novaro (1513) and Marignano (1515).[91] The carnage that he witnessed as chaplain made him to be critical of the Swiss practice of using mercenary soldiers to fight foreign wars, even in the name of the Pope.[92] In 1515 he met Erasmus, the emerging scholar and leading figure of humanism in Europe, and both

---

86. Holmes and Bickers, *Short History*, 136–37.

87. Holmes and Bickers, *Short History*, 148.

88. Grosshans, *Luther*, 7.

89. Lindberg, *European Reformations*, 170.

90. McEnhill and Newlands, *Fifty Key Christian Thinkers*, 269.

91. McEnhill and Newlands, *Fifty Key Christian Thinkers*, 270.

92. McEnhill and Newlands, *Fifty Key Christian Thinkers*, 270.

discussed the many abuses in the church and the overtly military nature of Pope Julius' reign.[93]

Zwingli went to Zurich in 1519 where he preached against the abuses in the church. In the same year he came in contact with Luther's work. Though he claimed to have been independent of Luther, contact with Luther's works no doubt intensified many of the issues he was addressing. Unlike Luther, he did not have trouble with conscience. In fact, he was said to have had sexual lapses even as a young priest. An accusation was brought against him in 1518 when he was called to be the preacher at the Great Minster in Zurich. In his defense, Zwingli regretted his failure to fulfill his vow of celibacy and argued that although he was guilty of sexual immorality, he had never defiled a virgin, a nun, or a married woman.[94] He demanded primacy of the Word, rejected the authority of the pope, clerical celibacy, invocation of the saints, fasting, the doctrine of purgatory and monasticism, and the sacrifice of the Mass. Zwingli became the leader of the Swiss reform. In 1525 the Roman Mass was abolished and replaced with Zwingli's communion service. Zwingli rejected the idea of real presence and accepted "symbolic" presence.[95] Zwingli is noted for the so-called Affair of the Sausages.

> During Lent of 1522, Zwingli was at the house of Christoph Froschauer, a printer who was laboring over the preparation of a new edition of the epistles of Paul. In order to refresh his dozen tired workers, Froschauer served sausages. Was it just coincidence that the number of participants and the manner of distribution recalled the Lord's Supper? This public breaking of the Lenten fast flouted both medieval piety and ecclesiastical and public authority. The Zurich town council arrested Froschauer, but not Zwingli, who himself had not eaten the meat. Zwingli, who held the eminent post of people's priest at the Great Minster church in Zurich, could have smoothed everything out. Instead, he made a public issue out of the incident by preaching a sermon, "On the Choice and Freedom of Foods" (23 March 1522), that was soon enlarged into a printed pamphlet (16 April 1522). Almost certainly influenced by Luther's earlier (1520) treatise on Christian freedom, Zwingli argued that Christians are free to fast or not to fast because the Bible does not prohibit the eating of meat during Lent. "In a word, if you will fast, do so; if you do

93. McEnhill and Newlands, *Fifty Key Christian Thinkers*, 270.

94. McEnhill and Newlands, *Fifty Key Christian Thinkers*, 271.

95. Holmes and Bickers, *Short History*, 139.

not wish to eat meat, eat it not; but leave Christians a free choice in the matter."[96]

John Calvin

John Calvin was born in the Cathedral city of Noyon (northeast of Paris) in 1509. His father was the notary and solicitor to the Bishop and Cathedral chapter at Noyon and he used his influence with the bishop to secure chaplaincies and benefices for Calvin and his other two brothers.[97] Calvin's father was excommunicated in 1528 because of suspicion of financial and other irregularities.[98] At the time of Calvin's birth in 1509, Henry VIII was king of England, Louis XII king of France, Ferdinand king of Spain, Julius II was pope, and the young Luther was twenty-six years old.[99] Calvin went to Paris in 1523 to continue his education. He enrolled in the Sorbonne in 1528. Soon after he left for Orleans to study law and completed this study in 1532.[100] Calvin soon came in contact with humanist philosophy and made friends like Pierre Robert and Melchior Wolmar who had identified themselves with the Reformation and were sympathetic to the ideals of reform in the church.[101]

After his studies, Calvin encountered a little problem with the local authorities, a problem that forced him to leave France entirely. But after his father's death in 1531 he returned to Paris to continue his literary studies and in 1532 published his first work, *De Clementia*, a work that betrayed his indebtedness to the humanist ideals.[102] "It is not clear, however, precisely when Calvin moved from being a humanistically inclined Catholic, with moderate intentions to reform the Church, to being someone who was wholeheartedly identified with the Protestant cause."[103] The only clue we have was his statement in the preface to the *Commentary on the Psalms* (1537) where he referred to himself as "someone obstinate in their attachment to the Church of Rome until God made his heart teachable."[104]

96. Lindberg, *European Reformations*, 169.

97. McEnhill and Newlands, *Fifty Key Christian Thinkers*, 91.

98. Holmes and Bickers, *Short History*, 141.

99. Holmes and Bickers, *Short History*, 141.

100. Holmes and Bickers, *Short History*, 141.

101. McEnhill and Newlands, *Fifty Key Christian Thinkers*, 91.

102. McEnhill and Newlands, *Fifty Key Christian Thinkers*, 92.

103. McEnhill and Newlands, *Fifty Key Christian Thinkers*, 92.

104. McEnhill and Newlands, *Fifty Key Christian Thinkers*, 92.

In 1534 Calvin fled France for Switzerland when the French authorities initiated a fresh persecution against the reformers and their allies. Calvin at first settled in the Swiss city of Basle where he published *The Institutes of Christian Religion* (1536), a systematic presentation of his reformed theology. In 1537 he went to Geneva and submitted to the city authorities his Articles on Ecclesiastical Organization.[105] The city authorities were not receptive to his confessional statement and he was forbidden to preach and banished from Geneva in 1538. Martin Bucer, one of the leading figures of the Reformation, invited him to Strasbourg. His association with Bucer put him in contact with the Lutheran scholar, Melanchthon, another leader of the reform movement. In 1541 he was invited back to Geneva by the city authorities to reform that city according to the principles of Holy Scripture.[106] In 1559 Calvin became a citizen of Geneva and became the head of the reform movement in the city. He was noted for his doctrine of predestination, his work on the Trinity, the Person and Work of Christ, the Word and Sacraments, and the church. He died in 1564, but not until he had transformed Geneva as the capital of Swiss reform.

John Knox (1513–72)

John Knox was born in 1513 in Scotland. He was educated in Glasgow where he came under the influence of the reformers. Knox fled England during the reign of Queen Mary Tudor. While in exile he met Calvin. He returned to England in 1559 after the death of Mary and continued his reformed policies. He persuaded the Scottish parliament to abolish the mass, reject papal authority and accept his Confession of Faith.

The English Reformation

The reformation going on in England was by and large different from that going on in the continent in that the reformation in England was an act of the state, under the leadership of the king, who was supported by the parliament.[107] Most historians agree that the English Reformation began more as a political rather than a religious dispute.[108] The Reformation began with Henry VIII, King of England (1509–47), who was far from being a religious

105. McEnhill and Newlands, *Fifty Key Christian Thinkers*, 92.

106. McEnhill and Newlands, *Fifty Key Christian Thinkers*, 93.

107. Holmes and Bickers, *Short History*, 148.

108. Feldman, *Merry Christmas*, 81.

revolutionary.[109] Though the Reformation began as an act of the state, the point also has to be made that neither England nor Scotland was isolated from the reformations taking place in the European continent, and as such the initiation and advance of reformation ideas and convictions did not begin with nor completely dependent on royal actions alone.[110]

The fifteenth-century church in England experienced the same abuses and problems as the rest of Europe: absenteeism, low moral standards, lack of education among the clergy, ignorance and superstition.[111] At the center of the English Reformation was King Henry VIII, who needed papal dispensation to have his marriage to Catherine of Aragon annulled so he could marry his new love, Anne Boleyn.

Though he was the King of England, Henry had some training in theology. In 1521, when he was still part of the Roman Catholic Church, Henry defended the sacraments of the Roman Catholic Church against Luther's attack in a work he published under the title, Assertion of the Seven Sacraments. At the time he received accolades from Pope Leo X who declared Henry the "Defender of the Faith." But a series of events that would scuttle Henry's love affair with Rome began when Henry needed a dispensation from the Pope to divorce Catherine of Aragon. Before he married Catherine in the first place, Henry needed a papal dispensation to marry Catherine, who was a widow of Henry's older brother. Now Henry needed another dispensation to divorce the same woman. He sought this dispensation in 1527 on two grounds. "First, he had fallen in love with Anne Boleyn; second, he wished to have a male heir. Catherine was unlikely to have any more children, and to that point she had borne Henry only one surviving daughter, Mary. Since divorce as we currently know it did not exist then, Henry claimed that from a religious standpoint, the marriage had been invalid at the outset and that the pope should therefore officially annul it."[112] When the pope, for political (the Emperor of the Roman Empire, Charles V, was Catherine's nephew, and the pope was not inclined to offend Charles V) and religious reasons, refused to grant this dispensation, Henry VIII, with the help of his Lord Chancellor Thomas Cromwell (1485–1540), transferred ecclesiastical jurisdiction from the hand of the pope to the crown and declared himself the supreme head of the Church of England. In August 1532, Henry divorced Catherine, and married Anne Boleyn in a secret marriage supervised by Thomas Cranmer, the Archbishop of Canterbury. Henry had

---

109. Feldman, *Merry Christmas*, 81.

110. Lindberg, *European Reformations*, 309.

111. Holmes and Bickers, *Short History*, 148.

112. Feldman, *Merry Christmas*, 80.

a daughter by Anne Boleyn, Elizabeth (who later became Queen Elizabeth). Pope Clement VII condemned Cranmer's action, denounced Henry's second marriage, and excommunicated him. Henry enacted series of legislations that led to the final separation with Rome.[113] He solidified England's break from Rome by procuring several key parliamentary enactments, the most important of which was the 1534 Act of Supremacy, which declared that "the king's majesty justly and rightfully is and ought to be the supreme head of the Church of England."[114]

John Wycliffe (1329–84)

Though the reformation in England was an act of the state, there were some notable individuals who worked relentlessly to bring about reform. One such man was the Oxford reformer John Wycliffe. Wycliffe was critical of the abuses in the church and did not hide his disdain for papal authority. He believed that everyone had the right to study the Bible, insisting that the Bible was the sole authority in a Christian's life. The medieval church used the Latin version of the Bible, the Vulgate. The Vulgate was prepared by St. Jerome, at the request of Pope Damasus (ca. 382 CE). Jerome translated the New Testament from the Greek, and in 405 produced Latin Old Testament translated from the Hebrew.[115]

Wycliffe made attempts to translate the Bible into English. "He and his followers, the Lollards, emphasized in their preaching the supreme authority of the Scriptures. But to 'search the scriptures' men needed a Bible in their own tongue."[116] Wycliffe and his followers made two translations of the Vulgate available in English. The first translation (1381–83) was a word-for-word rendering of the Vulgate, and the second translation (1395) was "less literal and less Latinate."[117] In 1408 the Synod of Oxford forbade translation of the Bible into English; failure to comply earned one the ignoble charge of heresy.[118]

---

113. Holmes and Bickers, *Short History*, 148.

114. Feldman, *Merry Christmas*, 80.

115. Thompson, *Bible in English*, 2.

116. Thompson, *Bible in English*, 2.

117. Thompson, *Bible in English*, 2.

118. Thompson, *Bible in English*, 2.

William Tyndale (1493–1536)[119]

The first real English translation of the Bible was undertaken by William Tyndale, and through the efforts of Miles Coverdale the first printed English Bible appeared in England in 1535.[120] William Tyndale was a student at Oxford where he earned his BA in 1512 and MA in 1515. After earning his MA Tyndale sought "the brighter air of Cambridge, where Erasmus had recently taught Greek (1511–14)."[121] At Cambridge Tyndale had the desire to translate the Bible into the vernacular, having been inspired by Erasmus' Latin translation of the Greek New Testament and Luther's German translation of the Bible. Tyndale sought the permission of the bishop of London, Cuthbert Tunstall, to translate the Bible into English. His initial attempt was rejected by the bishop, who was reputed to have said "we must root out printing or printing will root out us."[122]

Tyndale was thought to be a linguistic genius who spoke so many languages: Hebrew, Greek, Latin, Italian, Spanish, English, French, and German.[123] Tyndale needed the authorization of his bishop to proceed because the Constitutions of Oxford (1407–9) against Wycliffe's translations of the Vulgate were still in force.[124] When he could not obtain the support of the bishop of London for this task he accepted the financial assistance of a London merchant[125] and fled to Germany, where he could more freely publish his translations and get them smuggled back home.[126] In 1525 he translated the New Testament into English.

> Just as Luther had pointed out in the first of the Ninety-Five Theses that the sacrament of penance rested on a mistranslation of the Greek, so too did Tyndale translate the Greek metanoeite by "repent" instead of the Vulgate's "do penance" (*poenitentiam*

119. The actual year of Tyndale's birth seems to be in dispute. A newly discovered record of his ordination to the priesthood in 1515 suggests that he was born in 1491, not 1493. See Day et al., *Word, Church, and State*, ix. See also Brown, *William Tyndale on Priest and Preachers*.

120. Holmes and Bickers, *Short History*, 149. Although the Vulgate was in use in the medieval church it was not made official until the sixteenth century, when the Council of Trent declared it the authentic Bible (1546), and in 1592 Pope Clement VIII issued a revised and official text.

121. Day et al., *Word, Church, and State*, ix.

122. Lindberg, *European Reformations*, 313–14.

123. Lindberg, *European Reformations*, 314.

124. Day et al., *Word, Church, and State*, ix.

125. Grimm, *Reformation Era*, 290.

126. Day et al., *Word, Church, and State*, ix–x.

agite). Likewise, just as Luther consistently used "congregation" or "community" instead of "church," so Tyndale translated the Greek ekklesia as "congregation." The Catholic establishment was further undermined by Tyndale's translation of the Greek *presbyteros* as "elder" rather than as "priest."[127]

Tyndale also translated Luther's works (which had been banned) and made them available in English. He was arrested on October 6, 1536 and burned at stake. He was accused, among other things, of rejecting papal authority. A good number of his works, however, especially the first half of the Old Testament and the entire New Testament, was incorporated into the King James Bible.[128]

Miles Coverdale (1488–1568)

Miles Coverdale was originally an Augustinian friar at Cambridge. He worked with Tyndale to translate the Old Testament and was responsible for the first complete translation of the Bible in 1535.[129] He was born in either 1487 or 1488 in or very near the city of York.[130] It is not clear why Coverdale chose to join the Augustinians. But "in light of his youthful attitude toward learning, quite possibly the order's well-known respect for scholarly studies played a significant role in his choice."[131] He was ordained a priest in 1514 and was assigned to Cambridge. It was probably at this time that Coverdale came into contact with Tyndale.[132]

THE CATHOLIC REFORM

By the middle of the sixteenth century the reformers were beginning to win more and more converts and the Catholic Church was increasingly becoming disillusioning to many. In spite of Pope Leo X's initial dismissal of the Reformation as "nothing other than a drunken brawl among German Monks," there was a growing realization even among the hierarchy that the church was in need of renewal and reform.[133] The Catholics knew it was

---

127. Lindberg, *European Reformations*, 314.

128. Day et al., *Word, Church, and State*, x.

129. Day et al., *Word, Church, and State*, 315.

130. Worth, *Church, Monarch and Bible*, 43.

131. Worth, *Church, Monarch and Bible*, 43.

132. Worth, *Church, Monarch and Bible*, 43.

133. Lindberg, *European Reformations*, 335.

time to put their house in order. Historians refer to the Catholic reform movement as Catholic Reformation or Catholic Counter-Reformation. Perhaps it should be pointed out that the Catholic renewal movement was not necessarily a reaction, a Counter-Reformation,[134] for the fact that even before Luther the Church had produced reform-minded individuals who had set in motion the Catholic renewal movement. Giles of Viterbo, for instance, at the opening of the fifth Lateran Council, candidly addressed Pope Julius II and the other prelates present with the words: "Unless by this Council or by some other means we place a limit on our morals, unless we force our greedy desire for human things, the source of evils, to yield to the love of divine things, it is all over with Christendom."[135] This appeal for personal renewal as the key to reform and renewal in the Church was characteristic of the Catholic reform efforts both before and after Luther.[136]

The first reform movement in the Catholic Church began with the religious orders. The old Orders, the mendicants in particular, began to reform. The reform among the Franciscans, for instance, led to the emergence of the Capuchins. In 1574 the Capuchins received papal permission to establish houses outside Italy and in 1619 were recognized as a separate order distinct from the Franciscans. The French Cistercians also reformed in 1580 as well as the Benedictines. In Spain John of the Cross (1542–91) and Teresa of Avila (1515–82) led the reform of the Carmelites. New religious orders and congregations emerged at the end of the fifteenth century, mostly in Latin (as against Germanic) countries. They engaged in active, rather than contemplative, apostolate, devoting their attention to preaching, teaching and the needs of the poor. The most influential of the religious orders at this time was the newly formed Society of Jesus or the Jesuits who became the agent of Catholic-Reformation.[137]

The Society of Jesus was founded by St. Ignatius of Loyola (1491–1556). Ignatius was born in 1491 into a noble family in the Basque region of Spain. While fighting in the siege of Pamplona in 1521 he was severely injured. He went to Monserrat after recovering from his illness and began writing the *Spiritual Exercises* in 1522, which was to be the central core of Jesuit spirituality. His idea was to form soldiers who would find God in all things and do all things for the greater glory of God, i.e., people who would not acquiesce to the temptations and conflicting attractions of world culture.[138]

134. Lindberg, *European Reformations*, 335.

135. Olin, *Catholic Reform*, 57. See also Lindberg, *European Reformations*, 335.

136. Lindberg, *European Reformations*, 336.

137. Homes and Bickers, *Short History of the Catholic Church*, 162.

138. Olsen, *Beginning at Jerusalem*, 134.

The Society of Jesus was formally recognized in 1540. Their numbers increased in leaps and bounds and they sent members to such places as India, Brazil, Japan, and China. The Jesuits supported the papacy, founded colleges in Rome (1551) and France (1556) for the training of the clergy. They preached, often using the same methods as the Protestants, and became valuable instrument for the reform movement in the Church.[139]

The Catholic Church also responded to the Protestant Reformation by some controversial means. Pope Paul IV, who has been termed the first of the Counter-Reformation Popes and in whose pontificate the Catholic renewal movement centered on repression and earned the label, "Counter-Reformation," introduced the *Index Librorum Prohibitorium* (Index of Prohibited Books) in addition to the Inquisition, the juridical persecution of heresy by special ecclesiastical courts whose roots go back to the thirteenth century proceedings against the Catharist heresy.[140] Paul IV was convinced that effective thought control included not only burning the authors who propagated heresies, but their writings as well.[141] The *Index*, which was first published in 1559 under Paul IV and modified in 1564 by the Council of Trent, was to be an essential feature of Catholic Counter-Reformation until its final abolition in 1966. In 1571 Pius V established the Congregation of the Doctrine of Faith and transferred the duties of the Index to this newly found congregation.[142] The effect of the *Index* on culture, especially in Europe, is still debated to this day. Some have argued that it stymied exchange of cultural ideas, especially in Catholic countries, where its devastating effect was more apparent.

The other essential element of Catholic reform was by way of a General Council, the Council of Trent, which met in three major periods over the course of eighteen years. The Council first met from 1545 to 1547 and dealt with doctrinal and disciplinary matters. They dealt with such doctrinal matters as the sources of revelation, the role of the church as interpreter of Scripture, the Canon of Scripture, Original Sin and Justification (Joint Lutheran-Catholic Declaration on Justification, 1999, resolved this issue). The disciplinary issues they discussed include "pluralism" (holding several benefices), raising the standards of the clergy, importance of preaching, episcopal residence. The second period of the Council was from 1551 to 1552. They dealt with such doctrinal issues as the Eucharist, Penance, Extreme Unction (Anointing of the Sick). War broke out in Germany in

---

139. Homes and Bickers, *Short History*, 163.

140. Lindberg, *European Reformations*, 341.

141. Lindberg, *European Reformations*, 342.

142. Lindberg, *European Reformations*, 342.

1552, which led to the suspension of the Council. It did not reconvene until ten years later. The third period of the Council was held in 1562–63. The Council then issued teachings on the Eucharist, the Cult of the Saints, the veneration of relics, the use of Indulgences and the doctrine of purgatory.[143]

143. Holmes and Bickers, *Short History*, 167–70.

10

Islam

LIKE JUDAISM AND CHRISTIANITY, Islam traces its roots to Abraham and, like these religions, is known as an Abrahamic religion. Islam's historic religious and political ties to Judaism and Christianity "have been the source of mutual benefit and borrowing as well as misunderstanding and conflict."[1] Islam is the second largest religion in the world, second only to Christianity. There are over 900 million and counting Muslims all over the world, with sizeable Muslim populations in more than forty-four countries across Europe, Asia, Middle East, and Africa.[2] Although Muslims the world over belong to one community of believers and share a unity of faith in the one God, Allah, the guidance and message of Prophet Muhammad (PBUH),[3] and the divinely revealed Scripture, the Quran, there are two broad divisions in Islam: Sunni Muslims who constitute about 85 percent and Shia Muslims who constitute about 15 percent of Muslims.[4] This chapter will focus only on the shared beliefs of all Muslims.

---

1. See Esposito, *Islam*, 2.

2. Esposito, *Islam*, 1.

3. According to the Hadith, there are numerous benefits to be derived in bestowing "salaam" (peace) on the Prophets of Allah. As a mark of respect, Muslims traditionally invoke this blessing by saying *sal Allahu allayhi wa sallam* ("peace be upon him") each time the name of Prophet Mohammad is mentioned. The honorific blessing, abbreviated "PBUH" will follow in parenthesis each time the Prophet's name is mentioned.

4. Esposito, *Islam*, 2.

PRE-ISLAMIC ARABIAN PENINSULA

Islam emerged in some ways as a response to the chaotic social, political, religious, and economic climate of the seventh-century CE Arabian Peninsula. Jews, Christians, people who practiced ancient Egyptian and Mesopotamian religions, and even people of no faith, lived in the Arabian Peninsula at the time. The expansionist policy of Roman emperors, which brought political and economic growth to the empire, had begun to weigh heavily on the empire, which was becoming too large and too big to be efficiently governed by the central government in Rome. For practical purposes the empire was divided into two halves: East and West. The Eastern half, known as the Byzantine Empire, extended to far places like Egypt, Palestine, and Syria, up to the region of the Tigris—modern-day Iran. It shared close borders with the Persian Empire, which was at the time constantly at war with the Roman Empire. Arabia at the time was an isolated and poor region, mostly desert wasteland. It enjoyed complete autonomy because neither of the two superpowers that shared its boarder (i.e., Byzantine to the north and Persia to the northwest) was interested in controlling it.[5] What was then Arabia was a region of about a million square miles (about a third of the United States), mostly desert area and landscapes "dotted with oasis towns and cities."[6] Nomadic Bedouin tribes controlled a large portion of agriculture and commerce that took place in the desert.

Seventh-century CE Arabia was also an important trade center for the Silk Road (a trade network that connected the West to China and the Far East). The city of Mecca was particularly an important commercial center of this trading activity. Merchants who controlled trade became enormously rich and often at the expense of the poor whom they exploited. Rich merchants used camel and caravans to gain the upper hand. The Byzantine Empire also had a great influence on the trading activities that took place as they controlled most of the centers that linked the Silk Road to the Far East. Local tribes fought for control over trade. The rivalry was fierce and often led to banditry and armed robbery.

The Silk Road brought people of different ethnicities and religions to the Arabian Peninsula. Jews and Christians lived in the desert spots and in the Byzantine Empire. There were also Buddhists and Hindus who brought their religions from the Far East. But the predominant religion in Arabia was animism (worship of spirits and lesser deities). So there was animism on the one hand and polytheism (deriving from Hinduism) on the other

5. Foad, *Seerah of Prophet Muhammad*, 4.

6. Esposito, *Islam*, 2.

hand. Those who worshiped other deities relied on these deities for protection from armed robbers and gangs who laid siege on the trade routes. The city of Mecca was a center of activity for the worship of different deities. There was a large black stone (cubic-shaped building) known as the Kaaba that held a special status in the city. People came there for worship of deities and annual pilgrimage. A powerful myth or legend developed around the Kaaba. One legend tells that the Kaaba was consecrated by Abraham and his son Ishmael (who according to the Christian Bible was the son of Abraham by a slave woman Hagar) for the worship of the one God, Allah. Arabs consider Ishmael the legitimate son and heir to Abraham. They also consider Ishmael the father of all Arabs (not Isaac as Christians think). The ritual pilgrimage that developed around Kaaba brought Arabs and people from all works of life to Mecca. Most Arabs followed the religion of their forefathers Abraham and Ishmael before they deviated and started worshiping idols they themselves had crafted. Merchants made business out of the pilgrimage and exploited it for economic gains. Because the Arabs had lapsed into polytheism and deviated from the worship of the one true God that Abraham and Ishmael worshiped, the question of reform was just a matter of time.

The peoples of Arabia lived in tribal groups. "Social organization and identity were rooted in membership in an extended family. A grouping of several related families comprised a clan. A cluster of several clans constituted a tribe."[7] Emphases were placed on tribal ties and group solidarity, which provided identity, power, and protection in a society that had no central political authority or law.[8] Politically, Arabian society was hierarchically structured. There were three classes in the society: the nobles or "Ashraf," the allies who were under the protection of the nobles, and the servants or "Al-Abeed" who were poor and oppressed.[9] The tribe was the basic unit of society. The most famous of the tribes was the Quraish (sometimes spelt Koraish), which was in Mecca. They were the guardians of the Kaaba.[10] It was under this social and political situation, i.e., of an Arabian tribal society with a Bedouin polytheistic ethos,[11] that Prophet Muhammad (PBUH) was born and reared.

---

7. Esposito, *Islam*, 3.

8. Esposito, *Islam*, 3.

9. Foad, *Seerah of Prophet Muhammad*, 4.

10. Foad, *Seerah of Prophet Muhammad*, 3.

11. Esposito, *Islam*, 3.

Birth and Early Life of Muhammad Ibn Abdallah (PBUH)

Renewed interest in the life of Prophet Muhammad began in the twentieth century. Scholars had to piece together events of his life found in Islamic literature, particularly the Quran and the Hadith, as well as commentaries on these two. A few of the early chronicles of the life of Prophet Muhammad can be found in the works of the Medina-born historian and scholar Ibn Ishaq (704–67 CE) and his near contemporary, Ibn Hisham, who died around 833 CE. Ibn Ishak's biography of Prophet Muhammad was transmitted to us through Ibn Hisham. This biography is one of the most credible sources of the life of Prophet Muhammad.

Not much is known about the early life of Prophet Muhammad (PBUH). But we do know that his father, Abdallah, died when his mother Amina, was about two months pregnant with him. Muhammad (PBUH) was born in Mecca in 570 CE. His mother died when he was about six years old. According to the Quran (93:6), Muhammad (PBUH) was born an orphan, but Allah took care of him. Muhammad (PBUH) was born into a noble tribe, the Quraish. The Quraish trace their lineage to Ishmael and Abraham.

A Tradition about the Birth of Prophet Muhammad

Abdallah came into the house of another wife he had besides Amina, and he was stained with the clay he had been working in. He asked her to have sex, but she put him off because he was dirty. So he left her and bathed, washing away the clay that was on him. Then he went out intending to go to Amina. As he passed the other wife she invited him to come to her. He refused, since he wanted Amina. He went into her, had intercourse and she conceived Muhammad. When he passed the other wife again he asked if she still wanted him. She said, "No. When you just passed me there was a shining white spot between your eyes and I invited you, but you refused me and went to Amina instead, and she has taken it away."

Muhammad's grandfather raised him after his mother's death and when the grandfather passed away he was raised by his uncle Abou Talib. Abou Talib took him on several of his trading trips. Muhammad (PBUH) had to work as a driver in some of the trading caravans. It was while working in one of such caravans to Syria that he met a wealthy merchant and a widow from Mecca by name Khadijah d. Khuwaylid who hired him to work in her caravan. Impressed by Muhammad's honesty and spiritual qualities, Khadijah proposed marriage to Muhammad (PBUH) when he was twenty-five years old. She at this time was, at least, ten years older than Muhammad. Khadijah provided him a much-needed economic stability. Together they had two sons (Al-Qasim and Abdallah) and four daughters (Zaynab, Ruqaya, Umkulthum, and Fatima). Al-Quasim and Abdallah died young, but the four daughters all survived. Of the four daughters Fatima seemed to have lived longer. She was the only one that provided Muhammad (PBUH) the much-needed grandchildren, even though there were no boys among them.

Muhammad's marriage to Khadijah was a monogamous one and lasted for twenty-four years.[12] When Khadijah died Muhammad (PBUH) was forty-nine years old. He married Sawda bint Zam'a, the widow of one of his companions when Khadijah died. He married nine other women after emigrating to Medina.[13] Most of his wives were "widows of his Companions or of enemies killed in battle, and he seems to have married them primarily in order to give them protection."[14] Muhammad (PBUH) also had concubines, which he took for political reasons. There was Rayhana, a Jewish prisoner of war, and Mariya, a Coptic Christian that was given to him by the Byzantine governor of Egypt.[15] Muhammad's marriage to Zaynab, the divorced wife of his adopted son Zayd, has sometimes fuelled anti-Muslim polemic because non-Muslims wrongly think Zayd divorced Zaynab so Muhammad (PBUH) could marry her.[16] An account of the story is found in Quran 33:37. Some Muslim scholars who know more about the circumstances that led to the marriage between Zayd and Zaynab and who know more about the mismatch between the two when they were married interpret the revelation that Muhammad (PBUH) marries Zaynab to mean that God gave Zaynab to Muhammad (PBUH) in marriage "in order to establish an important social reform, the abolition of adoption."[17] The full explanation of this episode is beyond our scope here. Nevertheless, it is important to keep in mind these key points offered by John Esposito when addressing the issue of Muhammad's polygamous marriages:

i. The Semitic culture in which Muhammad (PBUH) lived permitted polygyny.

ii. Muhammad (PBUH) remained married to only one wife throughout the prime of his life.

iii. It was only after the death of his wife, Khadijah, that Muhammad (PBUH) took a number of wives.

12. Robinson, *Islam*, 92.

13. Robinson, *Islam*, 92.

14. Robinson, *Islam*, 92.

15. Robinson, *Islam*, 92.

16. Robinson, *Islam*, 92.

17. Robinson, *Islam*, 92.

iv. Most of Muhammad's eleven marriages, as was customary for Arab chiefs at the time, were political marriages meant to cement alliances.

v. Some of Muhammad's marriages were marriages to widows of his companions who had fallen in combat and in need of protection.

vi. Remarriage was difficult in the society in which Muhammad (PBUH) lived because the society emphasized virgin marriages. Aisha was the only virgin that Muhammad married.

vii. Muhammad's teachings and actions improved the status and lot of women.[18]

Piecing together the events of the early life of Muhammad (PBUH) is not easy to do because there were not many written accounts of his life. As we pointed out already, the earliest written account of the events of his early life was the *Sira* (biography) by Ibn-Ishaq (d. 767 CE), which was written about 125 years after the Prophet's death. The most definitive authority remains the Quran. But the Quran does not offer much either by way of biography, except for scattered references. In fact, the Quran only mentions Muhammad (PBUH) by name four times (Quran 3:144, 33:40, 47:2, and 48:29). But in spite of the paucity of biographical information, a lot is said or implied about Muhammad's status in the Quran.[19] We do know that he was a righteous man who Muslims believe to be the perfect example of men. They regard him as the last and the greatest of the messengers and prophet of God. The Quran addresses him as Prophet (Quran 8:64) and Messenger of Allah (Quran 5:41). It also mentions him in the same breath as Noah, Abraham, Moses, and Jesus (Quran 42:13) and describes him as "the seal of the prophets" (Quran 33:40).[20]

Other reliable sources for the life of the Prophet, apart from the Quran, are the compilations of the sayings of the Prophet put together by some of his companions and successors. The individual compilations of the sayings are called hadiths. Taken together collectively they are called Hadith. There are two main kinds of Hadith: the *musnad*—hadiths compiled on the basis of individual persons who compiled them and the *musannaf*—hadiths that are arranged according to the subject matter discussed.[21] Traditional Islamic societies, i.e., the way Muslims in traditional Islamic societies, "pray, conduct business, wage war, marry and divorce, rear their children, dress, greet

18. Esposito, *Islam*, 16–17.

19. Robinson, *Islam*, 85.

20. Robinson, *Islam*, 85.

21. Robinson, *Islam*, 86.

one another, eat and drink, or attend to matters of personal hygiene, are all largely determined by what the Prophet is deemed to have said and done, or tacitly approved or disapproved."[22] Muslims also look to Muhammad's example for guidance in other aspects of life, like what to eat or drink, what to wear, how to treat one's friends and enemies. These are called the Sunna (the trodden path)—the examples of the prophets that have been handed down by oral traditions and customs from generation to generation.[23]

THE CALL TO PROPHETHOOD AND THE BEGINNINGS OF REVELATION

According to Ibn Ishaq, before he received his call to prophethood, the young Muhammad used to spend a month every year in seclusion on Mount Hira to pray and practice *tahannuth*. *Tahannuth* was a religious practice or custom of the Quraish (the tribe of Prophet Muhammad). Each year, in observance of this custom, Muhammad would also give food to the poor, and before returning home, he would perform circumambulation of the Kaaba (walk around it about seven times). It was while observing this Quraish custom at Mount Hira one night that the angel Gabriel brought Muhammad God's message, when Muhammad was asleep. The text of the first message that was brought to Prophet Muhammad is found in Surah Al-Alaq 96:1–5. Ibn Ishak reports that after hesitatingly reading the text that the angel brought him, the angel departed and Muhammad, awoke from his sleep and descending the mountain, heard a voice from heaven: "O Muhammad! Thou art the apostle of God and I am Gabriel."[24] This happened in the month of Ramadan.

The year Muhammad (PBUH) began to receive revelations was 610 CE. He was about forty years old. There are different accounts of the nature of these revelations. Some depict the revelations as visions that came to Muhammad (PBUH) "like the brightness of daybreak" at his home in Mecca, while other accounts suggest that these events took place at Mount Hira, a secluded place outside of Mecca where the Prophet used to go and repair for solitude and prayer. Angel Gabriel would bring him revelations. The very day in the month of Ramadan in which first revelation occurred (Quran 2:185) was probably on the 27th or somewhere within the last ten days of the month. The night on which the first revelation occurred is referred to as *Lai lat al-Quadri* (the night of power or night of majesty, see Quran 97:1).

22. Robinson, *Islam*, 88.

23. Esposito, *Islam*, 11.

24. As cited in McAuliffe, *Islam*, 137.

"The revelations are explained by Islamic doctrine as the text of a divine book written by God in heaven, brought by the angel Gabriel, and recited by Muhammad."[25] Gabriel said to Prophet Muhammad: "Read in the name of your Lord who created man out of clot. Read and your Lord is the most generous" (Quran 96:1–3). Muhammad (PBUH) was not a lettered man yet the angel urged him to read (Quran 29:48). Muhammad was alone when he had this awesome experience which terrified him greatly. When he returned home trembling, the Prophet narrated the experience which caused him "great dread and anxiety" to his wife Khadijah who assured him that he is the prophet of God.

Muhammad (PBUH) received these revelations for twenty-three years. The first person to believe in Muhammad as God's Prophet and accept Islam was Khadijah his wife. Then there was his companion Abou Bakr, his cousin Ali (the son of Abou Talib), his children, and other companions and servants, like Belal, who all believed and accepted Islam. These early Muslims met privately with Prophet Muhammad (PBUH), learned from him, and prayed with him before the order came from Allah to Prophet Muhammad (PBUH) to proclaim openly Allah's message and warn his nearest of kin.[26] The revelation was for Muhammad (PBUH) to remind his people about the oneness and greatness of God and also to warn them of the judgment that will take place on the last day (Quran 74:2; 87:9). Prophet Muhammad (PBUH) "climbed to the top of Safa (a hill in Mecca) and called on the various branches of Quraish to invite them to worship Allah alone and to believe in him as Allah's messenger."[27]

Open Dawa and Hejira

When Prophet Muhammad proclaimed the truth of the message of God, his people disowned him. Not only did many refuse to believe him, they opposed him. Ibn Ishaq explains the reason as follows: "Prophecy is a troublesome burden—only strong, resolute messengers can bear it by God's help and grace, because of the opposition which they meet from men in conveying God's message."[28] So in the first three years of his call to serve Allah, Prophet Muhammad (PBUH) proclaimed the Dawa (call to serve Allah) in secret and only his family and close associates became Muslims. As we pointed out earlier, Khadijah d. Khuwaylid, the wife of the Prophet, believed

25. Carmody and Brink, *Ways to the Center*, 300.

26. Foad, *Seerah of Prophet Muhammad*, 15.

27. Foad, *Seerah of Prophet Muhammad*, 16.

28. As cited in McAuliffe, *Islam*, 138.

in him. Islamic literature records her as the first to accept Islam because she believed Muhammad was the prophet bearing the true message of God. Ali, the son of Abu Talib (the Prophet's uncle), i.e., the Prophet's nephew, was the first male to believe in him as the prophet bearing the true message of God. After Ali, the next male figures to accept Islam were Zayd, the Prophet's slave or servant and Abu Bakr b. Abu Auhafa, "a merchant of high character and kindliness."[29] After three years Prophet Muhammad was instructed to proclaim the Dawa publicly to the people of Mecca. Muhammad's preaching was initially not well received by the Meccans because it threatened both their polytheism and economic activities around the Kaaba. They feared that destroying their idols would put an end to the flood of pilgrims that came to Mecca and cripple their businesses. The leaders of the Quraish went to Abou Talib, the Prophet's uncle, and pleaded with him to intervene and stop his nephew from ridiculing their idols. They even tried to bribe Prophet Muhammad (PBUH) with money and promise of power and leadership. But Prophet Muhammad (PBUH) was not after money or fame, but only to proclaim steadfastly God's message.

When they could not stop the Prophet by bribe the people of Mecca began to persecute Muslims. In the fifth year of his revelations Prophet Muhammad (PBUH) encouraged some of his followers to emigrate to Habash (Ethiopia). Twelve men and four women, including Prophet Muhammad's daughter, emigrated to Ethiopia where they were offered protection by the king of Ethiopia. The king of Ethiopia was a Christian. The enemies of the Muslims, many of whom were from the Quraish tribe, sent delegates bearing gifts to the king of Ethiopia to repatriate the Muslims back to Mecca. But the king would not acquiesce. The king was so impressed with the Muslims when he heard their account of the state of decadence of Mecca before Islam and how Prophet Muhammad (PBUH) was turning things around by preaching belief in one God, Allah, prayer, and charity to the poor. The king turned down the Quraish delegations and told them that the Muslims were free to stay in his kingdom. The king's gesture encouraged more Muslims to emigrate to Habash. There were about eighty-three men and eleven women in the second emigration to Habash.[30]

The Meccan leaders did everything they could to discredit Prophet Muhammad (PBUH) and levelled all kinds of accusations against him. They claimed he was destroying their traditional religion and customs. They also accused the Prophet of sorcery, a baseless allegation particularly when one considers the fact that Prophet Muhammad's whole point in the first place

29. McAuliffe, *Islam*, 142.

30. Foad, *Seerah of Prophet Muhammad*, 24–25.

was to wipe out diviners and sorcerers. They also alleged that his revelations were a forgery (see Quran 25:4–5; 68:15) and that the Quran need not be taken seriously because it came, according to them, from the devil (See Quran 7:184; 15:6; 68:42). Muhammad (PBUH) responded to these charges by challenging his critics who claimed that he invented the Quran to produce something similar if the Quran was invented. Muslims hold that the Quran is sui generis and incapable of being imitated.[31] We shall discuss this point more later.

In spite of persecution from the Meccans, Prophet Muhammad's message gained much ground. Some warring groups from a nearby town called Yathrib accepted Islam and pledged their allegiance to the Prophet. In 622 CE Prophet Muhammad (PBUH) left Mecca for Yathrib to arbitrate a long standing dispute between two of the warring tribes. After the Prophet settled their dispute with revelation he received from Allah the people of Yathrib enjoined on him to stay. Muhammad (PBUH) stayed and became the religious and political leader of Yathrib. Later the name of the town was changed to Medina, meaning the city of the prophet. Muhammad's journey from Mecca to Yathrib (Medina) is known in Islamic history as the Hejira, a significant and turning point in Islamic history. Muslims call their calendar the *Hijri* calendar and use the designation *Anno Hejira* (AH), meaning "in the year of the Hejira." Since the emigration to Medina occurred in 622 CE, most likely the 20th of September (according to the Gregorian calendar), that year is considered 1AH in Islamic calendar. The Islamic calendar is a lunar-based calendar, consisting of twelve lunar months. Lengthwise, lunar months alternate between twenty-nine and thirty days, which means that the Islamic calendar has approximately 354 days, about eleven or twelve days short of the solar-based Gregorian calendar. Muslims today use both the Gregorian calendar (for civic purposes) and the Islamic calendar (for religious purposes) to determine when to kick start their annual fast, begin their annual pilgrimage, and celebrate Islamic festivals.

31. Kaltner, *Introducing the Qur'an*, 14.

Islamic Calendar Month	Meaning	Activity/Significance
Muharram	Muharram is derived from the term "haram," meaning "forbidden"	Considered unlawful to fight in this month. Believed to be the month in which Allah created the heavens and earth. Believed to be the month Allah created Adam and pardoned Adam and Eve for their transgressions. Believed to be the month Noah's Ark landed safely on Mount Judi. It is this month (680 CE/61 AH) that Prophet Muhammad's grandson, Imam Husain, together with his family and friends, were massacred in the battle of Karbala.
Safar	Means "empty" or "void"	Shia Muslims, who consider Imam Husain the third Imam, remember both the heroism and brutal murder of Imam Husain at Karbala on the 10th of Muharram. Muslims hold mourning ceremonies/prayer throughout the month of Muharram and Safar.
1st Rabi or Rabi-Ul-Awwal	The first month of Spring	Prophet Muhammad (PBUH) was born in this month. Emigration to Mecca occurred this month.
2nd Rabi or Rabi-Ul-Akhir	The second month of Spring	
1st Jumaada or Jumaada-Al-Oola	1st of Parched land	Prophet Muhammad (PBUH) married Khadijah in this month. Considered summer in pre-Islamic Arabia.
2nd Jumaada or Jumaada-Ath-Thani	2nd of Parched land	

Rajabi	Honor or Respect	The Miraj (Muhammad's night journey to heaven) took place on the 27th of Rajab.
		Sacred month in which fighting is forbidden.
Sha'ban	Scattered	Quibla (direction of prayer facing Mecca) was adopted in the 15th of Sha'ban, two months after Hejira.
		Fasting in the month of Ramadan was made compulsory on the 25th of Sha'ban, two years after Hejira.
Ramadan	Literally means "intense heat" or "burning"	The Quran was revealed on the 27th night of this month.
		Hasan, the grandson of Prophet Muhammad (PBUH), was born on the 15th of Ramadan, three years after Hejira.
		The Battle of Badr took place on the 12th of Ramadan, two years into the Hejira.
		Fasting month for Muslims.
Shawwaal	Means "breakage: or "raised." The name derives from a superstition among pre-Islamic Arabs who believed that any marriage that takes place in this month will in the end be unsuccessful.	The month of Hajj (pilgrimage).
		The first day of Shawwaal is Muslim festival of Eid-Ul-Fitri, a day when sins are forgiven.
		The Prophet's grandson, Husain (son of Fatimah) was born this month, four years after Hejira.
		The Battle of Uhud took place this month, three years after Hejira.
Dhul-Qu'da or Zul-Qa'dah	The one of Truce	One of the months of Hajj (pilgrimage).
		Another month in which war is forbidden.

Dhul-Hijja or Zul Hijjah	The one Pilgrimage or month of Hajj.	Another month in which war is forbidden.
		First ten days of this month are considered most virtuous days of the month. Hajj is performed within those ten days.
		Prophet Muhammad (PBUH) performed his "Farewell Hajj" and gave his "Farewell Sermon" this month.
		Umar, the second caliph, was killed 27th of this month, 26 AH.
		Uthman appointed third caliph this month.
		Uthman was killed 18th day of this month, 35 AH.

The people of Medina were by no means monolithic. They were diverse groups with diverse interests. They can be divided into four interest groups:

i. Muslims who emigrated from Mecca, known as the Muhajereen.

ii. Muslims resident in Medina, known as the Ansar.

iii. Arab groups resident in Medina who had yet to accept Islam.

iv. Jewish groups resident in Medina.

Regarding the latter, three different Jewish groups (Bani Quinuq'a, Bani An-adeer, and Bani Qoraiza) lived in Medina at the time of the Hejira. These Jewish groups had Arab names. Their cultures were similar to those of Arabs as well. They must have emigrated to Medina from Palestine to escape persecution. Nevertheless, they maintained their Jewish identity and controlled the commerce in Medina.[32]

Economically, Medina was poor. The continued influx of Muslims from Mecca was a drain on the economy of this poor town that was decimated by the two warring tribes of the Ansars—the Aws and Khazraj that fought each other for years with regularity.[33] Religiously, the Mosque built by Prophet Muhammad (PBUH) at Medina would serve as a symbol of unity for all the warring groups. Prophet Muhammad (PBUH) united the Muhajereen and the Ansar and they all saw each other as brothers and sisters in the faith. The Muslims met there regularly to worship and learn from Prophet Muhammad

32. Foad, *Seerah of Prophet Muhammad*, 74.

33. Foad, *Seerah of Prophet Muhammad*, 65.

(PBUH). "The mosque united the hearts of Muslims and served as the focal point in their lives. If one or more people did not show up, they were missed and the others would go and find why they had stayed away from the mosque or offer help if they were in need."[34] According to Salem Foad, Prophet Muhammad (PBUH) signed a non-aggression treaty and pact of cooperation between Muslims and non-Muslims in Medina and established there a Muslim state. The principal element of the agreement included the following five points:

i. All Muslims are equal in their rights and privileges. A believer also must not only help a believer, but must not help an unbeliever against a believer.

ii. Prophet Muhammad (PBUH) settled all disputes between the believers.

iii. The Muslim state was built on the best principles and rules that guaranteed peace.

Iv. Every citizen had the right to travel inside and outside of the state. Non-Muslims who wanted to live in peace with their Muslim counterparts were protected by the state. Their property was safeguarded and guaranteed and no one was forced to accept Islam.

v. The authority that safeguarded these rules was based on the belief in Allah and obedience to Prophet Muhammad (PBUH).[35]

RITUAL PRAYER AND MUHAMMAD'S NIGHT JOURNEY

We will get to Islamic ritual prayer later when discuss the five pillars of faith. The origin of the ritual prayer goes back to the angel Gabriel who Islamic scholars believe taught Prophet Muhammad the ritual prayer. Ibn Ishaq writes,

> A learned person told me that when prayer was laid on the apostle Gabriel came to him while he was on the heights of Mecca and dug a hole for him with his heel in the side of the valley from which a fountain gushed forth, and Gabriel performed the ritual ablution as the apostle watched him. This was in order to show him how to purify himself before prayer. Then the apostle performed the ritual ablution as he had seen Gabriel do it. Then Gabriel said a prayer with him while the apostle prayed with his

34. Foad, *Seerah of Prophet Muhammad*, 67.
35. Foad, *Seerah of Prophet Muhammad*, 73.

prayer. Then Gabriel left him. The apostle came to Khadija and performed the ritual for her as Gabriel had done for him and she copied him. Then he prayed with her as Gabriel had prayed with him, and she prayed his prayer.[36]

Muslims draw parallels between the life of Moses and that of Prophet Muhammad. One of the reasons has to do with Muhammad's night journey from Kaaba in Mecca to Jerusalem on a beast. According to the story, the angel Gabriel took the Prophet to the heavens. At the first point of entry, the angel introduced him to Adam who welcomed Muhammad to heaven as "the righteous son, the righteous Prophet." Then Gabriel took him to the second heaven and introduced him to Jesus and John the apostle who both welcomed Muhammad to heaven as "the righteous brother, the righteous Prophet." The angel took him from there to the third heaven and introduced him to Joseph who welcomed him to heaven as "the righteous brother, the righteous Prophet." Then the angel took him to the fourth heaven and introduced him to Idris who welcomed him to heaven as "the righteous brother, the righteous Prophet." From there the angel took him to the fifth heaven and introduced him to Aaron who welcomed him as "the righteous brother, the righteous Prophet." From there the angel took him to the sixth heaven where they met Moses who welcomed him as "the righteous brother, the righteous Prophet." When Moses saw Muhammad, he started weeping. When asked why he was weeping, Moses responded that he wept because after him (Moses) there had not been a prophet like Muhammad whose followers will enter paradise in great number. From there the angel took him to the seventh heaven where they met Abraham who welcomed Muhammad as "the righteous son, the righteous Prophet." The angel then showed Muhammad the beauty of heaven. Muhammad then received injunction that he and his followers must pray fifty times a day.

While he was descending from heaven, Muhammad met Moses again on the way. Moses asked him what had been enjoined upon him. Muhammad responded that he had been instructed to pray fifty times a day. Moses told him that his community cannot bear fifty prayers a day and that he should return and negotiate with God to reduce it. Muhammad went back and had the prayers reduced by ten. Moses urged him to go back negotiate to reduce it further. Muhammad did so and it was reduced again by ten. Again he returned to Moses who asked him to go back. He did so and it was reduced by ten again. He returned to Moses who again asked him to go and renegotiate it. This time Muhammad returned and had the prayers reduced to five prayers a day. When Moses asked him to go back again and have the

36. As cited in McAuliffe, *Islam*, 140.

prayers reduced further, Muhammad answered: "I have begged so much of my Sustainer that I feel ashamed. But I am content now, and I shall submit to God's will."[37] When Muhammad left, a voice from heaven confirmed the five prayers for Muslims. According to one hadith, someone asked Prophet Muhammad, "What is the most virtuous act a person can perform?" The Prophet replied, "To pray at the appointed times." Muslims understand this to mean that the performance of ritual prayer is the most virtuous, most sublime, and most significant thing a Muslim can do.[38]

Hadith and Sunna

Hadith refers to traditions about what the prophet said or did. The Sunna is "the Way"—the behavior and example of prophet Muhammad. Muslims believe that the pre-Islamic Arabs followed the sunna (example) of their fathers, but Muslims have to follow the sunna (example) of the prophet because the sunna of the prophet, according to the Quran, is in harmony with God's way:[39] "You have a good example in the messenger of God" (Quran 33:21). For a long time, the prophet's sunna was transmitted orally before it was finally committed to writing. Some of them became part of the hadith. "The three centuries following Muhammad's lifetime saw an exponential proliferation of hadith, not because new material about the Prophet and his Companions was discovered but because ever more widespread transmission multiplied versions of existing accounts as well as their chains of coveyance."[40] Because some hadiths were fabricated and forged, a conscious effort was made to scrutinize what hadith is to be regarded as credible. Hadiths that can be traced to the *sahaba* (early Companions of Muhammad) were more likely to be credible. Sunni Islam accept, at least, six hadith collections as canonical: *Sahih* of Muhammad ibn Isma'il al-Bukhari (810–70 CE), *Sahih* of Muslim ibn al-Hajjaj al-Naysaburi (821–75 CE), *Kitab al-Sunan* of Abu Da'ud al-Sijistan (817–89 CE), *Sahih* of Ahmad ibn Shu'ayb al-Nasa'I (d. 915 CE), *Jami'* of Muhammad ibn 'Isa al-Tirmidhi (d. 892 CE), and *Ktab al-Sunan* of Muhammad ibn Yazid ibn Majah (813–87 CE).[41] The Shia, on their part, consider canonical hadith transmitted through Ali ibn Abou Talib (599–661 CE), the prophet's first cousin that the Shia consider the first

37. See Al-Bukhari, *Hadith and Sunna: The Perfect Man Remembered as the Perfect Guide to Life*, cited in McAuliffe, *Islam*, 170.

38. Al-Jaziri, *Islamic Jurisprudence*, 223.

39. McAuliffe, *Islam*, 50.

40. McAuliffe, *Islam*, 50.

41. McAuliffe, *Islam*, 51.

Imam, as well as his successors.[42] Although there are similarities between the Sunni and Shia hadith, like their adulation of the family of the Prophet, there are also some significant differences. One significant difference is that while the Sunni hadith tends to "reflect the view of that community that after the death of Muhammad, leadership of the Muslim community, the caliphate, was properly to be awarded by acclamation within the community itself," in the Shia hadith tends to reflect "the infallibility of the imams and the genealogical primacy of Ali's claim to the caliphate."[43]

AL'QURAN

The Quran is revered as God's own word. Muslims believe it was divinely dictated (not merely divinely inspired) to Prophet Muhammad who only had to convey it verbatim to his followers. He received it in Arabic. The Quran is the "mother of all books" because it is the culmination of revelations God has been giving through Moses in Judaism and through Jesus in Christianity. Therefore, Muslims believe that the Quran contains the same divine message that was revealed to previous prophets and messengers of God. Muhammad (PBUH) is the last in this chain of prophetic figures that go back to Jesus, Moses, Abraham, and Adam. Muhammad (PBUH) is the last of these prophets, a reason for which he is called "the seal of the prophets." The Quran is, for Muslims, "the guarded tablet" (Quran 85:22) and "the mother of the Book" (Quran 43:4). Belief in the pre-existence of the Quran as "the guarded tablet" should be understood against the backdrop of beliefs in ancient Near East about the pre-existence of divinely revealed books, as in the example of Moses ascending the mountain to receive from Yahweh ten divinely revealed commandments that were inscribed on tablets.[44]

When the Quran was revealed the enemies of Islam who opposed the Prophet claimed it was a forgery. Muslims responded by urging them to produce something similar (Quran 28:49; 11:13). Their inability to do so reinforced Muslim believers' belief that the Quran is inimitable and that the inimitability (i.e., that the language, ideas, and style of the Quran cannot be reproduced) speaks to its divine origin.[45] For Muslims, the Quran is perfect, eternal, and unchangeable. In this regard it is the only miracle brought about by Prophet Muhammad (PBUH).[46] Some Muslim schol-

42. McAuliffe, *Islam*, 51.
43. McAuliffe, *Islam*, 51.
44. Robinson, *Islam*, 91–92.
45. Robinson, *Islam*, 59.
46. Esposito, *Islam*, 19.

ars also believe that the Quran is a copy of a heavenly original or urtext that resides with God in heaven and that God sent the Quran down to the prophet who in turn transmitted the words he heard. Muslims greatly revere the Quran for these reasons.

Thus, Muslims believe that the Quran is the divine message that was delivered orally to Prophet Muhammad (PBUH) by the angel Gabriel over a period of twenty-three years. The Prophet and his companions committed the message to memory and recited them during prayers. The first revelation occurred on "the night of power," in the month of Ramadan. The Quran does not say anything about what the experience of receiving revelations had on Prophet Muhammad (PBUH). "The matter is treated in non-scriptural sources that refer to various consequences of the revelatory state. Among the most commonly mentioned are that revelation was accompanied by the ringing of a bell and that Muhammad experienced physical symptoms, including a trance-like state, loss of consciousness, fatigue, perspiration, a change in skin complexion, and general physical discomfort."[47]

The Quran, at least in its Arabic form, is "primarily an aural-oral phenomenon. It exhibits rhyme, rhythm, assonance, alliteration and other poetic qualities which are lost when it is rendered into English."[48] The divine message that was revealed over a twenty-three-year period was revealed in stages: ten years of revelations in Mecca and thirteen years of revelations in Medina. During the Mecca revelations the Prophet repeated what was revealed to him to his companions who "jotted them down on loose leaves as aide memoire."[49] But in the Medinan period the Prophet "deliberately employed scribes" such that by the time the Prophet died in 632 CE "all the revelations had been memorized and were also available in written form."[50]

The Quran in its present form consists of 114 Surahs (chapters) of approximately six thousand verses. The Surahs are not arranged in chronological order. The first revelation, for example, that was revealed to Prophet Muhammad (PBUH) is placed in Surah 96 and the final revelation is to be found in Surah 5. This last divine message was revealed in 632 CE and was the subject of a sermon the Prophet preached at Arafat while performing his last pilgrimage there.[51] The first Surah of the Quran, the Al-Fatiha (the Opening), is often treated as a standard prayer. The final revelation, for Muslims, is a clear testimony to the perfection of the religion of Islam: "This day

---

47. Kaltner, *Introducing the Qur'an*, 13.

48. Robinson, *Islam*, 59.

49. Robinson, *Islam*, 60.

50. Robinson, *Islam*, 60.

51. Robinson, *Islam*, 63.

have I perfected for you your religion and completed my favor to you and chosen for you Islam as a religion" (Quran 5:3). The Prophet probably died shortly after this verse was revealed (about eighty-one or eighty-two days after). Mohammad (PBUH) is considered the last of the prophets because of his testimony of the perfection of the religion of Islam. The logic here is that if the religion has been perfected there is no need for a prophet after him.

Generally speaking, the Quran is arranged from the longest to the shortest chapters. From the arrangement of the Quran one cannot gain any certainty regarding the precise order in which all the Surahs were revealed. But "in most instances it is usually fairly clear from the contents of a given Surah whether it was revealed during the Meccan or the Medinan period."[52] There are some differences between Meccan and Medinan Surahs:

1. Generally speaking, the Meccan Surahs tend to be shorter than the Medinan Surahs.

2. The Meccan Surahs tend to have short verses (called Ayas).

3. According to Neal Robinson, Meccan Surahs contain six principal types of material:

    i. Messenger sections: addressed primarily to Muhammad the messenger of God, as message of comfort, rebuke, and encouragement.

    ii. Sign sections: that points to the wonders of God's creation, which should elicit gratitude on the part of the believer.

    iii. Polemical sections: that rebuke Arab pagans for worshiping false deities, rebukes them for their inordinate desire for material things, and chastises them for not caring for vulnerable members of the society.

    iv. Narrative sections: describes exemplary lives of believers like Joseph and Mary mother of Jesus and also describes how people who previously rejected God's divine message were punished.

    v. Eschatological sections: describes last judgment—the pleasures of Paradise and torments of Hell.

    vi. Revelation sections: describes the authenticity of the divine message revealed to Muhammad and rebuts accusations against the Prophet.[53]

52. Robinson, *Islam*, 63.
53. Robinson, *Islam*, 63–64.

4. Medinan Surahs often tend to be long and intricate, perhaps because they have universal significance. According to Robinson, the Medinan Surahs contain the same six types of materials that are in the Meccan Surahs but in a modified form:

 i. Messenger sections: often begin with the words "O Prophet . . . ," suggesting that Muhammad is not the author of the message but a transmitter of the message.[54]

 ii. Sign sections: because the Medinan revelations are addressed primarily to Muslims, Jews, and Christians who share similar belief in the creative acts of God the sign sections are rare because they are no longer necessary.[55] Nevertheless, the sign sections still "affirm that God is the sole Creator and that all around us there are abundant signs of His beneficence and power which should evoke our gratitude and awe."[56]

 iii. Polemical sections: polemic against Arabs gradually gives way to tirade against unbelievers. The section takes "human beings to task for their inclination to worship false gods who leave them free to indulge their selfishness and greed to the detriment of the weaker members of society."[57]

 iv. Narrative sections: "The narrative sections are no longer dominated by punishment stories about peoples who were utterly destroyed for their unbelief, but rather by stories of how God repeatedly forgave the children of Israel in Moses' time after chastising them."[58] It is also a "salutary reminder that past civilizations which sank to that level of degradation, and which rejected the upright prophets and messengers who tried to call the people to their senses, have vanished almost without trace."[59]

 v. Eschatological sections: the long eschatological section is now replaced "by much simpler stereotyped allusions to Paradise and Hell which are addressed to the believers."[60] Prophet Muhammad

54. Robinson, *Islam*, 65.
55. Robinson, *Islam*, 64.
56. Robinson, *Islam*, 65.
57. Robinson, *Islam*, 65.
58. Robinson, *Islam*, 64.
59. Robinson, *Islam*, 65.
60. Robinson, *Islam*, 65.

(PBUH) is also portrayed as having the same status as the other Hebrew prophets like Moses. The eschatological sections offer a dire warning that our society is heading the same way as that of the past civilization who rejected the message of the prophets.

vi. Revelation sections: the revelation sections are relatively rare. But it does "reinforce the Messenger sections by indicating that the message originated with none other than the Creator."[61]

5. The Medinan Surahs "contain a profusion of legal precepts and exhortations intended specifically for the believing community."[62]

6. Unlike Mecca where the Prophet had only a small group of followers in the early beginnings of the religion, in Medina the Prophet was an established religious and political leader and had to attend to matters of law and order as a religious and political leader. The Medinan revelations tend to reflect these hands-on useful matters, which for all practical purposes are the seeds of Islamic laws on social justice (inheritance, divorce, war, almsgiving, etc.). For example, the Medinan revelations prohibit gambling and usury (charging of interest on loans). The Medinan revelations also command the payment of compulsory charity (zakat) and institute the Ramadan fast as a way of mortification and inculcating self-discipline, and self-restraint.[63]

In terms of arrangement of the Quran, in some places some Meccan passages are interspersed with Medinan passages. But the central message of both the Meccan and Medinan revelations remain the same: that there is no God but Allah. Both the Meccan and Medinan messages were framed in a way that would appeal to Muhammad's contemporaries: "Hell is depicted as worse than a tropical desert in the heat of summer, with neither water nor shade, whereas Paradise sounds more enticing and refreshing than any earthly oasis."[64] Most scholars agree that the Quran went through an editing process, which may have been responsible for the arrangement of the book. The standard Egyptian edition of the Quran follows ancient traditions whereby each Surah comes with a heading that states whether the message was revealed in Mecca or Medina. Some English translations of the Quran have also copied this idea of giving a standard heading to each Surah.[65]

61. Robinson, *Islam*, 65.

62. Robinson, *Islam*, 65.

63. Robinson, *Islam*, 66.

64. Robinson, *Islam*, 65.

65. Robinson, *Islam*, 63.

THE FIVE PILLARS OF FAITH

So far we have seen that the Islam that emerged in the seventh century CE in Arabia "was not an isolated, totally new monotheistic religion."[66] Before Islam, Zoroastrianism, Judaism, and Christianity all preached monotheistic faith. These three religions "had been flourishing in Semitic and Iranian cultures for centuries preceding Muhammad's ministry."[67] Although these religions preached monotheism, community, fidelity, final judgment, etc., one of their main problems was that they had all, to some degree, "become associated with political power, that is, had become an official state religion: Judaism in the kingdoms of Judea and Israel, Christianity in the Roman (Byzantine) empire, Zoroastrianism in the Persian (Sassanid) empire."[68] Muhammad's essential claim was that he did not start a new religion but rather that his message was to call people back to the original message of the God that the people had deviated from. He thought that the "majority of Arabs lived in ignorance (*jahiliyya*) of Allah and His will as revealed to the prophets Adam, Abraham, Moses, and Jesus. Moreover, he believed that both the Jewish and the Christian communities had distorted God's original revelation to Moses and later to Jesus."[69] Thus, what Muhammad brought was not a new religion, but Islam (total self-surrender) to the will of Allah. This requires turning from unbelief to the straight path or law (sharia) of God.[70] For the sake of simplification it is not unusual to speak of Muhammad's message as the Five Pillars of Faith. These "pillars" are the bedrock on which Islam is built.

1. The Witness of Faith or *Shahada*

Pre-Islamic Arabia recognized the existence of God whom they called *alilah*, meaning "the god." They thought of this god as a high god or a remote deity who had little or no relevance to their everyday life. He was not, in their view, the sole deity, but one of many. They also thought this deity, *alilah*, had daughters (like the goddesses "Lat Manat" and "al-Uzza) and associates that could be appealed to for help.[71] But not all inhabitants of pre-Islamic Arabia were pagans. There were some Arab-speaking Jews and Christians who

66. Esposito, *Islam*, 4.
67. Esposito, *Islam*, 4.
68. Esposito, *Islam*, 4.
69. Esposito, *Islam*, 12.
70. Esposito, *Islam*, 12.
71. Robinson, *Islam*, 75.

recognized the moral demands God makes of us and know God properly as Allah. They are recognized by the Quran as the "People of the Book." There were also others who practiced Zoroastrianism, a religion that the Quran finds repugnant. Zoroastrianism was established in Persia around the sixth century BCE. It was founded by Zoroaster who lived from 628–551 BCE. Zoroaster taught a monotheistic doctrine. The name of the one supreme God is Ahura Mazdah. But Zoroaster's doctrine was dualistic—that there are two powerful and competing forces in the world. Zoroastrianism was the official religion of Persia (modern-day Iran) in pre-Islam Arabia. Under the threat of Islam Zoroastrians began to leave Persia and headed towards India where they founded a community. They were known as the Parsis in India. The remnants of the group who are still in Iran are referred to as the Gabars.

Although all these religious groups recognized the majesty of God, "some of them had unorthodox beliefs about Him."[72] The Christian belief in the Trinitarian Persons was considered one of these "unorthodox beliefs" about Allah. Islam explicitly condemns the thought of setting up a partner with God. This is called shirk or association, an offense the Quran says will not be forgiven (Quran 4:48, 116).[73] A person who engages in the sin of shirk is called a *mushrik*, meaning he or she associates something with God and violates the essential oneness of God.[74] It is good to be clear though that the Quran never considers Jews and Christians to be *mushrikun* because Jews and Christians, like Muslims, believe in one God and have God's word transmitted to them through the *Tawrat* (Torah) and the *Injil* (Gospels). This is why the Quran repeatedly refers to Jews and Christians as "People of the Book," meaning that they are the recipients of revealed texts.[75]

The Quran explicitly teaches God's unity (*tawhid*) or oneness of God. This explicit teaching about the oneness of God was preached by Adam, the first prophet, and continued down to the other prophets of Allah like Abraham, Moses, Noah, etc. "An uncompromising belief in the monotheistic nature of God is therefore not only the foundation of Islam, but also the first and foremost condition of being a Muslim."[76] The *Shahada* or the Muslim testimony that there is no god but the one God and that Muhammad is His prophet is the most devoted testimony to the absolute oneness of God.[77]

---

72. Robinson, *Islam*, 76.

73. Kaltner, *Introducing the Qur'an*, 44.

74. Kaltner, *Introducing the Qur'an*, 210.

75. Kaltner, *Introducing the Qur'an*, 211.

76. Nawaz, *Islam*, 10.

77. Nawaz, *Islam*, 12.

"It is a grave sin to generate or worship the images of God in any shape or form. It is unthinkable for a Muslim to conceptualize God as a figure with any biological or physical features."[78] The Quran ascribes different names to God to stress both the unity and eternity of God: beneficence, merciful, Self-sufficient, omnipotence, and omniscience, etc. The Quran teaches that this one God is Creator and that this Creator-God participates in human history. "The blind fatalism of the pre-Islamic Arabs is countered by the Quran's assertion that Allah determines when we are born, what calamities will befall us, and when we shall die. He knows everything we do and not even our innermost thoughts escape Him."[79]

2. Prayer or *Salat*

The second pillar of faith is *salat* (prayer). Islam recognizes that every religion practices some forms of ritual prayer. Islamic tradition believes that the purest form of ritual prayer was practiced by Abraham, Ishmael, Moses, and Jesus, but that generations after them watered down the ritual prayer which these prophets held in their sublime form. The Quran specifically denounces these watered down prayer, particularly the one that was practiced by the Arabs at Kaaba before Islam, describing it as "nothing but whistling and clapping of hands" (Quran 8:35).[80] Prayer in Islam is a way of reaffirming the majesty of God and seeking from God his help in walking the straight path of virtue, as against choosing the path of wrath and destruction.[81]

We already saw that according to tradition, Muhammad (PBUH) received revelation that he and his followers must pray fifty times a day, but because this would prove too arduous, Muhammad (PBUH) pleaded and bargained with God until the number was reduced to five. Following a Muslim's testimony to the oneness of God (the *Shahada*), "prayer constitutes the second of the obligatory duties that a believer must perform five times a day."[82] Prayer times are determined by the position of the sun and may vary depending on the season. In Muslim countries, prayer times are followed by an announcement that is broadcast from the minaret of the mosque by the adhan (call to prayer).[83] More important, however, is that the daily prayers be spread out throughout the day:

78. Nawaz, *Islam*, 12.

79. Robinson, *Islam*, 77.

80. See Robinson, *Islam*, 96.

81. Nawaz, *Islam*, 14.

82. Nawaz, *Islam*, 15.

83. Robinson, *Islam*, 98.

Fajr: the first of the five daily prayers performed at dawn or daybreak.

Zhuhr: the second of the five daily prayers performed at midday (see Quran 62:9–11).

Asr: the third of the five daily prayers performed late afternoon.

Maghrib: the fourth of the five daily prayers performed at sunset.

Isha: the fifth of the five daily prayers performed at night.

The proper place for obligatory prayer is the Masjid (mosque). Prayer can be performed individually or as a group. Group prayer is preferred because it shows the unity of the Muslim community. Muslims pray facing the Quibla—direction of the holy Mosque at Mecca. But a working or travelling Muslim can pray anywhere. All they need to do is find a clean place and make the place a suitable place for prayer. Sunni Muslims usually pray on a mat, while it is customary for Shia Muslims to pray on bare earth.[84] "In addition to finding a suitable place for prayer, a Muslim must be appropriately dressed. A man's clothing should cover his shoulders and the area between the navel and the knees. According to some authorities, his head should also be covered. A woman must cover her whole body, apart from her face and hands. Men and women alike remove their shoes."[85]

Prayer, for a Muslim, is not a mechanical or ceremonial act. The mechanical form is not as important as the spirit of righteousness.[86] One of the requisite demands for prayer is a clean state of mind. This means that a Muslim performing prayer must carry out prayer with a clear mind such that he or she understands the recitation and actions involved in prayer.[87] If a Muslim performs prayer without being pure and clean that prayer is not valid. The Quran lists some things that render a person unclean for prayer. If a person, for instance, has just had urination, defecation, and sexual intercourse they are considered ritually unclean (see Quran 4:43; 5:6). These require some ritual purification known as *At-taharah*, which in itself is of two kinds: Wudu (ablution) and Ghusl (full ablution). Ablution is not done randomly. Rather, it is performed diligently, according to a set of rules, by washing one's hands, feet, mouth, nose, face, forearms, and head. If a woman, for example, has just completed menstruation or is within forty

84. Robinson, *Islam*, 99.

85. Robinson, *Islam*, 99.

86. Nawaz, *Islam*, 18.

87. Nawaz, *Islam*, 16.

days of childbirth, she is required to perform ghusl (ritual washing of the whole body).[88]

How to Perform Wudu	How to Perform Ghusl
1. Must have the intention of performing Wudu.	1. Must have the intention of performing Ghusl.
2. Say: "Bismilahi Rahmani Rahim" (in the name of Allah, Most Gracious, Most Merciful).	2. Take full shower.
3. Wash hands, rinse mouth, and clean inside of the nose with water.	
4. Wash face.	
5. Wash arms up to the elbows, starting with the right arm.	
6. Rub the head and ears with wet arms.	
7. Wash feet up to the ankle, starting with the right foot.	
8. Say the *Shahada*.	

Friday is to Muslims what Sunday is to Christians. The Friday congregational or juma prayer has a special significance for Muslims.[89] All adult males are encouraged to attend the Friday congregational prayer. Women are also encouraged to attend, but their attendance is not obligatory. The mode of prayer, in general, consists of a sequence of movements called a raka, "standing upright, bowing from the waist, standing upright again, prostrating, sitting on the left hell, prostrating again, and then returning to the sitting position—accompanied by Qur'anic recitations and the utterance of set of expressions in Arabic."[90] The number of rakas to be performed vary according to the prayer time, i.e., whether it is morning prayer, afternoon prayer, or evening prayer.

3. Fasting or *Sawm*

Muslims are required to fast all year round, particularly in the month of Ramadan (the ninth month of the Islamic lunar calendar). The holy month of Ramadan is to the Islamic calendar year what prayer is to the daily life of a Muslim because the celebration of the Ramadan fast gives "the year

---

88. Robinson, *Islam*, 99–100.

89. Nawaz, *Islam*, 17.

90. Robinson, *Islam*, 100.

its rhythmic turning around God."[91] Ramadan holds special significance because it is the month in which the Quran was revealed. Fasting attunes the Muslim to God, making him or her aware of God's ever-presence. As a way of showing gratitude to God, the Muslim refrains from evil thoughts and evil actions. Fasting also helps the Muslim learn and practice self-denial and self-control. The Quran also prescribes fasting as a means of expiating one's sins (Quran 33:35).[92]

The Quran prescribes the fixed number of days of fasting, what is to be done and what is to be avoided during fast (Quran 2:183–185, 187). Fasting begins from sunset and lasts till sundown. No food, drink, or sexual activities are permitted during fast. Fasting is compulsory for all adult male and female Muslim in sound health. People with serious illness and elderly people are exempted from fasting. Children who have reached the age of puberty are encouraged to fast, but not compulsory.[93] "Those who are traveling or suffering from an ailment are allowed to make up for the missed days when they have completed their journeys and recovered from sickness."[94]

Before fasting in the month of Ramadan was made compulsory, Muslims who were with Prophet Muhammad (PBUH) in Medina used to fast with Jews, as a show of solidarity, on the day of Ashura (the tenth day of Muharram, the first month of the Muslim calendar), the Jewish Day of Atonement, and a day that Jews commemorate their liberation from Egypt. The Jewish Day of Atonement is commemorated on the ninth day after Rosh Hashanah (Jewish New Year). It was Jewish belief that God was closer to them on the Day of Atonement than on any other day.[95] When the practice of fasting in the month of Ramadan became mandatory after the Muslim break with the Jews, fasting on the day of Ashura became optional. But the idea of the nearness of God to the Muslim on this month is retained. Apart from the moral and spiritual significance of fasting in the month of Ramadan, there is also a socio-religious significance. "The method and timing of the fast distinguishes Muslims from Jews and Christians, marking them off as a distinct community. The fact that all Muslims fast during the same period and break the fast at the same time increases their sense of solidarity with each other at both the local and the international level."[96]

91. Carmody and Brink, *Ways to the Center*, 303–4.

92. Robinson, *Islam*, 117.

93. Nawaz, *Islam*, 36.

94. Nawaz, *Islam*, 36.

95. Robinson, *Islam*, 123.

96. Robinson, *Islam*, 124.

When does fasting in the month of Ramadan begin? The Islamic calendar, a lunar-based calendar, has twelve lunar months of twenty-nine or thirty days, which totals about 355 days (eleven days short of the Gregorian calendar). The month before Ramadan is called the *Shaban*. Muslims begin to look for the thin crescent of the new moon from the twenty-ninth day of *Shaban*. When the *qadi* (Islamic judge) determines that the new moon is out, Muslims are informed to begin fasting the following day.[97] This means that the beginning of Ramadan fast varies from country to country. Neal Robinson points out three potential problems this variation of the start of Ramadan fast poses for Muslims living in northern Europe and North America in contemporary world. First, the marked seasonal variation in number of daylight hours means "that when Ramadan falls in summer, the fasting period is far longer than it would be in Arabia, but that when it falls in winter it is far shorter."[98] Second, regarding the beginning and ending of the Ramadan fast, "because northern skies are often occluded at night, local Muslim communities usually take their cue from religious authorities in Saudi Arabia, Iran or Pakistan, rather than rely on local sightings of the new moon. Unfortunately this often results in different ethnic groups being out of step with each other by twenty-four hours, despite living in the same city."[99] Third, "against the clear skies of Arabia, the moon is visible night after night, and Muslims watch it wax and wane. They know for example that when there is a full moon they are half way through the month. In northern cities, however, the moon may be visible for as few as two or three days. For their inhabitants, the link between Ramadan and the lunar cycle is thus almost entirely severed."[100]

The Ramadan fast ends with the feast of *Eid-el-Fitr* that is celebrated on the first day of *Shawwal* (the tenth month of the Islamic calendar). *Eid* celebrations hold special significance for Muslims all over the world because it symbolizes their unity, brotherhood, and solidarity. "Every household with financial capabilities is required to donate a specific amount of money or its equivalent in kind (called 'Fitra') for charitable causes. In addition, people with ample monetary resources contribute generously to help the poor and the needy."[101]

---

97. Robinson, *Islam*, 119.
98. Robinson, *Islam*, 126.
99. Robinson, *Islam*, 126.
100. Robinson, *Islam*, 126.
101. Nawaz, *Islam*, 38.

4. Almsgiving or *Zakat*

Zakat is obligatory charity expected of a Muslim. The Quran prescribes prayer and charity, not as options, but as duties that help a Muslim purify his or her life. The word "zakat" originally meant "purity."[102] When *zakat* was first revealed, it was intended as a voluntary charity (Quran 73:20), but was later extended to mean an obligatory duty, because it serves as "a source of purification and sanctification of human soul, a vehicle of inner security, and a means of repentance from one's sinful actions (Quran 9:104)."[103] The obligation to do *zakat* is an obligation to donate a fixed percentage of one's income or wealth. *Zakat* is distributed to the poor and needy; never to be given to the rich or one's dependents. If a person is too poor to pay the obligatory *zakat,* he or she is still expected to act charitably.[104] At its root *zakat* has a spiritual significance in that it binds the giver and receiver in mutual respect and affection.[105] Giving a certain percentage of one's wealth helps one fulfill an important religious obligation and by so doing purifies one from greed and selfishness. In similar fashion, the one who receives *zakat* is purified because *zakat* saves the person from humiliation that comes from begging.[106] There is also the socio-economic function of *zakat*. "Together with the prohibition of usury, *zakat* discourages the hoarding of capital and stimulates investment in the means of production or merchandise, neither of which is usually regarded as zakatable."[107]

Besides *zakat*, Islam also encourages voluntary almsgiving known as *sadaqa*. Quran 9:60 lists eight categories of people that are eligible to receive *sadaqa*: the poor, destitute, captives who need to obtain their freedom, debtors, wayfarers, those employed to collect funds, those whose hearts are to be reconciled (perhaps may be referring to inhabitants of Mecca who were at first hostile to Islam but later converted when Mecca was conquered by Muslims), and those engage in holy war.[108]

---

102. Robinson, *Islam*, 111.
103. Nawaz, *Islam*, 39.
104. Robinson, *Islam*, 113.
105. Robinson, *Islam*, 115.
106. Robinson, *Islam*, 115.
107. Robinson, *Islam*, 115.
108. Robinson, *Islam*, 112–13.

5. Pilgrimage or *Hajj*

All Muslims, male and female alike, are required to do the obligatory *hajj* at least once in one's lifetime. There are many reasons for the *hajj*, all stemming from divine wisdom who wants all Muslims to come together in a single place to worship Him in sincerity of heart. "The hajj is an obligation that must be performed without delay: hence, whoever fulfills the conditions for its being obligatory but postpones its performance past the first year during which he would have been able to do so is guilty of wrongdoing."[109]

Muslims pray facing Mecca because for Muslims Mecca is "the center, the omphalos (navel) where the world was born."[110] The same inner logic is present in the obligation to make pilgrimage to Mecca at least once in one's lifetime.[111] The obligation to make pilgrimage to Mecca was instituted in the ninth year of the *Hejira* (Muhammad's flight from Mecca to Medina). Pre-Islamic Arabs made pilgrimage to the Kaaba in Mecca where they worshiped idols, particularly the three idols Al-Lat, Al-Manat, and Al-Uzza that were designated by the Koraish as daughters of Allah. The Quran denounces this idol worship as blasphemy. When obligatory pilgrimage was mandated for Muslims, Abou Bakr, one of the closest companions to Prophet Muhammad (PBUH), on the orders of the Prophet made a public announcement that "no polytheist shall be allowed to perform Hajj (pilgrimage) after that year."[112] This prohibition forbidden pagans and polytheists from performing pilgrimage to Mecca came approximately 631 CE. Prophet Muhammad (PBUH) led an exclusively Muslim *Hajj* in 632 CE. Today the area in Mecca known as the haram (sanctuary or sacred precinct) is clearly marked and non-Muslims are not allowed anywhere near the area. In this area is located the sacred mosque known as al-masjid al-haram. To the east of the sacred mosque are two hills Safa and Marwa that pilgrims have to pass through. At the center of the sacred mosque is the Kaaba (a cube-shaped building that pilgrims circumambulate counter-clockwise).

Muslims usually trace the origin of pilgrimage to Mecca to Abraham and Ishmael who performed true worship of Allah at the Kaaba. The Quran explicitly states that it was Abraham and his son Ishmael who erected the Kaaba and God ordained it to be a sanctuary or place of prayer (see Quran 2:124–29).[113] But with passage of time the followers of Abraham and Ish-

---

109. Al-Jaziri, *Islamic Jurisprudence*, 854.

110. Carmody and Brink, *Ways to the Center*, 304.

111. Carmody and Brink, *Ways to the Center*, 304.

112. Nawaz, *Islam*, 47.

113. Robinson, *Islam*, 129–30.

mael relapsed into idol worship.[114] Thus, Muslims perform pilgrimage to Mecca "to sanctify their true faith in Allah, the one and Absolutely One God without any partners or associates."[115] The *Hajj* is performed the second week of *Dhul-hijja* (the twelfth month of the Muslim calendar) and lasts for five days. The *Hajj* consists of series of rituals. Muslims performing the *Hajj* dress modestly to signify their renunciation of worldly vanities. The simple dress of all the pilgrims also signifies the unity of the believers—that there is no socio-economic or racial distinction. The Quran mentions that Safa and Marwa are among the places ordained by God for sacred rites (Quran 2:18).[116] The pilgrims run seven times between the hills of Safa and Marwa to "commemorate the agony of Hagar, wife of Abraham, running between the hills to find water for her son Ishmael. It also symbolizes the struggle of life which prompts human beings to enhance their efforts in seeking divine support."[117] There is the other ritual of throwing stones at the three pillars, which symbolizes Muslim rejection of the devil—the same devil who tried to dissuade Abraham from sacrificing his son as commanded by God.[118] At the conclusion of the *Hajj,* Muslims shave their head and slaughter an animal, in imitation of Prophet Muhammad and his companions who shaved their head and slaughtered a sacrificial animal at the conclusion of their own *Hajj.* The slaughtering of animal takes place on the third day of the *Hajj* when Muslims celebrate *Eid ul-Adha* (Festival of the Sacrifice). At the conclusion of the *Hajj* those Muslims who could afford it are encouraged to visit the Prophet's burial place in Medina, the second holiest city for Muslims.

Related to the *Hajj* is a lesser pilgrimage known as the *Umra.* The *Umra* is not an obligation, but it is encouraged. It can be performed at any time of the year. Pagan Arabs who performed *Hajj* also performed the *Umra* until they were forbidden to do these in 631 by the prophet. The series of rituals involved in *Umra* is about the same as that of *Hajj.*

FIQH AND MADHAHIB (THE FOUR LEGAL SCHOOLS)

In Islamic literature, law and legal reasoning are centerpiece, although complicated. While the Quran has important passages that shape the ethos of legal reasoning, these passages often do not convey explicit legal content. For example, the Quran provides guidance on such civil matters, like marriage,

114. Nawaz, *Islam,* 47.
115. Nawaz, *Islam,* 47–48.
116. Robinson, *Islam,* 130.
117. Nawaz, *Islam,* 51.
118. Nawaz, *Islam,* 51.

divorce, and inheritance, but provides no specifics on how these are to be handled.[119] What Muslims call *Fiqh* is a "human attempt to understand the divine will, or the intellectual exercise that translates the sources of divine guidance into prescriptive and proscriptive stipulations."[120] In employing *Fiqh*, Muslims try to differentiate between two actions: actions and duties that govern human behavior towards God and actions and duties that govern and regulate human interactions among humans.[121] For the Shia, after the Prophet, the divinely inspired imam is the sole interpreter of the divine will. What the jurists have to do, therefore, is study the imam's opinions and effectively communicate them to the community.[122] But the Sunni follow a rather different path. The Sunni do not place the interpretation of divine will squarely on the shoulders of one man. The Sunni believe in legal diversity and very early on developed four legal schools that over time became dominant in a given geographical area in the Muslim world. Each of the four schools derives its name from the great imam who was perhaps the first to set its principles of jurisprudence.[123]

a. The Maliki School, founded by the eighth-century Medinan scholar, Malik ibn Anas (715–95 CE): The stronghold of the Maliki School to this day is North Africa (Algeria, Tunisia, Morocco, Mauritania, Libya, and Egypt) and parts of sub-Saharan African countries, like Chad, Sudan, Nigeria, Niger, and Senegal. Some parts of Saudia Arabia, Kuwait, Bahrain, Dubai, and Abu Dhabi also follow the Maliki School.[124]

b. The Hanafi School, founded by Kufa scholar from Iraq, Abu Hanifa (699–767 CE): In the glory days of the Ottoman Empire, the Ottoman rulers adopted the Hanafi School, which they imposed on their subjects. This means that at the time of the Ottoman rule, present-day Turkey, some parts of Central Asia, the Balkans, Iraq, Afghanistan, Pakistan, India, Bangladesh, Syria, Jordan, Palestine, and Egypt, were all Hanafi.[125]

c. The Shafii School, founded by another Medinan scholar, Muhammad ibn Idris al-Shafi'i: The Shafii School has followings in Egypt and

---

119. McAuliffe, *Islam*, 52.

120. McAuliffe, *Islam*, 52.

121. McAuliffe, *Islam*, 52.

122. McAuliffe, *Islam*, 52.

123. See Al-Jaziri, *Islamic Jurisprudence*, xxiii.

124. Al-Jaziri, *Islamic Jurisprudence*, xxiv.

125. Al-Jaziri, *Islamic Jurisprudence*, xxiii.

North Yemen, East African countries of Ethiopia, Eritrea, Somalia, Kenya, Tanzania, and Uganda, and Southeast Asia countries of Indonesia, Malaysia, and the Philippines.[126]

d. The Hanbali School, founded by the Baghdad scholar Ahmad ibn Hanbal: The Hanbali School has most of its followings in Saudi Arabia, Qatar, Oman, and some parts of the Arab Emirates.[127]

No single school provides a dogmatically complete account of Islamic law; rather, each school represents "one possible reading of Muslim orthopraxis or of Islamic law (sharia), covering such fields as ritual law, family law, inheritance law, as well as laws dealing with economic and political practices."[128] Every one of the schools traces its historical origins to the differing approaches taken by the Companions of the Prophet and their direct disciples, approaches that allowed for diversity in application of Islamic laws. They "enshrine the principle of *ikhtilaf* (disagreement/difference), which permits a Muslim to choose the interpretation of the religious teachings that best suits his own circumstances and causes the least harm."[129] Overall, the Islamic ideal combines unity and diversity because according to Islamic tradition, Prophet Muhammad considered differences of opinion in the Islamic community as both a sign of divine favor and an act of mercy on the part of God who acknowledges that men of knowledge differ in opinion.[130]

ISLAM IN THE UNITED STATES OF AMERICA

Often neglected in the history of the Atlantic slave trade is the fact that the slave trade brought a significant number of black Muslims to the United States of America and the so-called New World. Before the Atlantic Slave Trade Islam flourished in many African Kingdoms, particularly in the Old Ghana Empire that reached its peak in the thirteenth century, the Old Mali Empire that reached its peak in the late fifteenth/early sixteenth century CE, and the late Songhai Empire that thrived in the sixteenth century. Islam was introduced to these kingdoms in the ninth and tenth century CE. Africa was connected to the Muslim world through the Trans-Saharan Trade routes that were controlled by Berbers from North Africa and Muslim traders from Tunisia, Morocco, Egypt, and Algeria. These Muslim traders traded in

126. Al-Jaziri, *Islamic Jurisprudence*, xxiii.

127. Al-Jaziri, *Islamic Jurisprudence*, xxiii.

128. Al-Jaziri, *Islamic Jurisprudence*, xxiii.

129. Al-Jaziri, *Islamic Jurisprudence*, xxiii.

130. Al-Jaziri, *Islamic Jurisprudence*, xxiii.

salt and gold with their sub-Saharan African counterparts. Trade brought a lot of cultural exchanges between the different trading partners. Islamic art, calligraphy, music, and ways of life were introduced to sub-Saharan Africa. One of the reasons for the growth of the early African kingdoms was Islam, which served as a means of unity and also provided social and political privileges. Many of the rulers, like Mansa Musa of Ghana, were devout Muslims who saw Islam as an opportunity to trade and connect with the Muslim world. Following the mandate that the religion of the king was the religion of the state, many Africans converted to Islam as soon as their leader became a Muslim. Timbuktu became a great center of Islamic learning. About three million of the African slaves that were brought to the Americas and the Caribbean islands in the seventeenth and eighteenth century were Muslims. About one million of these Muslim slaves made it to the United States. Many of the Muslim slaves captured in what is now Mali, Nigeria, Ghana, Senegal, Guinea, and Gambia were literate and learned. They kept aspects of their culture and Islamic religion when they were brought to the United States. From police records, plantation logs, and runaway notices that were kept by the courts and slave owners we know that some of these slaves practiced their Islamic religion openly while others practiced them secretly. For example, many of the slaves said their five daily prayers, fasted during the holy month of Ramadan, abstained from eating pork, bore Muslim names, and made Islamic calligraphy (artistic representation of Islamic faith). Some of the Muslim slaves even left journals.

The second wave of Muslim immigration into the United States was in the mid-twentieth century when Palestinian refugees began emigrating to Europe and the United States following the creation of the state of Israel by the United Nations in 1948. The Immigration and Nationality Act of 1952 (also known as the McCarran-Walter Act) also helped to accelerate the wave of Muslim immigration to the United States. The McCarran-Walter Act was put in place as a post-World War II and Cold War measure to check the influx of communists from Japan and the former Soviet Union (USSR) into the United States. While the goal of the Act was to reward notable Asian countries, like China, and assimilate them into the mainstream of US life, the Act was also an exclusionary measure meant to deny entry to the United States to people who refuse to be assimilated into the US economic and political structures. The McCarran-Walter Act was deemed exclusionary by critics and the controversy surrounding the Act, together with other factors, led to a revision of the US immigration laws in 1965. The 1965 Immigration and Nationality Act (also known as the Hart-Celler Act) abolished the national origins formula of the McCarran-Walter Act and instituted a new formula based on skill sets of immigrants. This new policy opened the floodgate of immigration for Muslims fleeing political and economic oppression in places like Palestine, Syria, Jordan, Pakistan, and Egypt. They established mosques in cities like Detroit, New York, New Jersey, and Chicago.

Wallace D. Farad, one of the immigrants from the Middle East, established a mosque in Detroit that attracted African-Americans. His message was a mixture of Islam and Black Nationalism. The movement thrived under his disciple Elijah Mohammed who made Chicago the capital of the movement. Many African-Americans saw this movement, which preached black pride and black emancipation from white rule, as a way to liberate themselves from poverty and racism. For these reasons, they converted in droves. This group got the attention of the world during the 1960s Civil Rights Movement. They were popularly referred to as Black Muslims. Malcolm X (formerly Malcolm Little), a student and disciple of Elijah Mohammed, exemplified what the movement represents with the credo "the white man hates us, so we should hate the white man back."[131] Malcolm denounced Christianity as a religion designed for slaves and defended Islam as the only religion that was not fixated on color differences or race. Malcolm argued, therefore, that black people have to be separated (not integrated) with white America and that it was only through separation that black people in America will discover their self-identity.

131. See Haley, *Autobiography of Malcolm X*, xvi.

PART TWO

Tribal Religions and the Non-Abrahamic Religions

11

Religious Rapprochement and African Traditional Religions

ACCORDING TO THE EVOLUTIONARY science of religion, religion is not a term with a fixed meaning, but a word whose meaning is always evolving and adapting. In its evolutionary sense, the word religion can convey different meanings to different people and can also represent totally different realities.[1] Most people who consider themselves religious accept the particular religion that they are born into. There are also those who self-consciously choose their own religion later on in life. But that is not to say that the two are mutually exclusive. A person can be born into a particular religion and still self-consciously choose it, making it a life-vision. In this chapter, we shall examine the Tribal religions, with particular attention to African Traditional Religions (ATRs), and with a view to highlighting the differences between "religion as clan-solidarity" and "religion as life-vision."[2] But before delving into this distinction it is important to highlight some key common features of the world religions.

WORLD RELIGIONS: COMMON THEMES

The three Abrahamic religions, i.e., Judaism, Christianity, and Islam, are religions that the British historian Arnold Toynbee (1889–1975) characterized as the religions of revelation. According to Toynbee, in spite of their

1. Fernando, "View of Jesus' Uniqueness," 70.
2. Fernando, "View of Jesus' Uniqueness," 70.

common historical root, these three religions have a tendency towards exclusivism and intolerance.[3] Toynbee also described these three Abrahamic religions as religions that ascribe to themselves ultimate validity. Building on this idea, the German theologian, Friedrich Heiler (1892–1967), suggested that what these religions in fact do is "transfer the absoluteness which is an attribute alone of the divine and eternal to their own system of faith without seeing that this divine absolute can also be comprehended in entirely different forms of thought and devotion."[4] The logical outcome of this is the danger of thinking of religions other than the Abrahamic ones as "second class" religions or not even ""religion" in the proper sense. To help correct this mistaken notion that the non-Abrahamic religions may have emerged as an "outgrowth of error, sin, and malice,"[5] it is good that we examine some common threads that hold the religions of the world (i.e., World Religions) together—Judaism, Christianity, Islam, Zoroastrianism, Hinduism, Buddhism, and Taoism.

World Religions differ from Tribal religions. Unlike tribal religions, World Religions are more global and spread out. They are not concentrated in one region or place. World Religions are also proselytizing religions—they are given to making converts. Another distinguishing factor is that World Religions usually have a founder and a written text that serve as scripture. The only exception to this is Hinduism, which has no founder, no divinely revealed scriptures, no creed or dogmas, no ecclesiastical organization or "church," and, in many of its forms, does not give importance to the concept of a personal divinity.[6] In general, however, all the World Religions have a common concern for cosmic harmony, inner peace, oneness with nature, the art of meditation as a way to the divine, asceticism and self-denial, the full use of higher human faculties, communication with the spirit world, and loyalty to one's family, community, and tradition.[7] Seven principal areas of agreement are worthy of attention.[8]

1. Reality of the Transcendent.

    All the World Religions acknowledge "the reality of the transcendent, the holy, the divine, the Other," who is assumed to be the eternal truth

---

3. See Toynbee, *Historian's Approach to Religion*.

4. See Heiler, "History of Religions."

5. Heiler, "History of Religions."

6. Kessler, *Eastern Ways of Being Religious*, 39.

7. Hellwig, "Rethinking Uniqueness," 77–78.

8. See Lonergan, "Future of Christianity," 149–63.

or "one without counterpart."[9] In Judaism this eternal truth is Yahweh. In Christianity, it is the Trinitarian Godhead—Father, Son, and Holy Spirit. In Islam it is the one God, Allah. Hinduism has an evolving polytheism that recognizes about 330 million gods, like Brahma (creator god), Vishnu (preserver), and Shiva (the destroyer). In Buddhism, although divinities of one kind or the other may play some role in stories and practices that shape the peoples' life, "the divine is essentially unimportant when it comes to understanding life, suffering, and the way to overcome suffering."[10] Taoism recognizes the Highest Venerable Lord—the manifestation of Tao or Way of Reality.[11] Zoroastrianism speaks of the one supreme God, Ahura Mazda who is called the Wise Lord.[12]

2. The Divine Transcendent is Immanent in Human Hearts.

All the World Religions find a creative balance for the tension between the transcendence and immanence of God. Jewish Scripture speaks of God in terms of both of God's transcendent and immanent qualities: "Am I a God nearby, says the Lord, and not a God far off? Who can hide in secret places so that I cannot see them? says the Lord. Do I not fill heaven and earth? says the Lord" (Jer 23:23–24). Christian Scripture speaks of the indwelling of the Holy Spirit among humans: "do you not know that your body is a temple of the Holy Spirit within you, which you have from God, and that you are not your own?" (1 Cor 6:19). Islam's distinctive virtue is to recognize the indwelling place of God in human hearts: "O you who believe! Answer (the call of) Allah and His Messenger when he calls you to that which gives you life; and know that Allah intervenes between man and his heart, and that to Him you shall be gathered" (Al-Anfal 8:24). In the Hindu pantheistic conception of God in the Upanishads, God is everything and everything is God. A person's goal is to be one with God (Brahma). In Taoism, humans are part of the cosmic process known as the Tao and the goal of human life, like that of all created reality, is harmony with the Tao.[13]

3. The Highest Good is the Final Goal.

9. Lonergan, "Future of Christianity," 149–50.
10. Kessler, *Eastern Ways of Being Religious*, 99.
11. Kessler, *Eastern Ways of Being Religious*, 227.
12. Carmody and Brink, *Ways to the Center*, 74.
13. Young, *World's Religions*, 118.

All the World Religions teach that the highest good is the final goal of all human striving.[14] Judaism, Christianity, and Islam all describe God as the ultimate and supreme good to whom all things tend and towards whom all humans strive. It is akin to the notion of *moksha* (liberation or release) from the world of suffering and cycles of life, death, and re-birth in Hinduism. In Buddhism it is nirvana—liberation from the cycle of suffering, birth, death, and re-birth. In Taoism it is transformation occurring within this life on earth.

4. The Reality of the Divine is Ultimate Love.

All the World Religions treat love as both the way of God and the way to God. In Judaism Yahweh's mercy is the same as Yahweh's justice and love. Christianity is a religion of love: "Beloved, let us love one another, because love is from God" (1 John 4:7). Love is the basis of relationship in Islam: "And among His Signs is this, that He created for you mates from among yourselves, that ye may dwell in tranquility with them, and He has put love and mercy between your [hearts]: Verily in that are Signs for those who reflect" (Al-Rum 30:21). Love is at the root of the Hindu ethic of *ahimsa* (non-injury to animals and all life forms) and Buddhist asceticism.

5. The Way to God is through Sacrifice.

All the World's Religions teach that the way to reach God is through sacrifice. The Jewish *Yom Kippur* (Day of Atonement) is a subdued and solemn celebration of fasting and reconciliation—a period in which one makes effort to reach out and reconcile with estranged members of one's family or community. Islam recommends fasting, especially in the holy month of Ramadan. Christians fast for forty days in Lent. Hindu gurus practice self-discipline. Many of them flock to Varanasi at old age, the site of the Hindu sacred river Ganges, to die and reflect the Hindu belief "that death in or near the Ganges at Varanasi results in Moksha, the final liberation from the endless cycles of birth and re-birth that is the ultimate spiritual goal of most Hindus."[15] Buddhism is called the Middle Way because Buddhists seek a middle way between excesses of sensuality and extreme asceticism.

6. Love of Neighbor.

14. Lonergan, "Future of Christianity," 150.
15. Kessler, *Eastern Ways of Being Religious*, 41.

The World Religions teach, not only love of God, but also love of one's neighbor. "All preach brotherly love, a love on which there are no limitations, a love that is to be extended even to enemies, a love that has its origin and source not in man himself but in God operating on man."[16] Christianity, Islam, and Judaism are religions that emphasize personal and communal salvation. The Hindu, Buddhist, and Taoist do not think of self in isolation from nature and society. Karma, which Hinduism and Buddhism preach, shows that what a person does or fails to do in this present life is going to determine his or her fate in this life or next. In other words, one's advancement or regression is going to be determined by the extent to which one has loved one's neighbor.

7. Love is the Ultimate and Supreme Way to God.

All the World Religions preach an ethic of love, i.e., love that has no limits, no qualifications. Jesus showed that love by dying on the cross. Love is at the heart of Gandhi's doctrine of non-violent resistance. Buddha showed it through the enlightenment that earned him nirvana.

TRIBAL RELIGIONS

Tribal religions are the religious systems of indigenous peoples—African Traditional Religions (ATRs), Native American religions, Australian Aborigines, and the Arctic peoples who inhabit the regions of Siberia to Alaska, to Canada, i.e., the Eskimos, Inuits, and Aleuts, etc. Tribal religions differ from the World Religions in many respects. The designation "tribal" is used to capture their form of social organization, which was usually a small band of hunters and gatherers who lived in an extended family structure or clan.[17] Hunting and gathering, their main economic activity, varied according to geographical and historical peculiarities.[18] Some anthropologists have taken to referring to tribal religions as prehistoric, pre-literate, and oral. These designations are meant to capture the fact that tribal peoples have no written records.

Modern mentality is far different from that of ancient cultures where history and culture were transmitted orally from generation to generation. But modern mentality requires writing "for a critical, objective, factual,

16. Lonergan, "Future of Christianity," 151.

17. Carmody and Brink, *Ways to the Center*, 27.

18. Carmody and Brink, *Ways to the Center*, 27.

trustworthy account of what happened."[19] It is helpful to understand that what makes these cultures tribal is their social organizations, which are based on tribes or clan. They are by no means "primitive" or "pagan" as some Western anthropologists sometimes pejoratively describe them. They may not have had technology in the modern understanding of the term, but they had a well-developed religious organization that addressed their most absorbing issues—those relating to survival, like birth, subsistence, and death.[20] They pondered life mysteries in terms of its implications to hunting. Hunting and gathering were, for them, sacred affairs that deal with nature's awesome powers concerning life and death.[21]

Common Areas

When a person is born and socialized into a religion, that religion can become for that person a form of "clan solidarity." Religion as "clan solidarity" is quite different from religion as "life-vision." The latter is a religion a person is "re-born to."[22] Tribal religions are good examples of "religion as clan solidarity." As a constituent element of culture, tribal religions fulfill an important sociological function that is vital for human existence.[23] Tribal religions, like culture's other constitutive elements—history of the clan, the geography of the clan, and the language of the clan—ensure clan solidarity.[24]

Like the World Religions, tribal religions have their own core common characteristics. As oral cultures, their sacred texts are not recorded in what may amount to holy books or scripture, but are contained in the memory of the people, particularly the elders of the community, and are transmitted through their traditional symbols, rituals, myths, and practices. Tribal religions are essentially religion as clan solidarity. As a form of clan solidarity, tribal religions are more provincial in their concerns. In other words, the characteristics that make them tribal are simply virtues that are culturally conditioned.[25]

1. The Sacred.

19. Carmody and Brink, *Ways to the Center*, 25.
20. Carmody and Brink, *Ways to the Center*, 27.
21. Carmody and Brink, *Ways to the Center*, 28.
22. Fernando, "Jesus' Uniqueness," 70.
23. Fernando, "Jesus' Uniqueness," 70.
24. Fernando, "Jesus' Uniqueness," 70–71.
25. Fernando, "Jesus' Uniqueness," 71.

In his book, *The Idea of the Holy*, the German Lutheran theologian, Rudolph Otto (1869–1937), analyzes the experience that underlies all religions. He calls this experience "numinous" and suggests that there are three components of this experience: *mysterium tremendum et fascinans* (mystery that is tremendous and fascinating). The mystery that is experienced, according to Otto, is unlike anything one experiences in ordinary life and because this mystery is "wholly other," it evokes silence and provokes awe or fear. The other part of this mystery or "awe" is that when provoked it does not dispel but attracts (fascinans).[26] Tribal religions experience the sacred in the Otto sense of *mysterium tremendum et fascinans*. The Pacific Island people of Papua New Guinea (known as Melanesians), for example, consider their deity to be sacred. They also consider their land to be sacred because it was given to them by their deity who created it from the remains of the sun and the moon.[27] This idea that certain things are set apart to be revered as sacred is common among tribal cultures. Emile Durkheim's (1858–1917) definition of religion as "a unified system of beliefs and practices relative to sacred things, that is to say, things set apart and forbidden,"[28] captures the essence of tribal religions.

2. Animism

Animism is the belief that all things, whether animals, plants, vegetation, seas, rivers, etc. have spirits or soul. Tribal cultures believe that there is a wide array of spirits out there with vested interests in human affairs and that the way one relates to the spirit world enhances or undermines one's life activities. This belief in spirits informs their worldview that spirits have to be worshiped or venerated. There are good spirits and bad spirits. Good spirits bring good fortune. Bad spirits bring bad fortune. Some cultures venerate the spirits of their dead ancestors, believing that such veneration will bring them good fortune. In Shintoism (the ancient religion of Japan) spirits are called "kami." Because they believe that "kami" exists in all natural things like lakes, rivers, mountains, oceans, animals, and plants, Shintos have shrines in several places for the worship of "kami." The British anthropologist, Sir Edward Burnett Tylor (1832–1917), developed the idea that religion

---

26. See Otto, *Idea of the Holy*.
27. Carmody and Brink, *Ways to the Center*, 52.
28. Durkheim, "Ritual, Magic, and the Sacred," 193.

at its core was animistic—that religion began as an attempt to explain ghosts.[29]

3. Exorcism

The belief in animism is related to the idea of exorcism—that bad spirits, which possess a person, need to be cast out. The duty of casting out evil spirits is not for everyone. It is usually the task of the high priest or shaman. The shaman is the medicine man who has good knowledge of the religious and cultural traditions of the people. Many indigenous cultures have female shamans. They ward off evil spirits through various means, like incantations and herbal medicine.

4. Healing

Exorcism is one way of procuring healing. But it is not only the one possessed by evil spirit that needs healing. There is a wide range of activities in tribal cultures that requires healing. A person who has committed a taboo, for example, or one who has fractured his or her relationship with the community, is brought back to the community only after going through a ritual sacrifice intended to heal or make whole.

5. Sacrifice

Sacrifice is a ritual performed to appease deity in tribal cultures. Sacrifices usually take the form of ritual offerings, like animal sacrifice, and in some societies, human sacrifice. The purpose of sacrifice is to restore harmony where the social fabric of society or community has been broken.[30] According to the French-born American philosopher of history and literary critic René Girard (1923–2015), human beings are prone to violence because violence is at the core of human nature. Human propensity towards violence is a conundrum for which human beings have to find a solution. From the beginning of human history, according to Girard, cultures have developed different methods of dealing with violence and one of this mechanism is religion. Religion, for Girard, therefore, is a mechanism which humans have developed to defend themselves against their own violent nature. The logic of Girard's argument is that tribal cultures lack a well-developed judicial system to deal with violence. Since each act of violence evokes

29. Carmody and Brink, *Ways to the Center*, 21.
30. Girard, "Violence and the Sacred," 244.

another, "to prevent this sequence, a victim—often a slave, king, or animal—is chosen. On this victim violence may be practiced without fear of reprisal."[31] Sacrifice, in the Girard sense, may be understood as a "regular exercise of good violence," which is used to overcome "bad violence."[32]

6. Taboo

A taboo, as understood in tribal societies, is a violation of prescribed action. It is also a morally reprehensible act. A person who commits a taboo incurs automatic punishment. Taboos are social mechanisms designed to establish some fundamental social values that are vital to society.[33] There are many types of taboos in tribal societies. Some taboos are designed for some specific occasions. Some cultures have taboos that are associated with farming or cultivation, for example. There are also taboos associated with harvesting, taboos for certain festivals, taboos to protect religious persons and places of worship, and taboos designed to keep women and children in certain places and at certain times. Like all religions (not excluding Judaism, Christianity, Islam, Hinduism, and Buddhism), tribal cultures have taboos that place restrictions on menstruating women. Prohibitions on menstruating women lead to prohibitions on "physical intimacy, cooking, attending places of worship, and sometimes requiring women to live separately from men" throughout their menstrual period.[34] In general, the sanctity of taboo is inspired by the idea that when a taboo is violated it may lead to disaster, not only for the individual violator, but for the society at large. The socio-cultural significance of taboo, therefore, is to confine the individual to the norms of society.[35]

7. Magic

As we saw already, sanctions always inevitably follow the breaking of taboos. When taboos are broken some tribal people turn to religious rituals to mitigate the wrong committed. Others at times turn to magic. Magic is an attempt to manipulate spiritual forces.[36] Un-

31. Girard, "Violence and the Sacred," 239.
32. Girard, "Violence and the Sacred," 239.
33. Banerjee, "Religious Beliefs and Practices," 155.
34. See Guterman et al., "Menstrual Taboos among Major Religions."
35. Banerjee, "Religious Beliefs and Practices," 155.
36. Carmody and Brink, *Ways to the Center*, 33.

like religious rituals, which usually take place in public and are often characterized by adoration and obeisance to the spirits, magical rites are often private, and like religious rituals acknowledge that all reality has some spiritual components.[37] Magic then is an attempt to interfere with the spiritual and make the spirits do human biddings. The Polish and British anthropologist, Bronislaw Malinowski (1884–1942), who was considered the father of Functionalism branch of anthropology (i.e., the idea that all parts of society work together to form a coherent meaningful whole) considered magic to be a precursor to religion. In other words, magic, for what he called "primitive" cultures, played the role technology plays for us moderns. According to him, "all peoples use the best technology available to them but turn to magic and religion when the problems they confront exceed that technology."[38]

8. The Profane

In the United States, like most of the Industrialized West, we are used to separation of church and state and hold the two realms in creative tension. Not so with indigenous societies. For them, religion and society are not two separate orders, but one and the same reality. The profane, for them, is the social order, i.e., the opposite of the sacred. But they do not understand the profane to be in opposition to the sacred. The distinction between the sacred and profane is, for them, just a way of speaking and demarcating two realms that are by no means opposed.

9. Rites of Passage

Tribal cultures have well-developed rites of passage. A rite of passage is a stage in life in which a person moves from one socially constructed role to another. Arnold Van Gennep (1873–1957) was the first to provide a scholarly definition of a rite of passage.[39] He defined rite of passage as "rites which accompany every change of place, state, social position, and age."[40] Rites of passage cut across all religions. Judaism is a good example of a World Religion with three well-defined rites of passage: Bris (infant circumcision), Bar Mitzvah (the coming of age ceremony for teen-age boys), and Kadish (funeral ceremony). Tribal

37. Carmody and Brink, *Ways to the Center*, 33.
38. Carmody and Brink, *Ways to the Center*, 21.
39. See Van Gennep, *Rites of Passage*.
40. See Turner, "Liminality and Communitas," 512.

cultures have rites of passage with striking similarities to those of the World Religions. There are basically four main rites of passage in tribal societies: birth (a ceremony initiates a child into the tribe), adolescence (ceremony that shows a person has moved from childhood to adulthood), marriage (a person becomes a responsible parent), and death (passage from this life to the next). "For every one of these events," Van Gennep wrote, "there are ceremonies whose essential purpose is to enable the individual to pass from one defined position to another which is equally well-defined."[41] Van Gennep went on to suggest that all rites of passage exhibit a pattern (or schema), which vary in importance, depending on the degree or the transitional phase that is being celebrated. The three patterns or schema are: separation, margin, and aggregation. The separation phase "comprises symbolic behavior signifying detachment of the individual or group either from an earlier fixed point in the social structure, from the set of cultural conditions or from both."[42] The rite of circumcision of a child will be an example of Van Gennep's separation phase. In the margin phase the person going through the ritual is in a liminal situation and because of this he or she manifests characteristics that are ambiguous.[43] The rites of adolescence or puberty will be a good example of the liminal stage. Finally, in the third phase, the one going through the ritual is in a relatively stable state and now has the same rights and obligations as others. He or she "is expected to behave in accordance with certain customary norms and ethical standards binding on incumbents of social position in a system of such positions."[44] An example here would be the rites of marriage.

Rites of passage in tribal societies are encoded in symbols. Symbols of course have different layers of meanings. The American anthropologist-linguist, Edward Sapir (1834–1939), spoke of two main classes of symbols. The first kind, Referential symbols, are for the most part cognitive in the sense that they refer to facts that are already known to the community or society. Examples of this are oral speech or a flag or code of arms of a community. The other class of symbol he called Condensation symbol. Ritual symbols in tribal societies are a good example of Condensation symbol.[45] The Brit-

41. Van Gennep, *Rites of Passage*, 3.
42. Turner, "Liminality and Communitas," 512.
43. Turner, "Liminality and Communitas," 512.
44. Turner, "Liminality and Communitas," 512.
45. Sapir, "Symbols," 492–93.

ish cultural anthropologist whose work on symbols revolutionized contemporary understanding of symbols, particularly as it pertains to our understanding of tribal societies, Victor Turner (1920–83), brings to our awareness the fact that symbols are polysemy (have many senses). Turner distinguishes three levels of symbolic meanings, which are important for understanding tribal ritual rites of passage. Turner calls the first level Exegetical meaning (understanding how the locals interpret their symbols). The second level is Operational meaning (understanding not only what the people say about their symbols, but also understanding what they do with their symbols). The third level is Positional meaning (understanding the meaning of the symbol in question in relationship to other system of symbols).[46] To understand tribal rites of passage one needs to investigate their rituals following these three levels.

10. Divination

Divination is an attempt to discern the will of deity or oracle for a particular course of action. It is also the practice of predicting or foretelling the future. Divination, in contemporary society, is akin to psychic hotline. Many people go to psychics today to get "answers" for their troubles, say marriage, illness, poverty, etc. In tribal societies divination "is similar to magic in that it is an occult, non-technological solution to life's problems, but whereas magic tries to manipulate future events, divination is the mere attempt to predict those events."[47] In many tribal societies, when someone is chronically ill and return to health of the sick person is hard to come by, many people take their sick ones to a shrine or oracle to meet a diviner for diagnosis and prognosis. Diviners use different methods, like looking at the entrails of animals (say sheep or goat), examining the flight path of birds, or reading cracks in the shell of tortoise.[48] Among the Yoruba people of southwest Nigeria, Ifa divination is very common. Ifa priests are well revered and respected by both the Yoruba and non-Yoruba people alike.

11. Creation Myths

According to a recent study in neurobiology, due to the structure of the brain, human beings inevitably construct myths to explain their

---

46. Turner, "Symbols in Ndembu Ritual," 526.
47. Carmody and Brink, *Ways to the Center*, 34–35.
48. Carmody and Brink, *Ways to the Center*, 35.

world.[49] A myth is usually a traditional storied form of explanation.[50] "A myth is an explanation of what has happened, and it is repeated because it expresses the tribe's identity and values. Peoples tell myths explaining how they came to be where and what they were."[51] According to the American mythologist, Joseph Campbell (1904–1987), there are four main functions of myth: (i) metaphysical function: to express a people's sense of awe before the absolute mystery; (ii) cosmological function: to account for the origin of the universe; (iii) sociological function: to provide support for the existing social order and integrate the individual into it; and (iv) pedagogical: to teach and guide the individual on how to attain spiritual growth and human flourishing.[52] Myths essentially help establish models of behavior,[53] and as narrative accounts of the acts of creation serve as models for ritual.[54]

12. Totems

A totem is an object that is considered sacred, which is used as the symbol of the family, clan, or tribe. It is usually made of an animal or plant that is revered by the family, clan, or tribe. The totem serves as an emblem on which the people rally together. It gives them a sense of pride and identity. The idea of using plant or animal objects is also to show the interconnectedness of all beings.

13. High God

Most tribal societies believe in deity and locate the heavens or sky as the abode of the high God. The location of sky as the abode of deity conveys the idea that the high God is centrally located. It also shows the power of this deity who is usually conceived in masculine terms. He resides in heaven and is in control of the galaxies—the moon, the stars, the planets—and all created realities. He is everywhere and oversees all things. Deity is addressed by a great variety of names. The Massai of East Africa, for example, address divinity "directly with a great variety of names which are metaphorical masks for the incomprehensible

---

49. See D'Aquili and Laughlin, "Neurobiology of Myth and Ritual."
50. Carmody and Brink, *Ways to the Center*, 35.
51. Carmody and Brink, *Ways to the Center*, 35.
52. See Campbell, *Occidental Mythology*.
53. Eliade, *Myth and Reality*, 8.
54. See Eliade, "Symbolism of the Center."

ground of all reality, the inscrutable mystery of life behind the visible universe."[55]

14. Afterlife

Belief in afterlife is a common feature of tribal religions. Life on earth is just the beginning of the life that is yet to come. The way a person lives and acts in this life will determine one's eschatological future. Tribal religions, more than all other religions, stress the importance of interwoven solidarity with one's kinsmen and women both past and present. Deceased relatives are not considered dead, but as having gone to take their place with the ancestors. The ancestors look after the tribe or clan from heaven.

15. Megaliths

In ancient times, particularly in Neolithic (New Stone Age) cultures, megaliths were carefully constructed centers of ritual, usually made of large stones. The notion of Megalith in tribal cultures is related to the reverence they have for their dead and ancestors. Stone in ancient times was a sign of fortress. People always sought refuge from life troubles by maintaining contact with ancestors and seeking from them strength and succor. Those who sought close communion with their dead ones often came to these ritual centers for both security and strength. Megalith then served as a "symbol of permanence—of resistance to change, decay, or death."[56] The Stonehenge in England is one of the world's famous megaliths.

16. Shaman

The Shaman is akin to a priest in contemporary society. The shaman is entrusted with cultic duties. He or she is essentially at the center of divination, healing, sacrifice, and even rites of passage. In many societies the shaman is reputed to have clairvoyance and clairaudience, i.e., has the ability to see and hear beyond the normal range.[57] According to Mircea Eliade, shamans play a great role in the defense of psychic integrity of the community. They champion anti-demonism by combating demons and diseases.[58] They uphold life, health, fertility and

55. Hillman, *Toward an African Christianity*, 51.
56. Carmody and Brink, *Ways to the Center*, 37.
57. Carmody and Brink, *Ways to the Center*, 38
58. Eliade, *Archaic Techniques of Ecstasy*, 508.

wage war against death, disease, sterility, disaster, as well as all forces of darkness.[59] They play these role so well because of their ability to travel to the supernatural world where they encounter superhuman beings (gods, demons, spirits of the dead, etc.).[60] Tribal people find it very comforting to know that their shaman has the uncanny ability to fight the forces of evil. They also find it reassuring to know that a member of their community, i.e., the shaman, is not only able to see what is hidden and invisible to others but can also bring back direct and reliable information from the spirit world.[61]

AFRICAN TRADITIONAL RELIGIONS

The word "religion," as we have pointed out repeatedly, is Western in origin. Although Africans have strong beliefs about God and the supernatural world, they do not have a word for religion in its Western sense. In traditional African society, like in all tribal religions, there was no wall of separation between church and state or religion and society. What religion accepted or forbade was accepted or forbidden by society. In a sense there was an overlap between the state and religion in matters of politics and morals. But if we are to speak of religion in the Western sense of the word *religio* (to perform ritual with care) or *religare* (to bind), it is safe to say that Africans have different activities and practices they do that parallel what the West means by religion. The African sense of Supreme Being, the spirit world, the relationship of ancestors to the spirit world, relationship of the person or individual to his or her clan, village, tribe, ethnicity, and culture, and belief in after life, are activities and practices that parallel activities we mean by religion in the Western use of the term.

Since religion permeates all aspects of African life, it is best to speak rather of African Traditional Religions (ATRs). We speak of African Traditional Religions (ATRs) in the plural because each ethnic group has its own traditional beliefs and practices. Ritual practices also vary from place to place and from one tribe to another. In sub-Saharan Africa alone there are hundreds of tribes and language groups. Sometimes it is easy to forget that there are stark differences in the religious practices and belief systems of the multitudinous religions we call ATRs. Sometimes these differences

59. Eliade, *Archaic Techniques of Ecstasy*, 509.
60. Eliade, *Archaic Techniques of Ecstasy*, 509.
61. Eliade, *Archaic Techniques of Ecstasy*, 508

can be very significant and well pronounced as in the differences between, say Christianity and Islam or differences between Judaism and Hinduism.

In spite of their differences, there are also common elements among ATRs. Like Islam and Christianity, all religions under the umbrella of ATRs ask questions that are fundamental to human existence: what is the meaning of human life? What does it mean to be human? Why do people suffer? Why sickness? Why do bad things happen to good people? Why afterlife? What will happen to people who live good life at the end of time and what will happen to people who live bad lives at the end of time? The questions of human origins, eschatology, and practical guides on how to survive the brutalities of life are contained in folklores, songs, hymns, and proverbs that are transmitted orally from generation to generation. Although ATRs are similar in the manner in which they pose these questions, they however do not answer them in the exact same way and their ritual prescriptions also vary significantly. Take the example of Christianity in the United States, in the early 1920s up to the 1960s when US Catholicism was still very much an ethnic immigrant church, it was common to see in the same locale a Polish Catholic Church, an Italian Catholic Church, an Irish Catholic Church, and a German Catholic Church, etc. Even though they shared the same Catholic identity, the Irish expressions of Catholicism were in some ways different from the Polish expressions of Catholicism, just as the German and Italian expressions of Catholicism were different from other ethnic expressions of Catholicism. Or take the example of Islam where in one city you can have some Sunni or Shia Muslims or even Ahmmadiya Muslims. Even though they all share the same fundamental beliefs of Islam, there may be slight differences in their ritual practices or differences in allegiance to authority. The same thing is true of ATRs. The differences in religious practices and belief systems of ATRs do vary according to tribes, ethnicity, and language. It is therefore helpful to examine some common practices/belief systems of ATRs.

SET OF NINE CORE BELIEFS

There are as many brands of local religions in Africa as there are tribes, as we have pointed out. Each local religion, as we have likewise pointed out, has its own specific religious beliefs and practices. But in general they have some common features that unify them and make it possible for us to speak of them as ATRs. In Islam it is common to speak of belief in Allah, fasting, praying five times a day, almsgiving, and pilgrimage to Mecca as five pillars of faith. This is a way of identifying the core beliefs of the followers of Prophet Muhammad (PBUH). ATRs do not have five pillars but several pillars. Here we approximate nine of them as a core set of beliefs.

1. Belief in Supreme Being

In the Western world it is not uncommon to find people who proudly self-identify as atheists. These people claim that they do not believe in any deity or Supreme Being. There may also be those who call themselves agnostics. Those who call themselves agnostics claim that it is not possible to prove whether or not there is God or deity and therefore we should doubt. In African society in general it is difficult to find any atheists or agnostics because Africans take the existence of God as a given. There is an African proverb that says you cannot show a child the palm of his hands. The palm of a child's hand is taken for granted because the child sees it every day and knows that it is there. The same idea is applicable when it comes to the existence of God—that God is a reality that the African sees every day. The African does not need a rational proof of God's existence in the face of empirical evidence. Religion in traditional Africa was a way of life that involved the whole community. Even if there were to be antireligious persons, they still had to be "involved in the lives of their religious communities, because in terms of African thought, life can be meaningful only in community, not in isolation."[62]

ATRs notion of God is that of a supreme being who is transcendent and distant. God is also a spirit and active force that is immanent in the world. Following the idea that God is an active force, Africans conceive the nature or essence of anything in the universe as "force." There are different categories of force, which Africans maintain follow a hierarchical order "such that God precedes the spirits; then come the founding fathers and the living-dead, according to the order of primogeniture; then the living according to their rank in terms of seniority."[63] God is called by various names in traditional Africa religions. The variety of names are "metaphorical masks for the incomprehensible ground of all reality, the inscrutable mystery of life behind the visible universe."[64] The name for God among the Massai of East Africa, for example, is "Enkai," meaning "the Originator." "Enkai" is neither male nor female, but still a personal helpful reality that is immanent and transcendent and with whom the people can and do enter

62. Moyo, "Religion in Africa," 317.
63. See Onyewuenyi, "Reincarnation."
64. Hillman, *Toward an African Christianity*, 51.

into relationships.[65] There are those who want to claim that Africans believe in plurality of gods and that they are polytheistic. This is not true across the board. Although Africans believe in the existence of other deities, they clearly distinguish these deities from the one supreme God who created and sustains all creation.

2. Belief in a Spirit World

ATRs attribute the creation of the world to God, the Supreme Being. God's creation is twofold: the visible world of the physical universe made up of humans, plants, and animals and the invisible world of spirits and deceased ancestors. There is interaction between the physical world of humans and the invisible world of spirits. This network of relationship is marked by cooperation and respect. Humans respect the spirit world by living in accord with deity's commands and in harmony with nature. The spirit world cooperates with the humans by looking after them and protecting them from the forces of nature and the harsh realities of life. Humans interact with the spirit world through worship, sacrifice, and divination. Prohibited acts called taboos are assumed to be criminal acts against society (lying, murder, sodomy, adultery, theft, etc.) and are punishable by communal sanctions. There are no written legal codes specifying what is permitted or forbidden. ATRs have no sacred books and no founder. Values, together with what is believed, are transmitted orally from generation to generation and for the most part everyone knows them.

3. Community

A person is a union of two forces: material and spirit. At death the spirit returns to the spirit world to join the company of the ancestors. For this reason a person is also not an individual alone, but a being in community—a community with a network of relationships to the ancestors and the spirit world. Community is the basis of morality. The community is hierarchically structured. The order of importance is determined by age—from the oldest to the youngest. Older people in the community are closer to the ancestors by virtue of their age and are accorded respect. They are also thought to be wiser than anyone else. Their role is to teach and mentor the young. Just as the community occupies a center stage in the tribe or clan, the family is also at the center of the community. The family, like society, is also

65. Hillman, *Toward an African Christianity*, 51.

hierarchically structured and almost always patriarchal. In every family the firstborn, especially if he is male, occupies a central role and is a chief decision maker in family matters. Men rule the family and have rights of inheritance.

4. Belief in a Personal God or "Chi"

In Christian teaching, there is belief in guardian angels. The concept of personal god or "chi" in ATRs comes closest to the Christian idea of guardian angels. Most Africans believe that everyone has a personal god, which is called "chi" among the Igbos of Southeast Nigeria. The general idea is that a person works in cooperation with his or her "chi." This is captured in the Igbo proverb that when a man says yes his chi says yes. But there is also the idea that a person's fortune, whether good or bad, is determined by his or her personal god. Some people believe that one's personal god, "chi," sets one's destiny and that one's destiny is always pre-determined because a person cannot rise above the destiny of his or her "chi." This idea that a person's "chi" sets one's destiny is always in dialectical tension with the individual quest to shape his or her own destiny. Chinua Achebe gives us a good example in his epic novel *Things Fall Apart*:

> [Okonkwo's] life had been ruled by great passion—to become one of the lords of the clan. That had been his life-spring. And he had all but achieved it. Then everything had been broken. He had been cast out of his clan like a fish onto a dry, sandy beach, panting. Clearly his personal god or chi was not made of great things. A man could not rise beyond the destiny of his chi. The saying of the elders was not true—that if a man said yea his chi also affirmed. Here was a man whose chi said nay despite his own affirmation.[66]

The idea that one cannot rise above the destiny of his or her "chi" can also be problematic. It seems to make "chi" the sole determinant and the one responsible for one's fortune. When things go well one can easily take responsibility or attribute it to the good fortune of one's "chi." But what happens when a person's bad fortune is as a result of one's obvious bad decisions and choices? Does the person lay it squarely on the feet of his or her "chi?" The consensus would be that every one's "chi" helps him or her to work out his or her destiny.

66. Achebe, *Things Fall Apart*, 131.

5. Ancestors

Africans accord a lot of respect to the ancestors. Respect for ancestors is the African way of expressing "fellowship, hospitality, and family continuity."[67] In many places ancestor worship is part and parcel of the people's folklore and mythologies. In some places people pray to the spirit of their dead ancestors for favors, like good health and good fortune.

6. Afterlife

Belief in ancestors is tied to the notion of afterlife. Traditional Africans are reminded every day about afterlife. A person's life is marked by a series of birth, death, and re-birth. We see a good example at the burial ceremony of a revered elderly man, Ogbuefi Ezeudu, in Chinua Achebe's *Things Fall Apart*. In the story, the one officiating at the funeral ceremony yelled to the dead man: "If you had been poor in your last life I would have asked you to be rich when you come again. But you were rich. If you had been a coward, I would have asked you to bring courage. But you were a fearless warrior. If you had died young, I would have asked you to get life. But you lived long. So I shall ask you to come again the way you came before."[68]

7. Elders

The elders are the closest to the ancestors. Traditional African society was theocratic in nature. The elders are considered human representatives of deity and the moral conscience of the community. When problems arise in the community, it is the role of the elders to adjudicate and establish order. They also establish what is right and what is wrong. In the following verse, an oracle, the Odu Obara Meji oracle of the Yorubas of southwest Nigeria, condemns disrespect for elders:

> If a child indulges in stubborn acts,
> if he sees an aged priest and slaps him,
> if he comes across an aged physician and beats him mercilessly,
> if he goes on and meets an aged priest and knocks him down,
> thus declares the oracle to the disobedient child,
> "Who says nobody could control him?"
> Orunmila says: "Don't you know that there is no long life for
> any child who beats an elderly priest, no long life for any child

---

67. See Onyewuenyi, "Reincarnation."

68. Achebe, *Things Fall Apart*, 123.

who slaps an aged physician. Any child who flogs an aged priest is seeking his own death. Respect for elders means long life."[69]

8. Rituals

The African worldview is permeated by rituals. "A man's life from birth to death was a series of transition rites which brought him nearer and nearer to his ancestors."[70] Ritual practices are used to offer logical explanations of phenomena. Ritual practices vary according to place and convention. There are rituals that pertain to worship. There are also rituals pertaining to festivals, marriage, death of a loved one, and birth of a new child. There are also rituals pertaining to the way to farm, the way to eat, and the way to treat one's guests or strangers. If a member of the community steals, for example, there is a ritual sacrifice to be performed to find out who the thief is and, if possible, recover the stolen property.

9. Theophoric Names

African names are loaded with messages and carry a lot of meanings and symbolism. By the time you know somebody's names you get to know practically their family history. In conferring names Africans also show the God-centeredness of ATRs by bringing God into the picture and making fundamental statements about themselves and their place in the world. Many African names are theophoric (God-bearing names) in that they either have "God" as a prefix or suffix. According to the African writer Theophilus Okere, Africans use the occasion of conferring names to tell their life story, make their profession of faith, pronounce judgment on the world, make fundamental statements about the meaning of life, celebrate their moral victories over their enemies, express their optimism for the future, and reassure themselves about the truth of things. They also use the occasion of conferring names to praise and lament, taunt and defy, dare, fawn, and pray.[71] The Igbos of southeast Nigeria, for example, have a variety of names that entreat God for favor or affirm their belief in God. God, for them is "Chukwu" or "Chineke." Some use the shortened form "Chi" to refer to this creator God. *Chidi* means "there is God"; *Chinwe* means "I am owned by God"; *Chima* means "God knows the hidden secrets

---

69. See Adewale, "Crime and African Traditional Religion."
70. Achebe, *Things Fall Apart*, 122.
71. Okere, "African Thought, Philosophy, and Spirituality."

and mysteries of life"; *Chinua* means "God fights on my behalf"; *Oge-chi* means "God's time is the best"; and *Onyeberechiya* means "bring your complaints to God."[72] The Yoruba of southwest Nigeria have similar ways of conferring names. They have a class of names they call *Oruko Amutorunwa* (literally, names a person brings from heaven). These names would depict all special events or unusual circumstances surrounding the birth of the child. For example, all twin-born children have specially designated names as the first of twins is called "Taiwo" and the second "Kehinde." A child born immediately after a set of twins is called "Idowu" and the one after "Idowu" is called "Alaba." They also have other classification of names. For example, a male child born after the father is immediately deceased is called "Babatunde" (literally "father has made a come-back"). A girl who is born to a family where the mother has recently been deceased is called "Iyabode" (literally "mother has made a come-back"). In all, the invocations in African names "offer infinite possibilities of prayer and communion with a God who is both Lord and master, friend and companion, judge and witness."[73]

ATRS IN POSTCOLONIAL AFRICA

Colonialism brought a lot of material benefits to Africa. It brought Western-style education, Western clothing, economic development, and Western religions and ways of life. Colonialism also brought Africa to the realities of modern world. Today a large number of Africans speak European languages, like English, French, and Portuguese, in addition to their own local languages. Those who receive formal Western education are more likely to speak either of these languages, while the uneducated ones are more likely to speak an adulterated version of these languages. For the sake of simplification local languages spoken in Africa can be grouped into five family groups:

(1). The Niger-Kordofanian family, which includes over 300 Bantu languages (like Swahili, Ganda, Kongo, Sesotho, and Zulu). These Bantu languages are spoken by Bantu people who live in central, eastern, and southern Africa. The Niger-Kordofanian language family also includes

72. Okere, "African Thought, Philosophy, and Spirituality."
73. Okere, "African Thought, Philosophy, and Spirituality."

some non-Bantu languages, like Igbo, Yoruba, and Akan, that are spoken in West Africa.

(2). The Nilo-Saharan family language (like Dinka, Nuer, Kanuri, and Massia) spoken by people who live in countries like Chad, Niger, Mali, Tanzania, Uganda, Kenya.

(3). The Khoihoi language family group (like San and Khoihoi), sometimes called click-languages because of the click-like sound of the language, spoken in Tanzania and South Africa.

(4). Afro-Asian languages, like Berber, Arabic, Amharic, Gall, Somali, and Hausa spoken in northern Africa and parts of West Africa.

(5). Indo-European languages, such as Afrikaans, which was developed by Dutch settlers in South Africa.

But the benefits of colonialism came with a price. The feeling among Africans in general is that colonialism brought a lot of exploitation and instability to the continent. Many of the nation-states created under colonialism are still politically and economic unstable. The general feeling is that these nations only received paper independence, not real independence. Many of them still depend on their colonial rulers for economic sustenance. Some who see colonialism as a massive failure have called for a return to traditional African belief systems and values. One of these was the Nigerian writer, Chinua Achebe, who expressed the clash between Western civilization and African belief systems in his novel, *Things Fall Apart*. Achebe meant his work as a response to Georg F. Hegel (1770–1831) and Joseph Conrad's Heart of Darkness, which depicted Africa as barbaric, cultureless, and uncivilized. In the novel Achebe shows how culturally superior Africans were before the contact with the West and how social institutions in Africa prior to European contact was solid and well-organized. On the political front, in the wake of the independence movement that was gathering momentum, some African political leaders began urging Africans to desert the colonial project and rediscover their humanity (which they believe the colonial project has stripped from them), and return to the African value systems, particularly the African sense of family. Some of these leaders attempted to build a political system that draws from traditional African values.

1. Kenneth Kaunda's African Humanism (1924–): Kenneth Kaunda who ruled Zambia from 1964–91 developed a socio-political and economic ideology he called African Humanism. Kaunda called on Africa to exercise caution in matters pertaining to Western technology and

discover and cherish African ways of being human. Kaunda thought that the two competing ideologies of the West (communism and capitalism) not only encourage violence but also dehumanize the African. Thus, Kaunda wanted to recover the African sense of community and the African sense of personhood.

2. Kwame Nkrumah (1909–72): Nkrumah ruled Ghana (then known as Gold Coast) from 1951 to 1966. He developed a philosophy of African personality he called "Consciencism." Nkrumah also thought that Western ideologies were dehumanizing and secularizing. He argued that the African sense of personhood is very spiritual and ennobling and therefore need to be re-discovered.

3. Leopold Senghor (1906–2001): Senghor was a poet and cultural theorist who ruled Senegal from 1960 to 1980. He developed a philosophy he called "Negritude." Senghor thought that the colonial system has produced in the African a split personality and an African who has lost true worth of self. Negritude will make the African appreciate his or her blackness and be a proud African.

4. Julius Nyerere (1922–99): Nyerere ruled what was then known as Tanganyika and later Tanzania from 1961 to 1985. He developed a socio-economic system he called "ujamaa," a Swahili word meaning "familyhood." *Ujamaa* is a brand of African socialism that takes the family as its centerpiece. Nyerere wanted to build a society in which the yardstick would be, not material things, but the progress of the people. What he calls *Ujamma* is different from the Marxist-inspired communism because it deplores violence and rejects class struggle. It is also different from liberal capitalism because it rejects exploitation of people.

These calls for a return to traditional African values were greeted with enthusiasm by some and skepticism by others. In Zaire, for example, Mobutu Sese Seko abandoned his Christian name Joseph Desire and opted instead for an African name. Mobutu also renamed his country from the Belgian Congo to Zaire. The city that was called Leopoldville he renamed Kinshasa and what was Elizabethville he renamed Lubumbashi.[74] Some countries, like Upper Volta, which became Burkina Faso, changed their names to more indigenous ones as part of this spirit of African nationalism or personhood. In the end, however, the call for rediscovery of African

---

74. Hillman, *Toward an African Christianity*, 15.

traditional values was met with stiff opposition. The project failed mainly for two reasons. First, the political leaders who advocated return to traditional African values were themselves corrupt. Some of them run a one-party state and looted state treasuries. Second, some of these ideologies, like the *ujamma* project of Nyerere, suffered from lack of organization and poor funding. All these made the philosophies expounded by these leaders seem like an empty slogan.[75]

There were also those who opposed the return to African traditional roots on academic grounds. These people argued that ironically it was the traditional African sense of familyhood and hospitality that made Africa vulnerable to foreign exploitation. These people "have no regrets about the loss of the African root, or its humane values, for they think that technologization, urbanization, and modernization cannot co-exist with those values."[76] They think that rather than return to traditional roots, Africa needs to fully embrace the modern world and catch up with the rest of the world in politics, economy, and technology. Some also dismiss the call to return to traditional African roots as amounting to nothing other than romanticization of the past. According to them, "the African past is characterized by such social habits and loyalties that are suspicious of innovation and hardened against change."[77] A return to such a society, while romantically desirable, is unrealistic and practically impossible.[78]

ATRs and Dialogue with Christianity

The Pontifical Council for Interreligious Dialogue underscored the importance of ATRs and called for greater pastoral attention to these religions for the following reasons:

1. ATRs is the religious and cultural context from which most Africans come and in which many of them still live.

2. ATRs is dynamic and ever-evolving. "Its vitality varies from country to country. In some African countries, some of the intellectual elite are declaring themselves to be adherents of ATR."[79]

---

75. Ehusani, *Afro-Christian Vision*, 25–26.

76. Ehusani, *Afro-Christian Vision*, 25.

77. Ehusani, *Afro-Christian Vision*, 26.

78. Ehusani, *Afro-Christian Vision*, 26.

79. See Pontifical Council for Interreligious Dialogue, "Pastoral Attention to African Traditional Religion."

3. Because of the church's respect for religions and cultures of other people the church wants to preserve what is noble, true, and good in those religions.

4. By understanding ATRs the church would better meet the needs of African Christians so that "the Church will be more and more at home in Africa, and Africans will be more and more at home in the Church."[80]

---

80. See Pontifical Council for Interreligious Dialogue, "Pastoral Attention to African Traditional Religion."

12

Chinese Ways of Being Human

DAOISM AND CONFUCIANISM

WHEN WE LOOK AT other people's religion, we often view it from an outsider's perspective, as opposed to an insider's perspective. An outsider's perspective can at times be judgmental, subjective, and even unhelpful. Unless we do it with some measure of openness, empathy, and goodwill, an outsider's perspective remains problematic. The study of religions requires human cultural wisdom, and foundational to human cultural wisdom is the capacity for openness, empathy, and goodwill.[1] Religious quest itself is a quest for self-transcendence. Self-transcendence is a precarious activity. It is dialectical in that it involves a tension between the self as transcending and the self as transcended.[2] The dialectical tension makes it all the more necessary to withhold judgment when we encounter belief systems or doctrines in religions different from ours. Rather than consider what we might not fully understand as aberrations or unreligious, we need to be mindful that religions deal with mystery that is unknown and mystery that no one has fully grasped yet.

We cannot study world religions without paying attention to Asia and Asian realities. About three-fourths of the world's population is in Asia. Also, all the major religions of the world either began in Asia or have deep roots in Asia. Not only is this true of Hinduism, Buddhism, Taoism, Confucianism, Zoroastrianism, Jainism, Sikhism, and Shintoism, it is also true of the three Abrahamic religions—Judaism, Christianity, and Islam. Each of

1. Lopez, *Buddhism*, 3.
2. Lonergan, *Method in Theology*, 106.

these religions gives meaning and direction to the lives of the Asian peoples that practice them. They also mold the lives and cultures of all who practice them.[3] In a nutshell, what we call religions of Asia might simply be Asian ways of being human, since their cultures and traditions are bound with them.

If we accept as basic, the idea that what we call religions of Asia are in fact the Asian ways of being human, then we must accept that what we call Chinese religions are equally Chinese ways of being human. In the main, there are three religious systems that have had profound influence on China. These are Confucianism, Daoism, and Buddhism. Buddhism is a proselytizing religion, like Christianity and Islam. It did not originate in China. Rather, it made its way to China very early on through the Silk Road in about the same fashion Christianity and Islam made their way to the Far East through the Silk Road. But Daoism and Confucianism are indigenous to China. Together with Buddhism, these two indigenous Chinese religions will help shape Chinese political and social life.

The three religious systems all began in the period known as the axial age. The German-Swiss psychiatrist and philosopher, Karl Jaspers (1883–1969), was the one who coined the term Axial Age. He used it to denote the period between 800 BCE and 200 BCE. This period, according to Jaspers, was a period of instability and chaos. Many great teachers, like Confucius in China and Socrates in Greece, emerged at this time to address the problem of stability and change. The Axial Age was also unique in that it distinguished ancient peoples from moderns. Many of the great teachers that emerged at this time were not interested in committing their teachings to writing. They simply gathered disciples and taught. We shall examine the impact of the Axial period in China before China opened itself to the Western world. In terms of the general features that characterized the Axial period, China of the Axial period was no different from any indigenous society. With respect to religion, it had no special realm it considered religious, as distinct from the secular or mundane. If anything approximated to being considered religious, it was the stress on nature. Nature was considered sacred in the sense that it is the arena in which all human activities with lasting implications play out. The goal of life in the traditional Chinese worldview is to seek harmony with nature. Inability to bring about harmony was considered the cause of chaos and disorder.

East Asia, as we will see, has so many philosophical systems and religious traditions. In the case of China, it is easy to miss the role these philosophical systems and religious traditions play in the life of the Chinese, if

3. Phan, *Asian Synod*, 73.

we view them strictly through the lens of our Western conception of reality. The Western mind is prone to dualism: body-mind, light-dark, and matter-spirit split. The Western mind tends to conceive things in terms of either-or, not both-and. Applied to religion, in the Western conception of religiosity, you are either a Christian or a Buddhist or Jew or a Muslim or a Hindu. There is no room for mix and match. But the Chinese idea is somewhat different. An analogy may help to put this in perspective. In the badger state of Wisconsin, USA, most people love the state's National Football League (NFL) team, the Green Bay Packers. The same people may also love the state's college football team, the Wisconsin Badgers; the state's basketball team, the Milwaukee Bucks; and the state's baseball team, the Milwaukee Brewers. In Wisconsin, like in many places in the United States, it is easy to be a fan of multiple teams, the Packers, the Bucks, the Brewers, and the Badgers, all at the same time. It does not go against the grain for one to say he or she is a passionate fan of all four teams. What we call religious traditions of China work the same way.[4] To quote Carmody and Brink who first offered a version of this useful analogy elsewhere, in terms of how to understand religions in China, "the right question to ask is not whether an individual is Confucian or Daoist but to what extent Confucian and Daoist traditions make that person's life relevant."[5]

EAST ASIA AND CHINESE WORLDVIEW

Our area of study is expansive and covers a great land mass. Some historians use the term North East Asia to refer to the areas we are describing as East Asia. East Asia is different from South East Asia, which itself covers about eleven modern independent nations, including The Philippines, Indonesia, Vietnam, Cambodia, Malaysia, Singapore, and Thailand. East Asia presently has five independent nations, not counting Hong Kong, Macau, and Taiwan. These independent nations of East Asia are China, Japan, South Korea, North Korea, and Mongolia.

Our study of ancient Chinese religions often takes things for granted. Apart from our many misconceptions of Chinese political and social life, we take for granted the enormity of the geographical location we call China. One writer called this the problem of a simplistic approach to China study.[6] The writer urges us to pause for a moment and consider the fact that about

4. I owe this analogy to Denise L. Carmody and T. L. Brink, who offered a similar analogy with respect to northern Californian football fans. See *Ways to the Center*, 165.

5. Carmody and Brink, *Ways to the Center*, 165.

6. Fairbank, *Great Chinese Revolution*, 10.

a billion people live in Europe and North and South America combined. These billion-odd people in Europe and America live in about fifty sovereign independent states. On the other hand, about 1.4 billion people lived in China in 2018, i.e., about 18.5 percent of the earth's total population. These people do not live in multiple countries, they live in one single state called China.[7] So it would be too simplistic to think these people who live in an entity we call China are homogenous just because they live in what seems like an autonomous single state. So we may say that anyone attempting to understand Chinese religions without attempting to understand the rich history of China and its revolutions is like a person who has committed to flying blind among mountains.[8] There is no denying that Europe has its own differences in culture and religion and attempts at unification of Europe were thwarted at various stages by these differences. But there is also an extent to which a common religion unified Europe, i.e., Christianity. A unified Europe was built on Christendom. The Chinese did not have a religion that could act as a unifying force the way Christianity aided Europe. The closest they came to having an analogous unifying force was the centrifugal pull they saw in their ruler. The ruler or emperor was both a military leader and exemplar of conduct. He was also revered as the dispenser of justice.[9] Up till about 1911, the emperor of China played this unifying role in the face of multitudes of peoples who were diverse in both language and culture.

China's neighbor, Japan, is an island nation in the Pacific Ocean with a population of about 127 million people. South Korea has a population of about fifty-one million people. Its northern neighbor, North Korea, has a population of about twenty-five million people. Mongolia, which derives its name from the thirteenth/fourteenth-century Mongolian Empire, founded by Genghis Khan, lies between China and Russia. It has a population of about three million people. Altogether, in 2018 East Asia had a population of about 1.6 billion people, i.e., 21.6 percent of the world's population. The region is the most densely populated part of the globe. It has multitudes of peoples and myriads of cultures and traditions. Just like in China where there was no single unifying religion to hold the people together, the whole of East Asia will encounter a similar problem. However, China would exercise a cultural dominance over the region, particularly through the spread of Confucianism. As we try to understand the religions of East Asia, in the light of the political and cultural dominance of China over the region, it is proper that we begin with a brief survey of Chinese dynasties.

7. Fairbank, *Great Chinese Revolution*, 10.

8. Fairbank, *Great Chinese Revolution*, 11.

9. Fairbank, *Great Chinese Revolution*, 10.

a. The Xia Dynasty (2700–1600 BCE). This was traditionally or mythically, as some would say, the first Chinese dynasty. The Chinese rulers of the early Bronze Age used bronze to strengthen their army by producing powerful weapons. The Xia dynasty lasted about five hundred years.

b. The Shang Dynasty (1600–1046 BCE). The Shang dynasty overthrew and succeeded the Xia dynasty. According to legend, Shang dynasty began when one Cheng Tang overthrew the last of the Xia despots. Some history books refer to the Shang as the Yin dynasty. The Shang or Yin dynasty made lots of technological innovations and transformed China into a highly organized society. They also introduced Chinese writing systems that made China a powerful force in the world.

In terms of religion, China at this time was very polytheistic. Belief in spirits permeated their worldview. There was also a widespread belief in ancestor worship. The reverential fear that was shown to spirits was extended to ancestors who at death became spirits. For this reason, ancestral spirits were venerated. Also, the Chinese of the Shang Dynasty had a common belief in an all-powerful divine force that rules the world. The name of this divine force was Shang Ti. Shang Ti was conceived as a personal god who could be reached only through mediums or diviners.

Politically, China was unstable. The kingdom was plagued by wars and unrests. The whole region was also beset by natural disasters, floods, earthquakes, and famine. Stability and change were a constant feature of life. The Chinese accounted for this dynamic by thinking of them as complementary. They thought of the cosmos in terms of a union of two complementary but nonetheless opposite principles, Yin-Yang. The Yin-Yang principles are represented by two dots in a circle. The Yin is a feminine principle. It represents night, cold, and the earthly realm. The Yang is a masculine principle. It represents light, heat, hot, and sky or the heavenly realm. The two principles are not in competition or opposition. Rather, they are thought to be complementary. Their union results in a cosmic harmony. The Yin-Yang principle dates back to the third century BCE. Ancient China used the Yin-Yang principle to denote the fact that human beings are part of nature and that they must interact with nature in order to survive life's harsh conditions and maintain cosmic harmony.

More recently, some feminist scholars are beginning to question the Yin-Yang principles' denotation of the feminine as dark, passive, and cold, in contradistinction to the male—bright, active, and warm. They suggest that this might be part of the early Chinese effort to subjugate women in Chinese society. They argue that it is only by invoking the Yin-Yang principle that women were fitted into the social and cosmic order. Regardless of whether one buys into their project, there is something to be said about a dualism in which there is an alternation of night and day and a contrast of the sun and moon. It is no wonder that these feminists see the contrast as "a ready-made matrix in which women could be confined."[10] Simply put, the ancient Chinese worldview had a well-buttressed philosophical system in which the inequality of the sexes was underpinned. It may have used this invention to keep women in their place.[11] In any case, the Shang Dynasty lasted more than six hundred years, but the philosophical underpinning of the Yin-Yang will outlive it.

The Yin-Yang symbol

c. The Chou or Zhou Dynasty (1046–256 BCE). During the Zhou Dynasty, agriculture and commerce flourished. Ancient China also made strides militarily, coming up with a very strong army. The Zhou thought they could unify the peoples of China by authorizing one unified language, the Old Chinese, for the people. The Zhou rulers also invented the mythical idea of *tianming* ("mandate from heaven"). This is the idea that the Zhou ruler could only be the ruler because there could only be one ruler at a time and that this Zhou ruler has the

10. Fairbank, *Great Chinese Revolution*, 68.
11. Fairbank, *Great Chinese Revolution*, 68.

blessings of the gods to rule. The mythical idea of *tianming* (mandate from heaven) would later become a basis for Chinese political ideology from the Zhou period up to the twentieth century.[12]

In spite of their attempt to unify the peoples of China through language and the mythical "mandate from heaven," ancient China was at times thrown into confusion because states within its axes fought each other continuously. Ancient China went through a series of wars known in history as the Warring States Period. It was in the context of this turmoil and disorder that the two great Schools of Chinese thought, Confucianism and Daoism, emerged. Confucius (551–479 BCE) began a series of philosophical teachings that would have a lasting impact on Chinese political and cultural systems.

d. The Ch'in or Qin Dynasty (221–207 BCE). The Qin Dynasty put a lot of effort into unifying China by emphasizing a strong central government. However, the emphasis on centralized system of government was considered imperial by many. The Qin were said to have made a lot of technological inventions, including paper-making and printing, the production of gunpowder, and compass. The Qin Dynasty, however, was one of the shortest of the Chinese dynasties, lasting only about fifteen years. But before its collapse, the rulers began building the four-thousand mile the Great Wall of China, a fortress that took over twenty years to complete. In terms of religion, the Qin Dynasty was anti-Daoism. Among their many blows to Daoism was the confiscation of Daoist temples, which the Qin authorities turned into schools and factories.[13]

e. The Han Dynasty (206 BCE–220 CE). Like the Qin Dynasty before it, the Han Dynasty was considered to be an imperial dynasty. Among the many achievements of this dynasty was the promotion of trade between China and the rest of the world through the Silk Road. The rulers of this dynasty were not kings, but emperors. They reinvented the Zhou idea of "mandate from heaven." They promoted Confucianism as the foundation of government and as the official state educational system in China. They also exported these systems to other countries. Towards the end of the Han Dynasty, due to trade and exchange of ideas between China and Europe that flourished through the Silk Road, Buddhism found its way into China. It was brought to China by

12. Gardner, *Confucianism*, 45.
13. Robson, *Daoism*, xxviii.

Indian gurus and missionaries. The Han Dynasty lasted for about four hundred years before it was overthrown. With the demise of the Han Dynasty China split into three kingdoms. During this time, Buddhism and Chinese Philosophical Schools began to spread fast in the three kingdoms.

f. Tang Dynasty (618–907 CE). After a period of interregnum, the Tang emerged as a major Chinese dynasty. They built what would properly be called an empire, not a dynasty. In what might be likened to a renaissance, they promoted Confucian ethic and systems of education, Chinese paintings, and poetry. Some consider the Tang era to be a golden age of Chinese Empire because of the cultural revival and the strong influence the empire had on its neighbors politically and culturally.

g. The Sung Dynasty (907–1279 CE). The Sung Dynasty continued the cultural revival of the Tang Dynasty and promoted Confucian and Buddhist ethics.

h. Yuan Dynasty (1279–1368 CE). It was during the reign of the Sung Dynasty that Kublai Khan, the grandson of the Mongol ruler, Genghis Khan, made his way to China and invaded the Chinese Empire. About the year 1200 CE, the Mongols, a series of tribes in the open Steppe to the West of Manchuria, under their charismatic leader Chingghis Khan (Genghis Khan), overran Central Asia, Persia, and south Russia, consolidated power and advanced as far as the Danube in Europe.[14] It was this expansionist policy that brought Kublai Khan to China during the Sung dynasty. He conquered the Sung Dynasty, founded the Yuan dynasty, and became the first Mongol ruler to rule over China. The Yuan rule was from 1260 to 1294 CE. The Mongols were different from the Chinese in many ways, particularly in customs and traditions. The Mongols were true nomads of the open steppe. They were not suited to a settled bureaucratic-commercial life.[15] Islam was already well established in Asia in the Mongol Empire, the ancestral home of Kublai Khan. When Kublai Khan established the Yuan Dynasty in China, he brought with him some of the Islamic merchants who had overseen economic policies in Mongol. As emperor, Kublai Khan received the Italian explorer and merchant, Marco Polo (1254–1324), when the

14. Fairbank, *Great Chinese Revolution*, 15.
15. Fairbank, *Great Chinese Revolution*, 16.

latter passed through China in his travels to the Far East. The Yuan Dynasty lasted almost a century.

i. Ming Dynasty (1368–1644 CE). The Ming Dynasty became the ruling empire in China when the Yuan Dynasty collapsed. The Ming Dynasty is considered one of the three golden eras or dynasties of China. The population of China at this time increased in leaps and bounds, almost doubling in the Ming era. They developed printing, and expanded trade and cultural ideas with the West. Fearing further attacks from the invading Mongolians, the Ming continued work on the Great Wall of China that was first begun in the late third century BCE, expanding and using the best architectural designs of the time to strengthen it. In the Ming era, China became a force in voyages. Their great admiral Zheng He, who is considered one of the great admirals in Chinese history, made seven epic voyages that took him to distant lands, including Arabia and Africa. His ship and his fleets were gargantuan, such that even when combined, those of the Italian explorer, Christopher Columbus (1451–1506), who made four voyages to the New World in the period between 1492 and 1502, and the Portuguese Vasco Da Gama (1460–1524), the first European to reach India by sea (1497–99), pale in comparison. In spite of its expansionist policy and outreach to the West, the Ming did not allow into Chinese territory European Christian missionaries who wanted to bring Christianity into China. The Ming rule lasted for about 276 years.

j. The Ch'ing or Manchu Dynasty (1644–1911). The Ch'ing is the last of the imperial dynasties to rule China. It is sometimes known as the Manchu Dynasty because of its ties to the ethnic Manchus who founded the dynasty with the invasion and capture of Beijing from the Ming. Their founding leader was Nurhachi. The secret of the Manchu rise and success was in the fact of their geographical position, ethnic composition, and their adeptness to precise features of warfare that can translate into political success.[16] When the Manchus first seized power, they put some Ming officials in strategic government positions, although most of the higher level officials remained ethnic Manchu. The strategy helped to pacify the Chinese population. The rule of the ethnic Manchu brought peace and prosperity to China after the brief period of instability that followed the fall of the Ming Dynasty. They expanded the Chinese territory and the population of the empire also

16. Fairbank, *Great Chinese Revolution*, 15.

significantly increased during the reign of the Ch'ing. The Ch'ing accepted Confucianism, Daoism, and Buddhism as the officially licensed religions of China. However, at some point, the pressure of increase population began to have its negative effect on the empire. Overpopulation aside, the empire began to witness severe flooding and farming. These led to some uprisings in both the north and the south. The empire had to deal with these rebellions, particularly the Taiping Rebellion (1850–64) and the Nian Rebellion (1853–68). The Ch'ing era also witnessed series of wars, particularly the Opium Wars. The First Opium War (1839–42) was fought between China and Great Britain. It was fought because of the embargo placed by the Chinese on the smuggling of opium into China. The British, on their part, thought they were fighting to resist trade imbalance, for the Chinese were exporting large amount of tea and silk to Europe, while still limiting massively the amount of European goods that made it to China. The Second Opium War (1856–60) was a war jointly fought by Britain and France against China. In these two Opium Wars, Great Britain and France were victorious. China had to sign some treaties with Europeans, most of which left China in a weakened position. One of these treatises was the Treaty of Nan-ching that ceded the important port of Hong Kong to the British and also opened several other Chinese ports to Britain and France. Great Britain controlled Hong Kong until it was given back to the Chinese in 1997. There was also a year-long war with Japan (1894–95), which emboldened factions within the empire to begin an uprising. The unequal treaties and concessions made to Western powers, Great Britain and France especially, and the series of rebellions, like the Chinese Secret Society or Boxers Rebellion of 1900, combined to weaken China politically and militarily. The last straw came on October 10, 1911, when the Republican revolution led by a radical group from southern China, forced the emperor, a six-year-old boy, to flee and abdicate the throne. The Republic of China was established on January 1, 1912. Sun Yat-sen (1866–1925) became the first provisional president.

With the establishment of the Republic of China in 1912, Daoism was condemned as a superstition. Later, in 1949, came the establishment of the Communist People's Republic of China, under the leadership of Mao Zedong (1893–1976): "With its aggressive early persecution of all religions, many in the West believed that the actual practice of Daoism had finally died out in its birthplace."[17] In spite of what the West thought, Daoism is still well and alive in China today.

The Four Great Chinese Dynasties

1. Han Dynasty (202–220 BCE)	2. Tang Dynasty: (618–907 CE)	3. Sung Dynasty (907–1279 CE)	4. Ming Dynasty (1368–1644 CE)
• The first of China's 4 greatest dynasties. • A golden age of Chinese cultural and economic achievement. • The three factors that led to the rise of this dynasty were: (a) Military might and expansion—introduced a new breed of horses that were bigger, faster, and stronger, which were used in wars as chariots; (b) political centralization—governed effectively from the center; and (c) cultural achievement—restored Confucianism as official state orthodoxy	• Trade along Silk Road flourished. • Revered both horses and camels—placed them (together with gold and silver) in the burial sites of royalties and aristocrats. • A highly creative period—invented gunpowder. • Opulent period in which painting and sculpture flourished in China.	• The dynasty was divided almost evenly into Northern (907–1126) and Southern halves (1227–79). • Produced ceramic in great proportion and mastered landscape painting. • The Northern half of the dynasty was peaceful. The peaceful era was characterized by philosophical and artistic development and economic growth. • The Southern half of the dynasty was quite the opposite—not stable and not peaceful. Marauding armies, particularly the Mongols, invaded from the north and drove the Chinese from their northern territory, forcing them to migrate south and establish a new capital city.	• Ming leaders revived a sense of cultural identity and respect for traditional artifacts and craftsmanship. • Made Confucius the patron of intellectuals and scholars. • Decreed that sacrifice be offered to Confucius in all schools in the land.

THE JESUIT INFLUENCE

A great deal of what the West knew about the Chinese religions in the sixteenth century was mainly due to the influence of Jesuit missionaries who traveled to the Far East for evangelization. In 1583, two Italian Jesuits, Matteo Ricci (1552–1610) and Michele Ruggieri (1543–1607), traveled to the Chinese city of Zhaoqing (present day Guangdong Province) for Christian missionary work among the Chinese. At the time, Portuguese missionaries

17. Robson, *Daoism*, xxviii.

already had a mission post in Macau. Ricci and Ruggieri spent time at Macau, studying Chinese language before Ruggieri returned to Italy in 1588, leaving Ricci there for almost thirty years. While in China, Ricci encountered Eastern religions, particularly Buddhism, Daoism, and Confucianism. He kept a journal about his findings. Many of what the West came to know about these religions would come from Ricci and his Jesuit companions who in China adopted a policy of accommodation to rectify Eastern religions with Christianity.[18] "The Jesuits saw possibilities for converting the Chinese through accommodation with Confucianism, since its main tenets—at least in the Jesuits' eyes—did not contradict or challenge Christianity."[19]

The policy of accommodation was hardly ever extended to Daoism. Many of the Western missionaries who worked in China in the sixteenth century had a negative view of Daoism, favoring instead Confucianism. "Not only did they collude with the Confucian elites in advancing certain Daoist texts as the reputable philosophy of the elite and denigrating the rest of Daoism as a benighted religion pandering to the superstitious beliefs of low-class villagers, but they also spread that skewed image around the world."[20] Ricci, for example, denigrated Daoism, just like he had vilified Buddhism earlier, characterizing Daoism as a deviant religion of the poor and powerless that is based on the idolatrous and superstitious beliefs and practices.[21]

DAOISM

The different interpretations of Daoism that have lingered to this day stemmed from Matteo Ricci and his companions. To understand Daoism, we have to rid ourselves of Western presuppositions that have long shaped its narrative. The Western conception has not only influenced the perception of Daoism, it has also created an artificial distinction between Daoism as part philosophy and part religion. But such a stark division between religion and philosophy made by Western polemicists is inaccurate and untenable.[22] That is not to say that we cannot grasp Daoism through the way we understand things with our Western mind. So long as we are mindful that our Western prejudices can at times be a hindrance, we can appreciate better what the Chinese mean by Daoism.

18. Robson, *Daoism*, 604.

19. Robson, *Daoism*, 48.

20. Robson, *Daoism*, 48.

21. Robson, *Daoism*, 48.

22. Robson, *Daoism*, 46.

In itself, the term "Dao" could be interpreted along many lines: ultimate reality, the way of nature, means to personal liberation, or a formula for harmonious living.[23] Either of these four terms could be appropriate, depending on the point of emphasis and which evolutionary trend of Daoism one is operating out of. However, it is hard to tell the origin of Daoism even though Ricci claimed that Laozi was the founder.[24] Even its parameters are difficult to define. What we know for sure is that Daoism (sometimes rendered Taoism) is a load of umbrella term for practices in the ancient Chinese life that include human interactions with nature, ethical codes regarding how to interact with nature and fellow humans, animism, shamanism, and ancestor worship, etc. We also know for sure that Daoism, like any living philosophy or system, has evolved over time. Contrary to how it is presented in popular literature, in the West at least, Daoism is not monolithic. It is not a single tradition with some core metaphysical teachings about how to gain salvation or free one's soul from earthly troubles. Rather, what goes under the umbrella term Daoism is "a set of texts with family resemblances concerned mainly with the questions of 'what Dao is' and 'how Dao function.'"[25] The Western depiction of Dao tends to suffer from two misunderstandings: one metaphysical, the other mystical. The metaphysical error, unfortunate as it is, depicts the Dao as a kind of transcendental reality or principle or even a Supreme Being that is distinct and distant from the world. Those who conceive Dao this way are merely imposing their Western metaphysical dualistic conceptions of reality into an ancient Chinese term. The related error, the mystical, tends to depict the Dao as some ineffable absolute Other beyond human reach that can be grasped only by mystical encounter.[26] Together the mystical and metaphysical errors transplant Western dualism or opposition between religion and philosophy, mythos and logos, secular and the sacred, and immanent and transcendent—dualism that are in themselves questionable—onto Daoist texts.[27] The point is not that the Dao may not be metaphysical or mystical in some sense, but that imposing a Western interpretation on a term that is more fluid than the Western denotation suggests can be misleading.

23. Carmody and Brink, *Ways to the Center*, 168.

24. Robson, *Daoism*, 605.

25. Storey, "Uses and Abuses of Metaphysical Language," 119.

26. Storey, "Uses and Abuses of Metaphysical Language," 119.

27. Storey, "Uses and Abuses of Metaphysical Language," 119.

Who Is the Founder of Daoism?

Daoism has often been traced to the legendary sage Laozi (sometimes rendered Lao Tzu). Whether or not Laozi existed in real life is still a matter of conjecture. Even some who question the existence of a historical figure Laozi leave open the possibility that a real person might be behind the legends.[28] If the legendary sage ever lived, he must have lived around 600 BCE. There are many legends surrounding the birth of the man his disciples call "the master." According to one legend, Laozi was born of a virgin woman. Not only was he born of a virgin woman, he was born old. Hence, he was nicknamed an "old child." Legend also has it that he was born full of wits. Many, including Confucius, came to him for wisdom. As an adult, he worked for the government as an archivist or librarian. But left the position when he realized that government laws and bureaucracies distort the simplicity by which humans should carry out their life.[29] When he left the government post, Laozi withdrew from society and lived a solitary life. It was probably in one of those reclusive times that many, including Confucius, visited him to tap into his wisdom. He traveled from one end of China to another, reaching as far as India, teaching and instructing people. Those who recognized him as a sage beckoned on him to write down some of his wisdom. He agreed and wrote a short book that came to be called the Daodejing. Although Laozi did not claim to have divine powers or be a god, some of his followers saw divine spark in him and worshiped him as a deity. They thought he was the Dao incarnated. According to another legend, Laozi never died. The reason why he never died was because he had the secret of immortality. Rather than die, he transformed his body in such a way that he could fly and then ascend to the heavens.

Terms and Their Variations

Chinese Term or Name	Chinese Variation	Description
Daoism	Taoism	The Way.
Daodejing	Tao Te Ching	Classic Daoist text attributed to Laozi.
Laozi	Lao Tzu	Legendary fifth-century BCE mystical Daoist sage.

28. See Young, *World's Religions*, 115.

29. Young, *World's Religions*, 115.

Zhuangzi	Chuang Tzu	Legendary fourth-century BCE mystical Daoist.
Yang Zhu	Yang Chu	Legendary hedonistic Daoist.
Kong Fuzu	Kong Qiu	Confucius—founder of Confucianism.
Zhu Xi	Chu Hsi	Twelfth-/thirteenth-century Historian and Confucian scholar.
Youzi		A disciple of Confucius.
Yan Hui		A disciple of Confucius.
Ji Kangzi		A disciple of Confucius.
Mao Zedong	Mao Tse Tung	Twentieth-century Chinese communist revolutionary leader.

Classical Texts of Daoism

Daoism, at least of the classical period, boasts of two classical texts that are worthy of examination here. The first is the classic work Daodejing, attributed to Laozi, and the second is the work of another recluse, Zhuangzi. The two texts can be traced back to the fourth century BCE. What the two texts call the Dao, the Way, though mysterious and nameless, refers to order in the universe.

a. The Daodejing

The authorship of the Daodejing (sometimes rendered Tao Te Ching), like the birth of Laozi, is still very much in the air. The text is estimated to have been written sometime between 350 BCE and 275 BCE, during the period of the Warring States (450–221 BCE). The way of life it presents was intended to restore harmony to a kingdom that was ravaged by wars and wanton destruction of life and property. The text of the Daodejing is critical of the uninhibited depravity of self-serving rulers. It is also scornful of social activism of self-seeking rulers because it considers it to be nothing more than an abstract moralism. The importance of this classic text cannot be overstated. It was considered by many to be a masterpiece comparable to other religious classics, like the Hindu *Bhagavad Gita*.[30] Its basic teachings can be summed up as follows:

---

30. Young, *World's Religions*, 116.

i. The Dao Is the Way: The Daodejing teaches that there is an order in the universe and that this order is indescribable. In fact, the Daodejing begins with a clear statement that we cannot linguistically describe the Dao. The opening chapter of the Daodejing reads,

> Dao (The Way) that can be spoken of is not the Constant Dao.
> The name that can be named is not a Constant Name.
> Nameless, is the origin of Heaven and Earth;
> The named is the Mother of all things.

The Dao is the origin of everything in the universe, although the Dao cannot be named. However, everything in the universe is a manifestation of the Dao. The Dao here does not mean God in the Judeo-Christian sense. In fact, the Dao is not only beyond description, it is nameless and it is not a person. The Dao is order in the universe that sets everything in motion. Its constant motion and rhyme keep the universe working as it should.

ii. Harmony with the Dao: The Daodejing teaches how to live harmoniously with the Dao. Since everything in the universe is a manifestation of the Dao, humans have to find a way to live harmoniously with the cosmos.

iii. How to Navigate Human existence: The Daodejing does not specifically deal with issues of suffering and death, like Buddhism does. But it recognizes that all organisms or *ming* are subject to death. It does not see any danger in dying a natural death, since death is the fate of all *ming* (organisms). Death is a necessary part of the continuous transformational process of the cosmos.[31] Suffering is inevitable in human existence. But it teaches how to navigate human existence by maximizing one's creative potential in the face of life's uncertainties. It teaches that it is only by returning to equilibrium or *jing* that one can avoid danger. The dangers to be avoided "are those superfluous dangers that are due to the tyrants and hierarchical political structures that coercively interfere with the lives of human [beings]."[32]

iv. Spontaneity in Nature: The Daodejing teaches that there is a natural flow of heaven and earth and teaches how to avoid

31. Bender, "Non-Coercive Action," 33.
32. Bender, "Non-Coercive Action," 34.

calamities by understanding the natural flow of heaven and earth.[33] It also teaches that there is spontaneity in nature and that we are part of the spontaneity of the cosmos. We have the power within us to grasp the spontaneity and natural flow of the universe. This power is achieved through wisdom. Anyone who possesses this power is a sage.

v. Contentment and Peace of Mind: The goal of human life is harmony with the Dao. To achieve this goal, a person has to learn how to live a simple non-complicated life. To teach humans how to avoid complications, the Daodejing gives practical guidance on how to manage wealth and be happy in life.

> Fame and life, which one is of intimacy?
> Life and wealth, which one is of importance?
> To gain one but to lose the other, which is of harm?
> Therefore, if one's desires are great, one would result in exhaustion.
> Overstock shall result in heavy loss.
> He who is contented will not suffer disgrace.
> He who knows his true nature will not incur danger.
> It is in this Way that one can long endure.

vi. Three Jewels of the Dao: The Daodejing rejects any notion of an independent, self-reliant self. There is no self divorced from others. The self exists only within an organic web of mutual influence. The Daodejing also identifies "three jewels of the Dao." These are the practices of non-coercive leadership, frugality, and compassion.[34]

> Dao gives birth to one.
> One gives birth to two.
> Two gives birth to three.
> Three gives birth to all things and all beings.
> All beings bear the negative physical form which is represented by Ying,
> and embrace the positive true nature which is represented by Yang.
> With the union of these two, they arrive at a state of harmony.
> Men dislike to be "the solitude," "the unworthy," and "the virtueless,"
> Yet the Lords and nobles call themselves these names.

33. Bender, "Non-Coercive Action," 33.
34. Bender, "Non-Coercive Action," 21.

Hence, things are benefited by being humble, and damaged by profiting.

What the ancients had taught, I shall also teach as such:

A man of violence who is in disharmony between Ying and Yang that is

the physical body and true self, shall die of an unnatural death.

This is the essential of my teaching.

The guiding motifs of the Daodejing are (i) the political—to be a handbook for political rulers; (ii) the religious—to be a guide to religious inquirers; and (iii) the practical—to be a practical guide to living in harmony with nature. These three motifs are not to be held in isolation.

b. Zhuangzi

Zhuangzi (also rendered Chuang Tzu), like Laozi, is legendary. We do not know much about his life and his writings, except that he lived around the fourth century BCE, during the Warring States period. Born around 369 BCE, Zhunagzi was a contemporary of the Confucian scholar, Mencius. The writing attributed to him takes after his name, Zhuangzi. This text is considered a definitive text of Daoism and more comprehensive than the Daodejing. Zhuangzi drew from and elaborated on the sayings of Laozi. Like the Daodejing, Zhuangzi taught about the Dao and how to live in harmony with the Dao. He taught that what can be known or said about the Dao is not the Dao because the Dao has no beginning or an end. Rather, life is an ongoing transformation of the Dao.[35]

Zhuangzi is sometimes referred to as a Daoist philosopher because of the elegance of his prose and the humor of his tales. He reportedly told a story of becoming a butterfly:

Once I, Zhuang Zhou, dreamed that I was a butterfly and was happy as a butterfly. I was conscious that I was quite pleased with myself, but I did not know that I was Zhou. Suddenly I awoke, and there I was, visibly Zhou. I do not know whether it was Zhou dreaming that he was a butterfly or the butterfly dreaming that it was Zhou. Between Zhou and the butterfly there must be some distinction. This is called the transformation of things.[36]

35. See *Encyclopedia Britannica*.
36. See *Encyclopedia Britannica*.

The story tells of Zhuangzi's uncanny ability to blur the difference between reality and fantasy, and between the past and the present.

EVOLUTION OF DAOISM

Daoism has evolved over time. Scholars have distinguished three basic types or patterns within Daoism. The three trends have different emphases but share a commitment to following the way of nature and rejecting social conventions.[37]

a. Hedonistic Daoism

Hedonistic Daoism is sometimes used as an umbrella term for those who gave up trying to save the social order in the time of chaos and disorder. These people instead chose to focus on saving themselves. One of the ways they did this was by fleeing from society and becoming a hermit: "leaving behind the chaos of the cities and the villages, the annoying and cumbersome obligations to government and family alike."[38] The hedonists usually tend to be pessimistic about society and the way things are. Unlike Greek hedonists who sought sensual pleasure, Daoist hedonists do not seek sensual pleasure. Their hedonism is in the pleasure of seeking to save only themselves in the wake of their pessimism about the organization of society. Yang Zhu (sometimes rendered Yang Chu) is a good example of hedonistic Daoist.[39]

b. Mystical Daoism

Mystical Daoism refers to those Daoist hermits, in the period of the Warring States, who developed a pantheistic conception of nature.[40] They "probed not only the natural functions of the Way and interior exercises that could align one with it, but also the revolt against conventional values that union with Dao seemed to imply."[41] Laozi and Zhuangzi are two examples of mystical Daoism.

c. Alchemical Daoism

37. Carmody and Brink, *Ways to the Center*, 168.
38. Carmody and Brink, *Ways to the Center*, 168.
39. Carmody and Brink, *Ways to the Center*, 168.
40. Carmody and Brink, *Ways to the Center*, 169.
41. Carmody and Brink, *Ways to the Center*, 169.

Alchemical Daoism attempted to synthesize elements from different schools of Daoism and blend them with metaphors they derived from Laozi and Zhuangzi. As their name suggests, they were preoccupied with extraordinary powers and magic, seeking by so doing to gain immortality. "Like medieval western alchemists who sought the patronage of kings by claiming to be able to change lead into gold, these Chinese alchemists sought the patronage of the noble and wealthy by promising to concoct an 'elixir of immortality.'"[42] In his diaries, Matteo Ricci notes how some Daoist priests, in their alchemical pursuit of immorality, performed magical rites to avert evil and accomplish other goals.[43]

CONFUCIANISM

Before taking up a discussion of Confucianism, we begin with the important question: Is Confucianism a religion or a philosophy? This is a question the West has not been able to answer properly and a question China has not dared to ask.[44] From the sketch of Chinese revolutions we offered in the previous section, one gets the idea that ancient China presented Confucianism, not as a religion or a philosophy, but rather as a code of wisdom and conduct for the Chinese gentleman scholar or the aspiring Chinese statesman.[45]

Kong Qiu or Kong Fuzu, anglicized Confucius (551–479 BCE), lived at the time of the Zhou dynasty, a time when China was split into small independent warring states (403–221 BCE). Feudal lords at the time maintained their authority "not through moral behavior and genuine concern for the welfare of the people, but through laws, punishments, and force."[46] Life was perilous and uncertainty ruled in the society in which Confucius lived. Confucius wanted a return to the pristine good old times, however idealistic that may be. The ancient Chinese venerated the ancestors and considered them closer to nature. Nature meant for them order and harmony in the way things are. Confucius wanted a return to the way things were at the time of the ancestors, which meant a return to harmony and order.

Confucius sought a moral basis for maintaining social order. His two basic assumptions are as follows: (i) All human beings by nature have innate

---

42. Carmody and Brink, *Ways to the Center*, 175.

43. Robson, *Daoism*, 605.

44. Robson, *Daoism*, xxvii.

45. Robson, *Daoism*, xxvii.

46. Gardner, *Confucianism*, 2.

moral sense. Since all are by nature disposed to moral malleability, all are therefore educable and can be moved by virtuous examples. (ii) Only a leader's virtuous conduct can make his subjects accept and follow his authority.[47] Thus, Confucius' ideals of proper behavior come down to these four words: *chung* (faithfulness), *hsin* (sincerity), *tu* (earnestness), and *ching* (respectfulness).[48] Confucius reportedly remarked to the feudal leaders, "If you can rule your own country, who dares to insult you? If we are unified, strict and sober, and if hundreds of measures are fostered, naturally the foreigners will not insult and affront us without reason."[49] Confucius was convinced that if good government and the four virtues he outlined had prevailed, the feudal wars would not have arisen. So he made it his mission to travel from one feudal state to another, hoping to find a receptive ruler who would embrace his vision, but to no avail. No ruler was willing to appoint him to a position of authority where he could share his vision.[50]

The feudal lords found Confucius' teachings to be idealistic and impracticable and never gave him a chance to try out his teachings in politics. Disappointed, Confucius turned attention to teaching. He gathered disciples, about seventy-two serious ones, and began to impart his knowledge to them, hoping that they would embrace his ideals and one day try them out in politics.[51] His disciples collected and codified his teachings into the *Analects*. In the second century BCE, three centuries after Confucius' death, the text of the *Analects* achieved its present form.[52] Together with the *Analects*, the *Book of Changes*, the *Book of Odes*, the *Book of History*, the *Book of Rites*, and the *Spring and Autumn Annals* are the classics considered canonical in the Confucian tradition. Confucians revere these works because they believe they convey basic principles of sage government, how to practice rituals, and how to perceive and relate to the cosmos. They think lessons from the history of the Spring and Autumn period (722–481 BCE), which are conveyed in the *Spring and Autumn Annals* are perfectly in accord with the Master's teachings.[53]

47. Fairbank, *Great Chinese Revolution*, 37.

48. Fairbank, *Great Chinese Revolution*, 106.

49. Fairbank, *Great Chinese Revolution*, 106.

50. Gardner, *Confucianism*, 2.

51. Gardner, *Confucianism*, 3.

52. Gardner, *Confucianism*, 3.

53. Gardner, *Confucianism*, 4.

Six Classic Confucian Texts

Name of Text	Other Names	Date of Composition	Description
The Analects	Analects of Confucius	During the Warring States Period (ca. 375–221 BCE) and finalized during the Han dynasty (ca. 202–220 BCE).	A collection of sayings and ideas of Confucius written by the followers of Confucius.
The Book of Changes	I Ching	Believed to have predated Confucius. Goes back to the Zhou dynasty—sometime around ninth century BCE.	An ancient text with philosophical-cosmological vision. It has gone through changes and refinements with time. Confucius was said to have recommended that his disciples follow the advice contained in the *Book of Changes*. It is one of the Five Classics of ancient Chinese literature. Legend has it that Confucius collected and edited the Five Classics.

The Book of Odes	Book of Songs or Book of Poetry.	Estimated to go back to the Zhou dynasty in the seventh century BCE.	Collection of (about 350) poetry and numerous diverse songs and eulogies. Traditionally thought to have been compiled by Confucius. One of the Five Classics of ancient Chinese literature.
The Book of History	Book of Documents	Second century BCE.	A collection of rhetorical prose that goes back to ancient Chinese history. Traditionally was thought to have been discovered in Confucius' estate. One of the Five Classics of ancient Chinese literature.
The Book of Rites	Classics of Rites or *Lijing*	Unknown	A collection of texts for social ceremonial rites. One of the Five Classics.
The Spring and Autumn Annals		Exact date of composition is unknown, but contains history that goes as far back as fourth and fifth century BCE.	One of the Five Classics. Contains historical record (such as royal ceremonies, marriage, death, and battles) of the over two-hundred-year history of the state of Lu, which is Confucius' own home state.

Confucius' Major Teachings

Unlike the founders of those religions that are concerned with the questions of afterlife and immortality, Confucius was not concerned with questions regarding whether human beings survive their death or are destined to absolute extinction at death.[54] He was more interested in cosmic harmony and unity in human relationships. Thus, his major ideas, which have been codified in a religious system that is named after him, can be summarized as follows:

1. Cosmological Vision

In the *Analects*, Confucius projects a worldview comprising of two realms: the human realm and the realm of heaven and earth. In the human realm, he assumes order must be actively created and nurtured by human agency. In the realm of heaven and earth, he assumes there is an inherent rhythm and harmony that spontaneously maintain a perfect balance among its many parts.[55] He thinks that there is an organic interconnectedness of being. Human ritual practice, therefore, must seek to sustain this harmony and interconnectedness of being. Confucius does not project any idea of creator God or any higher power responsible for the creation or sustenance of the universe. Rather, the cosmos operates automatically.[56] "It is not that a spirit world populated by nature deities and ancestors does not exist for Confucius; various spirits could assist human beings in controlling rivers and fields, villages and cities, and families and lineages. But there is no ultimate, omnipotent spirit or deity responsible for the creation of all that is and was."[57] Since the cosmos operates effortlessly to achieve balance and harmony among its parts, it is only the human realm that needs active regulation. Without regulation, politics and morality will continue to be in a wretched state.[58]

---

54. See Marcel, *Tragic Wisdom and Beyond*, 20.

55. Gardner, *Confucianism*, 13.

56. Gardner, *Confucianism*, 13.

57. Gardner, *Confucianism*, 13.

58. Gardner, *Confucianism*, 14.

2. Moral Vanguard

Confucius calls for a moral vanguard of community of persons. The moral vanguard begins with knowing one's mind, which according to Confucius must be encased in *ren* (sometimes rendered *jen*). *Ren* is a kind of love that generates a fellow-feeling and community-feeling. *Ren* not only makes living in community possible, it makes it attractive as well. *Ren* begins in the family and extends to the state or society. The Book of Mencius states clearly that "the foundation of the empire lies with the state; the foundation of the state lies with the family; the foundation of the family lies with the person."[59] A ruler should possess a virtue Confucius calls *de* (an inner virtue with a spiritual ethical transformative power). A ruler who possesses *de* has a moral suasion that attracts subjects to the ruler. Confucius compares a ruler who practices virtue to the Northern Star: "One who practices government by virtue may be compared to the North Star: it remains in its place while the multitude of stars turn toward it."[60] The moral authority of a virtuous leader is not a coercive power. Rather, it is a force that guides others in their movements, setting them in the right direction.[61] Confucius was so convinced of the transformative power of moral leadership that he purportedly said that with moral leadership even the Barbarians would turn from their crudeness and act right: "Guide them by edicts, keep them in line with punishments, and the common people will stay out of trouble, but will have no sense of shame. Guide them by virtue, keep them in line with ritual and they will, besides having a sense of shame, reform themselves."[62]

3. Formal Structure of Relationships

Confucianism sees the family as the microcosm of the state and the locus for learning about human relationships and the principles that govern these relationships.[63] Confucius taught that people are moved to proper behavior when they see good examples or good role models. He establishes five familial relationships: father–son, older brother–younger brother, older friend–younger friend, husband–wife, and emperor–subject. These relationships are not based on equality of rights, but on reciprocity of duties; the first of

---

59. See *Mencius* 4A.5; cited in Gardner, *Confucianism*, 16.
60. Gardner, *Confucianism*, 34.
61. Gardner, *Confucianism*, 34.
62. Gardner, *Confucianism*, 37.
63. Gardner, *Confucianism*, 29.

the relationships is the prototype and basis for others.[64] The father has the duty to care for the son, educate and nurture him. The son, in turn, has the duty to obey the father and then care for him in old age and all through his (the son's) life. The older brother has the duty to care for the younger brother almost the way a father would care for a son. The younger brother, in turn, has the duty to obey the older brother in all matters. The older friend has the duty to advise the younger friend wisely, but mostly by good examples. The younger friend has the duty to obey the younger friend, as well as following the good examples. The husband has the duty to provide for the wife and cater for all her needs. The wife has the duty to obey and follow the good counsels of the husband. The emperor has the duty to cater for the subjects and model good examples in virtue. The subjects are duty-bound to obey the emperor whose mandate to rule comes from the virtues he models.

Youzi, a disciple of Confucius, once said "One who is filial and fraternal but at the same time loves defying superiors is rare indeed. One who does not love defying superiors but at the same time loves sowing disorder has never existed. The superior man attends to the root. When the root is established, the Way issues forth. Filial piety and fraternal respect—are they not the root of true goodness?"[65] According to the *Book of Rites*, these five enduring relationships constitute the universal Way of the world.[66] A person's filial obligations to his or her parents, in Confucian thinking, do not cease with the death of one's parents, but continue throughout a person's entire life. It is expected that throughout one's life, one should live in a manner that would reflect well on the family's good name.[67]

4. Cultivation of Virtues

It is by practicing rituals and respecting the mutual responsibilities required to sustain the five relationships that one brings harmony to one's family, community, and the empire. Filial obligations do not play out within the web of family relations only, but are fully actualized in the larger network of social relations by a person's practice of good, virtuous acts.[68] "The prominent role played by the individual in creating good sociopolitical order explains why Confucian teachings, throughout the ages, give profound attention to the process of self-cultivation. Each and every human being is

---

64. Carmody and Brink, *Ways to the Center*, 167.

65. Gardner, *Confucianism*, 30.

66. Gardner, *Confucianism*, 26.

67. Gardner, *Confucianism*, 31.

68. Gardner, *Confucianism*, 31.

urged to engage in a process of moral refinement, as each and every human being has the capability to exercise a beneficial moral force over others."[69] Yan Hui, a famous disciple of Confucius once said, "The Master said, 'Hui! For three months his mind-and-heart would not lapse from true goodness. As for others, they might attain it for a day or for a month, but that is all.'"[70]

Throughout its refinements, Confucian teachings place emphasis on the process of self-cultivation of virtues. The reason why one cultivates virtues is to become a *junzi* (literally means a "ruler's son"). In ancient Chinese worldview, a *junzi* is a noble man or a socio-political elite. To be a *junzi* is to be an aristocrat.[71] "A *junzi* for Confucius is the *morally* superior person who, by according with the ritual code of the tradition, treats others with respect and dignity, and pursues virtues like humility, sincerity, trustworthiness, righteousness, and compassion."[72] Everyone, irrespective of class or social status, is encouraged to engage in a process of moral refinement and self-cultivation of virtues, if they are to be a moral force in the society. It is a Confucian belief that each and every human being already has the capability to exercise a beneficial moral force over others.[73] Self-cultivation of virtues is the starting point in a person's pursuit of the true Way. Self-cultivation of virtues is also the basis or the root of any attempt to regenerate civility, harmony, and ritual elegance in Chinese society.[74]

To show the importance of *junzi*, in the *Analects* Confucius draws a contrast between two people: the morally superior man, or *junzi*, and the "small man," or *xiaoren*. The small man does not adhere to the conventions of proper decorum and does not follow the Way—the moral path. According to Confucius, the *junzi* understands righteousness, but the *xiaoren* only understands profit.[75] The superior man's concerns are necessarily both guided by and expressed through a set of *li* (ritual propriety).[76] By showing that anyone can become a *junzi*, Confucius reinvents this ancient notion. "Whereas earlier a person could not strive to become a *junzi*—whether one was born into *junzi* status or not—now anyone, at least theoretically, could attain the status through successful self-cultivation. Here Confucius lays down a novel challenge to his contemporaries: through effort, any one

69. Gardner, *Confucianism*, 16.

70. Gardner, *Confucianism*, 24.

71. Gardner, *Confucianism*, 18.

72. Gardner, *Confucianism*, 18.

73. Gardner, *Confucianism*, 16.

74. Gardner, *Confucianism*, 18.

75. Gardner, *Confucianism*, 18.

76. Gardner, *Confucianism*, 25.

of you can *become* a noble person."[77] Confucius returns to his analysis of the good ethical thing a leader should do. He says a good virtuous leader is the consummate *junzi* because he is the perfect role model because he instructs and guides his subjects only through a charismatic moral example. The ruler can depend less on laws, edicts, and other routine tools of daily governance, said Confucius, if the ruler is morally right.[78]

The Chinese Philosopher Mencius (372–289 BCE)	The Book of Mencius
	The Book of *Mencius* (ca. fourth century BCE) is a collection of the sayings, conversations, and teachings of Confucius. Confucians use this text to build a political philosophy and advance these Confucian teachings: • *Ren* (Jen): a Confucian virtue that produces fellow-feeling and community feeling. • *De*: a transformative power or inner virtue a ruler must possess. • *Junzi*: a morally superior virtue. • *Xiaoren*: a morally inferior person. • *Li*: ritual propriety; it guides a superior person's actions.

5. Cultivation of Learning

The opening line of the *Analects* reads, "The Master said, 'To learn something and rehearse it constantly,' is this indeed not a pleasure?" Confucius reportedly said if there ever was anything that makes him different from all others, it is simply his devotion to learning.[79] The Confucian devotion to learning is well articulated in Zengzi's (one of Confucius' famous disciples) statement, "A learned man must be broad and resolute, for his burden is heavy and the journey is long. He takes true goodness as his burden: Is that not indeed heavy? And only with death does he stop: Is that not indeed long?"[80]

77. Gardner, *Confucianism*, 18.

78. Gardner, *Confucianism*, 36.

79. Gardner, *Confucianism*, 18.

80. Gardner, *Confucianism*, 24

One does not just become a *junzi* without learning about it. To become a *junzi*, one must cultivate learning. Unlike Plato, who advocated in the *Republic* that learning should be reserved only for the aristocrats who have been specially chosen to govern the state, Confucius taught that learning should be open to everyone. No one should be denied the privilege of learning. But he cautions that learning should not be mere accumulation of knowledge or listing of facts. Learning must be done inferentially.[81] Confucius thought that learning in his own day was distorted and reduced to accumulation of facts. Take, for example, Confucius' favorite disciple, Yan Hui. It is, in part, Yan Hui's exceptional inferential powers that explain Confucius' special affection for him:

> "The Master said to Zigong, 'Of you and Hui, who is the better?' He responded, 'Me? How could I dare compare myself to Hui? Hui hears one matter and understands ten; I hear one matter and understand two.' The Master said, 'No, you are not his equal. Neither of us is his equal'" (5.9). Further, the good student should know how to apply his inferential knowledge. "The Master said, 'Imagine a person who can recite the three hundred poems by heart but when entrusted with matters of governing cannot carry them out, or when sent on a mission to one of the four quarters is unable to exercise his own initiative. No matter how many poems he might have memorized, what good are they to him?'" (13.5). The message here is that book learning that devolves into mere memorization is sterile and useless and not the true learning that will enable self-transformation and the betterment of society.[82]

In addition, Confucius also taught that the good learning is one that leads to moral goodness or *Ren*—moral perfection or sagacity. Moral perfection or sagehood, however, is not a virtue one can acquire in isolation from others. Even the etymological derivation of the Chinese *ren* suggests that true goodness comes only in interaction with others.[83] Similarly, the Confucian idea of true goodness is only achieved in a community of persons and in interaction with others. "It is in concrete behavior that true goodness, as a virtue, is achieved. A filial son, for instance, 'enacts' his filial devotion by bowing before his father. True goodness is thus closely associated with ritual, for it is principally through the practice of ritual, the Master believes,

81. Gardner, *Confucianism*, 21.

82. Gardner, *Confucianism*, 21.

83. Gardner, *Confucianism*, 25.

that true goodness is given meaningful expression."[84] For those trained in Western Christian tradition of eremitical monasticism, this is where the Confucian idea of virtue differs from the Christian ascetical tradition. In eremitical tradition, Christian monks take refuge in the desert to live a life of virtue in isolation as hermits. The Confucian idea leaves no place for that.

The path to moral perfection, according to the *Analects*, must start with an unwavering commitment learning, just as Confucius the master did. Confucius reportedly said, "At fifteen, I set my mind-and-heart on learning. At thirty, I stood on my own. At forty, I had no doubts. At fifty, I knew heaven's decree. At sixty, my ears were in accord. At seventy, I followed the desires of my mind-and-heart without overstepping right (2.4)."[85] This is also the Confucian way of showing that true goodness requires a lifelong commitment and that it ceases only with death itself.[86]

6. The Practice of Ritual

When Confucius distinguished between a superior man and a small man, he was clear that it is the practice of *Li* or rituals that guides the superior man's actions. "A father, in practicing proper ritual, behaves as a true father should; a son, in practicing proper ritual, behaves as a true son should. Ritual thus promotes the actualization of the normative five relationships."[87] Ritual harmonizes or civilizes a person, whereas the absence of ritual turns a person backward, away from the Way. It is the practice of rituals that distinguishes a human person from beast. The *Analects* presents ritual practice as a means of manifesting one's humanity and a means of nurturing within a person the very qualities that make that person human.[88]

> The parrot can speak, and yet is nothing more than a bird; the ape can speak, and yet is nothing more than a beast. Here now is a man who observes no rules of ritual propriety; is not his mind-and-heart that of a beast? But if men were as beasts, and without the principle of ritual propriety, father and son might have the same mate. Therefore, when the sages arose, they framed the rules of ritual propriety in order to teach men, and cause them,

84. Gardner, *Confucianism*, 23.
85. Gardner, *Confucianism*, 22.
86. Gardner, *Confucianism*, 24.
87. Gardner, *Confucianism*, 26.
88. Gardner, *Confucianism*, 28.

by their possession of them, to make a distinction between themselves and brutes.[89]

What Confucius means by ritual should by no means be understood solely along the lines of what we think of ceremonial religious rituals. For Confucius, all facets of life, including the mundane, such as the way we eat, the way we entertain guests, the way we dress, and the way we conduct ourselves in public, are governed by a system of rituals.[90] "The instructive and transforming power of rituals is subtle: they stop depravity before it has taken form, causing men daily to move towards what is good and to distance themselves from vice, without being themselves conscious of it."[91] For example, by offering sacrifice one deepens one's feelings or reverence for the ancestors; through the act of bowing one deepens one's feelings of respect for elders; through one's decorous speech, dress, and table manners one deepens one's feelings of propriety and civility towards others.[92]

7. Maintaining Culture and Tradition

Confucius was an enforcer of culture and tradition. He suggested that culture and tradition are more effective tools of shaping human behavior than legal and penal codes.[93] Through moral suasion, a good ruler fosters a system of shared values, which regulates conduct in the society or state. It is these shared values and norms of behavior that bind people to the community, not edicts and penal codes.[94] "A person who uses his fingers rather than chopsticks to eat yellow fish, or curses his elderly father in public, or wears lavish clothing during the mourning period for a parent will likely be branded by others as uncouth and uncivilized. He has failed, after all, to learn what it means to be truly Chinese and now risks being marginalized by his fellow villagers."[95] This does not mean that Confucius did not see the place of edicts and penal codes in society. His point was that, should the leader lead by example, crime would be reduced to the barest minimum. By leading by example, the leader becomes the standard bearer of culture. "The good ruler is necessarily a good judge of character and selects as officials

89. Gardner, *Confucianism*, 26.
90. Gardner, *Confucianism*, 27.
91. Gardner, *Confucianism*, 27.
92. Gardner, *Confucianism*, 28.
93. Gardner, *Confucianism*, 37.
94. Gardner, *Confucianism*, 37.
95. Gardner, *Confucianism*, 37.

only those men who share his commitment to Confucian principles and the well-being of the people."[96]

We saw during the Zhou dynasty that the Zhou leaders introduced the mythical *tianming* (mandate from heaven) to justify their rule. Confucius insists that a leader does not need a" mandate from heaven" to be a leader. All a leader needs is virtue alone. Ji Kangzi, a disciple of Confucius, reported this exchange on government: "Ji Kangzi asked Confucius about government, saying, 'Suppose I were to kill the Way-less in order to promote those possessed of the Way. What would you say?'" With no little hint of impatience and even disdain for the usurper Ji Kangzi, Confucius answered, "You are governing; what need is there for killing? If you desire the good, the people will be good. The virtue of the superior man is wind; the virtue of the small person is grass. When wind passes over it, the grass is sure to bend."[97]

CONCLUSION

It is an error to think of Confucianism as a sort of unchanging monolith and its traditions as stagnant traditions with little or no changes since the time of its founder.[98] Like all major philosophical movements, like Platonism and Aristotelianism, and like other religions like Judaism, Christianity, and Islam, Confucianism is ever-changing and ever evolving. Like all major movements and religions in which the teachings of the founder are open to different levels of interpretations, all through history, the teachings of Confucius have been interpreted along many lines. Some have distinguished classical Confucianism, Mencian Confucianism, the Confucianism of Xunsi, Han Confucianism, Sung Confucianism, Wang Confucianism, Utilitarian Confucianism, and Neo-Confucianism.[99]

96. Gardner, *Confucianism*, 39.

97. Gardner, *Confucianism*, 34.

98. Gardner, *Confucianism*, 48.

99. Gardner, *Confucianism*, 49.

13

Hinduism

THE DOMINANT RELIGION IN South Asia is Hinduism. About eight hundred million of India's one billion people identify themselves as Hindu. Although Nepal declared itself a secular state in 2007, about 81 percent of its population also identify themselves as Hindu. Likewise, about 8.5 percent of Bangladesh's over fifteen million people is Hindu and about 12.5 percent of the population of Sri Lanka is Hindu. There are also millions of other Hindus scattered all over the world, including North America. Numerically, therefore, Hinduism is not only one of the largest, but also one of the oldest living religious and philosophical traditions of the world.[1]

Hinduism is a complex religious phenomenon. What the term is and what the term refers to are two different things. A critical study of Hinduism needs to distinguish what the term has been commonly understood to mean from what the term is and should be. For a religion that has about one billion and counting followers, it is not unusual to expect to find many different ways of understanding it.[2] One of the reasons for the complexity of this religion has to do with demographic changes. Indian culture and demographics have changed over the centuries, but the Hindus, on their part, have been unwilling and even unable to jettison old religious ideas and practices as they move forward.[3] Apart from tribal religions, whose origins cannot be separated from the founding narratives of the tribe itself, Hinduism ranks among the oldest religions the world has ever known. Its belief

1. Klostermaier, *Survey of Hinduism*, 1.
2. Matthews, *World Religions*, 83.
3. Llewellyn, "Problem of Defining Hinduism," 3.

systems are as rich and diverse as its peoples. Imagine this scenario: You are visiting a friend you just met through one of your social networks and you find yourself in a typical Indian city, say New Delhi or Bengal. Your friend welcomes you and introduces you to his mother and tells you his mother is a devotee of Lord Shiva. He introduces you to his father and tells you that his father worships at the temple of the goddess Durga. He introduces you to his brother and tells you that his brother goes to the devotional school of Lord Rama and that he occasionally visits the temple of Vishnu. He introduces you to his brother-in-law and tells you that his brother-in-law and his wife are fond of Lord Krishna and the god Hanuman. You are awed and perplexed because you have just been bamboozled by the many gods with whom this one family has ties. You are there stirring and trying to figure it out, but you can't seem to make a headway. Don't even try! Such is the complexity of the religious phenomenon we call Hinduism.

The complex nature of this religious tradition with historical roots that go as far back as five thousand years has led some to suggest, and correctly too, that we should perhaps drop the term Hinduism and refer instead to this vast and multifaceted religio-cultural phenomenon as "Hindu traditions."[4] If Hinduism is, as one scholar has argued, a victim of "the tyranny of some religio-cultural labelling game,"[5] then perhaps we might go a step further and add that we would better appreciate the religio-cultural traditions in India only if we see them as Hindu ways of being human in a complex world system. For a religious tradition that has within it elements of what we would call monotheism, polytheism, henotheism, animism, pantheism, panentheism, monism, and even atheism cannot be defined as if it were an integral system with a uniform set of belief systems. In addition to combining belief systems that appear contradictory, the significance assigned to belief systems by the Hindus themselves varies widely.[6]

The suggestion has been made that perhaps one of the reasons for the complexity of Hinduism is because the goal of Hinduism is beyond ordinary language.[7] Descriptors suggested as the goal of Hinduism have ranged from positive labels, like "God realization," "identification with the absolute," "supreme bliss," and "cosmic consciousness" to negative labels, like "release," "liberation," and "freedom."[8] This has led some scholars to

---

4. See Muesse, *Hindu Traditions*, xv.

5. See Lipner, "Meaning of 'Hinduness,'" 31.

6. Muesse, *Hindu Traditions*, 4–5.

7. Llewellyn, "Problem of Defining Hinduism," 4.

8. Llewellyn, "Problem of Defining Hinduism," 4; quoting Ellwood and McGraw, *Many Peoples, Many Faiths*, 60.

suggest that we desist from applying our Western derived categories to Hinduism because Hinduism does not necessarily conceive religious truth in dogmatic terms as we do, because for the Hindus, truth transcends all verbal definitions.[9] Moreover, Hinduism is not primarily concerned with the existence or non-existence of God. It does not probe whether there is one God or many gods.

> Hindus can choose to be monotheists, polytheists, atheists, agnostics, dualists, monists, or pluralists. They may or may not follow strict standards of moral conduct, spend time on everyday religious rituals, or attend a temple. Magic, fetishism, animal worship, and belief in demons coexist, supplement, and accompany profound theological doctrines, asceticism, mysticism, and esoteric beliefs.[10]

WHO INVENTED HINDUISM?[11]

There is still no agreement among scholars as to who invented "Hinduism." The essential arguments have varied from time to time. We know for sure that in the classical and medieval periods, Europeans traded with India for spices and textiles. The Portuguese Vasco da Gama arrived on the Malabar Coast at the end of the fifteenth century in search of spices. He was perhaps the most well-known of the European explorers.[12] The Dutch, British, and French soon followed the Portuguese to India, establishing trading companies in India in the sixteenth and seventeenth centuries, before the British eventually came to dominate India, at least, politically.[13] With Britain firmly secure in India, a number of European writers wrote tracts and books about India and its religion, at times with dubious intentions. The overarching motive being their desire to see India in European Christian image, evaluate India according to European Christian standards, and then benefit from India's riches—its goods and its culture.[14]

In fact, European missionaries and explorers brought with them to India their Christian presuppositions about what constitutes religion. One

---

9. Llewellyn, "Problem of Defining Hinduism," 4; referencing Nigosian, *World Religions*, 20.

10. Nigosian, *World Religions*, 20.

11. See Lorenzen, "Who Invented Hinduism?," 630–59.

12. Knott, *Hinduism*, 68.

13. Knott, *Hinduism*, 68.

14. Knott, *Hinduism*, 68.

writer has claimed that Christian presuppositions did in fact make it impossible for European writers to perceive religious plurality in India, leading them, therefore, to not only falsely conceive the religion, but also to employ the inadequate concept "Hinduism."[15] Also, some of the early European Christian missionaries, like the Italian Jesuit Roberto Nobili (1577–1656), were least interested in the religion of the Indians whom they thought were heathens, but more interested in the Indian culture and language systems. Nobili founded the Madurai mission in 1606 to help Jesuit missionaries in their work of "accommodation" and "adaptation" of Indian cultures to Christianity. His interest in Hinduism was not necessarily on the religion of Indians as such, but only insofar as it can serve the Jesuit interest in "accommodation."[16] It is hard, therefore, to dispute outside influences on Hinduism. Apart from the Europeans, there were also the Arabs and the Turks whose influences have helped shape our understanding of Hinduism. But the extent of its impact on the religion we know as Hinduism is still very much up for debate. To help us simplify the argument, we shall break it down to three different schools of thought, each offering a different opinion on the matter.

Constructionist School

The constructionist school thinks that what goes by the label Hinduism was constructed or invented or imagined by British scholars and colonial administrators in the nineteenth century and that whatever they put under the label did not exist in any meaningful sense before this date.[17] The idea of the constructionist school was systematically developed in 1962 by Wilfred Cantwell Smith. Smith claimed that the Hindus themselves do not think of themselves as practicing Hinduism. He, therefore, cautioned against reification of religions and against all attempts to make religion "an objective systematic entity."[18] Smith's statement, "There are Hindus, but there is no Hinduism,"[19] has been interpreted to mean that the term Hinduism is nothing but a foreign superimposition or invention on a religion with no clearly identifiable creed and no coherent organizational structure.[20] Thus, Smith's statement has been echoed in various ways by his other constructionist

15. Sweetman, "Unity and Plurality," 84.
16. Sweetman, "Unity and Plurality," 85–86.
17. Lorenzen, "Who Invented Hinduism?," 630.
18. Smith, *Meaning and End of Religion*, 51.
19. Smith, *Meaning and End of Religion*, 65.
20. Halbfass, "Idea of the Veda," 21.

colleagues who think Hinduism is a collective label produced by Western scholars for "the innumerable, partly cognate, partly divergent religious phenomena of one geographical and historical region."[21]

Modern restatement of the constructionist theory coalesces around the argument of Mark Muesse. Muesse argued that the Sanskrit term *Sindhu* (Hindu), in its original sense, had no religious connotations. Rather, *Hindu* was an old Persian word used to identify people who lived in the area flanking the Indus River, i.e., the region between northwestern India and modern-day Pakistan.[22] According to Muesse and members of the constructionist school, it was not until around 1200 BCE and 1500 BCE that the term was given a religious connotation to mean a person with a particular religious orientation. When it gained a religious connotation, "it was almost always used to identify those inhabitants of India who were not Muslims."[23] Around this time also, because of the geographical ties of Hinduism to the land of India, the term "Indian" was used almost exclusively for geographical identity, while the term Hindu was reserved almost exclusively for religious identification. Muesse, however, still noticed a problem with the religious identification of Hindu primarily because it has "no central core of teachings, scriptures, creeds, communities, or practices that could be specified as forming the essence of Hindu identity."[24]

Deconstructionist School

The Deconstructionist school rejects any notion that Hinduism was invented or constructed by European colonizers. They contend that long before the European colonizers made their foray into India in the nineteenth century that there was already in existence a Hindu religion that was theologically and devotionally grounded in Hindu texts, such as the *Bhagavad-Gita*, the Puranas (ancient stories), and philosophical commentaries.[25] The Deconstructionists also deny the claim of the Constructionists that the English word "Hinduism" is a nineteenth-century invention (first coined in 1829) of the British. They claim that what the Constructionists mean when they say Hinduism was constructed or invented by the British is deceptive because the Constructionists, according to them, are trying to suggest that

21. Halbfass, "Idea of the Veda," 22; quoting Hacker, *Kleine Schriften*, 480 and 290.

22. Muesse, *Hindu Traditions*, 2.

23. Muesse, *Hindu Traditions*, 2.

24. Muesse, *Hindu Traditions*, 2–3.

25. Lorenzen, "Who Invented Hinduism?," 631.

"the British imposed a single conceptual category on a heterogeneous collection of sects, doctrines, and customs that the Hindus themselves did
not recognize as having anything essential in common."[26] Thus the Deconstructionists think it ridiculous to suggest, as the Constructionist do,
that it was after the Hinduism was constructed by the Europeans that the
Hindus themselves adopted the idea that they all belong to a single religious
community known as Hinduism. While not himself a deconstructionist, the
deconstructionists cite the argument of the Hindu scholar, Ram Mohan Roy
(1772/4–1833), who purportedly made statements that have been used to
refute the constructionist argument. Ram Mohan was well vast in Persian,
Arabic, Greek, Latin, and English, as well as Bengali and Sanskrit. He also
had a good knowledge of Islam and Christianity, in addition to his own
Hindu religion. In fact, he is believed to be the first Indian to comment in
print on the British, their religion, and their place in the Indian context.[27]
Writing as a Hindu social reformer, Ram Mohan was critical of some Hindu
practices, such as idolatry, *sati*, child-marriage, and caste system, for which
he was vilified by his more orthodox Hindu peers.[28] However, a reference
to Hinduism he made in 1816 claimed that "the chief part of the theory
and practice of Hindooism . . . is made to consist in the adoption of a peculiar mode of diet."[29] In another related statement about Hindu deity in
1817, Ram Mohan claimed that "the doctrines of the unity of God are real
in Hinduism, as that religion was practiced by our ancestors, and as it is
well known at the present day to many learned Brahmins."[30] The deconstructionists use these statements to buttress their argument that Hinduism
was not constructed by anyone, but that it emerged naturally and grew and
developed organically over time.

Reform School

The Bengali Ram Mohan Roy is the main proponent of the Reform School
of Hinduism. There are also many other Hindus with a reform-minded view
of Hinduism. Before delving into this school and its ideas, a context may be
in order. The arguments of the deconstructionist aside, there is no denying
that by the nineteenth century, Hinduism was already saturated with a great
deal of European and Arab influences. Muslim contact with India goes as

26. Lorenzen, "Who Invented Hinduism?," 632.

27. Knott, *Hinduism*, 71.

28. Knott, *Hinduism*, 71.

29. Lorenzen, "Who Invented Hinduism?," 631.

30. Lorenzen, "Who Invented Hinduism?," 631–32.

far back as the eighth century when Islamic civilization spread as far as Asia. By the thirteenth century, Islam had become, not only a religious force, but also a political and economic power in the region. Many Indians were attracted to Islam's teaching of equality and economic and political protection and converted to Islam. Earlier we noted how Western powers, particularly Great Britain and France, made their way to India in the eighteenth century. The Western powers were very vocal in their criticisms of Hindu traditional practices.[31] It was largely these criticisms that gave birth to reform movements within Hinduism. One thing these reform movements have in common is their desire to distill what is most central to Hindu tradition and do away with what was considered, at least by the British standard, immoral, superstitious, and uncivilized practices. One of the eminent personalities at this time who sought to reform Hinduism was Ram Mohan Roy who founded the Brahmo Samaj (the society of Brahman) in 1828, a society that represented his vision of a reformed Hinduism.[32]

Mohan Roy was familiar with Western ideas and the Western system of education. Addressing the Western antagonists, Roy claimed that the essence of Hinduism is to be found in the Hindu philosophical texts, the Upanishads. Roy also claimed that in the Upanishads was revealed the One Nameless Absolute God of all peoples. This God is to be worshiped through meditation and a pious life. For Roy, such Hindu customs as image worship, pilgrimage, festivals, and the rules of the caste are to be considered superfluous in the service of this One Nameless Absolute God. Many at the time gravitated towards Ram Mohan's reform movement and his Brahmo Samaj, which attempted to institute "worship services and a type of piety that were rationalistic, humanistic, and devoid of distinctive Hindu symbols and customs."[33]

Like Mohan Roy, other reform-minded Hindu elites who had earlier embraced Western-style education, like the Bengali Ramakrishna (1836–86), Vivekananda (1863–1902), and Mohandas Karamchand Gandhi (1869–1948), took up the reform mantle. Vivekananda, a disciple of Ramakrishna, came to the attention of the Western world when he addressed the First World Parliament of Religions in Chicago in 1893. His reform program was enthusiastically received in Chicago. Vivekananda stressed the monistic teachings of the Upanishads. He also set up missionary centers in the West to foster the teachings and practices of Hinduism.[34] Mohandas

31. Kinsley, *Hinduism*, 20.

32. Kinsley, *Hinduism*, 21.

33. Kinsley, *Hinduism*, 21.

34. Kinsley, *Hinduism*, 22.

Gandhi, on his part, brought the themes of Hinduism to bear, particularly its stress on yoga and disciplined action. Gandhi stressed the Bhagavad-Gita's emphasis on involvement with the world through the technique of *Satyagraha* (truth force). Gandhi understood the Gita as upholding non-violent action, and therefore urged restraint, negotiation, and self-sacrifice in the face of political violence. Gandhi employed these techniques in his fight for Indian independence. He advocated a kind of Hinduism that emphasizes asceticism, renunciation of the world, and community service.

Hinduism went through more reforms in the twenty-first century with the rise of the Hindu right as a political force in India. In 1996, the Indian National Congress, led by high-caste Hindus who drew most of their support from low-caste Hindus, the party of Mahatma Gandhi (1869–1948), the father of independent India, and the party of India's first Prime Minister, Jawaharlal Nehru (1889–1964), was ousted by a coalition of Hindu nationalists, the Bharatiya Janata Party.[35] One of the complaints of the far-right Bharatiya Party was that the oppression of the indigenous people of India and their religion had not ceased even with independence and that the Indian National Congress had been busy catering for the needs of religious minorities, like the Muslims, to the neglect of Hindus themselves. They thought it was "time to give the Hindus their due and to put others, especially Muslims, in their place."[36] Although they did not oust the Indian National Congress until 1996, the revolt they began and a campaign they initiated a decade earlier led to riots that destroyed the Muslim house of worship, the Babri Masjid, in 1992. Their claim was that the Babri Masjid was built on the very spot that the Hindu god Ram was born and that the Masjid was occupying a space where a Hindu temple had stood.[37] Needless to say that the crisis precipitated by the riots that killed hundreds of Muslims and Hindus forced many to rethink what Hinduism really means.

ORIGINS OF HINDUISM

The three schools of thought we have examined, the Constructionist, Deconstructionist, and Reformed schools, differ in their approach to Hinduism. But they agree on the fact that Hinduism implies a unified system, irrespective of whether one thinks the many Hindu traditions are related to one another. The three schools also agree that Hinduism is an ever-evolving religion. Although it has a history which has helped to shape its religious

35. Llewellyn, "Problem of Defining Hinduism," 6.
36. Llewellyn, "Problem of Defining Hinduism," 7.
37. Llewellyn, "Problem of Defining Hinduism," 6.

traditions, i.e., the Aryanization or Brahmanization of the Indus Valley region (which we would discuss later), Hinduism does not trace its origin to a particular founder or to a historical person or figure. This is why the Modernist or Reform School think of Hinduism, not as a mere adaptation of Western superimpositions, but as "a reinterpretation of the traditional ideas and, in a sense, a hybridization of the traditional self-understanding" stemming from commitment to Vedic revelation.[38]

St. Francis Xavier, SJ (1505/6–1552)

Francis Xavier was born in 1505 or 1506 to a noble Basque family in Navarre, Spain. His father, Juan de Jassu, was a personal counselor of John III of Navarre (1469–1516). After an early education at Xavier, Francis left for Paris in 1525 for theological studies, at the age of nineteen. Paris at the time was one of the few prestigious theological centers in Europe. At the University of Paris at the time of Francis' arrival was a fellow Basque student and former soldier, Ignatius of Loyola, who had undergone a profound religious experience and who was mulling the idea of gathering together a like-minded band of brothers to form a new religious community to follow in the imitation of Christ. Francis and Ignatius must have met soon after Francis arrived in Paris. By 1533 Ignatius had convinced Francis to join his newly formed religious band of brothers, the Society of Jesus (Jesuits). The Jesuits were given papal approval in 1540 by Pope Paul III (who was the Pope from 1534–49). On August 15, 1534, i.e., six years before the Society of Jesus was formally approved, Francis Xavier took the religious vows of chastity, poverty, and obedience as a Jesuit with six other companions in a chapel at Montmartre, in Paris. Francis and the newly professed brothers worked in Italy for a while, though their long-term goal was to go as far as the Far East. Upon invitation from King Joao III of Portugal for the Jesuits to come to Lisbon and work as missionaries in Portuguese controlled territories in Asia, Ignatius of Loyola sent two companions, Simao Rodrigues and Nicolas Bobadilla. The latter took ill and was unable to go on the mission. Ignatius asked Francis to take his place. Francis left for Lisbon on April 7, 1541. After a few stops on the way that included a short stay in Mozambique, they arrived in Goa, India in 1542 where he preached the Christian gospel and converted the local

---

38. Halbfass, "Idea of the Veda," 28.

people to Christianity. After ministering in India for some years, Xavier attempted to cross into Japan but was unsuccessful. He then attempted to enter China surreptitiously in 1522 through the trading pot of Malacca to preach to the Ming Emperor, but was also unsuccessful. He died of disease on December 3, 1552 on Changchun Island, an Island off the coast of China. He died in the hands of his Chinese servant known simply as Antonio. Francis Xavier was at first buried on the beach before his remains were exhumed in 1553 and taken first to the Malay Peninsula and later to Goa for final burial. Throughout the ten years he lived in Asia (1542–52), Francis Xavier was noted for his wisdom and charity. Many reported miracles during his lifetime. There were also miracles associated with him after his death. In 1614, about sixty-two years after his death, Claudio Acquaviva, the Superior General of the Society of Jesus, upon the request of Pope Paul V, instructed the Jesuits in Goa, India, to exhume the body of Francis Xavier and remove his right arm for relics. Those present at this carefully orchestrated ceremony reported: "His right eye was open and so fresh that he seemed to be alive; and his cheeks were, too, and the fingers with which he held the divine sacrament." Francis Xavier was beatified in 1619 and canonized in 1622. He is known as the patron of Jesuit missions.

Regarding the differences between these schools, one way of resolving the difficulty is to ask whether the people who practice Hinduism (be it as a religion or as a way of life) see it the same way the outsiders who observe and study it see it.[39] In other words, we must distinguish between *devotees* (Hindus) and *scholars* (outsiders) of the religion. How the *devotees* (Hindus) see their religion should take precedent over how *scholars* (outsiders) who study it for different reasons view the religion. However, finding unanimity on how Hindus themselves view their religion is itself not an easy task either. Some Hindu ascetics, for example, claim that Hinduism involves renunciation of society and worldly pleasures in order to attain *moksha* (liberation) from this *samsaric* world. Unlike these ascetics who show disdain for rituals, the Brahmins locate the essence of Hinduism in performing Vedic rituals. They contend that one brings stability to the world when one performs rituals. We can see from this that Hinduism is a highly decentralized religion with no agreed articles of belief. No one particular belief system is considered essential.[40]

39. Knott, *Hinduism*, 2.
40. Kinsley, *Hinduism*, 6.

Many Hindus describe what they practice as the *Santana dharma* (eternal tradition or religion).[41] By this they mean that the origins of this eternal tradition "lie beyond human history, and its truths have been divinely revealed (*shruti*) and passed down through the ages to the present day in the most ancient of the world's scriptures, the *Veda*."[42] Some go as far as asserting that Hinduism is a divinely revealed truth that was first given to the Aryans who migrated from northwest India, which helped them to build a majestic Hindu civilization in India thousands of years ago.[43]

Before the Aryan conquest of the Indus Valley region, an area that stretches from modern-day India to modern Pakistan and beyond, a well-developed Harappa civilization (2500–800 BCE) was already in existence in the Indus Valley region. It was known as the Indus-Valley civilization and lasted up till the time the Aryan migrants entered northwest India. This civilization was largely an agriculture-based civilization. It was concentrated in two major cities: Harappa and Mohenjo-Daro. The people had religions that involved female figurines and worship of goddesses, temple rites, fertility cults, animal sacrifices, and ritual bathing in a large pool constructed of stone.[44] The civilization came to an end around 1500 BCE when the Indo-Aryans migrated into Northwest India and conquered the Harappans. The invaders settled in the towns and villages of the Harappans, particularly in the Ganges River area, and imposed their own Aryan civilization on the whole of the Indus Valley region, including their own deities, chief of which were Indra (a mighty warrior god), and Agni (god of fire and heat), and their scripture, the *Vedas*. During this period, which many history books refer to as the epic period, the Indo-Aryans composed two of their great epics: the *Mahabharata* and the *Ramayana*—two epics that deal with royal rivalries, "perhaps reflecting political turmoil during this period, and reflect, in their rambling ways, a tension between a religion aimed at supporting and upholding the world order and one aimed at isolating a person from society in order to achieve individual liberation."[45] We also learn from these epics, that the Aryans had disdain for the pre-Aryan Indians whom they described as "dark and snub-nosed," immoral, demon-possessed, and devoid of cultural achievements. The epics contain Aryan hymns of praise and myth—hyperbolic praise for heroic Aryan struggles and victory over their uncivilized and evil spirit-infested non-Aryan natives whom they conquered with the

41. Knott, *Hinduism*, 5.
42. Knott, *Hinduism*, 5.
43. Knott, *Hinduism*, 5.
44. Knott, *Hinduism*, 6.
45. Kinsley, *Hinduism*, 14.

help of the Aryan god Indra whom they praised as the "fortress splitter" and destroyer of citadels.[46]

Contrary to what the Aryan hymns depict, archeological evidence unearthed at the turn of the twentieth century suggests that the Harappa and Mohenjo-Dara civilization was a great civilization and that this civilization may not only have flourished around 2500–1500 BCE, but may also have been contemporaneous with the Sumerian culture in Mesopotamia and the first Egyptian dynasty.[47] Needless to say the Aryans, an Indo-European tribe of pastoral nomads that migrated outward from the steppes of Eastern Europe to the Indus Valley region, did not enter a cultural vacuum when they occupied the Harappa and Mohenjo-Daro cities.[48]

Traditionally, the Aryans developed four social classes or *Varna*. The *Rig Veda* lists them in the following hierarchical order: *Brahmana* (Brahmin), *Kshatriya* (Warriors), *Vaishya* (Commoners), and *shudra* (Servants). In the strict sense of the term, *Varna* (class system) is different from *jati* (literally means "birth"). However, the latter (i.e., *jati* or birth) is often made to fit into the four *varnas* the Aryans had developed. What it literally means is that the accident of birth fatally condemns one to a specified class. The Brahmins are at the top of the caste and the untouchables are at the other extreme and considered impure.[49] This social stratification of society is the Hindu way of articulating differences, which they see as hierarchically organized. There is a philosophical justification for this—*karma*, a concept akin to a law of cause and effect. Its basic idea is that a person is what he or she is now because of what he or she did in the past and that one's future existence is predicated on what one is doing at the present. In other words, whatever caste one belongs to should be seen as a moment in the endless drama of birth, death, and rebirth that will end only when one attains *moksha*.[50] The caste system reflects Hindu belief that there are a variety of ways or paths one can take to fulfill one's religious quest—that people are different from one another in their aptitudes, predilections, and abilities, but that it is through their differences that they fulfil their religious tasks.[51]

46. Kinsley, *Hinduism*, 14.

47. Kinsley, *Hinduism*, 4.

48. Kinsley, *Hinduism*, 4.

49. Knott, *Hinduism*, 22.

50. Kinsley, *Hinduism*, 7.

51. Kinsley, *Hinduism*, 6.

The Indian Caste System

Caste Group	Meaning	Essential Duties
Brahmin	priestly class	mediates between the gods and humans
Kshatriya	warrior class	fight wars and protect the state
Vaishya	producing class	engages in agriculture and commerce
Shudra	servant class	serves the three upper castes
Dalits	social outcastes and economically exploited called untouchables. They are outside of the caste system. The English meaning of the Sanskrit *Dalit* is "broken" or "exploited." They are the "broken" or "exploited" ones.	performs menial and low-skilled labors, like sweeping and mopping the floor, cleaning lavatories and getting rid of dead animals, etc.

AN EVER-EVOLVING RELIGION

We noted earlier that one thing the three schools of thought within Hinduism agree on is that Hinduism is an ever-evolving religion. Right from the time the Aryans invaded the Indus Valley region and imposed the Vedas as symbol of Hindu orthodoxy, the natives have always reacted to the changing patterns of cultural, social, and religious orthodoxy of the region. Sometimes these reactions have been provoked by some real or imagined violation of customs. Other times they have been provoked by some perceived threat to institutional purity of caste, duty, or status in society. The reactions have also at times been either fierce or massive. Other times it is both fierce and massive.[52] Oftentimes reactions that followed what the natives see as threats have been philosophical, intellectual, ideological, and polemical in character.

The Dharma

Dharma is an important concept in Hinduism. Although its translation in English has been varied, more properly, *dharma* connotes the idea of order, law, duty or obligation, and truth. In this wise, i.e., that *dharma* carries with it the idea of order, law, duty, and truth, both a general and personal

---

52. Frykenberg, "Constructions of Hinduism," 140.

application.[53] For example, everyone's *dharma* varies, depending on his or her *varna* (caste). In fulfilling one's *dharma*, according to one's caste or standing in society, the harmony of the world is maintained. "The maintenance of social order in the world and the relationship between humanity and the gods were the corporate responsibility of all, though each person's behavior in the service of *dharma* was different."[54] This is why Hindus speak of *varna-ashrama-dharma*—that there are ideal duties or obligations that befall a person, depending on their particular social class and stage in life.[55] "Men who were not 'twice-born' and had no access to Vedic teaching were not expected to follow the same stages of life as those in the higher groups. Married women's obligations were generally referred to as *stri-dharma*, the duties of the wife."[56]

It is clear from our discussion so far that there is hardly a single teaching or a comprehensive set of teachings in Hinduism that can be said to be valid for all Hindus.[57] However, a group of Hindu (religious) experts or elites known as the Brahman *pandits* whose origin dates back to the middle of the first millennium BCE claim to be authentic spokespersons for the truth and orthodoxy of the Vedic religion. They claim they alone know what Hinduism is and what a proper Hindu should believe and practice.[58] For them, a Hindu is "one who accepts the authority of the Vedas (texts composed, preserved, and interpreted by the Brahmans), follows the particular prescriptions for him or her in the *varnashramadharma* scheme (in which the Brahman class has placed itself at the top of the hierarchy), and accepts the Brahman class as the supreme earthly authorities on 'religion.'"[59] The Brahman *pandits* also insist that Hinduism has a doctrinal core, i.e., the Vedas. They consider anyone who deviates from the doctrinal core to be less of a Hindu, at least intellectually.[60] In some sense, the Brahman *pandits* have a point because even authorities in other Hindu sects, say the Shankara or the Mimamsa, have at one time or the other accepted the notion that they are all somehow linked to the Vedas and the Vedic past.[61]

53. Knott, *Hinduism*, 17.

54. Knott, *Hinduism*, 42.

55. Knott, *Hinduism*, 17.

56. Knott, *Hinduism*, 17.

57. Sweetman, "Unity and Plurality," 93; quoting Stietencron, "Hinduism," 32–53.

58. Smith, "Questioning Authority," 111.

59. Smith, "Questioning Authority," 111.

60. Smith, "Questioning Authority," 111.

61. Smith, "Questioning Authority," 111.

Revelation and Tradition

Hinduism is the only major religion of the world with as many scriptures and one of the major religions with unbroken and faithfully preserved tradition.[62] Unlike non-Hindus, Westerners especially, who view the Hindu scriptures as ancient literature, Hindus regard them as revelations bestowed on their ancestors.[63] The Hindu *shruti* (that which is revealed) refers to divine truths. For example, the *Vedas* (which contain accounts of creation and hymns to the gods) and the *Upanishads* (philosophical texts of Hindu mystics) are considered *shruti* literature and are believed to have been divinely revealed. These are different from *smriti* texts (that which is remembered or handed down). *Smriti* texts, such as the epics *Puranas* (ancient stories) and *Sutras*, which are taught by Hindu gurus or sages and remembered by their disciples, are human compositions that are based upon revealed truth or *shruti*.[64] Handing on of traditions is an important Hindu practice. Hindus have institutions they call *sampradaya* where they pass on theological and ritual traditions from one generation to another. *Sampradaya* are usually "places of great learning where monks train in Sanskrit and philosophy, and where ordinary Hindus come to worship and seek guidance from a guru. They are headed by renowned leaders known as *Shankara-acharyas* (*acharya* means 'leader' or 'master')."[65] These leaders are usually Brahmin gurus. In fact, before the revealed texts or *shruti* were written down, they first existed for a long time as oral traditions. They were passed on from one generation to another before they were finally committed to writing at a definitive point in history. Thus, the institutions described above are part of a long chain of authorities that have kept the oral tradition alive.

The Hindus do not consider their different sacred texts as holding the same degree of revelation. The level of authority of a text and its categorization were carefully developed by Hindu scholars over time.[66]

(a). The Vedas

It is hard to imagine a Hinduism without the Vedas, for Hinduism is inextricably linked with the Vedas. The Vedas consist of four collections or *samhitas*: (i) the Rig-Veda, a collection of about a thousand hymns addressed to various Hindu gods; (ii) *Samur-veda*, a collection of musical instructions deriving from the Rig-Veda for recitation; (iii) *Yahur-veda*, a book of Vedic ceremonies; and (iv) *Atharva-veda*,

---

62. Klostermaier, *Survey of Hinduism*, 45.

63. Klostermaier, *Survey of Hinduism*, 46.

64. Knott, *Hinduism*, 14.

65. Knott, *Hinduism*, 13.

66. Klostermaier, *Survey of Hinduism*, 46.

another collection of hymns.[67] Some scholars think that the role of the Vedas in traditional Indian society is at best paradoxical and ambiguous. The Vedas contain no Hindu dogma, no creed as such, and no clear guidelines on the Hindu way of life. They also provide no clear identifiable basis for understanding the doctrine of karma and rebirth, the principle of *Ahimsa* (non-injury to animals), and how to attain liberation.[68] Even the traditional order of society—castes and stages of life—are not delineated in the Vedas, at least in its original form.[69] In spite of the "highly elusive and ambiguous nature of the historical relationship between the Veda and Hinduism, the Hindu tradition has, for many centuries, defined itself in relation to the Veda."[70] Though it is true to say that the Vedas defy the *dharma* of Hinduism, it is also true that it is the Vedas that provide the *dharma* with its most significant point of reference and point of departure.[71]

(b). Upanishads

The Upanishads literature shows a development in Vedic religion. They show a movement or progression from philosophical to metaphysical concerns. Although the Upanishads vary and are diverse, overall, the mystics who developed the Upanishads were motivated by a concern for the truth, i.e., metaphysical truths that can liberate one from this samsaric world. Generally, the Upanishads are framed in forms of "dialogues between a teacher and a student, they usually take place away from society, and from time to time they criticize the performance of rituals as superfluous to the religious quest. Some of the texts extol renunciation of society and the performance of austerities that in later Hinduism become increasingly important techniques for liberation."[72] The fundamental reality, according to the Upanishads, is a spiritual force called Brahman. It teaches that the Brahman in essence is one and that a person's essential self transcends his or her individuality in space and time. Realizing this fundamental truth puts one on the path to realizing liberation from this samsaric world. Thus, the Upanishads advocate withdrawal from society and the practice of meditation.

(c). The Bhagavad-Gita

67. Klostermaier, *Survey of Hinduism*, 47.

68. Halbfass, "Idea of the Veda," 16–17.

69. Halbfass, "Idea of the Veda," 17.

70. Halbfass, "Idea of the Veda," 21.

71. Halbfass, "Idea of the Veda," 21.

72. Kinsley, *Hinduism*, 13.

Bhagavad-Gita are two separate words (*Bhagavad* = God and *Gita* = Song) the Hindus consider an eternal message or spiritual wisdom from God. The *Bhagavad-Gita* is a Hindu spiritual classic. The *Bhagavad-Gita* tells the epic story of Krishna whom the *Bhakti* movement (a devotional movement in India characterized by emotional attachment to a personal god) considers a god. There are many legends among Indians concerning the birth of Krishna whom many consider an avatar of Vishnu. In fact, some Hindus consider the *Bhagavad-Gita* a philosophical treatise of Krishna's life and a treatise on how to attain moksha. In the epic, Krishna is a warrior god who demonstrates to his disciples that the caste duty of a warrior is to fight. The epic portrays Krishna as having a conversation with his disciple, Arjuna, in the battlefield of Kurushetra. Krishna answers for Arjuna all questions concerning frailty of human life and existence and how to attain enlightenment. He teaches Arjuna how to avoid lust, anger, and greed—three concepts Krishna taught inhibit humans from gaining enlightenment. One with lust, anger, and greed remains in this samsaric world. Krishna teaches that the way to moksha are through meditation, caste duty, and personal devotion to a god.

DARSHANA—HINDUISM ORTHODOX SYSTEMS

The fifteenth- and sixteenth-century India saw a rise in devotional movements. On the one hand, several new movements were founded, and on the other hand, older traditions were either being refashioned or revitalized. On the basis of these revitalizations and emergence of new movements, scholars speak of six orthodox systems or *darshana* within Hinduism: *Samkhya* (dualistic and atheistic perspective), *Mimamsa* (focuses on the right course of action or teaching and he emphasizes the Vedas as source of inspiration), *Nyaya* (focuses on logic and liberation), *Vaisheshika* (atomistic analysis of Hindu teaching), *Vedanta* (exegetical system concerned with the Upanishads and emphasizes individual liberation), and the *yoga* or *Tantrism* (focuses on systems of discipline and liberation).

In all, these six orthodox systems contain rudiments or commentaries for liberating the self. They seek answers to the questions: what is the self? What is the relationship between the self and ultimate reality? In a religion that has a plethora of gods and goddesses, two main deities dominated the devotional moments: Rama and Krishna, two gods classical Hinduism considers avatars of Lord Vishnu.[73] "The worship of Rama was most popular in the Hindi-speaking areas of North India, whereas the worship of Krishna

---

73. Kinsley, *Hinduism*, 37.

was popular throughout the North, especially in Bengal. Devotion to both gods was extremely emotional and personal but differed quite significantly in accordance with their distinctive mythologies."[74]

These orthodox systems or schools became popular from about 600 CE to 1800 CE. They were characterized by their tendency to build temples for their *bhakti*, (which simply means devotion) and designate them as important religious centers or even dwelling places for the gods. These temples became important places for religious instruction. A celebrated Hindu story tells of a guru instructing his young disciple about the self. He employs an analogy of salt and water to demonstrate to the disciple how the same essence is in everything. He asks the disciple to put a chunk of salt in a water container and come back the next day. The disciple did exactly as he was instructed. When he returned the next day, the guru asked the disciple: "Did you put the chunk of salt in the water container yesterday?" The disciple answered "Yes." The guru asked him to bring the water container containing the salt. When the disciple brought it, the guru asked him to extract the salt from the water, but the disciple could not find the salt to extract, since it had dissolved completely. The guru then said to him, pointing to one corner of the water container, "Take a sip from here." When the disciple did, he asked him, "How does it taste?" The disciple replied, "Salty." The guru then pointed to another corner and said, "Take a sip from this corner." The disciple did so. The guru asked again, "How does it taste?" The disciple answered, "Salty." The guru pointed to the center of the water container and said, "Take a sip from the center." When the disciple did, he asked, "How does it taste?" The disciple replied, "Salty." After the experiment, the guru said to him, "Throw the water out and come back later." The disciple did as he was told and came back, finding that the salt was always there. The guru said to him: "although you could not see the salt, it was always there." The guru said to the disciple, "That's the way you are."[75] The guru used the experiment to teach the disciple a simple truth—the self is one with the world and the truth which underlies everything in its essence is also identical with one's self (*atman*). "This truth or self is the life force (*Brahman*) within both the world and humanity."[76]

Shankara, an eighth-century South Indian Brahmin, is considered the most brilliant and systematic exponent of the *Vedanta* school.[77] He was reputed to be skillful in philosophical exposition of the self. He considered

74. Kinsley, *Hinduism*, 37.

75. Knott, *Hinduism*, 28.

76. Knott, *Hinduism*, 28.

77. Kinsley, *Hinduism*, 19.

actions in themselves, whether good or bad, to be of no significance, because actions arise from a person's false sense of the self. He considered only a transforming knowledge, i.e., knowledge of one's identity with Brahman, to be the goal of the religious quest.[78] "To this day, Shankara is considered unrivaled in his expression of the vision of the unity of Brahman and Atman as the underlying essence of reality. Shankara is also taken as a model for those seeking divine self-realization."[79] The Bengali native Chaitanya (1486–1533) is thought to be the founder of the *Vaisheshika* School and one who systematized the devotion to Krishna.

In general, these devotional movements hardly criticize traditional Indian social structure. Quite often, they are indifferent to traditional society, which they consider confining or inhibiting in one's quest to reach God. Many of them claim that a person's ultimate spiritual goal is not achieved by or through one's social structure.[80] If any of the devotional schools came close to criticizing the traditional structure of society, it would be the Tantric school. They often criticize the religious practices of the Brahmins. They teach that the "individual is a miniature or microcosm of the cosmos and that by learning the sacred geography of one's body one may, by means of various yogic techniques, bring about one's own spiritual fulfillment, which in most Tantric texts is the result of uniting various opposites within one's body/cosmos."[81] Although the Tantras do not disregard traditional practices, such as Vedic study, Vedic rituals, pilgrimage, and puja, they consider them superfluous and not appropriate for the age. Thus, believing that people are often incapable of practicing the elaborate religious rituals of classical texts, the Tantras claim to introduce new techniques appropriate for the age that can lead one to liberation without going through the rigors of traditional practices and techniques. They "offer a variety of rituals that employ *mantras* (sacred formulas), *mandalas* (schematic diagrams), yogic techniques that are believed to achieve either complete liberation from the mundane world or extraordinary powers, such as omniscience and the ability to fly."[82]

HINDU DEITIES

Hinduism is a living tradition with a pantheon of deities. It is a religion with over 330 million gods. One of the intriguing facts about this religion

78. Kinsley, *Hinduism*, 19.

79. Kinsley, *Hinduism*, 45.

80. Kinsley, *Hinduism*, 19.

81. Kinsley, *Hinduism*, 19.

82. Kinsley, *Hinduism*, 20.

is, as one scholar has observed: "the god whom one Hindu adores with full devotion as the supreme deity and as the only Lord of the universe—that same god may be considered inferior or even totally insignificant in the eyes of another Hindu."[83] Much of what we know about early Aryan religion and their deities comes from the *Vedas* (literally "body of knowledge'), which are a collection of hymns to the gods. The early Vedic religion centered around divine powers or *devas*, which is translated into English as gods. The Vedas divide the *devas* into three categories: eleven celestial gods, eleven atmospheric gods, and eleven terrestrial gods, indicating by so doing their primary location and realm of activity and their close association with nature.[84] The Vedas address these Vedic gods as the only one, supreme, and greatest of gods. The Vedic notion of godhead neither conforms to our Western understanding of monotheism nor to our concept of polytheism. It was in the attempt to understand this puzzle that the German philologist and anthropologist Friedrich Max Mueller (1823–1900) coined the term *henotheism* to distinguish the Vedic idea of godhead from the Judeo-Christian notion of monotheism.[85] Aryans thought of the natural world as a realm of powers that affected and controlled their lives. These powers were also thought to be personal manifestations of divine will. The Indus peoples (with whom the Aryans mingled) may have worshiped natural powers, but the personal forces of nature, which they thought were apparent, manifested mainly in animals.[86] The *devas* or gods, therefore, control the forces of nature. Here are the classification of the *devas*:

a). The Celestial *Devas*: The oldest of the celestial gods was thought to be Dyaus Pitri (the Sky Father) that the Greek and Roman mythologies call Zeus and Jupiter.[87] There was also Varuna (an equivalent of the Greek Uranus) who is thought to be the guardian of cosmic order and regulator of morality.[88] It was Varuna who provided structure for the other celestial *devas*, like the sun god Mitra (equivalent of the Iranian sun god Mithra), and Varuna's chief assistant and friend, Vishnu, who traversed the earth and atmosphere in three strides.[89] Although he lives in the heavens, the great cosmic king god Vishnu periodically

83. Stietencron, "Hinduism," 36.

84. Hopkins, *Hindu Religious Tradition*, 11.

85. Klostermaier, *Survey of Hinduism*, 101.

86. Hopkins, *Hindu Religious Tradition*, 11–12.

87. Hopkins, *Hindu Religious Tradition*, 12.

88. Hopkins, *Hindu Religious Tradition*, 12.

89. Hopkins, *Hindu Religious Tradition*, 12.

descends on earth in various manifestations to maintain cosmic harmony.[90] His primary role in the divine economy is this maintenance of order and supervision of economy.[91] "Despite these qualities, however, he remained a subordinate figure in the early Vedic period, his powers largely subordinated by his role as friend and ally of the far more important god Indra."[92]

b). The Atmospheric *Devas*: The atmospheric gods are Indra (the god of thunder) who was the divine ally of the Aryans and the greatest of the Vedic gods, Vayu (the god of wind), Parjanya (the god of rain or cloud), Maruts (the storm god), and Rudra (another storm god and father of Maruts). "Most of these gods were closely connected with their respective atmospheric phenomena and seldom achieved independent personification. Only Rudra and Indra, for different reasons, were given importance in their own right."[93]

c). The Terrestrial *Devas*: Among the terrestrial gods are Indra (the warlike god and the ancient mythical dragon-killing hero of the Aryans), Agni (the god of fire), Brihaspati (the god of prayer and cultic sacrifice), and Soma (the god in charge of sacrificial ritual).[94] The Aryans so revered Indra that most of their early depictions of him capture his war-like heroism. "Of the more than one thousand hymns of the Rigveda about a quarter are addressed to Indra alone."[95] As other gods emerged in the post Vedic period and some of the existing Vedic *devas* gained more prominence, Indra and some of the early Vedic *devas* lost their importance as the Aryan worldview changed and their religious rites, which was dominated by fire sacrifice, began to wane.[96]

90. Kinsley, *Hinduism*, 2.
91. Kinsley, *Hinduism*, 18.
92. Hopkins, *Hindu Religious Tradition*, 12.
93. Hopkins, *Hindu Religious Tradition*, 12.
94. Hopkins, *Hindu Religious Tradition*, 13.
95. Klostermaier, *Survey of Hinduism*, 103.
96. Hopkins, *Hindu Religious Tradition*, 17.

Key Hindu Female Deities

Name of Deity	Essential Characteristics	Main Function	Other Information
Aditi	Primeval goddess known as the mother of many gods, particularly the celestial gods.	She is known as the personification of the infinite reality and the upholder of divine order.	Her sons are called *Adityas*. They are also "upholders of divine order."
Ardhanarishvara	She is depicted as a hybrid of male-female figure.	Signifies the inseparability of the male-female principles.	
Chandi	She is often depicted with eight or ten arms to show her wide reach.	She wards off bad spirits. Destroys demons.	She is called by different names and given attributes like "the Great Magician" or "the Fearless One."
Kali	Goddess of time and doomsday goddess. She is depicted with multiple arms.	She ensures fertility. She is the goddess of sexuality and motherly love.	Sometimes portrayed as naked; always in the nude and dancing. She is the wife of Lord Shiva. Shiva is the third of the Hindu trinity—the destroyer god.
Lakshmi	Often represented as smiling.	She is the goddess of wealth and fortune.	Wife of Lord Vishnu. Vishnu is the second of the Hindu trinity—the preserver and sustainer of life who is depicted with four arms to show his omnipotence and omnipresence.
Parvati	Often represented as a beautiful woman.	She ensures benevolence because she is benevolent herself.	Wife of Lord Shiva. Had two children with Shiva.

| Saptamatrika | The Sanskrit word *saptamatrika* is rendered in English as "Seven Mothers." | | This is a Hindu belief in seven mother goddesses. The seven goddesses are the female counterparts (goddesses) of the gods with whom they are associated: (i) the goddess Brahmani, the wife of Brahman; (ii) the goddess Maheshvari, the wife of Shiva; (iii) the goddess Kaumari, the wife of Kumara; (iv) the goddess Vaishnavi, the wife of Vishnu; (v) the goddess Varahi, the wife of Varaha; (vi) the goddess Indrani, the wife of Indra; and (vii) the goddess Yami, the wife of Yama. |

Other Notable Deities

i). The Hindu Trinity: Brahman, Vishnu, and Shiva.

Hindu texts speak of the triad of Brahma, Vishnu, and Shiva. Brahma is the first of the Hindu Trinity. He is the creator of the world, the Supreme Being, and the inner principle of the universe. According to an ancient myth, Brahma was born with five heads but one of Shiva's consorts in whom he was interested chopped off one of his heads, leaving him with only four. The four faces symbolize the completeness or fullness of his wisdom. Vishnu is the second of the Hindu trinity. Vishnu is the preserver god who is depicted with four arms to show his omnipotence and omnipresence. There are ten avatars or incarnations of Vishnu. The ascetic god Shiva is the third of the Hindu trinity. He resides in the Himalayas where he stores up energy he periodically releases into the world to refresh and reinvigorate it.[97] Some Hindu texts refer to all three as three separate names of the different aspects of the same being.[98]

ii). Lord Ganesha is the elephant-headed god who destroys all obstacles plaguing his devotees.[99] Lord Ganesha is the son of Shiva and Parvati. He is revered "for his kind attention to the requests of his devotees and his ability to remove obstacles."[100]

iii). Krishna is "the adorable cowherd god who frolics with his women companions in the idyllic forests of Vrindavana."[101]

iv). Hanuman is the monkey god. He embodies strength, courage, and loyalty.[102]

v). Durga is the warrior goddess. She periodically defeats the forces of evil in order to protect the world.[103]

vi). Kali is "the black goddess who dwells in cremation grounds and is served with blood."[104]

Ten Avatars (Incarnations) of Vishnu

Name of God	Avatar Position and Depiction	Event	Achievement
Matsya	First avatar of Vishnu. The god Matsya is depicted in combined human-fish form. The upper half human and lower half fish.	The Great Flood	Vishnu saved the world from great flood

97. Kinsley, *Hinduism*, 2.

98. Klostermaier, *Survey of Hinduism*, 108.

99. Kinsley, *Hinduism*, 3.

100. Knott, *Hinduism*, 48.

101. Kinsley, *Hinduism*, 3.

102. Kinsley, *Hinduism*, 3.

103. Kinsley, *Hinduism*, 3.

104. Kinsley, *Hinduism*, 3.

Kurma	Second avatar of Vishnu. The god Kurma is depicted in a human-animal form. The upper half is human and the lower half is tortoise.	The gods and the demons are in search of elixir of immortality.	
Varaha	Third avatar of Vishnu. The god Varaha is half-human and half-animal. He is depicted with the head of a boar and the body of a young man.	To rescue a boar. This is a creation legend.	Vishnu saves the world from primeval chaos.
Narasimha	Fourth avatar of Vishnu. The god Narasimha is depicted as half-man, half-lion.	An invincible demon, Hiranyakashipu, was a menace to the heavens and the earth.	Kills the demon that was troubling the heavens and the earth.
Vamana	Fifth avatar of Vishnu. The god Vamana is depicted as a dwarf.	The gods had lost their powers and demons ruled the earth.	Vishnu intervened to restore power to the gods.
Parashurama	Sixth avatar of Vishnu. Parashurama was the son of a Brahman sage and a Khastriya princess.	He cut off the head on the orders of his father who suspected her of infidelity. To avoid revenge of his mother's death by members of her tribe, Lord Parashurama killed all the males from that tribe.	Founder of Malabar.
Rama	Seventh avatar of Vishnu. The god Rama is depicted as the god of reason and virtue.		Hero of the Ramayana epic. Became focus of the Bhakti devotional movement.

Krishna	Eighth avatar of Vishnu depicted as the divine lover.		Became focus of the Bhakti devotional movement.
Buddha	Some Hindus assume Buddha to be the ninth avatar of Vishnu.		
Kalkin	Kalkin is yet to come. He will appear at the end of the world when he will destroy the wicked and usher in a new age.	Evil would have suppressed good and the wicked will reign, which will signal the end of the world.	

CONCLUSION

A lot of Hindu activities take place around the Ganges River. The Ganges is located in Benares. Pilgrims flock to this river for religious activities—ritual baths and to do *puja*, a Hindu practice of worshiping a personal god or deity they consider their favorite. The various religious activities that take place at the Ganges make it a beauty to behold. The Ganges region is also a home to many Hindu mystics. Some mystics live there permanently, while others wander around it temporarily. The activities that take place at the Ganges are too numerous to enumerate. They range from Brahmins performing their Vedic rituals to the singing and dancing of low-caste pilgrims visiting the temple of their personal god, and even to students learning from their masters the tenets of Hindu philosophy and practice.[105]

A familiar site at the Ganges River is the funeral pyres that burn constantly. Pious Hindus believe that anyone who dies at the Ganges or at least close to the Ganges is more likely to attain *moksha* or liberation. For this reason, the sick and the aged flock in their thousands daily to the Ganges River to die and gain their final liberation. If many of the funeral processions seem joyous, as they often do, it is to reflect the auspicious circumstance of the deceased liberation.[106] The constant funeral pyres at the Ganges also have other symbolisms. It reminds the gurus and ascetics that flock to the area for prayers and meditation of the transience of earthly existence.[107]

105. Kinsley, *Hinduism*, 4–5.
106. Kinsley, *Hinduism*, 3.
107. Kinsley, *Hinduism*, 4.

14

Buddhism

A SEARCH FOR TRANSCENDENCE

BUDDHISM STANDS UNIQUE (NOT alone) as a religion that promotes love and compassion, meditation, commitment to vegetarian diet, non-violence, and renunciation of excessive attachment to sensual pleasures. In spite of its commitment to a vegetarian diet, the founder of the ideas and practices Western scholars have called Buddhism not only ate meat, he did not forbid his early followers from eating meat either. Although the ideas of this mystic promotes non-violence and peace, ironically several wars have been fought by some Buddhist faithful in the name of Buddhism. Tibetan Buddhist sects have fought each other and have also fought adherents of indigenous religions of Tibet and other parts of South Asia—Thailand, Myanmar (Burma), and Sri Lanka. Some Buddhists have also waged holy wars against Muslims in defense of the dharma. Although Western scholars treat Buddhism as a major world religion, ironically again Buddhism was founded by a man who unequivocally declared that there is no God.

What we call Buddhism is in essence "a religion whose primary practice is to sit cross-legged on the ground and calm the passions."[1] Many today question whether Buddhism can be properly called a religion, since Buddhism does not profess belief in a God or deity. They claim that rather than calling it a religion that we should consider treating Buddhism as a kind of philosophy or at best a way of life. They claim that the principal tenets of this

---

1. Lopez, *Buddhism*, 45.

philosophy or way of life can be selectively adopted by anyone, regardless of one's religious affiliation.[2]

The founder of Buddhism shared many of the assumptions of Hinduism and Jainism, two religions that existed before Buddhism. The founder of Buddhism particularly accepted the Hindu and Jain assumption that human life is a sorrowful cycle of birth, death, and re-birth. He accepted the assumption that this sorrowful cycle is influenced by one's deeds in this life (karma) and that there is a need to escape this endless cycle of transmigration through meditation. But it was not all assumptions of Hinduism and Jainism that the founder of Buddhism accepted. He deviated from some Hindu beliefs, like the notion that there is a permanent self. He held firmly (unlike Hinduism) that there is no real self. Hinduism teaches that the self (Atman) was Brahman. But Buddhism teaches that there is no self (*Anatta*) and that it is when we succumb to the illusion that there is a real permanent self that we become more susceptible and fall victim to our desires and cravings.

Origin and Noble Search

The religious tradition that has come to be called Buddhism derives from the mystic Siddhartha Gautama whom his disciples would later call the Buddha. The exact date of his birth and number of years he lived remain a conjecture, notwithstanding that an important Buddhist text, the *Great Discourse on the Final Nirvana*, claims that the Buddha passed into nirvana when he was eighty.[3] The text situates the date of his passing on or around the year 400 BCE. Based on this estimate, the Buddha would have been born somewhere between 566 BCE and 536 BCE. The reason why the exact date of the Buddha's birth is difficult to calculate is because there was no known biography of the Buddha until about five hundred years after he passed into nirvana.[4]

Before Buddha, a number of philosophical movements and trends existed in India. Most notable among them were Jainism and Vedism, a Brahmin (priestly caste) of Hindu philosophical system. Jainism was founded around the sixth century BCE in India by a mystic, Jina Vardhamna Mahavira, after whom the religion took its name. Jainism is a nontheistic religion. It shares some of the assumptions of Hinduism, particularly beliefs in non-injury to animals and human life as a sorrowful life characterized by cycles

2. Lopez, *Buddhism*, 45.

3. Lopez, *Buddhism*, 48.

4. Lopez, *Buddhism*, 119.

of births and rebirth. Jainism, in fact, emerged as a reaction to the excesses of Vedic Hinduism, which was controlled by the Brahmin priestly caste of India. Many, including the Jains, considered the Vedic version of Hinduism to be racist because it places the Brahmin (priestly caste) on top of the social ladder. Nevertheless, belief in karma was integral to understanding the essential beliefs of both religions. The understanding was that bad karma leads to transmigration of souls (the souls of bad karma recurrently return to earth for purification). Its remedy is meditation—that meditation is a form of achieving *samsara* (liberation). This world of Jainism and Vedic Hinduism was the world in which Siddhartha, the man who would later become the Buddha, was born into.

THE BIRTH OF A PRINCE

Siddhartha was born to a noble family who lived outside the town of Kapilavatsu, modern-day Nepal. His father, Shuddhodana Gautama, and his mother, Mahamaya, were nobles from the tribe of Sakya. The family was a warrior caste, one of the layered levels of the Indian caste system. The many legends surrounding the birth of Siddhartha make it difficult to decipher truth from fiction. According to one of the legends, before his birth his mother dreamt that a white elephant had entered her side. Siddhartha, according to the legend, came out of that same side the elephant had entered and did so without causing his mother pain. Another legend has it that immediately after he came out of his mother's side, he stood straight and screamed "No more births for me!"[5] His followers understood this to mean that this baby boy would be an enlightened one who would bring a solution to the problematic of cycles of birth and rebirth that Jains and Hindus wrestled with. According to one legend, at the time of his birth, the astrologers of the time predicted that he would be either a great monarch or a great sage.[6] In any case, Siddhartha's mother died shortly after he was born. Following his mother's death, his father sheltered him and raised him in the palace. He surrounded him with wealth and did not want him to leave the palace.

At a very young age, probably about the age of sixteen, Siddhartha married a young noble princess his father had carefully selected for him. She bore him a son they named Rahula, which means "impediment." It was as if the son would foreshadow the "impediment" of life, at least as the Buddha saw it, an impediment which would lead Buddha to give up

5. Carmody and Brink, *Ways to the Center*, 222.

6. Lopez, *Buddhism*, 385.

his wealthy lifestyle for a monastic life. A Buddhist text that provides biographical information of the life of the Buddha, the *Ariyapariyesana Sutta* (the Noble Search), tells of a religious bemusement that will lead Siddhartha on a path of noble search.

Although Siddhartha's father did not want him to leave the palace, Siddhartha did make attempts to leave of different occasions. One of his successful attempts would become memorable because the adventure set off a chain of events that culminated in the founding of a new religion. When Siddhartha left the palace, he saw some people living in abject poverty, people who were afflicted with sickness and disease, and people battling old age and death. These led Siddhartha to go on a noble search for enlightenment. On his way in search of enlightenment, Siddhartha met King Bimbisara who offered him half of his kingdom, but which Siddhartha politely declined.[7]

In the *Ariyapariyesana Sutta*, the Buddha was said to have distinguished between two kinds of searches, one ignoble and the other noble. In the ignoble search, one who is subject to birth, aging, sickness, and death goes in search of what is subject to birth, aging, sickness, and death. In the noble search, one who is subject to birth, aging, sickness, and death goes in search of what is beyond birth, aging, sickness, and death—the search for nirvana. Buddha used this to tell the story of his own noble search, beginning with his departure from home, his wanderings in search of the truth, and his eventual discovery of enlightenment.[8] The *Ariyapariyesana Sutta* describes Siddhartha as "a black-haired young man endowed with the blessings of youth, in the prime of life"[9] when he gave up his ostentatious lifestyle, renounced his wife and child, and set out for a noble search. He probably was in his twenties at the time. He would later recount that his father wished otherwise and wept with tearful faces when he left the palace. "I shaved off my hair and beard, put on the yellow robe, and went forth from the home life into homelessness," he recounts.[10] The shaved head and ochre robe, in ancient India, were signs of one who had left the world in search of a condition greater than the world. While the Buddha may not have been the first to seek such a state, he would, however, be the most famous of those who claimed to have found it. An early Buddhist Chinese text, *Sishi'er* (translated "The Scripture in Forty-Two Sections"), speaks of the Buddha as giving the stamp of approval to this ancient idea of shaving one's head:

7. Lopez, *Buddhism*, 385.
8. Lopez, *Buddhism*, 120.
9. Lopez, *Buddhism*, 120.
10. Lopez, *Buddhism*, 120.

The Buddha said: Those who shave their heads and faces are *shramanas*. They receive the teaching, abandon worldly wealth and possessions, and beg, seeking only what is necessary. Taking a single meal at midday, and lodging a single night under a tree, they take care not to repeat either. That which makes men ignorant and derelict is passion and desire.[11]

His Enlightenment

Siddhartha wandered in the forest for close to seven years in search of enlightenment. He met up with Vedic gurus who taught him yoga and meditation. After he mastered yoga and meditation, he fasted and embraced severe asceticism but later renounced it because it did not lead to his desired enlightenment. Upon renouncing severe asceticism, he accepted a bowl of rice and a cup of milk that was offered him by a pious woman. After eating the rice and drinking the milk he regained his strength, sat under a Bodhi tree, determined that he would stay there until he gained enlightenment. While sitting under the Bodhi tree, a devious angel named Mara was concerned that if Buddha gained enlightenment he would teach others the path and humans would end the cycles of birth, death, and re-birth. Mara decided to pose an obstacle by unleashing temptations and a legion of demons to distract Buddha. But the Buddha withstood all the temptations Mara sent his way, remaining uncompromisingly steadfast and righteous. When he could not succeed in tempting Buddha, Mara pulled his last ace, sending his three daughters, Discontent, Delight, and Desire, to seduce Buddha. But the Buddha did not succumb and overcame the temptations dignifiedly.

Buddha's enlightenment came on a night of the full moon. On this night, he had three key experiences. In the first watch of the night, Buddha had a recollection of his past lives. In the second watch of the night, he had a grasp of the entire universe, i.e., how beings function, and understood therein the fickleness of human existence. In the third watch of the night, he understood the factors that lead to the endless cycles of birth, death, and rebirth. Thus, in the three watch of the night, the Buddha had a progressive clarification of consciousness,[12] ascending the four stages of trance: (i) calming of the passions and detachment from objects given to the senses, (ii) simple concentration, (iii) dispassionate mindfulness, and (iv) pure awareness and peace without pain.[13] During the trance, Buddha not

11. Lopez, *Buddhism*, 497.

12. Carmody and Brink, *Ways to the Center*, 223.

13. Carmody and Brink, *Ways to the Center*, 223.

only acquired knowledge of his previous lives, he also acquired a divine eye with which he saw the karmic state of beings that lead to the cycle of birth, death, and rebirth.[14] The vision helped him to realize "that good deeds beget good karma and move on toward freedom from *samsara*, while bad deeds beget bad karma and a deeper entrenchment in *samsara*."[15] The peak of the Buddha's mystical experience was reached when he grasped the Four Noble Truths and the Eightfold Path.

The end result of the Buddha's enlightenment is cessation of the cycle of birth and rebirth. This is called nirvana. Nirvana is considered the goal of Buddhism. It is a state of ultimate bliss in which desire and karmic *samara* cease. What the Buddha saw under the *Bodhi* tree was the formula for measuring life and curing mortal illness—nirvana.[16] The Buddha did not write down his teachings when he gained enlightenment, he simply taught them as any teacher would do. At the time of Buddha, the power of speech was revered. A learned person was not so much one who committed things to writing, but literally "one who has heard much."[17] Religious teaching was preserved orally. Writing was reserved mostly for mundane matters, like recording keeping and commerce. It was because religious traditions were preserved orally that people developed sophisticated mnemonic devices to preserve words accurately.[18] This was not exclusive to Buddhism alone. Hindu and Jain priests did the same. For example, Hindu gurus, some of whom were called "reciters of the long discourse," "reciters of the middle-sized discourse," and "reciters of the short discourse," preserved the Vedas literally by reciting the text forward and backward.[19]

As indicated earlier, two well-established religious systems in the form of Vedic Hinduism and Jainism were already dominant in India before Buddhism. Vedic Hinduism enshrined in India a caste system in which there was a fourfold hierarchical division of society led by the Brahmin. Buddha's attitude towards the caste was at best mixed. He did not reject it and did not have any intention of dispensing with the caste system of India altogether. He himself was from the Kshatriya or warrior caste. He accepted members of all four castes into the order of monks and nuns that he established. In fact, the majority came from the two highest castes of Indian society: the

---

14. Carmody and Brink, *Ways to the Center*, 223.

15. Carmody and Brink, *Ways to the Center*, 223.

16. Carmody and Brink, *Ways to the Center*, 324.

17. Lopez, *Buddhism*, 48.

18. Lopez, *Buddhism*, 48.

19. Lopez, *Buddhism*, 48–49.

Brahmin or priestly caste and his own Kshatriya or warrior caste.[20] When-ever Buddha did attack the caste, he directed his attack on the religious sys-tem controlled by the Brahmins, not the caste system. He only called into question the Brahmins so-called inborn superiority.[21]

THE BUDDHA'S FIRST SERMON

After gaining enlightenment, Buddha gave his first sermon at the Deer Park in Sarnath, near Benares. On the way to the Deer Park, the enlightened Bud-dha encountered a mendicant (monk) who asked him who his teacher was. The Buddha responded that he had no teacher because there was no one as enlightened as he (Buddha).[22] At first Buddha was reluctant to teach following his enlightenment. But he was persuaded to teach by the god Brahma who descended from heaven. Brahma made clear to Buddha "that though there are some beings with much dust in their eyes (who thus would be unable to per-ceive the truth that Buddha had seen), there are also beings with little dust in their eyes (and thus able to perceive the truth)."[23] It was after this that Buddha agreed to teach. When he accepted the invitation to teach, Buddha wanted the two old monks who taught him yoga and meditation to be the first to hear his sermon. But they had died. So Buddha opted instead for the five ascetics who had practiced an austere lifestyle with him but who had abandoned him when he accepted a meal from a pious woman against their will. Those five ascetics practiced extreme starvation and wanted Buddha to do the same, but Bud-dha chose a middle way instead. It was in trying to locate them that Buddha walked to the Deer Park, outside of Varanasi, a distance of about 150 miles. It was at Deer Park that Buddha gave his first sermon.

The Four Noble Truths

Buddha had grasped the essence of the Four Noble Truths during the third watch of his mystical experience under the Bodhi tree. The Four Noble Truths formed the basis of his first sermon at the Deer Park. They are as follows:

i). All life is suffering.

---

20. Lopez, *Buddhism*, 182.
21. Lopez, *Buddhism*, 182.
22. Lopez, *Buddhism*, 120.
23. Lopez, *Buddhism*, 177.

ii). The cause of suffering is desire.

iii). Stopping desire will stop suffering.

iv). The Eightfold Path is the best way to stop desire.

Buddha preached this sermon and titled it *Dhammachakkappavattana*, which means "Setting the Wheel of the Dharma in Motion." Buddha's teaching or the dharma is represented as a wheel (like that of a chariot) with eight spokes. Perhaps the symbolism of the wheel "is related to the wheel of the universal monarch (*charkravartin*), a figure of Indian mythology: this king possesses a magical wheel that rolls around the world, and every land that it reaches becomes part of his domain. When the Buddha teaches, he is said to turn the wheel of the dharma to set it rolling."[24]

The Middle Way/Eightfold Path

Earlier in his life, Buddha had fallen into two extremes: self-indulgent life as a prince and self-mortification as an ascetic with the group of five ascetics. Buddha rejected both extremes and sought a middle way. Buddhism is sometimes called the Middle Way for this reason. The Middle Way is the middle ground between these two extremes. Buddha's idea was that neither of the two extremes leads to peace and that only a middle way between them leads to nirvana. The Middle Way is captured in the tenets of the Eightfold Path:

- Right views (pertaining to having knowledge of the Four Noble Truths).

- Right intention (desirous of not inflicting any harm to all life forms).

- Right speech (pertaining to uttering only those words that uplift one and one's neighbors).

- Right action (pertaining to performing only those actions that are self-transcendent).

- Right livelihood (pertaining to living a life that causes no harm to others).

- Right effort (refraining from all malicious activities).

- Right mindfulness (refraining from all malicious thoughts).

- Right concentration (seeking and practicing mediation).

24. Lopez, *Buddhism*, 177.

Three of the Eightfold Paths pertain to ethical training necessary for liberation from rebirth: right speech, right action, and right livelihood. Three are necessary for training in meditation: right effort, right mindfulness, and right concentration. The other two are necessary for training in wisdom: right view and right intention.

Metaphorically, the wheel in Buddha's sermon *Dhammachakkappavattana* (Setting the Wheel of the Dharma in Motion) is thought to have eight spokes or even twelve spokes. Some think it is best to speak of this wheel with twelve spokes as Dependent Co-arising. In other words, it is a therapeutic analysis of what Buddha thought could cure people of their basic illness.[25] This Dependent Co-arising or wheel with twelve spokes is as follows:

> (1) Aging and dying depend on rebirth; (2) rebirth depends on becoming; (3) becoming depends on the appropriation of certain necessary materials; (4) appropriation depends on desire for such materials; (5) desire depends on feeling; (6) feeling depends on contact with material reality; (7) contact depends on the senses; (8) the senses depend on "name" (the mind) and "form" (the body); (9) name and form depend on consciousness (the spark of sentient life); (10) consciousness shapes itself by *samsara*; (11) the *samsara* causing rebirth depends on ignorance of the Four Noble Truths; and (12) therefore, the basic cause of *samsara* is ignorance.[26]

Like any chain, this wheel can be turned forward or backward. Regardless of how one chooses to turn it, the basic lesson to be derived from it is that "there is no single cause of the way things are. Rather, all things are continually rotating in this twelve-stage wheel of existence. Each stage of the wheel passes the power of movement along to the next. The only way to step off the wheel, to break the chain, is to gain enlightenment and so detach the stage of ignorance."[27]

The Middle Way

Training in Liberation from *samsara*	Training in Meditation	Training in Wisdom
Right speech	Right effort	Right view

25. Carmody and Brink, *Ways to the Center*, 324.

26. Carmody and Brink, *Ways to the Center*, 324–25.

27. Carmody and Brink, *Ways to the Center*, 325.

Right action	Right mindfulness	Right intention
Right livelihood	Right concentration	

THE BUDDHA'S LAST DAYS

When Buddha was eighty years old, he was frail and worn out. In spite of his frail condition, he traveled with his attendant and cousin, named Ananda, from Rajagaha to the town of Kusinara, teaching different audiences along the way. Buddha spent time with Ananda in the forest, using his powers of mindfulness to control his illness. One time when they were meditating in the forest, the Buddha told Ananda at least three times that a Buddha has the power to live for an aeon or until the end of an aeon, if asked to do so.[28] At another time in the same forest, Mara, the angel of death who tempted Buddha before his enlightenment, appeared to Buddha and reminded him of a promise he purportedly made long ago that he would pass on to nirvana once he had trained disciples to continue the dharma. Buddha responded to Mara that he would pass into nirvana in three months.[29] When Ananda heard this he remonstrated with the Buddha to remain until the end of the aeon. But Buddha scolded him for asking him to remain until the end of the aeon.[30]

Resigning himself to the fact that the Buddha was going to pass on to nirvana sooner than he wanted, Ananda asked Buddha where authority should reside after his death. Buddha explained to Ananda (together with a group of monks around him at the time) what he called "the four great authorities" (the authority of the Buddha, the authority of a senior monk in a sangha or community, the authority of a small community of several learned monks, and the authority of a single learned elder). Buddhists use these four great authorities to determine the authenticity of a Buddhist text or teaching. After this the Buddha received his last meal, "a pig's delight," from Chunda, a blacksmith. The Buddha was by no means a vegetarian. Many believe his last meal was a pork. The Buddha gave instructions during the meal that only he should be served the dish and that the rest should be buried. Following the meal, the Buddha suffered an attack of dysentery, leading some to believe that the meal was a potent poison. Ananda asked Buddha how his disciples should show respect to him after his death. The Buddha explained that they should visit four places of pilgrimage: the site of

28. Carmody and Brink, *Ways to the Center*, 159.

29. Carmody and Brink, *Ways to the Center*, 159.

30. Lopez, *Buddhism*, 158–59.

his birth, the site of his enlightenment, the site of his first teaching, and the present site—the site of his *parinirvana* (final nirvana). Anyone who dies while on pilgrimage to one of these four sites, the Buddha purportedly said, will be reborn as a god in heaven.[31]

The Buddha gave instructions regarding how he should be cremated when he dies—that his remains should be enshrined in a stupa and adorned with flowers and perfumes. The Buddha then uttered his last words: "All conditioned things are of a nature to decay—strive on untiringly."[32] Seven days after his death, the Buddha's body was cremated. At the time of the Buddha's death, members of his immediate family were either all dead themselves or had joined different order of monks, practically leaving the Buddha with no immediate family member to claim his body. Regardless, there were still about eight to ten claimants of the Buddha's body who wanted his relics for posterity. To avoid unrest, a Brahmin, named Dona, was invited to divide up the relics. "Dona kept for himself the urn that had held the relics; a ninth group was given the embers that remained from the funeral pyre."[33]

BUDDHIST ORIGINS OF MONASTIC LIFE

The early origins of monasticism in Buddhism remain quite fascinating. Traditionally, early Buddhist monks were wandering mendicants. Early Buddhist monks, including the Buddha himself, wandered from place to place all year round. They did not have a fixed place that they could call their home. Given the climatic conditions of India, they sought refuge with their lay Buddhist collaborators in the rainy season. But the lay Buddhists began to complain that the monks who sought shelter in the rainy reason were damaging their crops and stepping on worms and insects on their path, thereby creating negative karma. To address their concerns, the Buddha instituted what was called the "rains retreat." It was a period in which groups of monks would remain together in a particular place during the monsoon season. Laypeople provided those shelters during the rains retreat. These shelters later evolved into what we now know as Buddhist monasteries where monks reside all year round.[34]

The origin of the establishment of Buddhist order of nuns is also an interesting one. In ancient India, women were not permitted to take part in religious rituals. In rare cases where women were permitted to play a part

31. Lopez, *Buddhism*, 160.
32. Lopez, *Buddhism*, 160.
33. Lopez, *Buddhism*, 160.
34. Lopez, *Buddhism*, 228.

in ritual offerings, as in some sixth-century BCE yogic practice that dates back to Hinduism, they were only permitted a limited role. Following this ancient practice, the Buddhist monks were exclusively male until the Buddha visited his home town of Kapilavatsu after his enlightenment. As the story goes, during his visit, Buddha's aunt and stepmother, Mahapajapati, requested that he allow women to join the Buddhist order of monks, but Buddha refused. Buddha then left the city with his newly ordained monks (male of course). But unknown to Buddha and his men, they were followed by a group of women, most of whom were the wives the monks had left behind. The women had shaved their heads and donned monk's robes, their feet bleeding from walking very long in ascetic fashion that they were unused to. Looking back and seeing the throng of women following them, Ananda asked Buddha to allow the women to join the order of monks. Buddha refused. But after several entreaties, Buddha acquiesced and allowed the women to join the order of monks. He, however, came up with eight rules, sometimes called "heavy rules," for nuns—rules that placed the nuns in a subservient role to the monks.[35] The Buddha's "heavy rules" were built on rules governing women in traditional Indian society, in which a woman is said to be protected by her father in her youth, by her husband in her midlife, and by her son in old age:

> According to the rules of ordination, men required the consent of their parents, but not of their wives, to enter the order. Women, however, required the consent of their husbands. Thus, most of the illustrious female disciples of the Buddha are women who lack the protection of father, husband, or son: widows, courtesans, and unwed daughters of kings, as well as the abandoned wives of monks. When the Buddha's wife demands that he bestow upon their son Rahula his birthright, the Buddha ordains him as a monk; this is his inheritance. When the Buddha's recently widowed stepmother turns to her son for protection, he (eventually) ordains her as a nun.[36]

As Buddha was about to pass into nirvana, Ananda asked to know how men should behave towards women. The Buddha's reply was "Do not look at them." Ananda then asked how monks should behave if they happen to see women. The Buddha replied, "Do not speak to them." Ananda then asked the Buddha, "But if they speak to us?" The Buddha said, "Practice mindfulness, Ananda."[37]

35. Lopez, *Buddhism*, 232.
36. Lopez, *Buddhism*, 233.
37. Lopez, *Buddhism*, 232.

The Case against Ananda

After the Buddha had passed into nirvana, the order of monks in the community of arhats (holy persons) brought five charges against Ananda and asked him to confess to them. The first charge had to do with the Buddha's last days with Ananda. The Buddha had told Ananda that after his passing the monks could disregard the minor precepts. But Ananda failed to ask the Buddha which of the precepts were the minor precepts. Because he had failed to ask, all the precepts had to be followed by the monks. The second charge against Ananda was that he stepped on the Buddha's robe when he was sewing it. The third charge was that when the Buddha died and his body was being viewed, Ananda had allowed women to view the Buddha's naked body and that the tears of some of the weeping women had fallen on Buddha's feet. The fourth charge was that Ananda had failed to ask the Buddha to delay his passing into nirvana and live on for an aeon. The fifth charge was that Ananda had persuaded the Buddha to admit women into the order.[38]

The Three Jewels of Buddhism

In our treatment of Judaism, we pointed out that one is considered a Jew if one is born of a Jewish mother. Analogously in Islam, a Muslim is one who submits to the will of Allah and accepts the principles of Islam as found in the Five Pillars of Faith. With respect to Buddhism, what makes a person a Buddhist? Properly speaking, a Buddhist is one who takes refuge in the three jewels of Buddhism: the Buddha, the dharma (Buddha's teaching), and the sangha (community).[39] "Someone who says three times, 'I go for refuge to the Buddha. I go for refuge to the dharma. I go for refuge to the sangha,' is a Buddhist."[40] When Buddhists seek refuge in the Buddha, the dharma, and the sangha, it is their way of proclaiming that they need protection from the sufferings of life and that the best protection from those sufferings is provided by the Buddha, his teachings, and the community that grew out of his teachings. An Indian Buddhist text, *Sishi'er Zhang Jing* (literally, "The Scripture in Forty-Two Sections"), translated into Chinese at the request of Emperor Ming of the Han Dynasty (58–75 CE), underscores the Buddha's approval of the three jewels of Buddhism:

38. Lopez, *Buddhism*, 232.
39. Lopez, *Buddhism*, 45.
40. Lopez, *Buddhism*, 45.

The Buddha said: All beings consider ten things as good and ten things as evil. Three concern the body, four the mouth, and three the mind. The three [evil things] of the body are killing, stealing, and adultery. The four of the mouth are duplicity, slander, lying, and lewd speech. The three of the mind are envy, hatred, and delusion. He who lacks faith in the three honored ones [the Buddha, the teaching, and the community of monks] will mistake falsehood for truth. A lay disciple [*upasaka*] who practices the five precepts [not to kill, to steal, to commit adultery, to speak falsely, or to drink alcohol], without becoming lax and backsliding, will arrive at the ten [good] things [i.e., the antitheses of the ten evil things] and will ccertainly attain the Way.[41]

BUDDHIST TEXTS

The oral text of the Buddha's teaching was maintained for a long time until it was finally written down on the island of Sri Lanka to the south of India. There, a king whose name is unknown to us but who reigned from 29 BCE to 17 BCE, "fearing that the words of the Buddha might be lost if the monks who had memorized them died in a famine or a war, ordered that they be inscribed onto the dried palm leaves, the paper of the day—a relatively fragile medium for the preservation of the truth."[42] Thus, there was a four-century span between the death of Buddha and the first recording of his discourses—*sutra*. Even so, the first written version did not survive. It was not until the fifth century CE that the text of the Pali Canon that we have today was edited in Sri Lanka by the Buddhist monk Buddhagosa.[43] Buddhagosa whose name means "Voice of the Buddha" composed a massive work of about nine hundred pages called the *Visuddhimagga* ("The Path of Purification").[44]

Buddhists traditionally organize the Buddha's teachings into three groups called the *tripitaka*, meaning the "three baskets." These are the *sutras* (discourses of the Buddha), the *vinaya* (code of monastic discipline), and the *abhidharma* (special doctrine or pertaining to the doctrine).[45] "The *abhidharma* literature treats a wide range of topics, including epistemology, cosmology, psychology, and the function of the law of karma and

41. Lopez, *Buddhism*, 497.
42. Lopez, *Buddhism*, 48.
43. Lopez, *Buddhism*, 202.
44. Lopez, *Buddhism*, 249.
45. Lopez, *Buddhism*, 267.

mechanism of rebirth, as well as specific processes by which the practice of the path leads to liberation from rebirth."[46]

Three Marks of Reality

Buddhists who codify the Buddha's teachings sometimes reduce them to these three marks of reality:

1. The first mark of reality is based on the reality of suffering—that all life is painful. This is similar to the Platonic idea that happiness and pain are two sides of the same pole: one cannot experience happiness without pain lurking behind at the other end of the spectrum. For the Buddhist, the reality of sickness, disease, and death make life painful.

2. The second mark of reality is that life is fleeting. The early Ionian philosophers, Heraclitus especially, taught that all things change because of the fleeting nature of reality. For the Buddhist, the cycle of life is a movement from one fleeting stage to another. The fleetingness of life is seen in the cycles of birth, death, and rebirth. A tradition that goes back to the Buddha says the three *durgati* (bad migrations), i.e., worse or negative places of rebirth, are the realms of animals, the realms of ghost, and the denizens of hell.[47]

3. The third mark of reality is that there is no self—that the human person, mentally and physically, does not have an enduring nature. The Buddha taught that the human person is no more than "an impersonal collection of five interrelated aggregates: materiality, feeling, perception, mental formations, and consciousness."[48] A famous Indian Buddhist, Nagarjuna, who lived somewhere between 150 and 250 CE, helped to develop the Buddhist notion of fleetingness of life. He stated that nothing exists in and of itself and that everything lacks any kind of independent existence or intrinsic nature because everything is empty.[49] This void or emptiness is everywhere visible for us to perceive, propelling us therefore to strive towards being a bodhisattva—a Buddha.

---

46. Lopez, *Buddhism*, 267.
47. Lopez, *Buddhism*, 464.
48. Feldmeier, *Encounters in Faith*, 156.
49. Lopez, *Buddhism*, 367.

TYPES OF BUDDHISM

Not long after the Buddha's passing into nirvana, dissension and rancor among his followers split the community of monks he had established. This degenerated into a schism, leading to two types of Buddhism: Theravada Buddhism and Mahayana Buddhism.

Theravada Buddhism

The Theravada tradition of Buddhism is known as "the way of the elders" because of its ties to pristine early Buddhism.[50] It is also called the *Hinayana* (a name which means "small vehicle) tradition of Buddhism because of its claims "that each individual has to cross the river of suffering by his own efforts: Buddha only provides an example of how to do it."[51]

In a text of Theravada Buddhism called the *Mangala Sutta* ("Discourse on Good Fortune"), a sixteenth-century text, the Buddha is met by a radiant deity who, upon observing that both humans and gods seek good fortune but do not know what it is, asks the Buddha to describe what good fortune is.[52] The Buddha shrewdly chooses to answer, not by enumerating the Four Noble Truths and the Eightfold Path, but by enumerating those practices and virtues that lead to good fortune: hard work, humility, gratitude, and respect for one's parents.[53] Theravada Buddhists think practicing these virtues have apotropaic powers—the power to ward off evil spirits.[54] Something similar is found in the *Metta Sutta* ("Discourse on Loving Kindness"). According to the *Metta Sutta*, a group of monks went into the forest to meditate during the monsoon season when rains fell heavily in India, the spirits which inhabited the trees tried to disturb the monks and drive them away from the forest. The monks sought the Buddha's advice on this matter. The Buddha instructed the monks to fill the forest with thoughts of loving-kindness, which they did, and the spirits were subdued.[55]

One of the more important monks in Theravada Buddhism is the fifth-century scholar Buddhagosa (whose name means "Voice of the Buddha"). Tradition has it that he was born a Brahmin, near Bodh Gaya where Buddha got his enlightenment. As a Brahmin and Vedic Hindu, Buddhagosa was a

50. Carmody and Brink, *Ways to the Center*, 233.
51. Carmody and Brink, *Ways to the Center*, 233.
52. Lopez, *Buddhism*, 237.
53. Lopez, *Buddhism*, 237.
54. Lopez, *Buddhism*, 248.
55. Lopez, *Buddhism*, 248.

skillful debater. He converted to Buddhism only when he was defeated in a debate by the Buddhist monk Revata.[56]

Mahayana Buddhism

Mahayana Buddhism (literally, "Large Vehicle") teaches that the Buddha attained enlightenment long before he passed into nirvana and that he never died. The Buddha delayed his entry into nirvana to be an example of bodhisattva (an enlightened one). The Mahayana tradition of Buddhism began about five hundred years after the Buddha passed into nirvana. It is a theistic approach to Buddhism that views the Buddha as the captain of the large vehicle—that the Buddha is "a personal savior and all we have to do is get on his boat."[57]

One of Mahayana Buddhism's important sutras is the *Lotus Sutra*, whose author is still very much unknown, but most likely composed around the latter half of the first century CE.[58] One of the *Lotus Sutra's* bold claim is that everyone has the capacity to become a Buddha or bodhisattva because everyone has an inherent *tathagatagarbha* (translated "Buddha nature") in them. "No longer was the bodhisattva the rare being who decided to forgo the enlightenment of the arhat to follow the much longer path to Buddha-hood. Now everyone would follow the bodhisattva path and everyone would become a Buddha."[59] A Buddha is produced from wisdom and compassion and bodhisattvas exist to benefit sentient beings.[60]

The idea of *tathagatagarbha* (Buddha nature) seems to contradict the essential Buddhist doctrine that there is no self, since this Buddha nature sounds as though there is self. As the concept itself continued to spark controversy in Mahayana Buddhism, some scholarly schools found a way to explain it. One school in seventh-century China explained it this way: "In the degenerate age in which we live, it is impossible to take refuge in a particular Buddha, because humans are incapable of knowing who is enlightened and who is not . . . [Therefore] the Buddha encompasses all living beings, because all beings are equally endowed with the *tathagatagarbha*."[61]

---

56. Lopez, *Buddhism*, 249.

57. Carmody and Brink, *Ways to the Center*, 232.

58. Lopez, *Buddhism*, 278.

59. Lopez, *Buddhism*, 340.

60. Lopez, *Buddhism*, 487.

61. Lopez, *Buddhism*, 341.

Tara: A Woman Bhodisattva

The Mahayana tradition of Buddhism teaches that the ideal follower of the Buddha is a bodhisattva—one who has the wisdom and compassion of being a Buddha, i.e., an enlightened one who is capable of helping others attain enlightenment. In the pantheon of Buddhism, there is a plethora of bodhisattvas, male and female alike. One of such bodhisattvas, at least in Indian and Tibetan Buddhism, is a woman named Tara in Sanskrit. The historical origins of this woman whose name means "Star" or "Saving" is not very clear. In Buddhist iconography, she is represented as a beautiful sixteen-year-old maiden and as "the mother of all Buddhas" because of her wisdom and compassion.[62] There is a tale about how a group of monks met Tara and asked that she pray to be reborn as a man, to which Tara replied: "I developed bodhichitta as a woman. For all my lifetimes along the path I vow to be born as a woman, and in my final lifetime when I attain Buddhahood, I will be a woman."[63]

BUDDHISM IN CHINA

Buddhism entered China when China had fully developed as a political and cultural force in South Asia. This was about 100 CE. China, at the time, also boasts of its own sophisticated written language and philosophical tradition, Daoism. Buddhism entered China by way of the Silk Road that linked China with the West. Indian Buddhist missionaries who brought Buddhism to China gained foothold in China during the period of the Six Dynasties, a time of political discontent when Central Asian invaders attacked China from its northern border.[64] China would become Buddhism's new headquarters, second only to India, "providing the literature, the language, and much of the doctrine and institutional structure for Buddhism in Korea, Japan, and Vietnam."[65] Buddhist texts in Sanskrit were translated into Chinese and other East Asian languages.

When Buddhism first made it to China, some Buddhist teachings were not favorably received initially. Some of the teachings ran contrary to the Daoist teachings that Chinese culture was already steeped in. For example, the individualism of Buddhism, i.e., the focus on what the individual has to do to liberate oneself from the cycles of birth, death, and rebirth, was alien

62. Lopez, *Buddhism*, 487.

63. Lopez, *Buddhism*, 487.

64. Lopez, *Buddhism*, 492.

65. Lopez, *Buddhism*, 492.

to the community-centered ethos of the Daoist-Confucian ethic of China that focuses on reverence for ancestors. There is also the matter of Buddhist monastic life, which calls one to be a celibate, something that seemed to contradict the Confucian virtue of having children to continue the familial relationship and devotion to ancestors. The Buddhist monastic lifestyle also entails that one shaves one's head, in addition to renouncing one's family. To shave one's head in China was not looked upon kindly. To take monastic vows renouncing one's family violated the familial piety of Confucian ethic of China.[66] But with time, Buddhism found ways to overcome these obstacles through various adaptation techniques. The adaptations made the Chinese see ways Buddhism could be similar to Daoism. For example, many of the Buddhist's texts that were translated into Chinese during the Han Dynasty employed Daoist terminologies and Mahayana sutras that were translated in the period of the Six Dynasties also adapted the sutras to Daoist ways of thinking. During the Yuan Dynasty (1271–1368 CE) and the Qing Dynasty (1644–1911), when China was ruled by foreign invaders who were patrons of Tibetan Buddhism, the Mongols and Manchus, Buddhism received official state support in China.[67] The brand of Buddhism that flourished in China was the Mahayana type. Among monks, professional writers, and artists, the Mahayana school of meditation, known as the *Ch'an*, became influential, while the Pure Land movement, with its emphasis on devotion to the Buddha, flourished among the laypeople.[68] Thus, with time, Buddhism, together with Confucianism and Daoism, became one of the official "Three Doctrines" of Chinese culture.[69]

Buddhism in China experienced its golden age during the Sui Dynasty (581–618 CE) and the Tang Dynasty (618–907 CE).[70] It was during this period that Chinese Buddhism made its mark, particularly the Tiantai School of Chinese Buddhism, the Huayan School of Chinese Buddhism, and the Pure Land School of Chinese Buddhism. Each of these schools seeks "to understand the entire corpus of scriptures in light of a single text that they hold to be Buddha's highest teaching. Many of these schools took their own distinctive forms as Buddhist doctrine and philosophy was continuing to develop in India."[71]

---

66. Lopez, *Buddhism*, 492.

67. Lopez, *Buddhism*, 493.

68. Molloy, *World's Religions*, 159.

69. Molloy, *World's Religions*, 159.

70. Lopez, *Buddhism*, 492.

71. Lopez, *Buddhism*, 492.

Buddhism came under attack in China with the collapse of the Qing Dynasty and establishment of the Chinese Republic in 1912. The new rulers of China suppressed Buddhism and considered it a form of superstition. The situation degenerated with the Second World War. After the Japanese defeat of China and the founding of the People's Republic of China in 1949, many of the leading Buddhist scholars fled the country, many seeking refuge in Tibet.[72]

BUDDHISM IN TIBET

It is believed that Buddhism first made its way to Tibet in the seventeenth century. Like many of the legends surrounding Buddhism, it is sometimes difficult to distinguish fact from fiction. One legend has it that the king of Tibet was converted to Buddhism by his Nepalese and Chinese wives. However, what we do know for sure was that by the time Buddhism reached Tibet, the religion was already dominant in countries bordering Tibet, including India, Nepal, China, Sri Lanka, and Japan.[73]

There was no Tibetan written language before Buddhism made it to Tibet. A legend has it that the king of Tibet "sent a delegation of young men to India to study Sanskrit and then devise a Tibetan alphabet and grammar. Under another of the 'dharma kings,' a royal translation academy was founded where Tibetan scholars worked with Indian pundits to translate the vast literature of Indian Buddhism, both sutras and tantras, into Tibetan."[74] Buddhism received official backing from Tibetan kings for a long time, although there were a few kings who had adversarial relationship with Buddhism. Overall, Tibetan Buddhists maintained more ties with India than they did with China, Korea, and Japan, developing four major brands of Tibetan Buddhism over time: Nyingma, Kagyu, Sakya, and Geluk.[75] Each of these Tibetan Buddhist groups has its texts—texts that describe the Buddhist path from the beginning stage of dissatisfaction with a world of suffering to the advanced stage of meditation through which one can gain enlightenment.[76] An example of such text is the *Great Exposition of the Stages of the Path to Enlightenment*, a fifteenth-century text sometimes referred to as the *Summa Theologica* of Tibetan Buddhism.[77]

72. Lopez, *Buddhism*, 493.

73. Lopez, *Buddhism*, 677.

74. Lopez, *Buddhism*, 678.

75. Lopez, *Buddhism*, 678.

76. Lopez, *Buddhism*, 696.

77. Lopez, *Buddhism*, 697.

India call their mystics and sages guru. The Tibetans call their sages lamas. Leading lamas grew more in stature and importance as the religion became dominant in Tibet. More and more monasteries were built, many of them led by renowned lamas. They developed a unique form of succession: the institution of the incarnate lama:

> All Buddhist traditions believe in rebirth, and in the Mahayana it is said that buddhas and bodhisattvas intentionally return to the world again and again out of their compassion for all sentient beings. The Tibetans added to this idea the claim that after the death of a great master, his next incarnation could be identified, even when he was a young child. Eventually, some three thousand lines of incarnation developed in Tibet (a few of which are female), the most famous being the Dalai Lama. The institution of the incarnate lama would become a central component of Tibetan society, providing the means by which authority and charisma, as well as property, were passed from one generation to another.[78]

Earlier in our discussion of the revolutions in China, we saw how China was conquered by the Mongolian leader Kublai Khan, who introduced a Mongolian Yuan Dynasty in China. Tibet developed a client-patron relationship with Mongol. Under the terms of this patronage, Tibet provided the Mongols with Buddhist religious instructions and the Mongols provided Tibet with military and material protection. Even when the Manchu of the Qing Dynasty (1644–1911) ruled China, they retained the client-patron relationship with Tibet, exercising only a nominal authority over Tibet.[79] With military backing from the Mongols, Tibet, under the leadership of the fifth Dalai Lama, became a force to be reckoned with in the seventeenth century. The lamas wielded political authority and enshrined an institution of successive lamas who were appointed at young age. They ruled Tibet until 1959. Why did the rule of the lamas come to an abrupt end? In 1950, Mao Zedong's China conquered Tibet and exerted Chinese influence over this kingdom in the Hilmalayas that is twice the size of Texas. Many in the West interpreted the Chinese invasion as an annexation. The annexation of Tibet by China was a gradual process. When China invaded Tibet in 1949 and finally conquered it in 1950, at first it left intact the Tibetan social structure, in which the Tibetans were ruled by the lamas, but now under the authority of China. As Chinese influence over Tibet grew, some Tibetans resented Chinese control over the country and began an uprising. The uprising came

---

78. Lopez, *Buddhism*, 678–79.
79. Lopez, *Buddhism*, 679.

to a head in 1959 under the fourteenth Dalai Lama. who escaped to India for refuge on March 17, 1959. The rule under the lamas came to an end with the Tibetan uprising and the exile of the Dalai Lama. To this day, the Dalai Lama is considered a living Buddha, an embodiment of compassion, and a bodhisattva who renounced nirvana to remain in this samsaric world to help others attain their own enlightenment. Francisco Penas-Bermejo, a professor in the Department of Global Languages and Cultures at the University of Dayton, drew attention to a 2019 *Time* magazine cover of the fourteenth Dalai Lama in exile in India. Even in exile, the fourteenth Dalai Lama is seen as "the world's most famous Buddhist" today. Not only do people visit the Dalai Lama in his private chapel in India, they come with all kinds of requests. Many "brave the February chill to offer white *khata* scarves and receive the Dalai Lama's blessing. There's a group from Bhutan in traditional checkered dress. A man from Thailand has brought his Liverpool FC scarf, seeking divine benediction for the UK soccer team's 2018/19 premiership title bid. Two women lose all control as they approach the Dalai Lama's throne and are carried away shaking in rapture, clutching prayer beads and muttering incantations."[80]

BUDDHISM IN KOREA

Buddhism was brought to the Korean Peninsula around 372 BCE by some Chinese Buddhist missionaries. The dominant religion in Korea at the time was a variation of tribal religion otherwise known as Shamanism. Chinese Buddhist missionaries brought along with them their Chinese architecture, calendrical systems, and healing techniques.[81] By 668 BCE, Buddhism had become the state religion in Korea, entering its golden age by 918 BCE when the Korean rulers built monasteries and placed monks in influential governmental positions. However, the ascendancy of Buddhism in Korea did not go unchecked. Buddhism began to decline in the fourteenth century when the new Korean leaders, the Choson Dynasty, replaced Buddhism with Neo-Confucian ideology. "Buddhist lands were confiscated, monasteries were closed, and monks and nuns were banned from entering the city walls of Seoul."[82] It was not until Japan conquered Korea in 1910 and made Korea a Japanese colony that some of the restrictions against Buddhism in Korea were lifted, although the Japanese favored their own form of Buddhism, like

80. Campbell, "Test of Faith," 31.
81. Lopez, *Buddhism*, 581.
82. Lopez, *Buddhism*, 582.

Pure Land and Nichiren, which they imposed on Korea.[83] After World War II, when Korea regained its independence, it started practicing its own favored brand of Buddhism.

BUDDHISM IN JAPAN

Tradition has it that Buddhism was first introduced to Japan around 552 BCE by Korean Buddhist missionaries who came with their sutras and the image of the Buddha. Later, there would also be Buddhist missionaries from China who would make their way to Japan, introducing Zen Buddhism as a means of protecting Japanese rulers from their enemies. "In appealing for acceptance and support by the state, Buddhists have often made the claim that the practice of Buddhism, or the practice of a particular form of Buddhism, has the power to protect the nation from all manner of natural catastrophes, as well as from enemies both foreign and domestic."[84]

Zen Buddhism (known in China as *ch'an* before it was translated *Zen* in Japan) is an offshoot of Mahayana Buddhism that began in China. Its main emphasis was on meditation, as opposed to ritual. It claimed that the Buddha did not gain enlightenment through ritual, but through meditation. By the time Zen Buddhism found its way to Japan it had been stripped of its Indian ethos. The Mahayana Buddhism from which Zen derives places emphasis on the interpenetration of all beings and that nirvana is not something one could achieve by oneself alone. Zen followers favor following the technique of mediation that the Buddha himself adopted.[85] In Japan, the *zazen* (literally, sitting meditation) was favored as the fundamental Zen technique for reaching enlightenment. "It involves sitting in silence with one's back straight and centered, keeping the body still, and taking deep and regular breaths."[86] A Japanese monk, Eisai (1141–1215), who went to China to learn more about Zen teaching, wrote an essay upon his return to Japan about the new Zen teaching he brought back titled, *Promote Zen to Protect This Kingdom's Rulers*.[87] Like Eisai before him, Nichiren (1222–82) advocated Buddhism for state protection. Nichiren argued that all that the people needed to do was put their faith in the *Lotus Sutra* and "that chanting

---

83. Lopez, *Buddhism*, 582.

84. Lopez, *Buddhism*, 637.

85. Molloy, *World's Religions*, 167.

86. Molloy, *World's Religions*, 168.

87. Lopez, *Buddhism*, 637.

the title of the *Lotus Sutra* was the only way to gain liberation during the time of the decline of the dharma."[88]

Nichiren promoted the *Lotus Sutra* and denigrated other Buddhist texts as ineffectual, at times branding them heretical. When the Mongol invaders overran and occupied China and Korea, Nichiren warned that the conquest of Japan by the Mongols was inevitable unless the Japanese embrace the *Lotus Sutra*. He also implied that the various calamities suffered by Japan, including famine and pestilence, were as a result of the Japanese government's patronage of other heretical Buddhist sects.[89] Whatever happened to Nichiren, including his arrest and exile, is beyond our interest here.

88. Lopez, *Buddhism*, 637.
89. Lopez, *Buddhism*, 638.

Appendix
Review Questions

CHAPTER 1: THE COMPLEX MATTER OF RELIGION

1. How have individuals and communities understood the umbrella term "religion"?

2. What questions are more common during the time of distress, war, famine, or disasters?

3. What is the question "Who am I?" ultimately related to?

4. How do Western cultures conceive personal identity?

5. How do non-Western cultures conceive personal identity?

What Is Religion?

1. How did the indigenous peoples see religion? What did they use religion to address?

2. In what did the indigenous peoples embed their answers to the questions regarding the mysteries of life?

3. What is syncretism? Give an example.

4. What is acculturation?

5. What is theism? Give an example.

6. What is agnosticism? Give an example.

7. What is deism? Give an example.

8. What is monotheism? Give an example.

9. What is polytheism? Give an example.

10. What is pantheon? Give an example.

11. How is scientism different from rationalism?

Unconscious Religiousness

1. Who was Viktor Frankl?

2. What does Frankl mean by "unconscious religiousness"?

3. Who is the Austrian neurologist who later became the father of modern psychoanalysis?

4. What theory (existential analysis) did Frankl derive from his work in neurology?

5. What is the central theme of this existential analysis?

6. Why was Frankl prevented from treating any Aryan patient when the Nazis took over Austria in 1938?

7. What book did Frankl write in 1959?

8. What does Frankl mean by "self-actualization" or "self-transcendence"?

9. When do religious people think self-actualization is fully realized?

10. What does Karl Rahner mean by "transcendental experience"?

11. What is animism? Give an example.

12. What is henotheism? Give an example.

13. What is morphology? Give an example.

14. What is the difference between anthropomorphism and theriomorphism?

The Matter of Religion Reconsidered

1. Who was Raimon Panikkar?

2. What did Panikkar argue against and why?

3. Apart from strong systems of government and commerce, what else made ancient civilizations, like Egypt, Mesopotamia, and Babylon, great?

4. What is the name of the law code named after King Hammurabi?

5. What other ancient law codes are comparable to the law code named after King Hammurabi?

6. What is the Latin derivation of the word "religion" and what does it denote?

7. What does the word *religare* mean?

8. What did early Christian writers use the word *religio* to distinguish?

9. What is the broad definition of religion?

10. What is the subject matter of religion? Who is the object or goal of religion?

11. What is a sign?

12. How is the relationship between the sign and its representation determined?

13. What is a symbol?

14. Christians wear a cross around their neck to symbolize what?

15. Why do Muslims wear white robes during pilgrimage?

16. Why do Jews come to prayer wearing the *tallit*?

17. Are symbols meant to be believed? If yes, why? If no, why not?

18. What is a myth?

19. Are the truth-claims of myths to be verified? If yes, why? If no, why not?

20. What is a ritual?

21. What is the primary purpose of ritual?

22. In what are the ethical prescriptions of Jews and Christians contained? What is the ethical prescription of Buddhism called?

23. What is a doctrine?

24. What is the name of the Jewish fundamental statement about God taken from Deuteronomy 6:4–9 that an adult Jew is expected to recite?

Is Religion Different from Theology?

1. How is theology different from religion?

2. How is the subject matter of theology (God) different from that of religion?

3. What are the two Greek words from which the word "theology" is derived? What does theology mean?

4. How did Clement of Alexandria understand theology?

5. How did Christians of the third century understand theology?

6. When did theology develop into an academic discipline?

7. What are the five universities or centers of learning that emerged when theology became an academic discipline?

8. Who were the first to reflect on the nature of theology as a science and address the question of its definition?

9. Who is the author of the *Book of Sentences*?

10. What are the two major works for which Anselm is known?

11. What is Anselm's notion of God?

12. What is Anselm's Latin phrase that many Catholic theologians have understood as the classical definition of theology? What does the Latin phrase mean?

13. What are the two ways of knowing the truths about God, according to Thomas Aquinas?

14. How did Thomas Aquinas define theology?

15. What led to the demise of scholasticism?

16. What did Luther intend to achieve by his program of *sola fide, sola scriptura*?

17. When, according to Luther, did he make a complete break with Augustine?

18. What did the Catholic Church establish after the Council of Trent for formal training of priests and pastors?

19. Into how many areas was theology divided when it was no longer taught in the universities?

20. Who was John Macquarrie? How did he define theology?

21. Who was Bernard Lonergan? What are the names of his two famous books?

22. How does Lonergan integrate religion and theology?

23. Theological reflection, according to Lonergan, takes place in how many phases? Name them.

24. What are the eight distinct tasks a theologian performs, according to Lonergan? What name does he call these tasks?

25. Who was Shawn Copeland? What does she see as the failure of mainstream theology? What does she think theology can be used to contest?

CHAPTER 2: CREATION ACCOUNTS OF THE ABRAHAMIC RELIGIONS

1. What two things do physicists claim that we need to know to understand how the universe came into existence?

2. How did the universe come into universe, according to quantum theory?

3. When did the universe come into existence, according to the standard view of the Big Bang theory?

4. In what way do the three Abrahamic religions agree and differ with science regarding the origin of the universe?

5. What was the great legacy of Mesopotamia?

6. What early five civilizations developed in Mesopotamia? What did they use to account for the plagues and natural disasters they experienced?

7. What did ancient cultures use to explain the flux and instability they experienced?

8. What is the difference between civilizations that developed along rivers where the climate was unstable and civilizations that developed along rivers where the climate was stable?

Judeo-Christian Accounts

1. What is the Jewish name for the first five books of the Hebrew Bible? What do Christians call these books?

2. Do the first five books have the same author? Why do they have different translators?

3. What is the name of the first book of the Hebrew Bible? Where and when was it translated into Greek?

4. What is the Hebrew title of the first book of the Hebrew Bible?

5. What are the two natural divisions of the first book of the Hebrew Bible? What is the name of the first part of this book?

6. Do the narrators of the Genesis story intend to give a scientific account of history? How would you characterize their story?

Two Creation Accounts

1. How many creation accounts are in the primeval story? What are their names?

2. How do the creation stories differ?

3. When was the first creation account written and by whom?

4. In how many days did Yahweh complete the creation event, according to the first creation account?

5. What was the main goal of the writers of the first creation account with respect to human beings?

6. Which of the days of the week was given a special status, according to the writers of the first creation account, and why?

7. Who are the authors of the second creation account? What was their main concern?

8. What is the four-part story plot of the writers of the second creation account?

9. What is the name of the first human being God created? From what did God fashion him? Why did God have to create a partner for him?

10. What is the name of the woman God created for the first man? What does the name mean?

11. Where did God place the man and the woman? What tree did God instruct them not to eat?

12. Who tempted them to eat of the tree God forbade them? What was the punishment for their sin?

What Questions Does Genesis Try to Answer?

1. Who dominated the world militarily at the time the book of Genesis was written?

2. How would you characterize the two creation accounts of Genesis in the light of the military domination of the Israelite neighbors?

3. What is the name of the national god of the Babylonians?

4. What is the name of the wind god in Sumerian epic?

5. How do the two creation accounts complement each other?

6. What two things does the garden of Eden story tell us?

Creation Accounts in the Quran

1. In how many days, according to the Quran, did God create the world? How should these days be understood, according to the Quran, and why?

2. What word does the Quran use to describe the world?

3. Where are the creation accounts in the Quran located?

4. Does the Quran specify what was created in each day of the week?

5. How, according to the Quran, did God create?

6. Who, according to the Quran, made Adam and Eve to defy the divine commandment?

7. According to the Quran, what happened to Adam and Eve when they defied the divine commandment?

8. According to the Quran, what did Adam do, after his transgression? What did God do in return?

9. Who, according to the Quran, were with God when God created humans and what did they do when God wanted to create humans?

10. What dignified title did God confer on the first man, according to the Quran?

11. Who was the only one who was able to give the names of the creatures when God asked the angels to name them?

12. What is the name of the angel who refused to bow down to Adam when God commanded them to do so?

13. Why did the angel who refused to bow down to Adam refuse to do so? What did God do to this angel?

Proliferation of Sin in the Bible

1. What are the names of Adam and Eve's first two sons? What were they by profession?

2. Who killed who and why?

3. What is the name of Adam and Eve's third son?

4. What are the names of the two sons of Cain?

5. Who is described as a prototype of violent attacker and who boasted to his wife about killing a man?

6. What are the names of the three sons of Lamech and what are they by profession?

7. What did God do when God could no longer cope with human sinfulness? Whom did God spare?

Proliferation of Sin in the Quran

1. What sweet words, according to the Quran, did Satan whisper to Adam and Eve?

2. If Muslims believe that what happened in the garden was not "the fall," what do they think it was?

3. Since Muslims believe that it was God's plan from the beginning to put Adam and Eve on earth, what is their view of the garden?

4. What is the term used to explain what Muslims consider human nature at birth to be?

5. How is everyone, according to Muslims, born?

6. What, according to Muslim belief, make us deny our true nature?

CHAPTER 3: JUDAISM

1. When did the followers of Judaism begin to refer to themselves as Jews?

2. What is the meaning of the term "Jew"?

3. Who is considered a Jew?

4. Whose name did Yahweh change to Israel?

5. What are the two possible meanings of the term "Hebrew"?

6. Name three Jewish patriarchs.

7. What is the name of the second book of the Hebrew Bible? From what event does the book derive its name?

8. What is the Greek translation or meaning of "Exodus"?

9. At what mountain did the people of Israel enter into a special covenant with Yahweh?

10. Why do some people think Exodus is Israel's "Magna Carta"?

Sojourn in Egypt

1. What patriarchal material did the Yahwist group inherit?

2. What was the goal of the Yahwist in using this story?

3. Who deceived his father and stole his brother's blessing?

4. Who was the man who was sold into slavery by his brothers?

5. Whose descendants were called Israelites?

6. How did the Egyptians treat the descendants of Jacob after Joseph's death?

Moses and the Burning Bush

1. Where did Moses' mother hide him after his birth and why?

2. Who found Moses and took pity on him? Who was hired as his wet-nurse?

3. Why did Moses flee Egypt?

4. What is the name of Moses' wife? What is the name of Moses' father-in-law?

5. What did Yahweh tell Moses when he encountered Yahweh in the Burning bush?

6. What finally made Pharaoh to let the Israelites go?

The Passover Meal

1. What was the last plague that Yahweh sent to Egypt?

2. On what day did Yahweh slay the firstborn of Pharaoh and the Egyptians?

3. At what sea did Yahweh miraculously save the Israelites from the Egyptian army?

4. What is the name of the feast the Israelites celebrate to mark deliverance from Egypt?

5. What is the name of the wheat harvest the Israelites celebrate seven weeks after Passover?

6. What is the name of the fall harvest festival Jews celebrate by erecting straw?

7. What is the name of the Jewish Day of Atonement?

8. What is the name of the Jewish festival of lights?

9. Who led a successful revolt in 168 BCE against attempts to destroy traditional Judaism?

The Covenant

1. What is the Hebrew word for "covenant"?

2. What is the basis of the covenant in Jewish understanding?

3. Who is the French archeologist who discovered the law stele of the Babylonian king Hammurabi?

4. What are the two types of treaties in the ancient world? Which of the two treaties is more unilateral?

5. How many legal steps are in the ancient treaty that is more unilateral?

6. What kind of ancient treaty is the covenant between Yahweh and Israel patterned after?

7. What is the Decalogue?

8. What are the four covenants Yahweh made with Israel?

Law Codes in the Ancient Near East

1. What are the seven law codes in the ancient world that archeologists have uncovered?

2. What is *lex talionis*?

3. What two ancient law codes have *lex talionis*?

Apodictic or Case Law

1. What is a case or casuistic law? What two things does a case or casuistic law specify?

2. What is an apodictic law?

3. What is the term for Jewish dietary law?

4. What are Jewish dietary laws modeled after?

5. What do the animals that Jews consider unclean lack?

Exodus: A Creation Story?

1. How is the book of Exodus another creation story?

2. What is the name of the Babylonian creation story?

3. What is Bris?

4. What is Bar-Mitzvah?

5. What is Kaddish?

Prophecy and the Prophetic Books

1. What does Charlotte Buhler mean by human person is a being with intentionality?

2. Why is the pleasure principle misleading, according to Viktor Frankl?

3. What is the role of prophets in the ancient world?

Former Prophets and Latter Prophets

1. Where do the books of the Prophets appear in the Hebrew canon?

2. Which six historical books begin the Prophetic Books?

3. What is another name for the six historical books that begin the Prophetic Books?

4. Whose ideology shapes the six historical books?

5. What is the story behind the six historical books?

6. Who is regarded as prophet par excellence?

7. What is the name of the non-Israelite prophet who was hired to curse Israel, but chose instead to offer a blessing?

8. What are the names of the two court prophets during the time of King David?

9. When did the Latter Prophets emerge?

10. What are the names of the Latter Prophets?

Prophecy in the Ancient Near East and Israel

1. Israelite prophecy was dependent on prophecies in which part of the ancient world?

2. What was the role of *baru* in ancient Babylonia?

3. What was developed in the eleventh century BCE in Phoenicia?

4. Can you give an example of a prophet whose role was a "Seer" who received the word of God?

5. Can you name two prophets who lived with a band of prophets?

6. Where is the English word "prophet" derived from? Whose oracles were they connected to?

7. What is the Hebrew term for "prophet"? What does this term designate?

8. Who was the prophet who was a herdsman and a dresser of sycamore tree?

The Prophetic Books

1. How many major prophets are there and how many minor prophets?

2. Which prophet described his divine commission as coming "In the year that King Uzziah died"?

3. Which prophet directed his oracles against the ruling elites in Jerusalem?

4. Which prophet directed his oracles against the ruling class of Samaria?

Isaiah the Prophet

1. The prophetic material of the book of Isaiah stretches into how many centuries?

2. How many subcollections or books are found in the book of Isaiah?

3. Which chapters of the book of Isaiah are attributed to the eighth-century prophet who lived in Jerusalem?

4. Who are the authors of the other parts of the book of Isaiah?

A Divided Kingdom

1. Under whose reign did the nation of Israel split into two kingdoms?

2. What led to the split?

3. How many tribes became the Northern Kingdom and how many became the Southern Kingdom?

4. What are the names of the tribes that became the Southern Kingdom?

5. Which kingdom is often referred to as Israel and which is often referred to as Judah/Jerusalem?

6. What is the name of the great center of worship in the North that some prophets prophesied at?

7. Which kingdom is sometimes referred to by the prophets as Ephraim or Samaria?

First Isaiah (Chapters 1–39)

1. What is the name of the prophet to whom this material is attributed?

2. How many sons did he have?

3. What are the symbolic meaning of the names of the sons of this prophet?

4. Where was this prophet educated?

5. Which other prophets may have influenced him?

6. When this prophet prophesied, Israel was under the threat of what nation/power?

7. What are the names of the two kings under whom Isaiah prophesied?

8. What two powers invaded Judah at the time of this prophet and why?

Immanuel Prophecy

1. What are some of the themes of First Isaiah?

2. What dilemma was King Ahaz faced with?

3. What did Isaiah advise the king?

4. What sign did Isaiah promise the Lord will give?

Second Isaiah or Deutero-Isaiah (Chapters 40–55)

1. When did the Assyrian Empire that threatened Israel at the time of First Isaiah disintegrate?

2. Who was the new threat at the time of Second Isaiah? Under which leader?

3. Whom did Second Isaiah see as agent of Yahweh's restorative justice?

4. Whom did Second Isaiah consider agent of Yahweh's judgment?

5. Why was Second Isaiah disappointed with some of the captives in Babylon?

6. Why did Second Isaiah prophesy that there will be a new Exodus?

7. Why is Second Isaiah sometimes called the Book of Comfort?

8. What other themes or imagery are found in Second Isaiah?

Third or Trito-Isaiah (Chapters 56–66)

1. What century prophetic oracle is found in Third Isaiah?

2. What do we learn from the viewpoint of this prophet?

3. Who allowed the exiles to return to their homeland in 538 BCE and what edict did he enact?

4. What does Third Isaiah berate Israel for?

CHAPTER 4: THE CANON OF THE HEBREW BIBLE AND THE CHRISTIAN OLD TESTAMENT

Ancient Civilization and Israelite History

1. Who were the creators of civilization in Lower Mesopotamia in the Copper-Stone Age?

2. What kind of writing did the creators of civilization in Lower Mesopotamia in the Copper-Stone Age introduce?

3. Whose civilization was concentrated along the Nile River?

4. What kind of writing was introduced to the civilization along the Nile River?

5. What is the term for the Old Stone Age?

6. What is the term for the Middle Stone Age?

7. What is the term for the New Stone Age?

8. What is the term for the Copper Age?

9. What do the Hebrew Bible and the Christian Bible have in common?

10. What are some of the significant differences between the Christian Bible and the Hebrew Bible?

The Nature of the Bible

1. How would you define the Bible?

2. How many authors does the Bible have?

3. Who technically is the divine author of the Bible?

4. In what is God's first act of self-disclosure revealed?

5. Where does God definitively reveal God's self?

6. What is the term for the process of God's self-disclosure?

7. What is the meaning of the term "inspiration"?

8. What is meant by "inerrancy"?

9. What is the meaning of the term "canon" or "canonicity"?

The Hebrew Bible

1. What is the proper name for the Hebrew Bible? How is the term derived?

2. What is Nevi'im? What are some of the books of this collection?

3. What is Ketuvim? What are some of the books of this collection?

The Christian Old Testament

1. From where did Christians derive the term "Old" to speak of the Old Testament?

2. Who erroneously taught that the Old Testament has been rendered void by the New Testament?

3. How does orthodox Christianity view the Old Testament?

4. What is the Christian name for the first five books of the Old Testament? From where was the term derived?

5. Who was the first to use this Christian name for the Old Testament?

6. What is the term for the Greek translation of the Hebrew Scriptures that the Greek-speaking Christian community in Alexandria used?

7. What is the name of the second block of books in the Christian Old Testament?

8. What two books are in the Hebrew collection of Hebrew Ketuvim that are not considered part of this second collection of books in the Christian Old Testament?

9. What is the name for the third block of books in the Christian Old Testament?

10. What one book is found in the Christian collection of the third block of books that is not found in the Hebrew Bible and why?

11. How would you explain the Christian placement of this third block of books as the last collection in the Old Testament?

12. What is the name of the last book of the Christian Old Testament? Why does the Christian Church have this book as the last book of the Old Testament?

Catholic and Protestant Canons

1. In what language were most of the books of the Old Testament written?

2. Which books of the Old Testament were partly written in Aramaic?

3. In what language was the New Testament written?

4. What is the meaning of the term "canon"?

5. At what council did the Jews decide the books of their canon?

6. How many books are in the Hebrew canon of Scripture?

7. At what council did the Catholic Church decide their canon of Scripture?

Catholic and Protestant Canons of the Old Testament

1. How many books are in the canon of the Catholic Old Testament? How many in the canon of Protestant Old Testament?

2. What is the reason for the difference between the canon of the Catholic Old Testament and the canon of the Protestant Old Testament?

Deuteronomist History (DH)

1. What is primary history? Why is it called primary history?

2. Which book is pivotal to primary history, and why?

3. Which books are called Deuteronomist history, and why?

4. Who was the first scholar to develop the theory of Deuteronomist history (DH)?

5. Who are the three authors that developed the theory regarding DH? What was their theory?

6. What is Tetrateuch?

7. What is Hexateuch?

The Pentateuch and the Historical-Critical Method

1. Which two renowned historians mistakenly assumed that Moses wrote the Pentateuch?

2. On what was the assumption that Moses wrote the Pentateuch based?

3. When did people for the first time challenge the assumption of the Mosaic authorship of the Pentateuch?

4. What key passage disproved the Mosaic authorship of the Pentateuch?

5. Whose works brought to an end the view of Mosaic authorship of the Pentateuch?

6. What did the authors find in the Pentateuch that led them to disprove the idea of single authorship of the Pentateuch?

7. What is the Documentary Hypothesis?

CHAPTER 5: THE CHRISTIAN NEW TESTAMENT

The Gospels

1. What are the Greek and Latin terms for "gospel" and what do they mean?

2. How many Gospels are there? Which Gospel begins with a reference to the "gospel" of Jesus Christ?

3. The Gospels were written by what generation of Jesus' followers?

4. Around what period were the Gospels written?

5. What were the earliest Christian writings of the New Testament and when were they written?

Survey of the New Testament

1. What book did the early Christian communities read before the New Testament was written?

2. What we call Gospels first emerged as stories that circulated in the early church. In what three forms were these stories found?

3. The earliest Christian writings of the New Testament, which were composed by credible leaders of the various communities, were intended to serve as what for these communities?

4. What two sources does the Catholic Church insist on as the authoritative norms of the Christian life?

The Four Gospels and Criteria for Canonicity

1. Name five Gospels that were known and used by the early Church, which did not make it into the canon of the New Testament.

2. How far back did the early church recognize only four Gospels out of the many in circulation?

3. Which second-/third-century fragment attested to the existence of four Gospels?

4. What are the five criteria used for devising Scripture?

The Centrality of Mark

1. The present titles that the Gospels bear were added in what century?

2. To whom does tradition assign the authorship of the Gospel of Mark?

3. How did Papias describe the author of the Gospel of Mark?

4. How did Peter describe the author of the Gospel of Mark?

5. Whose authority was thought to be behind the Gospel of Mark?

6. How does Colossians 4:10 identify the author of the Gospel of Mark?

7. How does Acts 12:25 identify the author of the Gospel of Mark?

8. What is the name of the mother of the author of the Gospel of Mark? How was she described in Acts 12:12?

9. Where are the two possible places where the Gospel of Mark could have been written? In what year?

10. To whom was the Gospel of Mark addressed?

11. What did Saint Augustine think of Mark?

12. What is the literary device that is peculiar to the Gospel of Mark? Who discovered it?

13. What are some of the main emphases of the Gospel of Mark?

The Synoptic Problem

1. What is synoptic problem?

2. What is Triple Tradition?

3. What is Double Tradition?

Solution to the Synoptic Problem

1. What theory did G. E. Lessing propound in 1771?

2. What did Eichhorn propose?

3. How did J. G. Herder account for the interdependence among the synoptics?

Two-Source Theory or Two-Document Hypothesis

1. What is the two-source theory?

2. What is the Q hypothesis?

3. What is hypothetical M?

4. What is hypothetical L?

5. What is the Griesbach hypothesis?

6. Who revived the Griesbach hypothesis in 1964?

Critical Reconstruction of the Life of Jesus

1. What is the quest for the historical Jesus?

2. What is the argument of those involved in the quest for historical Jesus?

The Quest for the Historical Jesus

1. How are the Gospels different from other New Testament writings in their confession about Jesus?

2. How do the Gospels pose a historical problem?

3. To whom is it customary to attribute the origin of the quest for historical Jesus? What is the name of his book? When was it published?

4. What was the argument of the originator of the quest for historical Jesus? What influenced his views?

5. What are the four assumptions of the liberal view of early Christianity?

6. What was Friedrich Strauss's view? How is it similar and different from that of Reimarus?

7. Who revived the quest for the historical Jesus in 1953?

Non-scriptural Sources of the Life of Jesus

1. What is the Talmud? What information does the Talmud give about Jesus?

2. Who was Flavius Josephus? What information does Flavius Josephus give about the life of Jesus?

3. Who was Pliny? What information does Pliny give about the life of Jesus?

4. Who was Tacitus? What information does Tacitus give about the life of Jesus?

5. Who was Suetonius? What information does Suetonius give about the life of Jesus?

6. What are the agrapha? What information does the agrapha give about the life of Jesus?

7. What are apocryphal Gospels?

The Stages In-Setting of the Gospels

1. Who established the Pontifical Biblical Commission (PBC)? In what year?

2. What is the duty of the PBC?

3. What method does the PBC encourage? What does it caution against?

4. What are the three stages in the development of the Gospel tradition that interpreters must be aware of?

The Four Senses of Scripture

1. What, according to ancient tradition, are the two senses of Scripture?

2. What are the three subdivisions of the spiritual sense?

Hermeneutics and the New Testament

1. Where is the word "hermeneutics" derived from? What does it mean?

2. Who is the Greek (god) patron of communication?

3. What question does hermeneutics seek to answer?

4. What did ancient Greeks look for in their study of literature?

The Need for Hermeneutics

1. How does hermeneutics help us understand Sacred Scripture?

2. What are the three layers of a written or oral communication?

3. What is rabbinic exegesis?

4. What practice led to the practice known as the Targum?

5. What is Midrashim?

6. What method of interpretation of Biblical texts did the church fathers favor?

7. Who founded the Biblical Institute? In what year?

8. Who is the patron of Catholic biblical scholarship?

9. What document of the Second Vatican Council gave boost to Catholic biblical studies?

10. What two encyclicals define the involvement of Catholic Church in biblical studies?

Does Philosophical Hermeneutics Have a Place in Biblical Interpretation?

1. Which German philosopher's rationalistic philosophical thought undercuts true interpretation, according to the PBC?

2. Who was Friedrich Schleiermacher? What was his essential belief?

3. Who was Hans-Georg Gadamer? What was his thought about interpreting the text?

4. Who was Paul Ricoeur? What is the term for his hermeneutic?

The Historical-Critical Method and Biblical Analysis

1. Why does the PBC consider the historical-critical method "an indispensable method for the scientific study of the meaning of ancient texts"?

2. Who was Richard Simon? What did he draw attention to?

3. What is the documentary hypothesis? Whose work led to its development?

4. Who applied textual criticism and form criticism to the Synoptic Gospels?

5. What particular form of biblical analysis does the Pontifical Biblical Commission endorse?

6. What is rhetorical analysis?

7. What is narrative analysis?

8. What is semiotic analysis?

CHAPTER 6: TWO GREAT INFLUENCES

1. Name the two theologians whose influences were responsible for Christianity being synonymous with Western civilization in the Middle Ages.

2. Whose writings did Luther and some of the churches of the Reformation appeal to in the sixteenth century?

3. Whose writings did the Roman Catholic Church appeal to for synthesis between faith and reason?

4. Where was the hotbed of martyrdom at the time of Christian persecution in the early church?

5. Who was the twenty-two-year-old woman from a noble family in Carthage who became a martyr alongside her slave girl? What was the name of her slave girl?

Aurelius Augustinus (354–430)

1. Which three languages did the ancient Carthaginians speak?

2. How old was Augustine when he wrote *The Confessions*?

3. In what town was Augustine born? What culture was this town part of?

4. What are the names of Augustine's father and mother?

5. Why did Augustine move to Carthage?

6. What is the name of Augustine's son?

7. Whose philosophy was Augustine drawn to?

8. What sect did Augustine join in North Africa? How long did he remain with the sect? What are some of the teachings of this sect?

9. What particular teaching of the sect that Augustine joined fascinated him?

10. What are the degrees of membership in the sect Augustine joined? What level did he attain before he left the sect?

11. What is Neo-Platonism? Through whose Latin translations did Augustine learn Neo-Platonism?

12. What Neo-Platonic teaching was Augustine fascinated by?

13. What Neo-Platonic teaching would Augustine the Christian employ as harmonious with Christian teaching?

14. Who was the bishop of Milan when Augustine accepted a teaching position in Milan in 384 CE?

15. Where did Augustine spend eight months in solitude on his way to becoming a Christian?

16. What three factors, according to Augustine, led to his conversion?

17. Which other two people were baptized with Augustine?

18. What tragedy hit Augustine on his way back to Africa?

19. Augustine became the bishop of what city? At what age? How long did he hold the position?

The Donatist Controversy

1. Who were apostates?

2. Who were *dies traditores*

3. Why did the bishops from all of Numidia reject the consecration of Caecilian as bishop in 321 CE?

4. What distinguished the Donatists from orthodox Christianity?

5. Where did the Donatists get most of their converts from?

6. What was the main thing that distinguished the Donatists from the rest of the Church?

7. What did the Donatists demand of the lapsed Christians and clergy?

8. How did the Donatists interpret Scripture?

9. Why did Augustine compare the Donatists to "frogs in a pond"?

10. What does Augustine think the validity of the sacraments depended on?

The Pelagian Controversy

1. Who propounded a teaching that denied original sin?

2. What does Augustine teach about human nature?

3. What does Augustine think we need because of our fallen human nature?

4. What teaching of Augustine will be at the center of controversy in the sixteenth century?

Augustine's Writings

1. When did Augustine start writing *The Confessions*?

2. Into how many books is *The Confessions* divided?

3. What other two works is Saint Augustine known for?

The Middle Ages and Christianity

1. Which century is considered the golden age of church intellectual history?

2. What three important developments took place in the thirteenth century?

3. Which Jewish and Arabic philosophers made possible the discovery of Aristotle's work in the Latin West?

4. Why was the Latin West skeptical of the works of Aristotle when they were first discovered?

5. What are the three major reactions or responses to Aristotle?

6. Which two other great personalities emerged in the Middle Ages?

7. How did Pope Leo XIII describe the schoolmen?

8. Which two great saints embody the ideals of the schoolmen of the Middle Ages?

Thomas Aquinas (1224/5–1274)

1. What monastery did Thomas's father offer Thomas as an oblate?

2. When Thomas went to Naples for study what was he fascinated by?

3. What did Thomas do in 1244?

4. What did Thomas's brothers do to prevent him from carrying out his plans in 1244?

5. Under whom did Thomas study at the University of Paris?

6. What nickname did Thomas receive from his peers?

7. Whom did Thomas call "the philosopher"?

8. What experience did Aquinas have in Naples on December 6, 1273?

9. What happened to Aquinas after this experience?

Authority of Thomas Aquinas

1. What does the Code of Canon Law legislate for the clergy with respect to Thomas Aquinas?

2. What does Leo XIII's *Aeterni Patris* (1879) call for?

3. Who described Aquinas as "a model of fidelity to the Roman Church"?

4. Thomas Aquinas was given the titles *doctor communis* and *doctor Angelicus* and one other title. Which other title was conferred on him by Pope Pius V?

5. What did Leo XIII confer on Aquinas in 1880?

6. For whom does the church reserve the title *doctor ecclesiae*?

The Works of Thomas Aquinas

1. What are Aquinas's four major works in theology?

2. What is apophatic theology?

3. What are the two sources of knowledge around which Aquinas built his system?

4. How did Aquinas integrate the two sources of knowledge?

The Plan of the *Summa*

1. Why was Aquinas denounced as a heretic?

2. Why was Aquinas branded an Averroist?

3. What book did the *Summa* supplant as symbol of Catholic orthodoxy?

4. Why is Aquinas difficult to read for beginners not familiar with the scholastic method?

5. How is a conventional method of debate or medieval text structured?

6. Into how many parts is the *Summa* divided?

7. What are the Latin names of the different parts of the *Summa*?

CHAPTER 7: THE CHURCH, CHRISTOLOGY, AND SALVATION

The Problem of Evil

1. What moral evils and structural evils do we experience?
2. What is theodicy?
3. What is special transcendent knowledge?

Causes of Evil

1. How are human beings responsible for evil in the world?
2. In what way is ignorance—wrong or erroneous belief—responsible for evil in the world?
3. What kind of evil do Latin American liberation theologians spend their time challenging?
4. Who is Gustavo Gutiérrez? What are his three dimensions of true liberation theology?
5. Who are other Latin American liberation theologians?

Are We Responsible for Evil?

1. What does Buddhism suggest as a panacea for human suffering?
2. What does Bernard Lonergan mean by "our advance in understanding is also the elimination of oversights and misunderstandings"?

The Church

1. How did Jesus know himself while on earth?
2. What is the term for the special meal Jesus shared with his disciples?
3. What did Jesus command his disciples to do regarding the meal?

4. What did the followers of Jesus call themselves after his death?

5. What did the followers of Jesus receive at Pentecost? What did this gift do for them?

6. What did the different Christian communities founded by the apostles meet regularly to do?

7. What were their governmental structures like?

8. What, according to Karl Rahner, is one of the most difficult questions in church history?

9. What is the best way to speak of the church? Why?

10. Who was Avery Dulles? What did he offer?

11. What is meant by church as institution?

12. What is meant by church as community?

13. What is meant by church as sacrament?

14. What is meant by church as herald?

15. What is meant by church as servant?

16. What is meant by church as discipleship?

Christology

1. What is Christology?

2. Which Gospel is often referred to as the Fourth Gospel? How did this Gospel begin its prologue?

3. What is the cornerstone of the Christian faith?

4. What does the word "messiah" mean?

Early Christological Controversies

1. What were the first three patriarchates (theological centers) of the early church?

2. What is allegorical interpretation? Which two theologians used this method?

3. What school emphasized literal interpretation of Scripture?

4. In what year did the first Council of Nicea take place? What was it in response to?

5. In what year was the Council of Constantinople? What addition did it make to the Creed?

6. In what year was the Council of Chalcedon? What did the Council say about the two natures of Christ?

Church as Sign of God's Desire to Save Humanity

1. Who called the church "the basic sacrament of salvation"?

2. How many sacraments are there in the Catholic Church?

3. What are the sacraments of Christian initiation?

4. What are the sacraments of healing?

5. What are the sacraments of Christian vocation?

6. Which sacrament did Karl Rahner call the sacrament of the church "in a very radical sense," and why?

Catholic and Catholicism

1. What is the origin of the word "catholic" and what does it mean?

2. When used as a noun or an adjective what does the word "catholic" mean?

3. Who was the first to use the word "catholic"?

4. What two events in history made the word "catholic" problematic?

5. Apart from the Roman Catholic Church, which other six ecclesial communions call themselves Catholic?

Characteristics of Catholicism

1. What are the seven ways in which the Roman Catholic Church is different from non-Catholic churches?

CHAPTER 8: DEVELOPMENT OF CHRISTIAN DOCTRINE AND SPIRITUALITY

1. Jesus was born during the reign of which Roman emperor? Who was the king of Judea at the time? Who was the governor of Syria at the time?

2. What kind of education did Jesus receive?

3. At what age did Jesus begin his public ministry?

4. With whom did the Romans fight three Punic Wars?

5. What type of religion or worship did the Roman authorities mandate for all in the empire?

6. What did the Jews obtain from the Roman authorities through some political negotiations?

7. Who were the apologists?

Christian Communities in Asia Minor

1. What New Testament book gives a detailed account of the development of the church from its humble beginnings in Jerusalem to its growth in parts of the Mediterranean basin?

2. According to the story in the New Testament book that details the development of the church, where was the first Christian community located?

3. Who was chosen to replace Judas?

4. What event signaled the beginning of the Christian Church?

5. Which zealot Pharisee was an early Christian convert?

6. When he converted to Christianity, what did this zealot Pharisee see as his mission? How many missionary journeys did he embark on? Name any six of the communities he founded.

7. Where were the disciples of Christ for the first time called Christians?

8. Which apostle was linked to the community in Constantinople? Who was linked to the community in Rome?

The First Ministerial Position: The Diaconate

1. Name two external conflicts the early Christian community faced.

2. What was the complaint of the Hellenists?

3. What did the apostles decide with respect to the Hellenist complaint?

4. Which of the first seven deacons was stoned to death?

The Council of Jerusalem

1. What event led to the Council of Jerusalem?

2. When was the Council of Jerusalem? What was the decision of the Council?

3. In what year was the temple of Jerusalem destroyed?

Era of Formal Persecution of Christians

1. Whose reign signaled the era of formal persecution of Christians? Which two apostles died under this emperor?

2. Name three crimes, according to Tacitus, that Christians were accused of.

3. What group threatened Roman Empire from the western Mediterranean during the reign of Decius? What group attacked from borders of Gaul?

4. What edict did Decius enact?

5. How did the Roman authorities view Christians who refused to participate in the common expression of Roman pietas?

6. Apart from Nero's persecution, under which emperors did the other nine persecution of Christians take place?

7. Which persecution is called "the Great Persecution"?

8. Which persecution was the last of the formal persecution of Christians?

9. Whose reign was characterized by literary polemics against the church?

10. Who wrote the book *True Discourse*, which attacked Christians on the level of doctrine and practice?

11. Which group of Christian leaders began to defend the church against offensive literary attacks?

12. Who is the most famous of the Christian leaders who defended the church against offensive literary attacks and under which emperor did he die?

13. Who were the other notable apologists?

14. Which Roman emperor gave Christians a reprieve by enacting an edict of religious toleration?

15. What was the name of the edict of religious toleration and in what year?

Church Leadership and Organization

1. After Peter's death, and the death of the other apostles, which group took up leadership of the church?

2. Name some members of the group that took up leadership of the church after the death of the apostles.

3. Who was the first to use the term "Trinity" for the Godhead?

4. Which Germanic tribal group sacked Rome in 410 CE? Who was the last of the Roman emperors that was deposed by this Germanic tribe?

Internal Problems: Heresies

1. What was the capital of the western half of the Roman Empire? What language did they speak?

2. What was the capital of the eastern half of the Roman Empire? What language did they speak?

3. What is a heresy?

4. What is Gnosticism? In what way is Gnosticism in conflict with Christian teaching?

5. What is Marcionism? How is Marcionism in conflict with Christian teaching?

6. What is Montanism? How is Montanism in conflict with Christian teaching?

7. How did the church respond to the threats of Gnosticism, Marcionism, and Montanism?

8. Who championed the theory that the bishop of Rome was the successor of the apostle Peter?

Origin and Rise of Monasticism

1. Who moved the capital of the Roman Empire to Constantinople?

2. What was the most common expression of church architecture that developed around this time?

3. Why did some Christians flee to the desert? What is the Greek term for what they practiced?

4. Who began the Eremitical tradition of monasticism?

5. Who began the Cenobitical tradition of monasticism?

6. Name three people who championed the cenobitical tradition of monasticism and wrote rules for monks.

Early Ecumenical Councils

1. What is Arianism?

2. What controversy led to the Council of Nicea?

3. What year was the Council of Nicea? What was the decision of the Council?

4. Who were the three Cappadocian Fathers?

5. What was the teaching of Appolinarius?

6. What event led to the Council of Constantinople?

7. What year was the Council of Constantinople? What was the decision of the Council?

8. What addition to the creed became a source of argument and misunderstanding between the east and the west?

The Council of Ephesus

1. What is the title of the popular piety that emerged very early in the church's liturgical life in which Mary the mother of Jesus was venerated?

2. What honorific title for Mary was at the center of the dispute between the Bishop of Constantinople, Nestorius, and Cyril of Alexandria?

3. What aspect of Christ did the Alexandrian School emphasize? What aspect of the Christ was the Antioch School more concerned about?

4. When was the Council of Ephesus?

5. What event or dispute led to the Council of Ephesus? Who were the parties involved? What was their essential argument? What position did the Council of Ephesus adopt?

The Council of Chalcedon

1. What is monophysitism?

2. Who was behind monophysitism?

3. What year was the Council of Chalcedon?

4. What was the decision of the Council of Chalcedon?

CHAPTER 9: SCHISM AND REFORMATION

1. What metaphor did C. S. Lewis use to describe the history of the church?

2. Who was the twentieth-century Canadian Jesuit theologian whose work has been influential in Catholic reimagination?

3. What four factors contributed to the event of the Reformation?

The Great Western Schism and Conciliar Movement

1. What is Conciliarism?

2. What two factors gave momentum to the conciliar movement?

3. How many popes did the Great Western Schism produce?

4. Which council first attempted to end the Great Western Schism and how?

5. What pope was elected as the new pope at the end of the Great Western Schism?

6. What council finally ended the Great Western Schism? What two decrees did the council enact?

7. What are the three Gallican Liberties?

Growth of Humanism

1. Who began the humanist movement?

2. What is the goal of the humanist movement?

3. What did the humanist see as the only means of achieving their goal?

4. The humanist movement's love for music and the arts motivated Pope Sixtus IV to commission what chapel? Who painted the chapel?

5. What is the meaning of renaissance? What movement made it possible?

6. Whose work did the humanists use to propound their theory of city-state?

7. Who was Niccolò Machiavelli?

Johann Gutenberg and William Caxton

1. Who discovered the first printing press in 1450?

2. What is another name for the Gutenberg Bible?

3. Who introduced printing to England?

Erasmus and Thomas More

1. What bordered the humanist the most about the church?

2. Which two humanists refused to be part of the reform movement that severed ties with Rome? What did these two criticize about the church?

The Rise of Mysticism

1. What were the two general preconditions for mysticism?

2. Who began the Brethren of the Common Life?

3. Who was Thomas à Kempis and what book did he write?

4. To whom has the origin of German mysticism been traced? What did he emphasize in his mystical writings?

5. Who was John Tauler? What did his mystical writings emphasize?

6. Who was Henry Suso? What did his mystical writings emphasize?

7. Name two influential English mystics and their works.

Martin Luther (1483–1546)

1. In what town was Martin Luther born and what saint was he named after?

2. Where did Luther receive his bachelor's and master's degrees? What philosophical influence did he encounter there?

3. What monastery did he join at Erfurt?

4. What kind of conscience was Luther troubled by?

5. Who tried to help Luther overcome his fears?

6. What shocked Luther on his visit to Rome?

7. What did Luther realize in his famous "Tower Experience"?

8. Who paid a huge sum of money to the Curia to become the Archbishop of Mainz?

9. What was the name of the Dominican priest who was preaching indulgences?

10. What did Luther send to the Archbishop of Mainz and why?

11. What did Luther do when he did not receive a favorable response from the Archbishop of Mainz?

12. With whom did Luther debate in the Leipzig Disputation?

13. With whom did Luther debate on free-will that led to his publication of *De Servo Arbitrio* (1524)?

14. Whom did Pope Leo X send to try Luther?

15. What is the name of the secular ruler of Saxony who refused to extradite Luther?

16. What year did the pope excommunicate Luther?

17. What was Luther's argument in "An Open Letter to German Nobility"

18. What was Luther's argument in *The Babylonian Captivity* (1520)?

19. What did Luther stress in "The Freedom of the Christian"?

20. Whom did Luther marry when he severed himself from the church?

Ulrich Zwingli (1484–1531)

1. In what city did Zwingli preach against the abuses in the Church?

2. What did Zwingli insist on in his argument against the Church?

3. What did Zwingli abolish in 1525 and what did he replace it with?

4. What did Zwingli substitute for "real presence"?

5. What was the so-called Affair of the Sausages?

John Calvin

1. In what city was John Calvin born?

2. Why did Calvin leave France for Switzerland in 1534?

3. What is the title of the work Calvin published in the Swiss city of Basel?

4. Calvin became the head of the reform movement of what city?

5. What doctrine was Calvin most noted for?

The English Reformation

1. How was the English Reformation different from that of the rest of the continent?

2. What abuses and problems did England experience that the rest of the continent also experienced?

3. From whom did Henry VIII need annulment so he could marry someone else? Whom did he marry instead?

4. What two factors led Henry VIII to seek dispensation for his marriage to Catherine of Aragon?

5. What is the name of the daughter Catherine bore for Henry?

6. What two reasons made the pope not to grant Henry's request for dispensation?

7. What is the name of the Lord Chancellor who helped Henry to transfer jurisdiction from the hands of the pope to Henry?

8. What is the name of the Archbishop of Canterbury who supervised Henry's secret marriage to Anne Boleyn?

9. What is the name of the daughter Henry had by Anne Boleyn?

10. What key parliamentary act did the archbishop of Canterbury help Henry enact to make Henry the supreme head of the Church of England?

John Wycliffe (1329–84)

1. What is the name of the Oxford reformer who believed that everyone had the right to study the Bible?

2. What is the name of the Latin version of the Bible that was used by the medieval Church?

3. Who translated the Latin version of the Bible used by the medieval Church?

4. Who translated the Latin Vulgate into English?

William Tyndale (1493–1536)

1. Which two other English men made attempts to translate the Bible into English?

2. What happened to William Tyndale after he was accused of rejecting papal authority?

The Catholic Reform

1. What did the reform among the Franciscans lead to?

2. Who led the reform of the Carmelites in Spain?

3. Which religious group was the most influential of the religious orders that became agents of Catholic counter-Reformation? Who founded this order?

4. Who wrote the *Spiritual Exercises* (1522)?

5. What controversial measures did Pope Paul IV introduce to Catholic Counter-Reformation?

6. What did Pius V establish in 1571?

7. What council was convoked to deal with the issues of reform? In how many periods did this council meet?

CHAPTER 10: ISLAM

Introduction

1. Why is Islam known as an Abrahamic religion?

2. Which religion is the second-largest religion in the world?

3. What are the two broad divisions in Islam?

Pre-Islamic Arabian Peninsula

1. What kind of people lived in pre-Islamic Arabia in the seventh century CE?

2. What tribal group controlled agriculture and commerce in the Arabian Desert?

3. What city was an important commercial center in the trade network that connected the West to China?

4. What was the predominant religion in the Arabian Peninsula?

5. What was the name of the black stone in the city of Mecca?

6. Who, according to legend, built the Kaaba?

7. Whom do Arabs consider the legitimate son of Abraham?

8. Which tribe was the most famous of the tribes in Arabia?

Birth and Early Life of Muhammad Ibn Abdallah (PBUH)

1. Which Medinan-born historian and scholar wrote a biography of Prophet Muhammad?

2. What are the names of the father and mother of Prophet Muhammad?

3. What year was Prophet Muhammad born and in what city?

4. When did Prophet Muhammad's father die?

5. How old was Prophet Muhammad when his mother died?

6. Who raised Prophet Muhammad when his father died?

7. Into what tribe was Prophet Muhammad born?

8. What was the name of the wealthy widow merchant who hired Prophet Muhammad to work in her caravan?

9. How many children did Muhammad and the wealthy widow merchant have?

10. Which of the daughters lived longer?

11. How old was Prophet Muhammad when his wife died?

12. What is the most definitive authority with respect to the biography of Prophet Muhammad?

The Call to Prophethood and Beginnings of Revelation

1. What was the name of the religious practice of the Quraish that the young Muhammad took part in every year?

2. Where did Muhammad often go in seclusion to pray?

3. How old was Prophet Muhammad when the angel first brought him divine revelation? In what year?

4. In what chapter of the Quran is the text of the first message found?

5. What is the name of the night on which the first revelation occurred?

6. When Muhammad went home and narrated his experience who assured him he is the prophet of God?

7. How many years did Prophet Muhammad receive revelations?

8. When revelation came for Prophet Muhammad to proclaim openly Allah's message, what hill did he climb to proclaim the message?

Open Dawa and Hejira

1. Who was the first to accept Islam?

2. Who was the first male to accept Islam?

3. Which two other male figures accepted Islam early on?

4. How many years after revelation did Muhammad make the first public proclamation?

5. Why was the Prophet's preaching not initially well received by the Meccans?

6. Where did the first followers of Prophet Muhammad emigrate to in the fifth year of revelation and why?

7. What happened in 622 CE? What is this event called?

8. Approximately how days are there in Islamic calendar?

9. What are the names of the four interest groups in Medina?

Ritual Prayer and Muhammad's Night Journey

1. Who taught Prophet Muhammad ritual prayer?

2. With whom do Muslims draw parallel with Prophet Muhammad?

3. At first how many times were Muslims instructed to pray before it was reduced to five?

4. What, according to Prophet Muhammad, is the most virtuous act a person can perform?

Hadith and Sunna

1. What is hadith?

2. What is Sunna?

3. How many hadith collections does Sunni Islam accept?

4. How many hadith collections does Shia Islam accept?

Al Qur'an

1. In what language was the Quran dictated?

2. What do Muslims mean when they refer to the Quran as "the guarded tablet"?

3. What do Muslims mean when they call the Quran "mother of all books"?

4. What is meant by inimitability of the Quran?

5. If Prophet Muhammad brought one miracle, according to Muslims, what was it?

6. The Quran was revealed in a period of how many years?

7. How many surah does the Quran have?

8. In what surah is the first revelation found?

9. In what surah is the final revelation found and in what year was it revealed?

10. Where did the Prophet preach his last sermon?

11. What is the name of the first surah of the Quran?

12. How many days after the final revelation did the Prophet die?

The Five Pillars of Faith

1. What was the official religion of Persia in pre-Islamic Arabia?

2. What is *shirk*?

3. Who is a *mushrik*?

4. What does the Quran call Jews and Christians?

5. What is *tawhid*?

6. Who, according to the Quran, was the first prophet?

7. What is the *Shahada*?

8. What is *salat*?

9. What determines prayer times?

10. How many times a day do Muslims pray? What are the names of the prayer times?

11. Where do Muslims face when they pray?

12. What are the two kinds of ritual purification Muslims perform before prayer?

13. What month do Muslims usually fast?

14. What feast do Muslims celebrate after a month of fasting?

15. What is the name of the obligatory charity every Muslim is expected to perform?

16. What is the name of the voluntary alms-giving expected of Muslims?

17. Who are those forbidden to make pilgrimage to Mecca? What year was this prohibition instituted?

18. When do Muslims perform the obligatory pilgrimage to Mecca and how long does it last?

19. During pilgrimage, between what hills do pilgrims run and how many times do they run?

20. What two things do Muslims do at the conclusion of the obligatory pilgrimage?

21. What feast do Muslims celebrate on the third day of obligatory pilgrimage?

22. What is the name of the lesser pilgrimage Muslims are encouraged to perform?

Fiqh and Madhahib (The Four Legal Schools)

1. What two actions do Muslims try to differentiate through fiqh?

2. For the Shia, who is the sole interpreter of the divine will?

3. How many legal schools do the Sunni recognize?

4. Name the legal schools and identify their strongholds.

CHAPTER 11: RELIGIOUS RAPPROCHEMENT AND AFRICAN TRADITIONAL RELIGIONS

World Religions: Common Themes

1. Who is Arnold Toynbee? Which religions did he characterize as the religions of revelation and why?

2. Who is Friedrich Heiler? What is his view about the religions of revelation?

3. What are the distinguishing factors of world religions?

4. Which world religion does not have a founder and does not give importance to the concept of personal deity?

5. Which religion recognizes one supreme God whose name is Ahura Mazda?

6. What are the seven common areas of the world religions?

Tribal Religions

1. What are some examples of tribal religions?

2. What makes tribal religions tribal?

3. Why is it not proper to call tribal religions "primitive" or "pagan"?

Common Areas

1. What is the difference between religion as clan solidarity and religion as life-vision?

2. How is tribal religion a good example of religion as clan solidarity?

3. What are the distinguishing factors of tribal religions?

4. What, according to Rudolph Otto, are the three components of experience of the "numinous"?

5. What does it mean to say tribal religions experience the sacred?

6. What is animism?

7. Which religion believes that *kami* exists in all natural things?

8. Who held the view that religion, as it developed, was at its core animistic—that it was an attempt to explain ghosts?

9. What is exorcism? In tribal cultures who performs exorcism was and by what means?

10. What is the function of healing in tribal religions?

11. What is the function of sacrifice in tribal religions?

12. Who is René Girard? What does he say is at the core of human nature? What does he think cultures developed to deal with it?

13. What is a taboo? What are some of the taboos in tribal religions?

14. What is magic? When do tribal cultures turn to magic?

15. Who is considered the father of functionalism in anthropology? What does he consider to be the precursor to religion?

16. What is the meaning of profane in tribal religions?

17. What is a rite of passage in tribal cultures? Who was the first to provide a scholarly definition of rite of passage?

18. How many rites of passage are there in tribal religions? Name them.

19. Who was Edward Sapir? What are his two types of symbols?

20. Who is Victor Turner? What are his three types of symbols?

21. What is the function of divination in tribal religions? What kind of methods do diviners use?

22. Why do tribal religions repeat myths?

23. Who is Joseph Campbell? What according to him are the four functions of myth?

24. What is totem in tribal religions? What is it usually made out of? Why?

25. Where does the high god reside in tribal cultures? What is the significance of this location?

26. What do tribal religions believe about after life?

27. What is a megalith in tribal religions? What is it usually made of? What does it symbolize for tribal religions?

28. Who is the shaman in tribal religions? What powers is the shaman reputed to have?

CHAPTER 12: CHINESE WAYS OF BEING HUMAN

Introduction

1. Which three religions have had profound influence on China?

2. What is the Axial Age?

3. What is the Western mind prone to that is not found in the Chinese worldview?

East Asia and Chinese Worldview

1. Name five independent nations of East Asia.

2. What is meant by the "problem of simplistic approach to the study of China"?

3. How many people lived in China in 2018?

4. What unified Europe in the Middle Ages?

5. In what did ancient China find a unifying force?

6. What percentage of the world's population lived in East Asia in 2018?

7. How was China able to exercise a cultural dominance over East Asia?

8. What Chinese dynasty is traditionally considered the first dynasty and how long did it last?

9. What did the Shang Dynasty introduce to China to make China a powerful force in the world?

10. What was the name of the all-powerful divine force during the Shang Dynasty?

11. What kind of natural disasters plagued China during the Shang Dynasty?

12. How did China think of the cosmos?

13. What is the Yin and what is the Yang?

14. What problem has been raised by feminist scholars with respect to the Yin-Yang principle?

15. What did the Zhou rulers invent to maintain their power?

16. What two great schools of Chinese thought emerged during the Warring States period?

17. What great landmark was started during the Qin dynasty?

18. What Zhou idea did the Han Dynasty reinvent?

19. What religious system did the Han Dynasty promote as the official state educational system?

20. What religious system made its way to China by way of Silk Road during the Han Dynasty?

21. What Mongolian leader invaded China during the Sung Dynasty and established the Yuan Dynasty?

22. Which Italian explorer visited China during the Yuan Dynasty?

23. Who made epic voyages to Arabia and Africa during the Ming Dynasty?

24. Which three religious traditions were promoted during the Ch'ing or Manchu Dynasty?

25. What two rebellions did the Ch'ing or Manchu Dynasty have to contend with?

26. The First Opium War was fought between China and who?

27. The Second Opium War was between China and who?

28. What port was ceded to Britain by the treaty of Nan-ching?

29. Who was the first provisional president of the first Republic of China?

30. What year was the Communist People's Republic of China established? Who was the first ruler?

The Jesuit Influence

1. Which two Italian Jesuit missionaries traveled to the Far East and encountered Eastern religions in their missionary work?

2. What policy did the Jesuits adopt to convert the Chinese?

3. Why did the Jesuit missionaries favor Confucianism over Daoism?

Daoism

1. Who made an artificial distinction between Daoism as part philosophy and as part religion?

2. What four possible meanings or interpretations are there for the term "Dao"?

3. What two misunderstandings do the Western depiction of the Dao tend to suffer from?

Who Is the Founder of Daoism?

1. To whom has Daoism been traditionally traced?

2. Why did Laozi abandon his government position?

3. What did Laozi do when he abandoned his government position?

4. What book was Laozi thought to have written?

Classical Texts of Daoism

1. Who are the authors of the two classical texts of Daoism?

2. What is the Daodejing critical of?

3. What does the Daodejing say about describing the Dao?

4. What, according to the Daodejing, is inevitable in human existence?

5. What does the Daodejing say happens to all organisms or *ming*?

6. Who, according to the Daodejing, is a sage?

7. What, according to the Daodejing, is the goal of human life?

8. What are the three jewels of the Dao?

9. What are the three motifs of the Daodejing?

10. Around what period was Zhuangzi born?

11. What, according to Zhuangzi, is life?

Evolution of Daoism

1. How many trends within Daoism have scholars distinguished?

2. What is hedonistic Daoism?

3. Name one hedonistic Daoist?

4. What is mystical Daoism?

5. Name two examples of mystical Daoists.

6. What is alchemical Daoism?

7. Who are some alchemical Daoists?

Confucianism

1. How did ancient China present Confucianism?

2. Under what dynasty did Kong Fuzu live?

3. Why did Kong Fuzu seek a return to the pristine old times?

4. Which four virtues were Confucius's ideal of proper behavior?

5. Which six classics are considered canonical in Confucianism?

Confucius's Major Teachings

1. What does Confucius mean by *Jen*?

2. What does Confucius call *de*?

3. What are the five familial relationships in Confucianism?

4. When does a person's filial obligations to one's parents cease?

5. What is *junzi*?

6. What is *xiaoren*?

7. What is *Li*?

8. Who was Zengzi?

9. Who was Han Hui?

10. What, according to Confucius, should learning lead to?

11. In what way is the Confucian idea of cultivating virtues different from the Western Christian notion of cultivating virtues as found in eremitical tradition of monasticism?

12. What, according to Confucius, does the practice of ritual do?

13. What, according to Confucius, does a leader need to justify his or her rule?

CHAPTER 13: HINDUISM

1. How many people in India practice Hinduism?

2. Which other country in South Asia has a Hindu majority?

3. What are the reasons for the complexity of Hinduism?

4. What elements, other than polytheism, can be found in Hinduism?

5. What descriptors have been suggested by scholars as the goal of Hinduism?

Who Invented Hinduism?

1. Which European explorer arrived on the Malabar Coast at the end of the fifteenth century?

2. Which other European explorers followed the Portuguese to India in the sixteenth and seventeenth centuries?

3. What was the main motive of the Europeans who went to India?

4. Which Italian Jesuit missionary founded the Madurai Mission?

5. What work were the Jesuit missionaries doing in India?

6. Apart from Europeans, which other groups influenced our understanding of Hinduism?

7. What is the view of the Constructionist School regarding Hinduism?

8. Who systematically developed the idea of the Constructionist School?

9. According to Mark Muesse, what was the original meaning of the Old Persian word Hindu?

10. When, according to the Constructionist school, did the term "Hindu" acquire a religious connotation?

11. What is the Deconstructionist view of Hinduism?

12. Who do the Deconstructionists cite to show that Hinduism was not constructed by the British?

13. Where does Ram Mohan Roy claim the essence of Hinduism is to be found?

14. What group did Ram Mohan Roy found?

15. Which three other Hindu elites attempted a reform of Hinduism?

16. Who brought his reform movement to the attention of the World Parliament of Religions in Chicago in 1893?

17. What did Gandhi stress in his reform movement?

18. What led to the rise of further reform in Hinduism in the twentieth century?

19. What was the complaint of the Hindu right?

20. Why was the Babri Masjid destroyed in 1992?

Origins of Hinduism

1. What two points do the three schools of Hinduism agree on?

2. What is the difference between *devotees* and *scholars* in the study of Hinduism? Which one should take precedence?

3. What do Hindu ascetics claim Hinduism revolves around?

4. What do Brahmins think is the essence of Hinduism?

5. What civilization developed along the Indus Valley region before the Aryan conquest of the region?

6. What was involved in the religion of the pre-Aryan civilization of the region?

7. What are the names of the deities the invading Aryans brought with them?

8. What scripture did the invading Aryans bring with them?

9. What are the four *Varna*, according to the Rig-Veda?

10. What is the philosophical justification of the *Varna*?

The Dharma

1. What does dharma mean?

2. Which group claims to be the spokespersons for Hinduism?

3. Who is a Hindu, according to the spokespersons of Hinduism?

4. In what do the spokespersons of Hinduism locate the doctrinal core of Hinduism?

Revelation and Tradition

1. How do Hindus view their scriptures?

2. What is *Shruti*?

3. Name two *Shruti literature*.

4. What do Hindus consider *Smriti*?

5. What is the name of the institution where theological and ritual traditions are passed on from one generation to another? Who heads these institutions?

6. The Vedas consist of how many collections? Name them.

7. Why do some scholars think that the role of the Vedas in Indian society is at best paradoxical?

8. What, according to the Upanishads, is the fundamental reality?

9. What does the Upanishads advocate?

10. What is the Bhagavad-Gita?

11. Whose story does the Bhagavad-Gita tell? Who is he the avatar of?

12. What, according to the Bhagavad-Gita, are the three things to avoid?

13. What three things, according to the Bhagavad-Gita, lead to salvation?

Darshana—Hindu Orthodox Systems

1. How many orthodox systems or movements are there within Hinduism? Name them.

2. Which two deities dominated the devotional movements?

3. What is the one factor that characterizes the orthodox systems within Hinduism?

4. Who is considered the most brilliant exponent of the *Vedanta* school?

5. Who is the founder of the Vaisheshika School?

6. Which of the six devotional schools came close to criticizing traditional structure of Indian society?

Hindu Deities

1. Into how many categories do the Vedas divide the *devas* (gods)? Name them.

2. Who coined the term "henotheism" and why?

3. Who control the forces of nature?

4. Who is the oldest of the celestial gods?

5. Who is considered the guardian of the cosmic order and regulator of morality?

6. Which of the atmospheric devas is the god of thunder?

7. Who is the god of fire?

8. Which three deities are considered the Hindu version of the trinity?

9. Who is the elephant-headed god?

10. Who is the monkey god?

Conclusion

1. Where do a lot of Hindu activities take place and why?

2. What do pious Hindu believe about dying at the Ganges?

3. What is the symbolism of the funeral pyres at the Ganges?

CHAPTER 14: BUDDHISM

1. Why do some people question whether Buddhism should be called a religion?

2. What are the names of the two religions whose assumptions the founder of Buddhism accepted?

3. What two assumptions of these religions did Buddhism share? In what way is Buddhism different from these religions?

Origin and Noble Search

1. At what age, according to the Buddhist text, the *Great Discourse on the Final Nirvana*, did Buddha pass into nirvana?

2. What is the name of the mystic who founded Jainism?

3. What religion did Jainism emerge as a reaction to and why?

4. What, according to Jainism and Hinduism, lead to transmigration of souls?

5. What, according to Jainism and Hinduism, can help one achieve *samsara*?

The Birth of a Prince

1. Siddhartha's parents were nobles from what tribe?

2. What caste group did Siddhartha's parents belong to?

3. What dream, according to legend, did Siddhartha's mother have before his birth?

4. What, according to legend, did Siddhartha scream when he came out of his mother's side?

5. How did Siddhartha's family raise him?

6. At what age did Siddhartha marry? What is the name of his son?

7. What three things did Siddhartha see when he left the palace?

8. Who offered Siddhartha his kingdom when he began his noble search?

9. How does *Ariyapariyesama Sutta* describe Siddhartha's condition when he began his noble search?

His Enlightenment

1. How many years did Siddhartha wander in the wilderness in search of enlightenment?

2. What two techniques did Siddhartha master in his wanderings?

3. Why did Siddhartha renounce asceticism?

4. Under what tree did Siddhartha sit?

5. What devious angel tempted Siddhartha and why?

6. What three last temptations did the devious angel put before Siddhartha?

7. On what night did the Buddha's enlightenment come?

8. What did the Buddha grasp at the peak of his enlightenment?

9. What was the end result of the Buddha's enlightenment?

10. What was the Buddha's attitude towards the Indian caste system?

The Buddha's First Sermon

1. Where did Buddha give his first sermon?

2. Who did Buddha want to be the first to hear his sermon?

3. What was Buddha's first sermon?

The Four Noble Truths

1. What are the Four Noble Truths?

2. What does *Dhammachakkappavattana* mean?

The Buddha's Last Days

1. What is the name of the Buddha's cousin who attended to him and traveled with him when he was old?

2. Where did the Buddha say authority should reside after his death?

3. What was the Buddha's last meal called?

4. What four places did the Buddha instruct his disciples to visit after his death?

5. What last words did the Buddha utter before his death?

Buddhist Origins of Monastic Life

1. What is "rains retreat"? Why did the Buddha institute it?

2. What event led to the establishment of the Buddhist order of nuns?

The Case against Ananda?

1. How many charges were brought against Ananda by the order of monks of arhats?

2. What were they?

The Three Jewels of Buddhism

1. Who is a Buddhist?

2. What are the three jewels of Buddhism?

3. What is the name of the Indian Buddhist text that was translated into Chinese at the request of Emperor Ming?

The Buddhist Text

1. On what island was the text of Buddha's teaching first written down?
2. How many centuries elapsed between the death of the Buddha and the first recording of his discourse?
3. When was the first text of the Palin canon edited? By whom?
4. Into how many groups do Buddhists traditionally organize the Buddha's teaching? Name them.

The Three Marks of Reality

1. What is the first mark of reality?
2. What is the second mark of reality?
3. What is the third mark of reality?

Types of Buddhism

1. What type of Buddhism is known as "the way of the elders"?
2. What four virtues, according to this tradition, did Buddha enumerate as leading to good fortune?
3. What are apotropaic powers?
4. Who is the fifth-century scholar that is considered an important monk of Theravada Buddhism?
5. What is the literal meaning of Mahayana Buddhism?
6. What type of Buddhism is a theistic approach to Buddhism?
7. What bold claim is found in the *Lotus Sutra*?
8. What is *tathagatagarbha*?

Buddhism in China

1. By what road did Buddhism make its way to China?
2. Who were the first to bring Buddhism to China? Under what dynasty?

3. Why were Buddhist teachings not initially well-received in China?

4. Most of the Buddhist texts were translated into Chinese at the time of what dynasty?

5. During which dynasty did Buddhism receive official state support in China?

6. What two brands of Buddhism flourished in China?

7. What flavor did this brand of Buddhism take among Chinese monks and professional writers? What flavor was popular among the lay people?

8. Under which dynasty did Chinese Buddhism experience a golden age?

9. Why did the rulers of China suppress Buddhism after the establishment of the Chinese Republic in 1912?

10. Which country did many of the leading Buddhist scholars flee to for refuge after the founding of the People's Republic of China in 1949?

Buddhism in Tibet

1. In what century did Buddhism first make its way to Tibet?

2. What name do Tibetans call their mystics?

3. What group, under the backing of the Mongols, ruled Tibet until 1959?

4. What happened to Tibet in 1950?

Buddhism in Japan

1. Why was Zen Buddhism introduced to Japan?

2. What was the favored Zen technique for reaching enlightenment in Japan?

3. Who advocated Buddhism in Japan for state protection?

4. Who promoted the *Lotus Sutra* in Japan and denigrated other Buddhist texts as ineffectual?

Bibliography

Achebe, Chinua. *Things Fall Apart*. 50th anniversary ed. New York: Anchor, 1994.

Adewale, A. S. "Crime and African Traditional Religion." *Orita* 26 (1994) 54–66.

Al-Jaziri, 'Abd al-Rahman. *Islamic Jurisprudence according to the Four Sunni Schools*. Vol. 1, *Acts of Worship*. Translated by Nancy Roberts. Louisville: Fons Vitae, 2009.

Amiot, Francois. "Jesus, an Historical Person." In *The Sources for the Life of Christ*, edited by Francois Amiot et al., translated by P. J. Hepburne-Scott, 7–12. New York: Hawthorne, 1962.

Anderson, Bernhard W. *Understanding the Old Testament*. 4th ed. Englewood Cliffs, NJ: Prentice-Hall, 1986.

Anderson, Janice Capel, and Stephen D. Moore. "Introduction: The Lives of Mark." In *Mark and Method: New Approaches in Biblical Studies*, edited by Janice Capel Anderson and Stephen D. Moore, 1–28. Minneapolis: Fortress, 1992.

Anselm of Canterbury, Saint. *Proslogion*. In *Anselm of Canterbury: Volume 1*, edited and translated by Jasper Hopkins and Herbert Richardson. 4 vols. New York: Edwin Mellen, 1974.

Aquinas, Thomas. *Summa Theologica*. 5 vols. Translated by the Fathers of the English Dominican Province. Allen, TX: Christian Classics, 1981.

Arbuckle, Gerald A. *Culture, Inculturation, and Theologians: A Postmodern Critique*. Collegeville, MN: Liturgical, 2010.

Bailey, Lloyd R., and Victor P. Furnish, eds. *The Pentateuch: Interpreting Biblical Texts*. Nashville: Abingdon, 1981.

Bainton, Roland H. *Christianity*. Boston: Houghton Mifflin, 1987.

Bandstra, Barry L. *Reading the Old Testament: An Introduction to the Hebrew Bible*. 2nd ed. Belmont, CA: Wadsworth, 1999.

Banerjee, Bikash. "Religious Beliefs and Practices among the Bokars of Arunachel Prandesh." In *Understanding Tribal Religion*, edited by Tamo Mibang and Sarit Kumar Chaudhuri, 143–58. New Delhi: Mittal, 2004.

Barton, J. *Isaiah 1–39*. T&T Clark Study Guides. Sheffield: Sheffield Academic Press, 1995.

Beardslee, W. A. *Literary Criticism of the New Testament*. Philadelphia: Fortress, 1970.

Beck, Hans-Georg, et al. *History of the Church*. Vol. 4, *From the High Middle Ages to the Eve of the Reformation*. Edited by Hubert Jedin and John Dolan. Translated by Anselm Biggs. New York: Crossroad, 1980.

Bejczy, István Pieter. *Erasmus and the Middle Ages: The Historical Consciousness of a Christian Humanist*. Leiden: Brill, 2001.

Bender, Jacob. "Justice as the Practice of Non-Coercive Action: A Study of John Dewey and Classical Daoism." *Asian Philosophy* 26 (2016) 20–37.

Benjamin, Don C. *The Old Testament Story: An Introduction.* Minneapolis: Fortress, 2004.

Blake, Norman Francis. *Caxton and His World.* London: Andre Deutsch, 1969.

Blenkinsopp, Joseph. *A History of Prophecy in Israel.* Louisville: John Knox, 1996.

———. *The Pentateuch: An Introduction to the First Five Books of the Bible.* New York: Doubleday, 1992.

Boadt, Lawrence. *Reading the Old Testament: An Introduction.* New York: Paulist, 1984.

Bright, Pamela. "Church, North African." In *Augustine through the Ages: An Encyclopedia,* edited by Allan D. Fitzgerald, 185–91. Grand Rapids: Eerdmans, 1999.

Brown, Andrew J. *William Tyndale on Priest and Preachers.* London: Inscriptor Imprints, 1996.

Brown, Raymond E. *An Introduction to the New Testament.* New York: Doubleday. 1997.

Brown, Raymond E., et al., eds. *The New Jerome Biblical Commentary.* Englewood Cliffs, NJ: Prentice-Hall, 1990.

Brueggemann, Walter. *The Creative Word: Canon as a Model for Biblical Education.* Philadelphia: Fortress, 1982.

———. *Hopeful Imagination: Prophetic Voices in Exile.* Philadelphia: Fortress, 1986.

———. *Isaiah 40–66.* Louisville: Westminster John Knox, 1998.

———. *Theology of the Old Testament: Testimony, Dispute, Advocacy.* Minneapolis: Fortress, 1997.

Caird, G. B. *The Language and Imagery of the Bible.* Philadelphia: Westminster, 1980.

Campbell, Charlie. "Test of Faith." *Time,* March 18, 2019.

Campbell, Joseph. *The Mythic Image.* Princeton: Princeton University Press, 1974.

———. *Occidental Mythology.* New York: Penguin, 1991.

Carmody, Denise Lardner, and T. L. Brink. *Ways to the Center: An Introduction to World Religions.* 6th ed. Belmont, CA: Wadsworth/Thomson Learning, 2006.

Carson, D. A., et al. *An Introduction to the New Testament.* Grand Rapids: Zondervan, 1992.

Carter, Stephen L. *The Culture of Disbelief: How American Law and Politics Trivialize Religious Devotion.* New York: Anchor, 1993.

Catechism of the Catholic Church. 2nd ed. New York: Doubleday, 1995.

The Catholic Study Bible. New York: Oxford University Press, 1990.

Chenu, M. D., and Ellen Bremner. "The Plan of St. Thomas' *Summa Theologiae.*" *CrossCurrents* 2 (1952) 67–79.

Cohn-Sherbok, Dan. *The Hebrew Bible.* London: Wellington, 1996.

Cone, James. *A Black Theology of Liberation.* 20th anniversary ed. Maryknoll, NY: Orbis, 2006.

Conzelmann, Hans, and Andreas Lindemann. *Interpreting the New Testament: An Introduction to the Principles and Methods of N.T. Exegesis.* Peabody, MA: Hendrickson, 1988.

Copeland, Shawn. "Guest Editorial." *Theological Studies* 61 (2000) 604–5.

Cunningham, Lawrence. *The Catholic Heritage.* 1995. Reprint, Eugene, OR: Wipf & Stock, 2002.

Davies, Stevan L. *The New Testament: A Contemporary Introduction.* San Francisco: Harper & Row, 1980.

Davis, Philip G. "Mark's Christological Paradox." In *The Synoptic Gospels: A Sheffield Reader*, edited by Craig Evans and Stanley Porter, 163–77. Sheffield: Sheffield Academic Press, 1995.

D'Aquili, Eugene, and Charles Laughlin. "The Neurobiology of Myth and Ritual." In *The Spectrum of Ritual: A Biogenetic Structural Analysis*, 153–82. New York: Columbia University Press, 1979.

Day, John T., et al., eds. *Word, Church, and State: Tyndale Quincentenary Essays*. Washington, DC: Catholic University of America Press, 1998.

Dempsey, Deidre A. "2 Samuel 7." In *Introduction to Theology*, edited by John Laurance, 7–10. Boston: Pearson, 2000.

Dines, Jennifer. "Imaging Creation: The Septuagint Translation of Genesis 1:2." *The Heythrop Journal* 36 (1995) 439–50.

Douglas, Mary. *Leviticus as Literature*. Oxford: Oxford University Press, 1999.

———. *Purity and Danger: An Analysis of the Concepts of Pollution and Taboo*. New York: Pantheon, 1966.

Doyle, Dennis. *Communion Ecclesiology: Vision and Versions*. Maryknoll, NY: Orbis, 2000.

Duling, Dennis, and Norman Perrin. *The New Testament: Proclamation and Parenesis, Myth and History*. 3rd ed. Fort Worth: Harcourt Brace College, 1994.

Dulles, Avery. *Models of the Church*. Garden City, NY: Doubleday, 1974.

Dumbrell, William. *The Faith of Israel: A Theological Survey of the Old Testament*. 2nd ed. Grand Rapids: Baker, 2002.

Durkheim, Emile. "Ritual, Magic, and the Sacred." In *Readings in Ritual Studies*, edited by Ronald L. Grimes, 188–93. Upper Saddle River, NJ: Prentice Hall, 1996.

Eckhart, Meister. *Selected Writings*. Translated by Oliver Davis. London: Penguin, 1994.

Ehrman, Bart. *The New Testament: A Historical Introduction to the Early Christian Writings*. 3rd ed. Oxford: Oxford University Press, 2004.

Ehusani, George Omaku. *An Afro-Christian Vision: "Ozovehe!" Toward a More Humanized World*. Lanham, MD: University Press of America, 1991.

Eliade, Mircea. *Archaic Techniques of Ecstasy*. Translated by Willard R. Trask. Princeton: Princeton University Press, 2004.

———. *Myth and Reality*. Translated by Willard R. Trask. World Perspectives 31. New York: Harper & Row, 1963.

———. "The Symbolism of the Center." In *Cosmos and History: The Myth of the Eternal Return*, 12–27. New York: Harper & Row, 1953.

Ellwood, Robert S., and Barbara A. McGraw. *Many Peoples, Many Faiths: Women and Men in the World Religions*. Upper Saddle River, NJ: Prentice Hall, 1999.

Enchiridion Biblicum. http://www.catholicscripture.net/enchiridion/.

Esposito, John L. *Islam: The Straight Path*. 3rd ed. Oxford: Oxford University Press, 1998.

Fairbank, John King. *The Great Chinese Revolution, 1800–1985*. New York: Harper & Row, 1986.

Fanning, Steven. *Mystics of the Christian Tradition*. New York: Routledge, 2001.

Farmer, W. R. *The Synoptic Problem: A Critical Analysis*. 2nd ed. Macon, GA: Mercer University Press, 1976.

Fee, Gordon. "A Text-Critical Look at the Synoptic Problem." In *The Synoptic Problem and Q: Selected Studies from Novum Testamentum*, compiled by David Orton, 163–79. Brill's Readers in Biblical Studies 4. Leiden: Brill, 1999.

Feldman, Stephen M. *Please Don't Wish Me a Merry Christmas: A Critical History of the Separation of Church and State.* New York: New York University Press, 1997.

Feldmeier, Peter. *Encounters in Faith: Christianity in Interreligious Dialogue.* Winona, MN: Anselm Academic, 2011.

Fenton, Terry. "Israelite Prophecy: Characteristics of the First Protest Movement." In *The Elusive Prophet: The Prophet as a Historical Person, Literary Character and Anonymous Artist,* edited by Johannes C. de Moor, 129–41. Oudtestamentische studiën 45. Leiden: Brill, 2001.

Fernando, Anthony. "An Asian's View of Jesus' Uniqueness." In *The Uniqueness of Jesus: A Dialogue with Paul F. Knitter,* edited by Leonard Swidler and Paul Mojzes, 68–73. 1997. Reprint, Eugene, OR: Wipf & Stock, 2007.

Fitzgerald, Allan D., ed. *Augustine through the Ages: An Encyclopedia.* Grand Rapids: Eerdmans, 1999.

Foad, B. Salem. *The Seerah of Prophet Muhammad.* New York: Vantage, 2001.

Francisco, Clyde T. "The Moral Message of the Hebrew Prophets." *Review and Expositor* 45 (1948) 435–44.

Frankl, Viktor. *Man's Search for Meaning.* New York: Pocket Books, 1984.

————. *The Will to Meaning: Foundations and Applications of Logotherapy.* New York: Penguin, 1988.

Freed, Edwin D. *The New Testament: A Critical Introduction.* Belmont, CA: Wadsworth, 1986.

Frykenberg, Robert Eric. "Constructions of Hinduism at the Nexus of History and Religion." In *Defining Hinduism: A Reader,* edited by J. E. Llewellyn, 125–46. New York: Routledge, 2005.

Gamble, Harry Y. *The New Testament Canon: Its Making and Meaning.* Philadelphia: Fortress, 1985.

Gardner, Daniel K. *Confucianism: A Very Short Introduction.* Oxford: Oxford University Press, 2014.

Girard, René. "Violence and the Sacred: Sacrifice." In *Readings in Ritual Studies,* edited by Ronald L. Grimes, 239–56. Upper Saddle River, NJ: Prentice Hall, 1996.

Goldingay, John. *Old Testament Theology: Israel's Gospel.* Downers Grove: InterVarsity, 2003.

González, Justo L. *Church History: An Essential Guide.* Nashville: Abingdon, 1996.

————. *A History of Christian Thought.* Vol. 3, *From the Protestant Reformation to the Twentieth Century.* Rev. ed. Nashville: Abingdon, 1987.

Goodacre, Mark. *The Synoptic Problem: A Way through the Maze.* London: Sheffield Academic, 2001.

Grabbe, Lester L. *Priests, Prophets, Diviners, Sages: A Socio-historical Study of Religious Specialists in Ancient Israel.* Valley Forge, PA: Trinity, 1995.

Grimm, Harold J. *The Reformation Era: 1500–1650.* New York: Macmillan, 1954.

Grosshans, Hans-Peter. *Luther.* London: Collins, 1997.

Gunkel, Hermann. "Fundamental Problems of Hebrew Literary History." In *What Remains of the Old Testament and Other Essays,* translated by A. K. Dallas, 57–68. 1928. Reprint, Eugene, OR: Wipf & Stock, 2016.

Guterman, Mark A., et al. "Menstrual Taboos among Major Religions." *The Internet Journal of World Health and Societal Politics* 5 (2007). https://ispub.com/IJWH/5/2/8213.

Hacker, Paul. *Kleine Schriften*. Edited by Lambert Schmithausen. Wiesbaden: Steiner, 1978.

Halbfass, Wilhelm. "The Idea of the Veda and the Identity of Hinduism." In *Defining Hinduism: A Reader*, edited by J. E. Llewellyn, 16–29. New York: Routledge, 2005.

Haley, Alex. *The Autobiography of Malcolm X*. New York: Ballantine, 1999.

Halivni, David. "Aspects of Classical Jewish Hermeneutics." In *Holy Scriptures in Judaism, Christianity and Islam: Hermeneutics, Values and Society*, edited by Hendrik M. Vroom and Jerald D. Gort, 77–97. Amsterdam: Rodopi, 1997.

Heiler, Friedrich. "The History of Religions as a Preparation for the Cooperation of Religions." In *The History of Religions: Essays in Methodology*, edited by Mircea Eliade and Joseph Mitsuo Kitagawa, 132–60. Chicago: University of Chicago Press, 1959.

Hellwig, Monkia K. "Rethinking Uniqueness." In *The Uniqueness of Jesus: A Dialogue with Paul F. Knitter*, edited by Leonard Swidler and Paul Mojzes, 74–78. 1997. Reprint, Eugene, OR: Wipf & Stock, 2007.

Helms, Randel McCraw. *Who Wrote the Gospels?* Altadena, CA: Millennium Press, 1997.

Henn, William. "Hermeneutics and Ecumenical Dialogue: BEM and Its Responses on 'Apostolicity.'" In *Interpreting Together: Essays in Hermeneutics*, edited by Peter Bouteneff and Gagmar Heller, 47–91. Geneva: World Council of Churches, 2001.

Hillman, Eugene. *Toward an African Christianity: Inculturation Applied*. Mahwah, NJ: Paulist, 1993.

Hogan, Richard. *Dissent from the Creed: Heresies Past and Present*. Huntington, IN: Our Sunday Visitor, 2001.

Holmes, J. Derek, and B. W. Bickers. *A Short History of the Catholic Church*. New York: Continuum, 2002.

Honoré, A. M. "A Statistical Study of the Synoptic Problem." In *The Synoptic Problem and Q: Selected Studies from Novum Testamentum*, compiled by David Orton, 70–122. Brill's Reader's in Biblical Studies 4. Leiden: Brill, 1999.

Hopkins, Thomas J. *The Hindu Religious Tradition*. Encino, CA: Dickenson, 1971.

Houtepen, Anton. "Hermeneutics and Ecumenism: The Art of Understanding a Communicative God." In *Interpreting Together: Essays in Hermeneutics*, edited by Peter Bouteneff and Gagmar Heller, 1–18. Faith and Order Paper 189. Geneva: World Council of Churches, 2001.

Huff, Margaret C., and Ann K. Wetherilt. *Religion: A Search for Meaning*. New York: McGraw-Hill, 2005.

Isichei, Elizabeth. *A History of Christianity in Africa: From Antiquity to the Present*. Grand Rapids: Eerdmans, 1995.

Jeanrond, Werner. *Theological Hermeneutics: Development and Significance*. New York: Crossroad, 1991.

John Paul II, Pope. *Ecclesia in Africa*. September 14, 1995. http://www.vatican.va/content/john-paul-ii/en/apost_exhortations/documents/hf_jp-ii_exh_14091995_ecclesia-in-africa.html.

Johnson, Luke Timothy. *The Writings of the New Testament: An Interpretation*. Rev. ed. Minneapolis: Fortress, 1999.

Jones, A. H. M. *Constantine and the Conversion of Europe*. Toronto: University of Toronto Press, 1978.

Kaltner, John. *Introducing the Qur'an: For Today's Reader*. Minneapolis: Fortress, 2011.

Kapr, Albert. *Johann Gutenberg: The Man and His Invention*. Translated by Douglas Martin. Brookfield, VT: Ashgate, 1996.

Kessler, Gary. *Eastern Ways of Being Religious*. Mountain View, CA: Mayfield, 2002.

Kinsley, David R. *Hinduism: A Cultural Perspective*. Englewood Cliffs, NJ: Prentice-Hall, 1982.

Klein, William W., et al. *Introduction to Biblical Interpretation*. 2nd ed. Nashville: Nelson, 2004.

Klostermaier, Klaus K. *A Survey of Hinduism*. 3rd ed. Albany: State University of New York Press, 2007.

Knitter, Paul. "Five Theses on the Uniqueness of Jesus." In *The Uniqueness of Jesus: A Dialogue with Paul F. Knitter*, edited by Leonard Swidler and Paul Mojzes, 3–16. 1997. Reprint, Eugene, OR: Wipf & Stock, 2007.

Knott, Kim. *Hinduism: A Very Short Introduction*. New York: Oxford University Press, 2000.

La Due, William. *The Chair of Saint Peter: A History of the Papacy*. Maryknoll, NY: Orbis, 1999.

Landry, David, and David Penchansky. "The Primeval Story." In *The Christian Theological Tradition*, edited by Catherine Cory and David Landry, 19–28. 2nd ed. Upper Saddle River, NJ: Prentice Hall, 2003.

Laurance, John, ed. *Introduction to Theology*. Boston: Pearson, 2000.

Lemche, Niels Peter. "Hebrew." In *The Anchor Bible Dictionary*, edited by David Freedman et al., 3:95. New York: Doubleday, 1992.

Leo XIII, Pope. "Encyclical Letter *Aeterni Patris* (1879)" ["On the Restoration of Christian Philosophy According to the Mind of St. Thomas Aquinas, the Angelic Doctor"]. In *Summa Theologica*, translated by the Fathers of the English Dominican Province, 1:ix–xviii. Allen, TX: Christian Classics, 1981.

Lindberg, Carter. *The European Reformations*. Oxford: Blackwell, 1996.

Lipner, Julius J. "Ancient Banyan: An Inquiry into the Meaning of 'Hinduness.'" In *Defining Hinduism: A Reader*, edited by J. E. Llewellyn, 30–47. New York: Routledge, 2005.

Llewellyn, J. E. "Introduction: The Problem of Defining Hinduism." In *Defining Hinduism: A Reader*, edited by J. E. Llewellyn, 1–12. New York: Routledge, 2005.

Lonergan, Bernard. "The Future of Christianity." In *A Second Collection*, edited by William F. J. Ryan and Bernard J. Tyrell, 149–63. Toronto: University of Toronto Press, 1974.

———. *Insight: A Study of Human Understanding*. Edited by Frederick E. Crowe and Robert M. Doran. Collected Works of Bernard Lonergan 3. Toronto: University of Toronto Press, 1997.

———. *Method in Theology*. Toronto: University of Toronto Press, 1971.

———. *Philosophy of God, and Theology*. Philadelphia: Westminster, 1973.

Lopez, Donald S., Jr., ed. *The Norton Anthology of World Religions: Buddhism*. New York: Norton, 2015.

Lorenzen, David N. "Who Invented Hinduism?" *Comparative Studies in Society and History* 41 (1999) 630–59.

Lowe, Mary Elise. "Woman Oriented Hamartiologies: A Survey of the Shift from Powerlessness to Right Relationship." *Dialog: A Journal of Theology* 39 (2000) 119–39.

Lührmann, Dieter. "Q: Sayings of Jesus or Logia?" In *The Gospel behind the Gospels: Current Studies on Q*, edited by Ronald A. Piper, 97–116. Leiden: Brill, 1995.

Machiavelli, Niccolò. *The Prince, and the Discourses*. Translated by Luigi Ricci. New York: Modern Library, 1950.

Macquarie, John. *Principles of Christian Theology*. New York: Scribner's, 1977.

Malina, Bruce, and Richard L. Rohrbaugh. *Social-Science Commentary on the Synoptic Gospels*. 2nd ed. Minneapolis: Fortress, 2003.

Marcel, Gabriel. *Tragic Wisdom and Beyond: Including Conversations between Paul Ricoeur and Gabriel Marcel*. Evanston: Northwestern University Press, 1973.

Masson, Robert. *The Charmed Circle: Theology for the Head, Heart, Hands and Feet*. Kansas City, MO: Sheed & Ward, 1987.

Matthews, Warren. *World Religions*. 3rd ed. Belmont, CA: Wadsworth, 1999.

McAuliffe, Jane D. *The Norton Anthology of World Religions: Islam*. New York: Norton, 2015.

McBrien, Richard P. *Catholicism*. New ed. New York: HarperCollins, 1994.

McDermott, Timothy, ed. *Summa Theologiae: A Concise Translation*. Westminster, MD: Christian Classics, 1989.

McEnhill, Peter, and George Newlands. *Fifty Key Christian Thinkers*. London: Routledge, 2004.

McGonigle, Thomas D., and James F. Quigley. *A History of Christian Tradition: From Its Jewish Origins to the Reformation*. New York: Paulist, 1988.

McGrath, Allister E. *Theology: The Basics*. Oxford: Blackwell, 2004.

McKnight, Edgar. *Jesus Christ in History and Scripture: A Poetic and Sectarian Perspective*. Macon, GA: Mercer University Press, 1999.

Miller, John W. *Meet the Prophets: A Beginner's Guide to the Books of the Biblical Prophets*. New York: Paulist, 1987.

Molloy, Michael. *Experiencing the World's Religions: Tradition, Challenge, and Change*. 4th ed. Boston: McGraw-Hill, 2008.

Moyo, Ambrose. "Religion in Africa." In *Understanding Contemporary Africa*, edited by April A. Gordon and Donald L. Gordon, 335–70. 4th ed. Boulder, CO: Lynne Rienner, 2007.

Muesse, Mark W. *The Hindu Traditions: A Concise Introduction*. Minneapolis: Fortress, 2011.

Murphy, R. E. "Introduction to the Pentateuch." In *The New Jerome Biblical Commentary*, edited by Raymond E. Brown et al., 3–7. Englewood Cliffs, NJ: Prentice-Hall, 1990.

Nawaz, Muhammad. *Islam: Religion of Peace and Justice*. Bloomington, IN: AuthorHouse, 2003.

Nigosian, S. A. *World Religions: A Historical Approach*. 3rd ed. Boston: Bedford, 2000.

Nissinen, Martti. "What Is Prophecy? An Ancient Near Eastern Perspective." In *Inspired Speech: Prophecy in the Ancient Near East; Essays in Honor of Herbert B. Huffmon*, edited by John Kaltner and Louis Stulman, 17–37. London: T. & T. Clark, 2004.

Oakes, Edward T. *Pattern of Redemption: The Theology of Hans Urs von Balthasar*. New York: Continuum, 2005.

Okere, Theophilus. "African Thought, Philosophy, and Spirituality." Unpublished Paper.

Olin, John. *Catholic Reform: From Cardinal Ximenes to the Council of Trent, 1495–1563*. New York: Fordham University Press, 1990.

Olsen, Glenn. *Beginning at Jerusalem: Five Reflections on the History of the Church*. San Francisco: Ignatius, 2004.

O'Meara, Thomas F. *Thomas Aquinas Theologian*. Notre Dame: University of Notre Dame Press, 1997.

Onyewuenyi, Innocent. "Reincarnation: An Impossible Concept in the Framework of African Ontology." In *African Belief in Reincarnation: A Philosophical Appraisal*, 33–45. Enugu, Nigeria: Snaap, 1996.

Orji, Cyril. *The Catholic University and the Search for Truth*. Winona, MN: Anselm Academic, 2013.

———. *A Semiotic Approach to the Theology of Inculturation*. Eugene, OR: Pickwick, 2015.

Orlandis, José. *A Short History of the Catholic Church*. Dublin: Four Courts, 1994.

Otto, Rudolph. *The Idea of the Holy*. 2nd ed. Oxford: Oxford University Press, 1950.

Panikkar, Raimundo. "The Invisible Harmony: A Universal Theory of Religion or a Cosmic Confidence in Reality?" In *Toward a Universal Theology of Religion*, edited by Leonard Swidler, 118–53. Maryknoll, NY: Orbis, 1987.

Paul VI, Pope. *Dei Verbum*. November 18, 1965. http://www.vatican.va/archive/hist_councils/ii_vatican_council/documents/vat-ii_const_19651118_dei-verbum_en.html.

———. *Nostra Aetate*. October 28, 1965. http://www.vatican.va/archive/hist_councils/ii_vatican_council/documents/vat-ii_decl_19651028_nostra-aetate_en.html.

Phan, Peter, ed. *The Asian Synod: Texts and Commentaries*. Maryknoll, NY: Orbis, 2002.

Pontifical Biblical Commission. "Instruction on the Historical Truth of the Gospels." *The Catholic Biblical Quarterly* 26 (1964) 299–312.

———. *The Interpretation of the Bible in the Church*. Boston: St. Paul's Books & Media, 1993.

Pontifical Council for Interreligious Dialogue. "Pastoral Attention to African Traditional Religion." *Bulletin* 68 (1988) 102–6.

Pontifical Council for Justice and Peace. *Compendium of the Social Doctrine of the Catholic Church*. Washington, DC: USCCB, 2004.

Portier, William L. *Tradition and Incarnation: Foundations of Christian Theology*. New York: Paulist, 1994.

Rahner, Karl. *Foundations of Christian Faith: An Introduction to the Idea of Christianity*. New York: Crossroad, 1997.

Rhoads, David, et al. *Mark as Story: An Introduction to the Narrative of a Gospel*. 2nd ed. Minneapolis: Fortress, 1999.

Robinson, Neal. *Islam: A Concise Introduction*. Washington, DC: Georgetown University Press, 2007.

Robson, James, ed. *The Norton Anthology of World Religions: Daoism*. New York: Norton, 2015.

Rolle, Richard. *The Fire of Love*. Translated by F. M. Compar. London: Methuen, 1914.

———. "The Form of Living." In *The English Writings of Richard Rolle*, edited by Rosemary Allen, 152–83. London: SPCK, 1989.

Sanneh, Lamin. *West African Christianity: The Religious Impact*. Maryknoll, NY: Orbis, 1983.

Sapir, Edward. "Symbols." In *Encyclopedia of the Social Sciences*, 14:155–69. 15 vols. New York: Macmillan, 1933.

Schwarz, Hans. *Theology in a Global Context: The Last Two Hundred Years*. Grand Rapids: Eerdmans, 2005.

Schweitzer, Albert. *The Quest of the Historical Jesus*. Edited by John Bowden. Minneapolis: Fortress, 2001.

Schweitzer, Don. *Contemporary Christologies*. Minneapolis: Fortress, 2010.

Shannon, Thomas A. "Grounding Human Dignity." *Dialog: A Journal of Theology* 43 (2004) 113–17.

Sigmund, Paul E., trans. and ed. *St. Thomas Aquinas on Politics and Ethics: A New Translation, Backgrounds, Interpretations*. New York: Norton, 1988.

Smith, Brian K. "Questioning Authority: Constructions and Deconstructions of Hinduism." In *Defining Hinduism: A Reader*, edited by J. E. Llewellyn, 102–24. New York: Routledge, 2005.

Smith, J. MacDonald. "Can Science Prove That God Exists?" *The Heythrop Journal* 3 (1962) 126–38.

Smith, Wilfred C. *The Meaning and End of Religion: A Revolutionary Approach to the Great Religious Traditions*. New York: Macmillan, 1963.

———. *The Meaning and End of Religion: A Revolutionary Approach to the Great Religious Traditions*. London: SPCK, 1978.

Sparks, Kenton. *Ancient Texts for the Study of the Hebrew Bible: A Guide to the Background Literature*. Peabody, MA: Hendrickson, 2005.

Stietencron, Heinrich von. "Hinduism: On the Proper Use of a Deceptive Term." In *Hinduism Reconsidered*, edited by Günther-Dietz Sontheimer and Hermann Kulke, 32–53. Delhi: Manohar, 1997.

Storey, David. "The Uses and Abuses of Metaphysical Language in Heidegger, Derrida, and Daoism." *Comparative and Continental Philosophy* 3 (2011) 113–24.

Swanston, Hamish. *The Kings and the Covenant*. London: Burns & Oates, 1968.

Swartley, Willard M. *Israel's Scripture Traditions and the Synoptic Gospels: Story Shaping Story*. Peabody, MA: Hendrickson, 1994.

Sweetman, Will. "Unity and Plurality: Hinduism and the Religions of India in Early European Scholarship." In *Defining Hinduism: A Reader*, edited by J. E. Llewellyn, 81–98. New York: Routledge, 2005.

Talbert, Charles, ed. *Reimarus: Fragments*. Translated by Ralph Fraser. Chico, CA: Scholars, 1985.

Tatum, W. Barnes. *In Quest of Jesus*. Rev. and enl. ed. Nashville: Abingdon, 1999.

Thompson, Craig R. *The Bible in English, 1525–1611*. Washington, DC: Folger Shakespeare Library, 1958.

Thompson, L. A., and J. Ferguson, eds. *Africa in Classical Antiquity*. Ibadan: Ibadan University Press, 1969.

Torrell, Jean-Pierre. *St. Thomas Aquinas*. Vol. 1, *The Person and His Work*. Translated by Robert Royal. Washington, DC: Catholic University of America Press, 1996.

Toynbee, Arnold. *An Historian's Approach to Religion*. Oxford: Oxford University Press, 1956.

Tuohey, John F. "The Gender Distinctions of Primeval History and a Christian Sexual Ethic." *The Heythrop Journal* 36 (1995) 173–89.

Turner, Victor. "Liminality and Communitas." In *Readings in Ritual Studies*, edited by Ronald L. Grimes, 511–19. Upper Saddle River, NJ: Prentice Hall, 1996.

———. "Symbols in Ndembu Ritual." In *Readings in Ritual Studies*, edited by Ronald L. Grimes, 520–29. Upper Saddle River, NJ: Prentice Hall, 1996.

Ullmann, Walter. *The Origins of the Great Schism*. London: Burns & Oates, 1948.

Van Gennep, Arnold. *The Rites of Passage*. Chicago: University of Chicago Press, 1960.

Vassiliadis, Petros. "The Nature and Extent of the Q-Document." In *The Synoptic Problem and Q: Selected Studies from Novum Testamentum*, compiled by David Orton, 138–62. Brill's Readers in Biblical Studies 4. Leiden: Brill, 1999.

Walsh, James, ed. *The Cloud of Unknowing*. London: SPCK, 1981.

Ward, Benedicta. "The English Mystics." In *An Introduction to Christian Spirituality*, edited by Ralph Waller and Benedicta Ward, 47–64. London: SPCK, 1999.

Weaver, Walter P. *The Historical Jesus in the Twentieth Century, 1900–1950*. Harrisburg, PA: Trinity, 1999.

Westermann, Claus. *Isaiah 40–66: A Commentary*. Philadelphia: Westminster, 1969.

Widyapranawa, S. W. *Isaiah 1–39: The Lord Is Savior; Faith in National Crisis*. Grand Rapids: Eerdmanns, 1990.

Wilson, Robert. *Prophecy and Society in Ancient Israel*. Philadelphia: Fortress, 1984.

Worth, Roland H. *Church, Monarch and Bible in Sixteenth-Century England: The Political Context of Biblical Translation*. London: McFarland, 2000.

Wrede, William. *The Messianic Secret*. Translated by J .C. G. Greig. Greenwood, CT: Attic, 1971.

Wright, Addison G., et al. "A History of Israel." In *The New Jerome Biblical Commentary*, edited by Raymond E. Brown et al., 1219–52. Englewood Cliffs, NJ: Prentice-Hall, 1990.

Wright, N. T. *The Challenge of Jesus: Rediscovering Who Jesus Was and Is*. Downers Grove: InterVarsity, 1999.

———. *The Contemporary Quest for Jesus*. Minneapolis: Fortress, 2002.

Young, William A. *The World's Religions: Worldviews and Contemporary Issues*. 2nd ed. Upper Saddle River, NJ: Pearson Prentice Hall, 2005.

Index

N

O